BEN NIGHTHORSE CAMPBELL

ALSO BY HERMAN J. VIOLA

Thomas L. McKenney

The Indian Legacy of Charles Bird King

Diplomats in Buckskins

Exploring the West

The National Archives of the United States

After Columbus

Seeds of Change (editor)

The Memoirs of Charles Henry Veil (editor)

Little Bighorn Remembered

Warrior Artists

BEN NIGHTHORSE CAMPBELL

AN AMERICAN WARRIOR

UPDATED

HERMAN J. VIOLA

Johnson Books
BOULDER

First paperback edition 2002

Copyright © 1993, 2002 by Herman J. Viola

Originally published in hardcover by Orion Books, a division of Crown Publishers, Inc., New York, New York.

Published by Johnson Books, a division of Johnson Publishing Company, 1880 South 57th Court, Boulder, Colorado 80301. E-mail: books@jpcolorado.com.

9 8 7 6 5 4 3 2 1

Cover design by Debra B. Topping
Cover photo courtesy of Senator Campbell

Library of Congress Cataloging-in-Publication Data
Viola, Herman J.
    Ben Nighthorse Campbell : an American warrior / Herman J. Viola.— 1st paperback ed.
        p. cm.
Originally published: New York : Orion Books, c1993, in series: The library of the American Indian.
Includes index.
    ISBN 1-55566-322-2
    1. Campbell, Ben Nighthorse, 1933– 2. Cheyenne Indians—Biography.
3. Legislators—United States—Biography. I. Title.
    E99.C53 C359 2002
    973.91'092—dc21

                                        2002010688

Printed in the United States by
Johnson Printing
1880 South 57th Court
Boulder, Colorado 80301

To Mary Incollingo
and
Mary Vierra Campbell,
two immigrant girls
who believed in the American Dream

CONTENTS

ACKNOWLEDGMENTS

Special thanks go to my wife, Susan, whose willingness to tackle the federal census rolls provided the key to unlocking the secrets of Campbell's family history. She spent the better part of a year conducting research in libraries and archives in California, Colorado, New Mexico, and Washington, D.C., and it was her reading of newspapers and census rolls that paid remarkable dividends.

Thanks are also due to my three sons, Joseph, Paul, and Peter, who each contributed in his own special way to the successful completion of this book, thereby turning this project into a real family affair.

I'm grateful to Campbell's classmates from grade school and high school, especially to Jeanne Dickow Rood, who shared her memories and her photographs; to the Black Knights, Lowell Heimbach, who gave me a guided tour of Weimar, and Cyril Daniels; to Noel Bergun, Campbell's train-hopping companion; to Vic Roberts, the Weimar postmaster; to Sylvania Besana, his teacher; to Roberta Hall, his secretary; and to James Fales, his principal at Daylor High.

Thanks are due Campbell's fellow warriors from the world of judo—Phil Porter, Mel Augustine, Don Savage, John Vinson—but especially his Olympic teammates George Harris, Paul Maruyama, and, particularly, James Bregman, whose candor and care so greatly enriched this part of the story of Campbell's life.

From the world of jewelry, thanks to Leon Hodge, Victor Gabriel, and Herb and Peggy Puffer, who also shared their memories and photographs.

Thanks also to the transcribers of nearly one hundred hours of tape recordings: Pat McDonald, Liz Roach, John Danis, and India Lee Worley of CATS.

Special appreciation goes to my fellow archivists, whose lifelong care and knowledge of our nation's documentary heritage make such research both exciting and rewarding. Campbell's family history would still be shrouded in mystery and speculation were it not for archivists in Colorado and New Mexico, especially Sandra Jaramillo Macias, whose intimate knowledge of New Mexico's Spanish and Indian records and her willingness to go the extra mile made it possible to trace Campbell's family tree from Richard Campbell to Vencezlado Valdez. Thanks also to Robert Kvasnicka of the National Archives, who found Albert Baldez on the rolls of the Crow Agency boarding school; to Pat Mendoza, who convinced me that the Black Horse shot at Darlington was Ben Campbell's Black Horse; to Felix Lowe of the Smithsonian Institution Press, who liked the idea of a Campbell biography from the very beginning.

To the staff of Johnson Books, especially Stephen Topping, who shares my appreciation for the history and culture of America's native peoples, and to Jan Danis, my editor and friend of twenty-five years.

To my friends and Campbell's relatives in the American Indian community, especially Dennis Limberhand, and to the Senator's family, Shanan, Colin, and above all Linda, who added the burden of helping with this biography to an already overwhelming schedule complicated by open heart surgery in the middle of her husband's first Senate campaign.

Thanks are also due to Campbell's cheerful and zealous staff, past and present, including Kenneth L. Lane, Carol C. Knight, and Jane E. Wilson, who were so important to the first edition; and, for the present edition, special thanks go to Ginnie Kontnik, chief of staff; and also to David Devendorf, Alton Dillard, Deborah Kalb, Ricardo La Fore, Michael J. Russell, Michael Schooler, Alberta Vega, and Larry Vigil.

PREFACE

By any standard of measurement, Ben Nighthorse Campbell is a remarkable individual. His is a fascinating story that deserves to be told. But how I came to be the one to tell it is also an unusual story. I met the then congressman because he liked one of my books, *Diplomats in Buckskins*, an account of our government's official dealings with American Indian leaders, especially those who came to the nation's capital as members of tribal delegations, which has been a standard way of conducting business with the native peoples of North and South America since Christopher Columbus took a wrong turn on his way to the Indies.

I followed *Diplomats in Buckskins* with another book, *After Columbus*, which describes the changes that affected the indigenous peoples of North America since 1492. One of those changes is the direct participation of Indian peoples in the administration of the United States itself.

What better person, then, to make a few kind remarks about *After Columbus* at a reception marking its publication? I had walked up to Capitol Hill and given both an invitation to the party and a copy of the book to Kimberly Craven, his assistant for Indian issues, and was proceeding back down the hall of the Longworth Building when I was hailed. "Herman, wait!" Kimberly shouted. "The congressman wants to meet you."

I was immediately ushered into Campbell's office and met him for the first time. He was not the polished politician I expected. He was wearing a western-cut shirt and denim trousers, a bolo tie, and cowboy boots. As we shook hands, I noticed a copy of *Diplomats in Buckskins* on his desk. "I have wanted to meet you for some time," he said warmly, "just so I could tell you how much I enjoy your book on Indian delegations. I must confess I haven't read it from cover to cover, but I do enjoy reading snatches of it when I have a free moment, just to see how the old-time Indians dealt with Congress. It's a fascinating story. I'd be happy to say a few words about your new book at the reception as long as I can do it without missing a roll-call vote in the House," he assured me before I left.

Campbell never got to the party in the Smithsonian Castle, although he made an attempt. Midway through the reception, Kimberly came rushing up to me and blurted, "He's not coming." The gate on Independence Avenue was locked and he told the cabby to go back to his office. "That's just the way he is," Kimberly confessed with an embarrassed shrug. "He's a very impatient man."

At that moment, which was rescued by Rick West, the new director of the National Museum of the American Indian, who spoke in Campbell's place, I naturally assumed I had seen the last of Campbell. Not so. A couple of weeks later, I answered my office telephone and discovered Campbell on the other end of the line. He was not calling to apologize, but to invite me to lunch in the House restaurant. "When can you come? I want to talk to you about something." One thing I had learned after twenty-five years as a government employee: when a congressman has a request you listen, even if it is one at whom you are slightly peeved.

We met as scheduled a few days later. All I could imagine was that he wanted some more free copies of my new book. "I read *After Columbus*," he immediately informed me, "and I really like it." Uh-oh, I thought; here comes the pitch. Again Campbell surprised me. It was not books he wanted but *a* book, his own. "Lots of people keep asking me if they can write my biography," he said, "and I always turn them down, but after reading *After Columbus*, I've decided you're the one to do it if you're willing. You have an obvious feeling for Indians, and I have checked you out. Everyone gives you a high recommendation for scholarship, integrity, and friendship to Indians. What do you think?"

Since he could read the shock in my face, he quickly added, "Oh, yeah, you probably don't know anything about me. You eat lunch and I'll tell you something about my background. Then make your decision."

Campbell's life story surprised me even more than his unusual request. As you, too, will discover upon reading this book, his is a unique story. By the time he finished talking I had come to a preliminary decision to write the biography, but I had a few questions and conditions. Was he seeking a political potboiler to use for further political advancement? "No," he replied, "I'm getting out of Congress after my next term to return to making jewelry full time. If the Colorado governorship opens up, I might be tempted. Herman, just think of the irony. Me, a Cheyenne, the governor of Colorado, the state responsible for the Sand Creek Massacre—some of my ancestors died there. You know, there's a town named Chivington in honor of the bastard responsible for the atrocity. If I became governor, I wouldn't mind working to get that name changed. But I expect my political career to end in 1994, probably before the book even comes out."

The real reason he wanted the book written, Campbell insisted, was so young Indian and inner-city kids would have a suitable role model. "I started at the bottom and look at where I am today," he said, in the same calm, understated, self-assured tone with which he always talks about his remarkable achievements. "I want every kid in America to know that this great country will give them the opportunity to make something of themselves, if they are willing to work for it."

Fair enough, I replied, but before accepting the challenge of writing his life story, he had to accept the fact that I would publish what I found, warts and all. "That's fine with me," he laughed. "I'm as clean as a hound's tooth except for the few speeding tickets and some trouble I got into as a kid."

This book is the culmination of that conversation. The only curve ball turned out to be Campbell's decision to run for the Senate when Tim Wirth of Colorado abruptly decided to leave office after one term. "I guess I haven't done you any favors," Campbell admitted upon breaking the news to me. "The fact is, I just couldn't resist the opportunity. With only six months to go until the November election, I see it as a win-win situation for me. I only have to campaign for six months, which means I don't have to raise nearly the amount of money a Senate campaign normally costs—you have to figure it is a two-year process—and if I win I am a senator. If I lose, I can go back to making my jewelry. Either way I win!"

Campbell's decision to make the Senate race caught his family and his staff by surprise as well. But people who know Campbell find it easy to understand why he did it. He simply cannot resist a challenge. He lives to compete, and a Senate race seemed to be the ultimate challenge, although I for one would not be surprised to see him reach for—and attain—still higher office. He has amazing charisma, charm, ability, and energy. But it is not the job itself that appeals to him. It is the competition.

What initially attracted me to Campbell was the search for his Indian roots. When we started, Campbell owned no documentary evidence of his Indian background. I began with a tattered copy of his father's Army discharge and roughly one hundred pages of Campbell's personally dictated recollections of his life story. Although his recollections all panned out and he has an uncanny ability to pull names from the deep recesses of his memory, his memory for dates is not so precise. An invaluable biographical resource, however, was a series of scrapbooks filled with clippings of his exploits kept by his proud mother, Mary. In them are a few greeting cards and photographs, but otherwise they consist of newspaper clippings of her son and his friends. The scrapbooks were later continued by Ben's wife, Linda, who recognized the value of saving her husband's news stories once he got elected to public office, even though she has never been able to bring herself to do more than tolerate the limelight herself.

Fortunately, it was fairly easy to flesh out most of Campbell's life before politics because he was involved in—and succeeded in—such high-profile activities. Everywhere Campbell has gone he has left behind a trail of friends. It was impossible to find anyone who had a harsh word to say about him, even off the record.

His Indian story was much more difficult to unravel, but thanks to the help of several archivists and librarians and my own wife, who insisted we leave no page unturned or reel of microfilm unscanned, I was able to fill out Campbell's family genealogy with remarkable completeness. The only piece of the puzzle left unanswered is how his father, Albert Campbell, got from Pagosa Springs to the Northern Cheyenne Reservation. My hope is that one of Campbell's many relatives will come forth after reading this book and supply that missing fact. In my own mind I am convinced that Albert was, in fact, related to the Black Horse family, although it probably will be impossible at this late date to establish the actual relationship through documentary evidence.

The other part of Campbell's story that appealed to me was its power for America. Since 1987 I had been developing the program commemorating the Columbus Quincentenary anniversary for the Smithsonian's National Museum of Natural History. I had become immersed in the issues that surfaced regarding the events of 1492—multiculturalism, political correctness, pluralism—and Campbell's story could not have been more appropriate for the time. His mother was a young emigrant girl from Portugal; his father was part American Indian and part Hispanic with a smattering of Scottish. A new world of human relations was the true legacy of Columbus, and Ben Nighthorse Campbell perfectly symbolized it. Indeed, lost in all the hoopla over the fact that Campbell is one of the few Indians ever to serve in the Senate is the fact that he is the first U.S. senator of Portuguese descent.

As readers will see, this is an approving biography. Ben Nighthorse Campbell is a self-made man whose life exemplifies much that Americans admire and like to call their own and rightly affirm.

ONE

THE BLACK KNIGHTS

Ben Campbell's early life is not easy to trace, and what is known of his background is like a patchwork quilt, bits and pieces stitched together with little obvious pattern, yet an attractive design nonetheless. Before assisting with this book, Ben knew very few facts about his family history. His father, Albert Valdez Campbell, claimed to be a Cheyenne Indian who, about the age of twelve, ran away from home in Pagosa Springs, Colorado, and went to join his relatives on the Northern Cheyenne Reservation in southeastern Montana. Albert joined the U.S. Army not long after the First World War, went overseas, and returned as an alcoholic.

Upon his discharge from the Army, instead of going back to the reservation, Albert Campbell ended up in Placer County, California, in a little town called Weimar, where he obtained a job as an orderly at the Weimar Joint Tubercular Sanitorium.

According to local legend, Weimar is named for Chief Weimah of the Maidu Indians, who once called this lovely spot home. The town is nestled in the pine-covered foothills of the Sierra Nevada, some fifty miles below Donner Pass along the banks of the American River. Weimar owes its existence to the land rush launched in 1849 by the discovery of gold at Sutter's Mill, located about twenty-five miles to the south on the American River. The Maidu, as did all the other native inhabitants of Northern California, lost their lands to the thousands of gold seekers who swarmed into the region's countless little river valleys like army ants. Thanks to the numerous streams that flowed off the Sierra Nevada, the most productive means of obtaining the elusive grains of gold was a process known as placer mining, which involved dredging or washing large quantities of mineral-rich sand and soil. Although most gold miners got little more than calluses for their efforts, they did leave behind a rich legacy of colorful place names—Ground Hog's Glory, Miller's Defeat, Whiskey Diggings, Hell Hole, Bogus Thunder, Humbug, Poverty, Deadman's Bar, in addition to Placer County and Weimar Crossroads.

Even today, Weimar is no more than a wide spot in the road, although it once sat strategically along old Highway 40, which linked Sacramento to Reno, Nevada, 134 miles away. Highway 40 and Weimar were muscled aside in the 1950s by Interstate 80, a modern expressway six lanes across that each weekend disgorges thousands of Californians onto the ski slopes and gaming floors of Lake Tahoe at the Nevada state line. Weimar, now an exit along I-80, is little more than a bedroom community for Auburn, the seat of Placer County about ten miles south.

Although the gold craze fizzled out, Weimar always had a pleasant climate, making it an ideal location for a tubercular hospital. The only known treatment for TB at the turn of the twentieth century was fresh air, sunshine, good food, and rest, and the popular setting for tubercular hospitals was the mountains of the West. At about 2,300 feet above sea level, Weimar was "above the fog and below the snow."

Established and supported by fifteen California counties, Weimar Joint Sanitorium opened its doors to 125 patients on November 17, 1919. Patients lived in long, narrow wards or cottages lined with glassless windows—for maximum exposure to fresh air and sunshine. Canvas covers kept rain and dew off the bedding, while stoneware hot water bottles heated each bed during cold weather. The garbage disposal system was a herd of pigs. Virtually a city unto itself, the sanitorium included a nursery, grade school, and high school, which provided care for the children of mothers with tuberculosis. At its peak in 1948, the sanitorium housed 550 patients in fourteen buildings and was the major employer, by far, for the people of Weimar, pumping a monthly payroll of $125,000 into the local economy. Thereafter, thanks to the control of TB by modern drugs, the need for the sanitorium gradually declined. It became a thoracic health care center in 1957 and then a general hospital three years later. Weimar Sanitorium closed its doors for good in 1972. Today the site is a health and education facility operated by the Seventh-Day Adventists, but visitors are still welcome to tour the grounds and cemetery, the final resting place for some fifteen hundred patients, many of them lying in unmarked graves.

Most of the patients were in residence at the sanitorium for only a year or so, but a few remained there as long as fifteen to twenty years. One of these long-term patients was a Portuguese immigrant girl named Mary Vierra, who became Ben Campbell's mother.

Mary Vierra was born in the Azores off the coast of Portugal on September 6, 1898. Her father, John Vierra, stowed away on board a ship that had put into Faial with a broken rudder. John told the family in later years that when he jumped ship in New York City, he had only a loaf of bread and three dollars to his name and could not speak a word of English. Somehow, by hopping freight trains, hitching rides on carts and wagons, and walking, he reached Sacramento, California, which had quite a large Portuguese colony in the early 1900s. After working in the Sacramento area for several years and saving his money, he sent for his family, which consisted of his wife, Maria, five sons—Joseph, John, Manuel, Frank, and Marshall—and his daughter, Mary. The family came through Ellis Island in 1906 and continued to Sacramento.

According to welfare records, Mary Vierra fell victim to tuberculosis in 1917. For two years she took rest treatments at a hospital in Colfax and then was transferred to the Weimar Sanitorium as soon as it opened in 1919. She remained there as a patient and an employee for approximately twenty-two years. Sanitorium records, which are incomplete, indicate she was a patient on at least three different occasions between 1919 and 1930. Her longest known stay as a patient was June 2, 1924, to August 15, 1927. When not actually a patient, she worked as a practical nurse and ward maid, for which she received a monthly salary of fifty dollars plus free room and board. After her children were grown, however, she suffered relapses that required additional treatment and hospitalization. She never led what could be called a normal life.

While at the sanitorium she met and fell in love with Albert Campbell, whom she married in August 1929. The couple had two children, a daughter Alberta, who was born on her father's birthday, July 12, 1930—just four months after Mary was released as a patient for the third time, with her condition listed as "improved"—and Benny, who was born on April 13, 1933. A devout Catholic, Mary had both of her children baptized at birth.

One of the first things the newly married couple did was to buy property along Highway 40 near the sanitorium at the rural intersection then called Weimar Crossroads. The six acres were for sale for fifteen hundred dollars, and the former owner, George Ludwig of Auburn, held the mortgage. Albert Campbell put up three cabins, the rentals from which provided a total monthly income of fifteen dollars. In addition, the Campbells bought seven hundred young chickens in hopes of starting a prosperous business.

Although America was supposedly the land of opportunity, it did not prove so for this young family. Mary was trapped by tuberculosis, and Al was trapped by a taste for alcohol. From glimpses provided by various welfare records, it is obvious that Mary had difficulty simultaneously dealing with an alcoholic husband, raising two children, and coping with her illness, not to mention tending seven hundred chickens.

Less than two years after Benny's birth, she requested permission to place her children in St. Patrick's Home for Children, a Catholic orphanage on Meadowview Road outside Sacramento. According to a report provided by Monsignor Michael J. Hynes of Colfax and dated February 20, 1935, Albert Campbell had deserted the family two weeks earlier.

The administrators of St. Patrick's Home were sympathetic but unable to help because Benny was too young. The minimum age for admission was four. Since the two-year-old would have to go to a foster home anyway, their recommendation was to place both children in a foster home, which could be done for twenty dollars per month for each child, to be paid for by Catholic Charities. "However, inasmuch as your children are so young," wrote one official, "it would be very much better for them to remain in their own home with you. Would it be possible for you to arrange for a housekeeper to take of the children at home while you are absent at work?"

Mary somehow managed this because, a year later, she appealed once again to St. Patrick's Home to take her children. On this occasion Monsignor Hynes made a detailed report of the Campbell family's plight. "Albert Campbell," he wrote on August 13, 1936, "is in perfectly good health, but he seems to be run down from excessive drinking. For this reason, also, he is unable to hold a job. He is very well thought of . . . as an orderly at the Weimar Sanitorium. He has a very good personality and is liked by everyone with whom he comes in contact." Nonetheless, continued Monsignor Hynes, Albert was obviously "very careless" about his Catholic faith and was "in general" in a state of demoralization. There was no accusation of infidelity to Mrs. Campbell, however. "He is simply a problem drinker. He is unable to hold his job and maintain his position as head of the family."

Monsignor Hynes very much hoped St. Patrick's Home could come to the family's assistance because he was being pressured by Dr. Mildred Thorne, the superintendent of Weimar Sanitorium. Dr. Thorne was "particularly interested" in the case, he explained, because Mary Campbell had been one of the original patients at the sanitorium and "has been a very faithful worker" ever since. "Dr. Thorne recommends that the children be placed in an institution or a foster home and that Mrs. Campbell come to live at the sanitorium and work. Her pay will be $50 a month as when she was living in her own home."

Dr. Thorne urged this arrangement because the Campbell home was not a fit place to raise children "on account of the conduct of the father." Furthermore, Mrs. Campbell's health would not bear up much longer under the strain and tension of trying to maintain a home while continuing to work at the sanitorium. Placing the children at St. Patrick's would be only a temporary measure, claimed Dr. Thorne, because the shock of it would bring Mr. Campbell "to his senses" and force him "to rebuild the home into a place where it may function as a normal institution."

Still reluctant to take Benny because of his age, the Reverend T. R. Markham, executive director of St. Patrick's Home, decided to confront Albert Campbell instead. "For the first time [he] was faced with the threat of his home being broken up," Markham later reported. "It was explained to him that the pressure of public opinion would demand that the children be changed to a different environment if he did not change his conduct." This had the desired effect, Markham believed, because "it was the first time he had ever been brought face to face with the situation, and also that is the first time that he has ever really made a promise to amend his way of life." Based on that promise, Markham gave Albert two weeks to think things over.

Meanwhile, Father Markham also had a chance to think things over. "The children should be kept in their home at all costs," he informed Monsignor Hynes less than a week later. "If Mr. Campbell does not amend his ways, he should be clapped in jail and County aid should be contributed to the support of the children in their home with the mother." Admittedly, County aid would provide only twenty dollars per child per month, which meant a net loss to the family of ten dollars a month based on Mrs. Campbell's wages at the sanitorium, but "considering that the chickens may be rendering a little profit later on, this solution may work out."

Two years passed before Mary once again approached St. Patrick's Home for assistance. During that time Albert had continued to be less than a model husband, and Dr. Thorne, frustrated at trying to deal with Catholic and state welfare officials, simply let Mary bring the children to live with her at the Weimar Sanitorium, since it had facilities there for the children of tubercular patients. Benny lived at the sanitorium for at least one year. Understandably, he has only a vague recollection of the time he spent there: "We could never touch our mothers or be with them, but at least we could see them and wave to them or talk to them through a window."

Matters finally came to a head in November 1938. Albert was in the Placer County jail in Auburn convicted of drunkenness and failure to provide for his family; and Mary, unable to find a suitable person to care for her children, requested permission to place them in St. Patrick's for the rest of the school year. During that time she hoped to find a more suitable solution for her child care problems. "She will become nervous," wrote Miss A. M. Coughlin of St. Patrick's, "if the present situation continues in her home, and she may not be able to carry on with her position."

This time Mary got her wish. On January 16, 1939, she delivered Benny and Alberta to St. Patrick's Home in Sacramento. From there the children were taken for a physical examination to Sacramento County Hospital, where Benny, aged five and a half and weighing forty-six pounds, was determined to be in good health except for slightly enlarged tonsils. Later that day the Campbell children were placed in the Sacramento Children's House for a three-day stopover before being admitted, at last, to St. Patrick's Home.

Mary saw St. Patrick's as a temporary solution. A letter to Miss Coughlin, dated February 21, reveals her anxiety to be near her children. Mary had been trying to find a family in Auburn that would take both Benny and Alberta, but thus far her search had been fruitless. Even a home in Sacramento would be acceptable, if it were on a bus or streetcar line so that visiting the children would be easier than at St. Patrick's. "My trips to see them are a problem," she confided. "I mean the expense. It's not the fare from here to Sacramento, but the price for the taxis to get out to St. Patrick's and back nearly floor me. $4.00 round trip. $4.50 and $5.00 if they wait 5 or 10 minutes."

"I realize the difficulty you have in reaching St. Patrick's Home," replied Miss Coughlin. "We have a new application from a fine Catholic family close to the bus lines . . . for a boy and a girl. I plan to call there today and if the lady is willing to take children as young as yours, we will consider their placement there."

On reconsideration Mary decided against a change. "I was in Sacramento last Saturday," she wrote Miss Coughlin on March 6, "and met with an old friend who kindly offered and insisted on taking me to St. Patrick's any time I was down there."

This evidently resolved Mary's dilemma because there is no further correspondence until June 3, when she excitedly informed Miss Coughlin that she had finally found someone to care for the children in Weimar. "I promised the children I would bring them home for their vacation and I have a very nice lady who will care for them days. That way I can have them to myself nites and my days off. If this lady proves satisfactory at the end of the two months [summer vacation] I would like to keep the children. What do you think about it?"

"I think it is splendid for you," Miss Coughlin immediately responded. "If the plan works out well I see no reason why you should not have the children with you all the time. Any child is better off with a good mother than away from her. Please let us know the exact day you plan to come for the children, so that Sister may have their clothing ready."

"I will be [there] . . . about 11:30 or 11:45 on Saturday, the 17th. I would like to bring all of the children's things. [I] Will take them back in case the children have to go back," Mary replied, closing out her correspondence and her relationship with St. Patrick's Home for Children.

Campbell himself can shed little light on this troubled period in his early life. His oldest memory is dragging a pan down Route 40, the two-lane highway that ran past his home in Weimar. "I was about three. It was a big dishpan, and I took off down the road dragging it along. I can still remember cars honking at me and my mother hauling me back into the house with that pan. That's the earliest recollection I have."

Campbell can also remember how hard his mother struggled to keep their family together while his father was off drinking. "It was all she could do, sick and weak herself, to take care of her little family." Sometimes, Campbell says, the only food in the house was a can of beans. "I remember one day, in fact, when my mother opened a can of peas and gave half of them to my sister and half to me. All she kept for herself was the juice in the can."

His most vivid memory, however, is the winter day Mary Vierra Campbell bundled up her children, packed each of them a suitcase, and took them to St. Patrick's. "When my mother wanted to go to Sacramento, which was about fifty miles away, she used to hitch a ride with the person we called the mail woman. Her name was Mrs. Worter, and she delivered mail, but she used to take passengers. They can't do that anymore. I thought we were just going for a ride. When we got to the place, Mom told Alberta and me to stay in the car. She got out and started talking to these nuns and a priest. I knew something was up. Then she came to get me and left my sister in the car. She took me by the hand and walked me up onto this porch and said I was going to have to stay there. By then I was kicking and screaming and she was crying. She got me inside but I broke loose and managed to scramble out a window. I climbed down through some brush and ran back to the car. The trunk was open so I jumped in and closed the lid down on myself hoping they wouldn't find me, but they did. Boy! Talk about abandonment. I think the experience left some real scars; to this day I have a little bit of fear about being abandoned. I don't blame my mother for that. She had nothing. My dad was off drinking. She didn't have any choice."

Benny had little contact with Alberta at St. Patrick's because the boys and girls were segregated. He could catch a glimpse of her once in a while, but they could not visit each other or be together.

Generally, Campbell says, the priests and nuns treated the children well, but an orphanage is not a home. "I got scolded and spanked pretty regularly, but I probably deserved everything I got." One rule that caused him considerable difficulty was the requirement for clean hands at meal-time, not an unusual problem for a five-year-old boy. "At mealtime we had to line up and put our hands on a brick bannister as we walked into the dining room. If our fingernails were dirty, a nun would hit the back of our hands with a ruler and call us dirty little kids. The edge of a ruler is really painful. Some of the nuns were nice, but this one was mean. One day she thought my hands were especially dirty. 'If you want to be like a pig,' she said, 'you can live with the pigs.' " The orphanage operated a farm with cows, pigs, and other animals. "That nun," Campbell scowls, "took me right over to the pigpen and threw me in with the hogs. Do you know how big a hog is to a little kid? And they're meaner than hell, too. Luckily one of the hired hands was nearby and saw what happened. He threw some feed into the trough, and the hogs just knocked me down as they ran over to eat. Then he dug me out of the hog pen. That is one real vivid memory I have of that place. I still get a funny feeling if I look at my fingernails and find they are not clean."

There were good nuns, too, Campbell remembers. "They used to play baseball with us. If we were sad or sullen, they'd try to help us a little bit, you know."

He can also remember being hungry. "Some of the kids would be so hungry they'd eat orange peelings. I don't ever remember being that hungry myself. But I do remember this one kid who got a box of oranges from home. As he ate them, he would throw the peelings on the ground, and other kids would pick them up and eat them."

At the orphanage, the children lived in large dormitories—boys in one, girls in another—with as many as forty in a room. "The bad thing about it was all ages were in the same room," Campbell declares. "With us tiny kids were some older boys, teenagers as old as sixteen or seventeen, and there were a couple of child molesters. At the time, I didn't know what they were. I just knew they kept trying to get me and other little kids into the bathroom. Some of the other older kids would tell me, 'Don't ever go in there with those guys. Those guys will hurt you.' Not until years later did I realize what it was all about. I never had an incident myself because I ran and hid when they tried to bother me."

Ben's mother came to see him only a couple of times, he recalls; his father never, probably because he was still in jail. "It was a long way from Weimar. Even though fifty miles does not seem like much, in those days it was hard, and we didn't have a car."

By the time the family stabilized in the early forties, Campbell claims, "Alberta was a stranger to me. We never formed much of a bond." Her way of escaping the unhappy home situation was to marry James Reid, one of her classmates, in her senior year of high school. "Some conjecture at this around," noted the district nurse on her transcript. Conjecture soon gave way to confirmation with the birth of Alberta's son a few months later. As a result of her pregnancy, Alberta did not graduate from high school, and she never succeeded in getting her life on track.

Alberta is an elusive figure. A family album contains a few cards she sent to her parents, which reveal an insecure, shy, and sensitive person. Her handwriting is small and timid. Most of the cards are signed "Sis," or simply "Alberta." All are undated. "Dear Mom and Dad," she wrote on one: "Wishing you a happy valentine's day, if I wasn't broke I'd have boughten you a box of candy, but this year I hope just a card will do. I love you both very much." On a Mother's Day card, signed "Lots of love," she added: "P.S. I'll get a Mother's Day present when I go to work Mom." The note on another Mother's Day card is simply: "I love you Mom." On a Christmas card she wrote: "I love you both, Sis." Another reads: "Merry Christmas to wonderful parents, Lots of love." Only one message is directed solely to her father: "Dad, I sent for a shirt for you but it hasn't arrived yet, so your Father's Day gift will be a little late, Happy Father's Day, I love you." Last in the group is a birthday card. "Dearest Mom," Alberta wrote. "Just a few lines . . . to say Happy birthday and I love you." Pasted next to it in the album is a memorial notice that reads:

Alberta M. Reid, A native of California, Born July 12, 1930, Died January 9, 1975, Weimar, California. Services Quinn's Sierra Chapel, Colfax, California, Monday, January 13, 1975, at 2:00 P.M. Officiating Rev. Ralph Gardner, Organ selections Mrs. Lola Hood, Private Interment Colfax District Cemetery.

Alberta died from a combination of sleeping pills and alcohol at age forty-four. She left no suicide note, but Ben is convinced her death was deliberate because she had previously attempted to take her life. It was a sad end to a troubled life. "I guess we never were as close as we would have been had we grown up together. She was a beautiful and wonderful girl," Campbell says. "It was just a tragedy that her life was marred so much as a child, too."

Sadly, Alberta seems to have crumbled under the same pressures that made Ben strong. Although the orphanage experience may have contributed to her destruction, Ben thinks he benefited in some ways. " 'That must have been so terrible,' people always tell me, but as I look back on it I think it was one of the best things that happened to me. It made me very self-reliant and independent. If you have nobody to rely on, then you have got to do it yourself. Another thing people should remember: I wasn't the only one in there. A lot of kids went through those places."

Despite the reunion these were still not happy times for the Campbell family. Ben's mother tried to provide a loving and caring home for the children, but her poor health and her husband's chronic drinking were major obstacles. In fact, Ben's dominant memory of his father is his alcoholism. A binge drinker, Albert Campbell sometimes would disappear for weeks, even months at a time. Albert never struck the children, but his restraint did not extend to his wife. She could give as well as take, however. One time after Al slapped her, Mary knocked him cold with a heavy frying pan. "She was a mite of a woman, but she sure packed a wallop," Ben chuckles. "We used that pan, with its telltale dent, for years afterwards."

Fighting seems to have come naturally to the Vierra family; this perhaps helps to explain some of Ben's lifelong combativeness and interest in sports. All of Mary's brothers became professional boxers; one, Marshall, next to the youngest, did fairly well in the ring. He and Jack Dempsey were friends and boxed on the same card in late 1917 and 1918. Marshall later fought for the world lightweight title and lost on a technical knockout.

Albert Campbell was no one to tangle with, either. Sometimes when Al did not come home for an extended period of time, Mary would send her children out looking for him. Alberta would drive to skid row in Sacramento, where she and Ben would turn over drunks lying on the sidewalks until they found their father. They would then get him on his feet and take him home. One time, however, they stepped into a bar and witnessed a wild fight between their father and two other drunks. As Albert knocked one fellow down, the other one stabbed him in the head with an ice pick. Albert then turned around and knocked him down too. Before anyone could react, Ben and Alberta rushed their father out of the bar and took him to the emergency room of the hospital with the ice pick still impaled in his head. The injury, it turned out, was not serious. The pick had glanced off his skull and was lodged in the tissue between the scalp and the bone. "He was so drunk, however, I don't think he was feeling any pain from that ice pick at all," Ben marvels. "We got him sewed up and took him home, but that's the sort of thing Alberta and I lived with as youngsters."

As Ben grew older, he usually went alone on these hunts for his father. One time he found him at a bar in Roseville. When Al saw Ben come in, he told the bartender, "Give the kid a beer." Ben stomped out in disgust, got in the family Buick, and drove home, leaving his father there.

Most folks in Weimar knew of Albert Campbell's drinking problem, but they did not know he was an Indian. "No one suspected it," Vic Roberts, the former postmaster, says, "because he didn't want anyone to know." The family knew he was Indian, but Albert Campbell insisted they keep it a secret. "We don't talk about that," he would admonish the children. Ben still does not fully understand why his father worked so hard to deny his Indian identity. "He was ashamed. There was a great deal of prejudice in California at that time against people of color, especially Japanese and Indians. As a result, we just didn't say very much about it. My dad had some Indian friends who would come to the house once in a while, but most of the people we associated with were non-Indian. It was just our secret."

People in that small and close community naturally felt sorry for Mary and the family, so they would try to find work for Albert even though he seldom held a job very long. One regular employer was the Weimar Joint Sanitorium, where Albert frequently worked as an orderly. According to Roberts, folks around Weimar used to say that "anyone who had ever had Albert's care at the sanitorium would rather have him drunk than anyone else sober."

Because of his severe drinking problem, Albert Campbell was well acquainted with the local jails. Most of his arrests were for fighting, driving under the influence, or public drunkenness, but once he was convicted of grand larceny. Thanks to someone's influence, Albert got a job at the ice plant in Auburn. Since he had no way to get to work, the company loaned him the use of an ice truck. Things went well until the day Albert and the truck disappeared. He evidently had sold the truck and used the money for booze, because he was roaring drunk when the authorities found him. The people who had the truck when it was located (much the worse for wear) claimed Albert had sold it to them. The result was a stay in the state penitentiary. As Ben explains, all of his dad's problems were alcohol-related. When sober he could be a "pretty decent guy."

Although Mary eventually divorced Albert, they did not remain apart for long. His mother, Campbell says, was too devout a Catholic for her own good. She always felt guilty about the divorce, so when Albert showed up at the door one day claiming to be a reformed person, she took him back even though they remained legally divorced.

One person who knew the family very well was Vic Roberts. Ben was about seven years old when the postmaster first met the boy, hiding under a bush and crying. "My sister hit me in the face with a flyswatter," he sniffed, "and she's in the fourth grade." At the time the two children were into so much mischief the authorities warned Mary to take better care of them or risk losing them. Roberts thinks it was an attempt to provide a better life for her children that made her decide to open a grocery store and restaurant in her home.

Mary did not have an easy time of it. During the war supplies were very difficult to obtain. Once, she told Roberts, she took in fourteen cents the whole day. Ben remembers she would buy packaged goods for the store from trucks en route to larger towns in the area. Out of sympathy for her some of the drivers would open cases of goods and sell her a can or two at a time because she seldom had money enough to buy in bulk. At first she managed to make a go of the store, Ben believes, only because the neighbors felt sorry for her and tried to help her out. She also used her home as a diner, serving meals to patrons in her front room, as a way of making ends meet.

As time passed things improved for the family. Mary's brother Frank bought a house across the road, so he was able to help with the business and the children, and Albert Campbell finally was able to pull himself together. As a result, the family began to prosper. With the help of relatives and neighbors, they built a tiny store out of cinder block in front of their two-room cabin at the crossroads. Their real break, however, came when the government needed a site for the Weimar Post Office and offered to place it in the store if the Campbells added a room. This bit of federal largess was followed by the decision to replace Highway 40 with Interstate 80. "Can you believe it?" Campbell marvels. "Years after they'd built that little store, a damn freeway goes right in front of it, with a major off-ramp right beside it. You know what that does for business and property values. That's how they could borrow to upgrade their store. They weren't born with money, and I never gave them any. In fact, they helped me, even in college. Although I had the G.I. Bill and I drove a truck, I'd get real broke sometimes, and they would send me a little cash to help out. My dad had settled down by then and was working hard. That's how they could afford the Buick they bought me when I came back from Korea. It was just blind luck they happened to build in a place that skyrocketed in value. We eventually got two hundred thousand dollars for the place after my mom died."

Vic Roberts watched Ben and Alberta grow up. Alberta grew into a beautiful but distant teenager; Ben, although he had a serious side to him, was always outgoing and sociable with a ready smile.

In time Ben and the postmaster became buddies. Roberts liked to carve and so did his young friend. When postal duties permitted, they would sit on the post office stoop, each hard at work on a whittling project. Roberts gave Ben advice about his carving and tried to help with his problems, such as what to do about the red-tailed hawk that had taken a fancy to the Campbell chickens. Ben solved the problem himself by tying a mother hen to a stake and lying in ambush with his .22 rifle. The hen sensed danger before Ben did. Squawking and flapping her wings, the chicken frantically tugged at the stake as the hawk suddenly swooped across the yard. Caught by surprise, Ben still managed to fire a few shots in its direction. "I missed but so did the hawk. He never bothered my chickens again, I can tell you that."

Ben says Roberts taught him to carve. "I don't recall doing it," Roberts says. "What I do remember is trying to teach Ben how to use a bullwhip that he had won as a door prize at a rodeo." Ben recalls that incident very well. Roberts saw him trying to crack the whip and showed him how it was done. When the lesson was over, Roberts challenged Ben to hold a balloon while he broke it with the whip. "Of course, I missed the balloon and hit him on the wrist instead, but it didn't affect our friendship."

Indeed not. Roberts had not seen Ben for about thirty years when his wife read in the newspaper that Congressman Campbell was being honored that day in Sacramento with a display of his jewelry. Eager to see him yet anxious that he had forgotten them, they rushed to the store. They had nothing to fear. "Vic Roberts! He about half raised me! " Ben yelled from across the room as they came through the door.

As a youngster Ben had two pets, a roan mare named Redwing and a tailless little mongrel dog named Peanuts. The three of them went just about everywhere together, remembers Roberts, who once whinnied as Ben rode past the open window of the post office. Redwing stopped dead and peered into the window. "He thought you were a real horse," Ben laughed, as he continued on his way.

Campbell's memories of Redwing are not quite so nostalgic. "That was the meanest old horse in the world. The rotten thing would buck me off and drag me around with daily regularity," he recalls. Ben solved the problem by befriending a horse rancher named Bob Webb from Murdo, South Dakota. Each summer Webb shipped a boxcar or two of horses to Weimar for sale to farmers in the area. Ben, then about twelve years old, one day asked the rancher for advice about training his cranky horse. Webb looked at Redwing and then at the earnest boy. "Well," he said, "what if I just trade you a horse that will be a little more gentle?" The trade was made. Webb got a worthless horse but a friend for life. "When I got elected to Congress, I wrote to Bob Webb, who was still living in Murdo. The old man sure was thrilled to know that the kid who used to shovel manure for him and groom his horses had come a long way."

Peanuts, on the other hand, had a habit that ensured him an early death. He liked to chase cars. One warm summer evening as Ben and Peanuts were playing on the front lawn, a pickup truck came flying past. Peanuts rushed to the challenge as usual but in the darkness misjudged the truck's speed. There was a thud, the truck screeched to a stop, and the driver hopped out. Instead of assisting the dying dog, however, the driver checked his front fenders for possible damage. This so enraged Ben that he rushed into the house for his rifle. By the time he got back outside, truck and driver were long gone. "I would have shot the bastard, I swear it. That dog was all I had in the world."

For spending money, Ben had to work. Fruit ranches were plentiful in Placer County, and there was always need for help at harvest time. Ben started working at the packing sheds when he was only twelve years old. A frequent employer was a man by the name of Howard Margoulias, whose family still has a huge ranch called Sun World near Palm Springs.

Many of the fruit pickers and packers were of Japanese descent. "I identified pretty strongly with them," Campbell declares. "They were still being discriminated against quite a bit in those years right after the Second World War, and so were half-breed Indian kids like me."

When Campbell got older he began working in the tall timber country around Truckee, some eighty miles north of Weimar near the Nevada state line. To get there he would hop Southern Pacific freights that rumbled through Weimar several times each day. His companion was frequently Noel Burgan, a former classmate who now catches wild horses in Nevada and raises mules for a living. Noel, it so happens, was also part Indian—Sioux—and like Campbell he was a loner who chose his friends carefully. "Someone honest, trustworthy, strong-minded, adventurous, and about half crazy is what I looked for in a friend, and Ben pretty much fit the bill."

When they were not hopping freights they were chasing girls or, as Noel prefers to remember it, the girls were chasing them. "His father bought a Buick convertible, so we would cruise in style after Ben got his driver's license. We had to beat off girls with a stick," Noel insists. "We never really figured out whether they were chasing us or the car, but we really didn't care, as long as they kept chasing."

"Noel and I did some wild things all right," Ben admits. "We had our share of brawls, we stole a car or two and went joyriding, but perhaps the most exciting thing we did was to hop freights to work with the loggers in the high Sierras. Summertimes we worked in the sawmills around Truckee, and in the early winter we cut Christmas trees for a guy named Jim McIver, a real old-time pioneer. We'd drag the trees out on horseback and put them on the trucks that took them to the cities for sale. We used to stay with the rest of the loggers at Pete Lazarro's Star Boarding House, which is still in Truckee. Those lumberjacks—big, strong guys—were pretty rough. They were always fighting, carousing, and raising hell, probably because they drank too much of Pete Lazarro's homemade wine. He made barrels of the stuff and we could have all we wanted. It was always on the table, where we all ate together Italian family style. Those old lumberjacks liked to get Burgan and me just schnockered as hell—'Here, kid, have one more. Let me fill that for you.' Of course we tried to keep up with them, and we'd end up roaring drunk."

Since Noel and Ben much preferred cutting trees to attending class, they missed more than their share of school. "We would hop a freight on a Sunday night or real early Monday morning to get up there in time for cutting. We'd work until Friday and then jump a freight back home for the weekend."

To board the freights they used "torpedoes," Campbell explains. These were little squares of dynamite with iron clips that held them to the rail. The torpedoes, which exploded when a train wheel hit them, were used to send signals to the engineer. One explosion meant slow down; two meant stop. "We would swipe torpedoes from the section crews and put one on the track when we needed a lift to Truckee. We could get off easy enough because the steam engines always stopped in Truckee for water. It was the return trip that was the damn problem. Man, those suckers would highball it coming out of the Sierras! I remember one time Noel and I were coming back on top of a boxcar through rain and snow. By the time the train hit Weimar we were soaked to the skin, but the train was flying at that point. We were afraid to jump off. It was still cruising when we got to Auburn, but we decided to take our chances and jump. We must have rolled fifty feet. Luckily, neither one of us broke anything, but we were at least twelve miles from home. All we could do was wait out the night and hitchhike home in the morning."

Once, when the railroads were shut down because of snow and ice, Ben and Noel returned home in a stolen car. "We had to get back and the trains weren't running," says Campbell, "so we started walking. We must have walked eighteen or twenty miles when we finally reached a resort called Nyack's Lodge. We were so damn cold and tired we decided to steal a car, if we could find one with keys in it. Well, we found one—a brand-new Hudson. We drove it three miles past Auburn and left it parked with the motor running along the road facing Sacramento. We wiped everything clean, so the police wouldn't find our fingerprints, and then we stomped a few yards in the mud and snow alongside the road to make it look like we were heading for Sacramento before we doubled back toward Weimar." This was not the only time they "borrowed" a car, Campbell admits, but it was the only one they took very far.

"We really weren't the sort of kids to steal cars ordinarily or to get into serious trouble," remembers Burgan. "But on that night we were just unbearably frozen." Every one of the few cars that passed threw up slush on the boys, and they were exhausted when they reached Nyack's Lodge. "When we got back to Auburn, we spent the rest of the night at my aunt's house. We were still so scared we slept under the bed."

Truckee was about eighty miles from Weimar, and the trip up the grade by steam engine usually lasted about four hours. Sometimes Ben and Noel got to ride inside boxcars. Occasionally they sat inside an automobile; once or twice they got to sit on bulldozers; but usually they had to travel, exposed to the elements, on top of boxcars. "By the time we got off we'd look like raccoons, just eyeballs and soot."

Noel still has vivid memories of the first freight they ever hopped, which was probably during their sophomore year in high school. "I can't remember exactly what finally made us do it. I guess we had sat in that train yard and watched too many of them come and go. I know we both felt it was our destiny to become part of the excitement and adventure of hobo life, and it's certainly a great feeling, I can tell you. As you stand on top of a boxcar you can see the whole train, and it reminds you of a huge snake slithering its way slowly to the top of the pass."

Everything went well until the train began to crawl through the miles of sheds that covered the Southern Pacific tracks completely to protect them from the heavy snows that fall in the high Sierra Nevada each winter. Before long Ben and Noel found themselves gasping for air because the smoke from the coal-burning steam engines had turned the snowsheds into a dark, elongated gas chamber. To compound their problems, the train came to an abrupt halt and sat for what seemed like hours. Eventually the boys crawled along the tops of the boxcars in the pitch darkness until they reached a gondola filled with rocks, which they had remembered seeing a few cars back. "By the time we got there," Noel says, "the smoke was hanging lower and lower and it was really hard to breathe. We each dug a hole in the rocks, stuck our face into it, and unknowingly made a filter of sorts." When the train finally emerged from the sheds it was evening. The stars were twinkling, and a whole new world had opened to them. "We climbed back on top of one of the cars and began soaking up the night," recalls Noel, who must be a poet as well as a wrangler. "You have never seen a moonrise until you have watched it from atop a boxcar in the Sierra Nevada overlooking Donner Lake. As the moon came up, it lit up the tops of the pine trees and made the tracks behind us look like two ribbons of quicksilver. God meant for us to see it, and seeing it the *first* time is something that comes around only once in life. Ben and I took many freight rides together, but that first one was the best."

When Ben Campbell lived there, Weimar boasted no more than a couple of hundred residents. From the Campbells' store only three other houses were visible. The nearest town, population 1,000, was Colfax, about five miles north along Highway 40. Auburn, the seat of Placer County, was ten miles away and had a population of about eight thousand.

Despite its limitations, Weimar must have been a wonderful place to be a child. Jeanne Dickow Rood, for one, paints a picture of a pastoral way of life that now exists only in memories and movies. "Weimar," she writes, "was a tiny country town like many in rural California in the early 1940s. Ranches were small. People raised their own chickens, vegetables, fruit trees, and, usually, a few cows or horses. A two-lane road ribboned through the hills that connected all of us to Colfax and Auburn. The eight grades of New England Mills Elementary School met in a brick house that had two rooms. Four classes, seated in rows by class, were in each room. I always wanted to sit in the 'upper' room with Ben and the rest of 'the big kids.'

"We all walked the miles to school and learned country shortcuts. Some of us had horses. If anyone had a bicycle it was a luxury. There was an irrigation canal that flowed at a good pace, and we loved to get in it during hot days and be swept along. My childhood mind thought Ben was rich and lucky because his family had a store by the *big highway,* and he could read all those comic books on the rack. Twenty years after we each left Weimar our paths crossed again, and we learned how much our interests paralleled—sports, art, and a search for our roots. Ben found his on the reservation, and I found mine in Spain." Rood is today a successful artist and photographer living in Lafayette, California. Like Ben, who was her childhood heartthrob—"I shoulda married him," she quips—she also hid her true heritage from her classmates. She used her middle name, Jeannie, instead of her first name, Dolores, which she thought was too typically Mexican.

Two of Campbell's closest friends in Weimar were Lowell Heimbach and Cyril Daniels. Lowell still lives in the area and guided me around all their old haunts. He, too, remembers Weimar as a great place to be a kid. "We did a lot of crazy things, fun things for kids, like horsing around on the Southern Pacific tracks nearby. We played baseball and football and we roughhoused in the water grass—it would bend down and be slick. We would play, and we would talk. We liked to hang out at the Grange Hall and at Melba Rodolfi's place. She was a beautiful lady, still is. We hung around there before the six-lane highway went through and changed things."

Lowell felt especially close to Ben, who was about three years older. "We were both loners," he says. "We both knew a lot of other kids and got along with them, but we were close to each other and not others." Lowell says he did not have much of a family life. He was a solitary child whose father had died and whose mother seemed to have no interest in him. As a result, he became very attached to Ben, who played the role of an older brother. "Ben was quiet and never pushed himself on anyone. When he talked, it wasn't something useless, it usually meant something." Everything Ben did, Lowell tried to imitate, even to writing left-handed. "His handwriting seemed so beautiful," he says, "I tried to copy him. I still write backhand. I admired him and, in turn, I came to like what he liked."

Lowell also has very fond memories of the Campbell family, especially Alberta. "I always had a crush on her, she was so pretty. But I was a little turkey then, and she never noticed me." Ben's mom was petite and pretty, his father looked Indian—slender, with high cheekbones and a hawk nose—and he favored cigars. "When you talked to Al, he would sometimes take the cigar out of his mouth, but most times not. He was also very quiet and only spoke when spoken to, but he was always pleasant to us kids. I just remember them as being good parents and a nice family."

Both Lowell and Cyril knew Ben was an Indian and that he was very proud of it. He was always drawing pictures of Indians, they recall, and he liked to make Indian things like beaded shirts, leggings, and moccasins. Together they would sit in his bedroom above the garage where Ben taught them to draw and to make Indian clothes out of buckskin and to fashion bows and arrows. "These were not toys," Daniels declares, "but real hunting bows capable of felling a deer." Daniels still owns a black leather quiver with red beads that Ben made for him.

Naturally, three such close friends would form a secret club. Even though its members dressed as Indians and stalked deer, grouse, and rabbits in the woodlands around Weimar with bows and arrows, the club was named the Black Knights. The members had a secret meeting place, complete with benches and candles, in an abandoned gold mine in the hills above town by the railroad tracks.

The only untoward incident to blot the escutcheon of the Black Knights occurred the afternoon they agreed to admit a new member, a neighbor boy named Dale Rutter. As an appropriate initiation, Ben,

Cyril, and Lowell decided to tie Dale with rope and leave him in the darkened mine tunnel for a while. As luck would have it, the Black Knights had a short attention span and promptly forgot their initiate until Dale's sister came to Lowell's home that night asking if anyone knew the whereabouts of her brother. Cyril and Lowell immediately rushed up to the tunnel and untied him, but the damage had been done. "Dale never talked to me again after that," Lowell grins. "But it was probably a good thing, because we had a pretty exclusive club, Ben, Cyril, and I."

The episode that most stands out in all their memories, however, is the time they ran away from home. Ben and Cyril were now sixteen and juniors in high school; Lowell was in the eighth grade. The idea to run away came from Cyril, whose father had beaten him severely for a bad report card—all Fs. His father, a guard at the Weimar Sanitorium, was a "heavy-duty bully," Cyril says. He was a former prizefighter who liked to knock people around, especially him. Once he beat Cyril with a flashlight. Ben wanted to leave, his friends recall, because his father had been drinking again and abusing his mother. "But Ben's father was nothing compared to my father, I can tell you that," Cyril insists.

The escape was well planned. Over a period of several days the boys assembled their supplies and gear. Canned goods, cereal, and candy disappeared from the shelves of the Campbell grocery store as did several jars of preserves from the Heimbach basement. Besides blankets, sleeping bags, lanterns, extra clothing, and foul-weather gear, the boys also assembled a small arsenal—it was their intention, as experienced woodsmen, to live off the land—consisting of their hunting bows and arrows, a shotgun that belonged to Cyril's father, the .30/30 carbine that Ben's dad used for deer hunting, and a .22 rifle and pistol that Lowell owned. They had too much equipment to carry at one time, so they stashed much of their gear in a drainage ditch under the railroad tracks, where it could be retrieved at leisure the night of their escape.

Even the best-laid plans can go awry, they soon learned. Their crucial mistake was saying good-bye to some of their classmates. Although sworn to secrecy, someone told his parents, who promptly told the boys' parents. The result was quite a surprise when they went to

23

retrieve their gear and found most of it gone. The adults, it turned out, had confiscated the cache of goods, fully expecting the boys to abandon their plan now that it had been discovered.

The Black Knights were made of sterner stuff, even though they were now left with only the few things they had taken when leaving their homes that night—their guns, a little food, two blankets, and (unknown to Cyril and Lowell) a notebook in which Ben recorded their adventures. Titled "Log of Cyril Daniels, Ben Campbell, Lowell Heimback," it describes a series of escapades worthy of Tom Sawyer and Huckleberry Finn and makes us regret the passing of a time when young boys could take to the woods and be Robin Hood, the Deerslayer, or even Black Knights without risking assault by social workers, clinical psychologists, and various juvenile authorities of one stripe or another.

Undaunted, the boys proceeded with their plan even though it meant a cold and restless night as they tried to sleep on the slope above the railroad tunnel on the southbound tracks. "I was littlest and slept in the middle," Lowell remembers, "so Ben and Cyril kind of fought for who got most of the blankets, rolling back and forth. It was not too pleasant an evening for them, but I was nice and warm."

The next morning they moved farther up the canyon along the American River and visited the abandoned homestead of the De Busk family. The De Busks, whose sons were classmates, had recently moved to town. Not wanting to spend another cold and cheerless night, however, the boys decided to risk returning to town that evening so they could retrieve some of the food and bedding confiscated by their parents. As Ben describes the adventure in his diary, however, running away was turning out to be more than they bargained for.

March 1. We three woke up very scaird from running the night before from a number of people. Made two trips with food, camping equipment to Debusks, down through hydrolic diggings and down near the bottom of cod fish canyon, here we decided to make a permement camp for it wasnt to far from town or the river.

We wanted to stay on top the diggings in a miners cabin but it was occupied. After supper we talked and wished for the sleeping bags witch had been found the night before and the bows and arrows that were hidden by the track. We finally drifted into a troubled and very cold sleep since we had only two blankets left for three of us. We were still very scaird.

March 2. Morning found us very cold and hungry. We built a nice warm fire and had breakfast. Lowell hunted in the morning for us but had no luck.

About 10:30 we started for town hoping to get more blankets and food. On the way up we found some leather for mocasins at De busks and were almost caught while starting to make mocasins. Got to Weimar at 2:00. We made our way to Lowell and Cyrils after hiding guns in the bushes. Cyril stealthely snuck into Lowells room and got some blankets while we kept watch as Cyrils folks were both home. After makeing our way back down to tracks we hid blankets in bushes and started to get hidden preserves under tracks. About halfway there we had the scair of our lifes when Cyril and Lowells mothers start yelling "there they are, come quick Ted." At the first yell we vaulted a four foot fence, crashed through the thickly wooded area as fast as possible. Thought we lost Lowell but found him at top of hill. Kept crawling, crashing, and running till we thought we were safe in the Sanitarium grave yard about two miles away. Got a drink, hid from sherifs plane that was circleing overhead and waited in woods till dark. Quitely made our way to find Ray at scout meeting to get him to buy us food as we had nothing to eat since breakfast. After eating we went to Bens to get food and blankets but couldn't make it. Went back to Lowells to agian get the blankets that they had found. Also got some preserves and canned chicken. Makeing our way towards camp we found it to cold to make it without coats so we stayed at De busks for the night. Still scaird from second chase we went to sleep.

25

March 3. Woke up from De busks feeling safe from chase the day before. We were about to leave and we found out a mouse ate a hole in the bread. Found the camp safe on our return and then had a very large breakfast. After that we washed dishes and started for the American river. On the way down we saw a water snake, two hawks, numerous frogs and fish.

In one place we found one of the most buetiful water falls we had ever seen, and a cave not far from it. Cyril fished and got one strike but no fish. We hunted a while and then came back to camp.

Had a large supper and played cards till 10:00. Went to sleep hoping it wouldnt rain.

March 4. Lowell and Cyril got in a fight and Lowell wanted to go home. Cyril talked him into staying and every thing was alright agian. Went up to meet kids at De Busks where we got latest news of town. Lowell missed a jack rabbit twice, right after we got done seeing five deer and numerous quail. Found out Lowells mom was sick so he decided to go home that night.

Came back to camp and ate. Then left for town where we dodged more people. Lowell thought he heard some one calling during the day but wasn't sure. Cyril and Ben came back with some preserves. Found numerous quail roosting in bushs by camp but couldn't catch them. Came back and went to bed. During the day we saw mountian lion and coyote tracks around camp which scared us.

At least Lowell and Cyril were scared. "We had a reasonably good supper that night, and then we told stories about wild animals and such before crawling into our sleeping bags," Lowell remembers, "when we heard this awful, awful scream, as we were dozing off. It scared the hell out of me and Cyril, but Ben wasn't the least bit fazed by it. The next minute he was breathing deeply and sound asleep, but not us. Cyril got his shotgun and I got my .22 rifle and my pistol and we sat up all night."

The mountain lion had merely been letting out a nervous yell because the boys were probably too close to her den, they later surmised, but at the time they were convinced she was waiting to pounce on them as soon as they fell asleep.

March 5. Woke up and found it raining. Fixed camp so it wouldnt get wet and ate breakfast. Went scouting for new camp sight. Found two but one was to far away from Weimar soe we worked on the other. Cyril kept guard upon "Big Pikes Peak" but saw no one. Three friends came to camp and visited us during the afternoon. They told us the latest events in town, also told that we were almost caught twice at DeBusks but we didn't know it. We then had a large supper and decided to stay in tent and play cards since it was raining and hailing.

March 6. Got up early in the morning and started moving camp. Got most of the stuff up and had lunch up there.

What makes this diary especially interesting is the fact that it is about the only personally written thing Campbell ever saved until he entered politics. Neither Cyril nor Lowell ever saw Ben writing the diary, so it tickled them immensely to receive such a unique souvenir of their youth.

Although their parents may have been worried, the boys were seldom far from their friends. One visitor was Garth Rutter, uncle of the prospective fourth Black Knight. Garth, a victim of muscular dystrophy, could not walk, so he went everywhere on horseback. He told the boys that the sheriff planned to leave them alone because of their arsenal. "Everyone knew we had a mess of weapons," Lowell laughs. "They didn't want to provoke us into doing something foolish like shooting at them. We might do something crazy all right, but none of us had thoughts like that." His sentiments were echoed by Cyril, who admits, "We were kind of ornery kids, not really troublemakers, just unpredictable."

The trips into town were necessary because they had such poor luck as hunters. The first foray was especially interesting. "There we were in the basement of my house scarfing food," Lowell laughs, "while our mothers were overhead discussing what should be done if we came back. Cyril and Ben were already real big fellows, full grown, but I was just a little turkey." That was the evening they were spotted and chased by Cyril and Lowell's parents and a few other people including the Weimar police. It was a close call, and they only managed to elude their pursuers by jumping into an open grave in the cemetery next to the Weimar Sanitorium. It proved to be too good a hiding place, Ben remembers; it was so deep they had real difficulty in climbing out.

"We snuck into town a couple of evenings," Lowell recalls. Once they went to the Grange Hall and pulled his brother Ray out of a Boy Scout meeting and asked him to buy them sodas and junk food. Another time they visited Jerry Stern's store, which was also the pool hall and a good place to get all the news.

The first to call it quits was Lowell. After a friend told him his mother had gotten quite sick worrying about him, he says, "I thought I better get my tail back out of the canyon." Besides, he did not really have a good reason for running away in the first place, and living off the land had lost its charm.

According to Vic Roberts, Ben and Cyril returned two days later. "One of the mothers talked a neighbor child into showing her where they were holed up in an old mine shaft. She went up there and persuaded them to come home."

All in all, nobody was the worse for the experience, Lowell and Cyril remember. "There were no punishments or repercussions, even though Ben's dad was probably mad at us for taking his canned goods," Lowell says. "Al never mentioned it, though." Even Cyril suffered no ill effects. While the boys had been away, the sheriff had warned Cyril's father to behave himself. "Everyone knew about my father," Daniels says. "There already had been a couple of chats with the welfare department people, so the sheriff eased the way for me to come back home in safety."

Al and Mary Campbell were not really concerned, Ben says, because he had frequently gone off alone into the hills for days at a time. They knew he could take care of himself. Less tolerant, however, were his teachers. On his high school transcript is the notation that he cut classes from March 1 to March 8. Ben did not care what his teachers thought; he did not figure on staying in school much longer anyway. In fact, he left before the year was out.

Considering his stressful and at times traumatic youth, Campbell appears to have been well adjusted as a youngster with few obvious psychological scars. Certainly, this is the impression left by his grade school counselor. According to the counselor, who provided a personality profile to Placer High School in Auburn in September 1947, the fourteen-year-old freshman was "resentful and hypersensitive, but otherwise pleasant. Physically and socially adjusted, [he] likes to play baseball, kickball, but [shows] no evidence of unusual skills or likes." In grade school his "mother [had been] very cooperative" and he had been "fairly regular in attendance," but he seemed to have trouble concentrating "due to home conditions." She noted the tuberculosis in the family. Although "gifted in art and story writing, [Ben] does not wish to take [an] art course, but should be encouraged to do so as soon as he has an elective," the counselor advised.

Despite showing promise, Ben did not get on well in high school. He and school were not meant for each other, he says, and his record verifies his judgment. Ben's grades for his freshman, sophomore, and junior years reflect an indifferent student—no As, three Bs (art, shop drawing, and woodworking), a smattering of Cs, a preponderance of Ds, but only one F (in U.S. history).

Ben's underachievement did not go unnoticed. On his high school transcript an English teacher noted: "Makes no effort. Is conveniently absent when assignments are due." Another teacher scored Ben "good" in integrity but "poor" in work habits and class attitude. She summed him up in one word: "Dreamy." Even gym class was evidently too burdensome for the young man who was later to find fame as an athlete. "Ben always has an excuse written out to get out of taking gym," observed Sylvia Besana, his physical education teacher and the assistant principal. "I doubt that [he has] been ill so much but due to fact Mother has T.B. may be afraid to take chances."

Besana may have been onto something. Ben was, in fact, afraid to take chances. "As a kid, the times we were together as a family, all I ever heard about was catching my mom's TB. We could never eat out of her plate, and she could never eat out of ours. All of her silverware, all her utensils, her plates, everything had to be boiled. Not just washed, but boiled. Everything belonging to her had to be boiled and kept separate. That was standard procedure for tuberculars in those days, and that experience affected me far more than I realized at the time. In fact, it became a problem when I got married, years later. My wife Linda comes from a family that did everything together, even to eating off each other's plates. 'Oh taste this,' they tell each other. 'Let me try that.' I had a real emotional problem with that sort of thing for a long time after our marriage," Campbell confesses. "I couldn't do it, I just couldn't do it. Now I've kind of gotten over it, but that fear lasted for years. I couldn't eat from someone else's plate. Something inside of me stopped me. I was really scared. Maybe that was part of my not wanting to take gym," he shrugs. "I don't know."

Unexpressed fear could explain his problems with gym, but Campbell offers no excuse for the rest of his academic difficulties. "I was probably the world's worst student," he laughed ruefully when reviewing his high school transcript. "I was really running the wrong way and not doing well at all in civics, history, and all the other solids. I was at odds with just about every teacher at Placer High School except those who taught art, shop, and physical education." Not so, says Sylvia Besana. "He was Mr. Personality, a very pleasant young man. Why, he even took one of my advanced dance classes." As for his friends, they struck her as nice boys, not serious troublemakers but simply very active teenagers, especially Cyril Daniels, who was "a real pistol." Another teacher who saw merit in Ben was Mr. Gein, a shop teacher: "Born 100 yrs. too late! " he noted on Ben's transcript in an entry dated June 1, 1950. "Should have been Dan'l Boone's pal. [Has] many abilities not appreciated by modern life or school. A fine boy."

The only thing Campbell really enjoyed in school, he says, was art. "I had always done art as a child, and I began using my hands at a very early age. In fact, any toys I ever had I made myself." Ben credits his father for this, because Albert liked to make jewelry, a skill he learned from Navajo friends, and taught his son the rudimentary skills of shaping, soldering, and piercing metal. If Albert had a real gift as an artist, however, it went to waste. He worked only sporadically as a jeweler, making only enough to trade for food once in a while. Ben loved to watch him at work and often tried to help him, something his dad did not always appreciate. "He used to tease me," Ben says, "by saying that my showing up was like having two good men leave." By age twelve Ben was making his own jewelry, a skill that one day would become his profession as well as his passion.

Looking back on his early years, Campbell can now see the threads of three major life interests beginning to develop. "I was going on three tracks at the same time—horses, sports, and art—yet I never fully understood or appreciated it. Instead, all I knew was that I did not like school."

He also felt he was heading nowhere good very fast. "I was running with some very tough kids in those days," he admits. "Several of them had spent time in reform school, and I was picked up a couple of times myself." Once he spent two weeks in Juvenile Hall with his cousin Francis Vierra and a third youngster from Sacramento whose name he has long since forgotten. "But he was a tough son of a gun," Campbell remembers. They were arrested for stealing gasoline and detained pending trial. When the police arrested and searched them, however, they missed the .38-caliber pistol his cousin's friend had shoved down the front of his pants. All during their stay in jail the young man kept his gun. He even had extra bullets rolled up in the cuffs of his pants. During the trial, he managed to slip the pistol to his sister right in the courtroom. The three of them were fined and released, but the incident made Campbell think, especially when his father showed up one day.

"How do you like it in here? " Albert asked.

"Not very much," Ben admitted.

"I never liked it either," the elder Campbell replied, "so you better make sure it doesn't become a habit."

Lacking direction and not one to seek advice, Ben decided to quit school and enlist in the military service. "I saw no reason to stick around." Getting a diploma certainly held no appeal. Besides, Uncle Sam needed him. It was 1950, and the Korean War had just started. As soon as football season ended—he played center and tight end—Ben Campbell joined the United States Air Force.

Although he passed the GED high school equivalency test while in the Air Force, being a school dropout later bothered Campbell very much. In June 1991 he asked the principal of Placer High School if he could return for his diploma and march with the class. The senior class, consulted about the idea, welcomed Campbell to the graduation provided he would be the commencement speaker. Quite a few of his high school classmates turned out for the occasion, including Lowell Heimbach. He had not seen his childhood chum for almost four decades, but he saw that Ben had changed little over the years. "Ben loved to joke as a kid and he had a beautiful smile. When he came back for his diploma, I could see he still had that same smile, and it brought tears to my eyes."

GENTLE BEN

The key to Ben Campbell's success is the sport of judo. Judo gave his life purpose, it channeled his aggressions, and it taught him self-discipline. Judo became an obsession for Campbell as a young man, and it has remained a force in his life to this day.

Campbell's introduction to the sport in the 1940s was physical and very dramatic. "Summers we kids around Auburn earned pocket money working at fruit-packing plants. I worked in Newcastle in a fruit shed as what they called a 'shook boy.' My job was to feed the nails into the box-making machine." Working with Ben at the time was a small, wiry Japanese youngster who claimed to be a judo expert. "I wasn't convinced such a squirt could handle me, so I took him on. I don't even remember how it started. I think we just bumped into each other. I do remember that I took a swing at him and immediately ended up on the floor. That this little shit could do something like that surprised the hell out of me, but I couldn't get a hold of him. I couldn't do anything to him. He made a believer out of me, a convert for life."

Through this youngster Campbell met other Japanese judoists. The boy, who invited Ben home to dinner, lived in Penryn, a Japanese enclave near Newcastle. He had relatives in both communities, and in each there was a judo club, consisting of little more than a mat or two in someone's garage. "I was a young teenager then, but I liked the rough stuff in those days, and that's how I became interested in judo."

Translated literally, judo means "gentle way," with "way" referring to the way of life itself. The sport traces its origin to Jigoro Kano, a frail student at Tokyo Imperial University, who took up the ancient art of self-defense, jujitsu, as a means of coping with the harassment of fellow students. Kano saw in jujitsu the potential for developing one's mind and body, but he also saw that its dangerous and crude techniques were not appropriate as a sport or physical fitness program. Kano selected what he considered the most suitable jujitsu techniques from the various training schools of the period and, in 1882, founded the Tokyo Kodokan, or "school of studying the way."

By the time he established the Kodokan, Kano had become a recognized educator in Japan. He made many notable contributions to athletics and education in the ensuing years. He was the founder and first president of the Japan Athletic Association, the first Asian member of the International Olympic Committee, and the holder of many governmental posts in the field of education. In fact, when Kano died in 1938 at the age of seventy-eight the IOC had just awarded the 1940 Olympic Games to Tokyo, but the outbreak of World War II forced their cancellation. Twenty-four years were to pass before Tokyo was chosen again, and Japan became the first Asian nation to host the Olympic Games. Judo was offered as an Olympic sport for the first time in 1964 as a courtesy to Japan not only because it was, by then, the country's national sport, but also because it had attracted a host of zealous practitioners like Ben Campbell the world over.

International judo competition and its terminology still reflect its Japanese origins. Judo is practiced in a room or building called a *dojo*. The judoist is a *judoka* and wears a suit called a *judo-gi,* consisting of loose-fitting but tightly woven cotton trousers and jacket. The jacket is tucked under a long cloth belt, which is wrapped around the waist twice.

The belt, which may be white, brown, or black, denotes rank. Beginners wear a white belt until successfully completing a course of study and earning a sufficient number of wins in open competition. The judoka is then awarded a brown belt, whose holders must work through three ranks—third to first—before attaining the black belt. The black belt is akin to the master's level of judo with degree rankings from one to ten. Since its founding in 1882, Kodokan judo has awarded only twelve tenth-degree black belts. The last holder of the tenth-degree black belt, a very respected judoka named Kotani, died on October 19, 1991, at age eighty-nine. In the United States today there are fifteen thousand active black-belt holders; in Japan the total is above four hundred thousand.

At the time Campbell first became interested in judo, there were no weight divisions, and the sport was in its infancy in the United States; now, American judoists compete in eight weight divisions.

Judoists enjoy no shortcuts to success. Progress depends on dedication, commitment, instruction, and—as Campbell likes to joke—"a high threshold for pain." Simply put, a judoist uses basic principles of physics to defeat an adversary by turning the strength and aggression of his opponent against him. When attacked, a judoist retreats and tries to get his opponent off balance while keeping his own. Theoretically, a skilled judoist can and should defeat a larger and stronger opponent who is either untrained in the art or less skilled. The key to success is mastering how to fall. Without this ability broken bones and wrenched joints are inevitable.

A judoist can win a match in one of four ways—a throw, a hold down, an arm lock, or a choke. The most common throw and the one first taught is the *osto-gari* or outside leg throw. The *seoinage* or shoulder throw comes next, followed by the hip throw and more advanced skills. Eventually, the judoist will master a repertoire of about fifteen main throws and an assortment of variations. Then come the mat holds, chokes, and arm locks. These require increasing levels of mastery to learn and apply. The arm lock, for instance, can only be used against a holder of the black belt because serious damage to the elbow joint will result if improperly applied.

Although "gentle" may be somewhat of a misnomer to describe the sport, judo is an effective skill for self-defense and competition and an excellent means of keeping mentally alert and physically fit. Campbell had no idea that he would ever become any good at judo, but its rough-and-tumble nature appealed to him. As he points out, "For a lot of youngsters who come up from hard times and through hard circumstances, rough contact sports are attractive. If I hadn't gone into judo, I probably would have become a boxer, as my uncles were."

Once introduced to judo, it became a lifelong love affair. "In high school," Ben recalls, "I was playing football and running track, but neither sport satisfied me. I was too small for football, and track felt rather mechanical. These are two fine sports, but they weren't suited to me, that's all." His lack of enthusiasm for organized sports was obvious to those around him, as this comment on his high school transcript indicates: "Likes to play baseball and kickball, but [shows] no evidence of unusual skills or likes."

Ben's success and sustained interest in judo surprised even him. Because of his initial success, he decided to stick with the sport when he entered the Air Force in 1951. Although he had the option of becoming a model maker, he opted for a billet with the Air Police because judo was part of the training. Upon graduating from police school at Tyndall Air Force Base in Panama City, Florida, in April 1952, he was assigned to Amarillo Air Force Base, Texas, where he spent only six months before getting transferred to Korea, where he served a year as a military policeman directing traffic, guarding prisoners, and protecting military property. His first assignment was guarding a storage area for radar parts near Seoul, but he was there only a short time before being transferred to a base near Pusan.

There Campbell met a Korean physician named Chang Han Ju. Dr. Chang had been raised in Japan, but after World War II he had returned to his homeland, where he not only practiced medicine but also taught judo. Dr. Chang had a brother about the same age as Campbell named Chang Han Sin. Since the brothers were avid judoists, Ben started training with them in downtown Pusan. For eight months Ben devoted five hours a day, six days a week to judo.

The club was about ten miles from Campbell's military base, which meant he traveled back and forth in uniform, armed with a Thompson submachine gun. His boots he had to leave at the door, but the gun he could take inside.

Usually he could hitch a ride downtown from someone leaving the base, but getting home was another matter. Most nights, after two and a half hours of practice, he had to walk back. By then it would be dark, and he would have to sneak through some heavily damaged parts of Pusan rife with gangs of homeless, desperate people as well as North Korean guerrillas. Once he had to walk back to his base barefoot because someone had stolen his boots. That was also the night he had broken a toe in practice. To further complicate matters, as he hobbled along he soon realized he was being followed, so he crawled under a building and hid there for the night.

Coming and going was a piece of cake compared to the judo practice itself. During the *kangeihu,* or winter practice, for example, the athletes sometimes had to sweep snow off the practice mats before they could begin. Afterward, when exhausted and drenched with perspiration, they had to pour ice water over each other to inspire the proper fighting spirit. It was very rough training even in the best of weather. "My gosh," Campbell groans, "I dislocated my back twice and bruised every part of my body."

To Ben the pain was a small price to pay for the training he had received. At the end of eight months Dr. Chang awarded him a diploma and the brown belt. Then, his tour of duty completed, Airman Campbell returned to the United States.

After leaving Korea and, subsequently, the Air Force, Ben spent the next five years in California attending college. A couple of friends from his grade school days, Jeannie and Dick Rood, gave him the idea. The Roods were now living near Lake Tahoe, and Ben sometimes visited the family on weekends. Jeannie, who had just graduated from high school, was enrolled at San Jose State, and she urged Ben to attend as well. Since San Jose State perennially fielded one of the strongest judo teams in the United States and since he wanted to continue in judo, his decision was not a hard one.

Before gaining admittance as a regular student, however, Campbell first had to make up some academic deficiencies and demonstrate his capacity to work at the college level. Consequently he attended San Jose City College for a year. He tackled a challenging slate of courses that included economics, psychology, English composition, U.S. history, business mathematics, accounting, and one apparent ringer—beginning piano, in which he earned a B. His overall average was a B– for thirty-two credits. He then enrolled at San Jose State as a police major.

Campbell did not remain a police major very long, however. In looking for a place to live, he answered a newspaper ad for a room near campus and met a man named Robert Byers who, it turned out, had been a charter member of the California Highway Patrol in the early 1900s. Byers immediately proceeded to persuade his young tenant that civilian police work would not be a wise career path. In the best of times being a policeman could be a very tough and dangerous job. Byers had begun his career in the days before policemen had radios or any other modern telecommunications, in the days when being a state trooper was like being an old-time western marshal transported from horseback to a car. "After Bob showed me all the scars he had received from being stabbed, shot, and run over by assorted bad guys, I decided that I did not want to be a policeman after all."

Career choices might be postponed, but bread was a daily need. Scholarship money was nonexistent in the world of collegiate judo. Campbell had some support from the G. I. Bill, and to stretch his resources he worked as a truck driver during the summers and on weekends when there was no judo competition. "I used to run big eighteen-wheelers to Los Angeles on Friday nights, come back on Sundays. If there was a meet, I wouldn't work that weekend." In the wintertime and on occasional weeknights Campbell worked in the yards— switching loads, tying down cargo, cleaning trucks. "I still have a Teamsters union card," Campbell boasts.

Credit for San Jose's great success in judo goes to Yosh Uchida, a Japanese American who began coaching the sport while a student at the school. Beginning with only five students in 1946 (at the time only police majors could register for the sport), Uchida began a powerhouse program that came to dominate college judo by the 1950s. Ben Campbell was one of his best students.

Uchida, a quiet-spoken man in his sixties who still coaches the San Jose judo team, can recall their first meeting. Ben struck him as a nice young man, clean-cut, earnest, and "anxious to set the judo world on fire." Coach Uchida tried to explain that there were many excellent young players on the team and that it would be difficult to make the squad; by the time he graduated Campbell had become the dominant player, not only on the San Jose team but in the entire nation.

Mentally strong and indifferent to pain—he simply taped himself up when injured—Campbell would always be ready and in good condition for tournaments. When he lost a competition, he would work even harder at the next practice to overcome the mistake that had cost him the match. Ben was a perfectionist who was always working, always trying to increase his strength and his technique, Uchida recalls. "He would work the pulleys, always trying to find a way to strengthen his grip. He would ask me to watch, to tell him if this twist or that repetition would help him improve, so he could defeat larger, stronger opponents. This," Uchida believes, "was one of the reasons why he worked so hard at the sport. Judo gave him confidence and increased his self-esteem by showing him how to throw and defeat a much larger opponent."

By any standard, Ben Campbell had a spectacular college athletic career. He was captain of the team, Amateur Athletic Association Pacific Coast champion (as well as three more times after college), and in his senior year, only little more than a year after earning his third-degree black belt, he attained the rank of fourth degree. By doing so, he not only became the youngest holder of the fourth degree in the United States, but also the first to earn it through actual competition and the first to win it while still in college.

"As with any sport," Campbell says modestly, "if you practice hard you're bound to get better, and I was no exception. Judo training strongly emphasizes discipline and that appealed to me. But what appealed to me most, I guess, was still that same old rough-and-tumble stuff that I had enjoyed as a youngster. Whatever the reason, I did train very hard at San Jose, and I got better with each passing year."

For Campbell college was merely the prelude to greater athletic achievements. Nonetheless, he did well as a student. Uchida required his athletes to maintain a B average, and Campbell, valuable as he was to the team, was no exception. Despite the fact that he had been a high school dropout, he did well in college because he tackled his courses in the same way he tackled everything else. He worked at it. He did not breeze through, but he did finish in good fashion, earning a solid B average in physical education, which became his major after he dropped police studies.

Campbell's best friend in college was his teammate Emilio "Mel" Augustine. Ben and Mel bonded for several reasons. Both were military veterans, both were on the G.I. Bill and thus had more money than the younger students, and both had Portuguese mothers. "In fact," Augustine says, "our mothers looked very much alike." Mel did not know much about Ben's Indian ancestry at the time, even though Campbell referred to it on occasion. "In those days, lots of people said they had Indian blood, but few made much of it."

Of more importance to Mel was the fact that Ben was an all-American guy with definite goals. "He had a flair for the good things in life, but he was willing to work hard to get them." Each drove a fancy car—Ben's was a golden yellow Buick convertible, Mel's a wine-colored Pontiac two-door sedan. Each dressed well. Each favored Kentucky colonel string ties. Each was a lady-killer.

No matter how hard they trained or how much they studied, they found time for women. "I have never considered myself a lady's man," Campbell says, but he never suffered the absence of female companionship, even in his college days. "My God, after the Korean War, there were five girls to every guy at San Jose State. Girls were always around us."

Not all of the interest in him was romantic, he eventually discovered to his chagrin. At first he thought San Jose State was one of the friendliest places he had ever been because of the number of invitations to college parties he received. Since the beer flowed freely on these occasions, someone invariably would have too much to drink, and Ben did not take it amiss if the hostess asked for his help in removing the unruly guest. Sometimes the guest did not wish to leave and things got a little physical, like the time Ben tossed a San Jose football player from a second-floor balcony, inadvertently breaking his arm—"I felt bad when I later saw him on campus, but he was so drunk at the time he never remembered who had done it to him." Only later did Campbell discover the party invitations were for his brawn and not his brain or social graces. "Oh, dear, who will be our bouncer, if you can't come?" a sweet young thing responded when he turned down her invitation to a sorority party.

Campbell's friends at San Jose State called him "Cho-Cho," a nickname he got from a Japanese waitress. While in Hawaii on a road trip, the San Jose judo team dined one evening at a Japanese restaurant where the waitresses wore kimono-style outfits. The members of the judo team spoke some Japanese, and the girls spoke a little English, so they were able to communicate well enough. When Ben asked one of the waitresses for a date, she refused. "You're so good-looking, you are probably like a butterfly going from flower to flower."

"Then go out with me," Mel suggested.

"Only if you carry the lantern for us," she laughed, indicating Campbell and herself. Thereafter, to his teammates Augustine was known as "Cho-chi-mo-chi," the lantern carrier, and Campbell was "Cho-Cho," the butterfly.

Ben's good looks and athletic prowess attracted plenty of women at home also. Rather than sow wild oats like his teammates, however, he always preferred the companionship of one person. Perhaps he felt dating distracted too much from his judo regimen. More likely, he had an unrecognized need to come home to a loved one, a need that lingered from his troubled days of childhood when he felt abandoned by his mother. Whatever the explanation, Campbell has married three times—impulsively in every case. Fortunately for him, his third wife is a person with tenacity, inner strength, moral character, and solid family values.

His first wife, whom he married when he was twenty-two, was a young woman endowed with considerable physical assets but little else. "It was purely physical," says Campbell, who was older than his undergraduate classmates and seldom socialized with them. He was a loner in college, and he has remained pretty much a loner. Both of them soon realized a mistake had been made. They did not live together for more than a few months, nor did they have any children. "She was a Catholic," Ben explains, "so a divorce was out of the question." Instead, they requested and received an annulment. "That's why," Campbell jokes, "I can tell folks I have only been divorced once."

One reason the marriage failed—as did his second—is that Campbell put judo first. Augustine, who was probably the better athlete, put girls first. When they first met, Mel claims, he could handle Campbell easily. In one of their first tournaments, for example, Mel defeated Ben even though he was in considerable pain from some muscles along his rib cage. "Ben cannot take defeat," Mel laughs. "As a result, he trained and trained until he could beat me, whereas I just practiced on a regular basis; judo was not my sole interest."

Campbell, on the other hand, trained incessantly. He trained evenings and weekends. He trained with the San Jose State judo team and with the nearby San Jose Buddhist judo club. He trained anytime and anywhere he could. "His way of dealing with the training was to practice as hard as possible," Mel recalls. "He just had the drive that he could be good and would be good."

Campbell was also compulsive about trying anything that might give him an edge in a match. Thus, when Mel said he had slept with a girl the night before a championship meet and won, Ben attempted the same thing. At the next Pacific Coast championship tournament, he spent the night before his match with a cooperative coed and then proceeded to lose the match. The next day he came after Mel with fire in his eyes. "You son of a bitch," he snarled, "if it hadn't been for you, I would have won. Here I spend the night in the sack and the next day I don't have anything left. You go out and you win."

"We can laugh about it now," Mel says, but at the time Ben was as serious as he could be. "From then on, I am sure, Ben abstained from sex before a tournament. That's how he trained, even in Japan. Training was always foremost in his mind. Nothing got in the way. Not sex. Not women. Nothing."

Another example of Campbell's dedication to training was his constant effort to compete against superior players. One of his favorite practice partners was a student from Japan named Kenichi Hatai, who had transferred to San Jose State from Meiji University in Tokyo. Hatai had been a member of the Meiji judo team, which was equivalent in this country to being a starter on the Notre Dame football team.

Once Ben discovered Ken could handle him easily, Hatai had no peace. Ken and Mel lived with three or four other judo players in the Faculty Club. Their only duties in return for free housing was to keep the place clean and to provide fresh coffee and doughnuts for the faculty members who used the club between classes. "Consistently," Mel recalls, "Ben would wake us up Saturday and Sunday mornings and make us go down to the gym with him to train." Ben also pestered another college student named Haru Imamura, an excellent judoka from Tenri University in Japan. Imamura, however, lived in Fresno, more than a two-hour drive away. Nevertheless, when Ken was unavailable, Ben thought nothing about hopping into his car and driving to Fresno, just for the opportunity to work out against a better technician.

So determined was Campbell to defeat Ken Hatai, he kept his picture on the wall of his room. "I will beat you," Ben would yell at the picture, and finally he did. The occasion was the finals of the 180-pound division in the Pacific AAU judo tournament in 1957. Ben's first victory over Ken Hatai gave him the Pacific Coast championship. "Ken was beside himself," Mel chuckles.

Another opponent whose defeat became an obsession with Campbell was a fantastic national competitor named George Harris, a sergeant in the U.S. Air Force. One of the few black athletes in judo, Harris was a year older than Campbell and much larger—six feet five inches tall and 240 pounds. Ben kept George's picture inside the door of his locker. Whenever he changed into his judo-gi, Campbell would look at that picture, slam it with his fist, and yell, "I'll get you, you son of a bitch. Wait and see."

Besides Campbell's determination, Mel Augustine remembers his appetite. "Ben ate. He ate and ate and ate. Whenever he could, he would eat. He consumed pints and quarts of milk, milkshakes, french fries, hamburgers, junk food, any food, in order to gain weight. He wanted that weight so he could beat guys like Harris and the other top athletes in judo."

Campbell graduated from San Jose State in June 1958, but he did not leave the area immediately. For two years he worked toward a master's degree and taught art in public schools in the nearby Campbell Unified District. Even while teaching Campbell pursued a training schedule that would have buckled the toughest Marine drill instructor. Dawn would find him at a nearby dam running up and down its steep concrete slabwork to toughen his leg muscles and build up his endurance. After a light breakfast and a day in the classroom, he resumed his training—4 to 5:30 P.M. in the gym working out with weights. Five nights a week, he spent the hours from 7:30 to 9:30 at the Buddhist Temple Annex in downtown San Jose working out with the local judo club. In between, he found time to skip rope, lift weights and pulleys, vault parallel bars, and do situps and pushups and the other usual exercises with which athletes love to drive themselves.

By now absolutely committed to judo, Campbell began thinking seriously about moving to Japan. "My first love is judo. Work comes second," he told a reporter. If he hoped to succeed on the international level, he had to train with the "big boys." Campbell also knew that in 1964, judo would be for the first time one of the sports included in the Olympic Games in Tokyo.

The decision cost him his car, his home, and his life insurance policy. It also cost him his wife. When Campbell made the decision to move to Japan he was twenty-seven and had remarried. His second wife was Elaine Morgan, an attractive student he met during his senior year at San Jose State. Like his first marriage, it was a short relationship. Looking back, Campbell says the couple had little in common, and she left him soon after they moved to Tokyo.

Elaine, it appears, wanted more out of life than the spartan existence of an aspiring Olympic gold medalist. The couple lived in a small, semifurnished, walk-up apartment about forty minutes by express train on the *Chuo* (center) line from downtown Tokyo. The apartment consisted of two rooms and a bathroom with a sunken tub and a shower. Furniture was little more than a table and chairs and a few tatami mats for beds. "Ben was like a man possessed," recalls his friend Phil Porter, a longtime judo associate stationed in Japan with the U.S. Air Force at the time. "Everything was directed to his goal to be champion. He even shunned beds because sleeping on the floor was the way of a true judoka." Elaine left because she simply got tired of competing with her husband's exclusive commitment to judo, Porter claims. "You've got a giant for a husband," Porter counseled her. "Stay with him. It will all be worth it one day."

Losing his wife seemed a small price to pay for improving his judo skills, because Ben Campbell had a long way to go if he hoped to compete effectively on an international level. "The training I had done in the United States was kid stuff compared to what I went through the next four years. It was by far the hardest, most disciplined, most painful thing I ever did. I mean, God, you hurt all the time. It was really brutal training."

Thanks to Ken Hatai, who sponsored him, Campbell was able to enroll at Meiji University, located in downtown Tokyo. Meiji consistently produced judo champions, and Campbell wanted to work out with the best. For its freshman class, the Meiji team each year scoured Japan for about three hundred of the country's "meanest, biggest, strongest, and roughest judo players," says Porter, who today is president of the U.S. Judo Association. "These were the toughest kids to be found and only one in four completed the program. That's the kind of a cement mixer Ben Campbell was thrown into. It was a butcher shop."

Meiji University did produce the best athletes, but at a tremendous personal price. The goal of Japanese training was to drive players to the wall emotionally and physically. Judoists would delight in rendering their opponents unconscious by employing subtle pressure on an opponent's neck. Then, like a cat playing with a wounded mouse, the pressure would be eased enough to let the victim gain consciousness before he would be rendered unconscious again. This could go on indefinitely, or until the dominant player tired of his sport. It was not unusual, Porter claims, for Campbell after a typical hour session to hang his head out of a window, "vomiting and retching until he didn't have anything left inside. Then he'd go back and fight some more."

As part of training, the Japanese disregard injuries. If a judoka cannot practice, then he is expected to stand at attention and watch the others. "If your legs aren't black and blue from the ankles to the knee," Porter claims, "then you're not training hard. If you don't have blisters and great huge calluses on all of the knuckles of your fingers, if you don't have cuts all over, especially on your ankles, elbows, knees, and sometimes your shoulders, then you're a softy. It was just horrendously difficult training and this, I believe, is the crucial matrix of Campbell's character."

Japanese judoists also train in the skill of persistence. At Meiji Campbell watched an old teacher twist the arms of an upperclassman until he grimaced in pain. Then the teacher bent back his arms, his fingers, and strangled his neck. When Campbell asked him about it, the judoka said very simply, "I'm practicing not giving up." In Japan, Campbell warns, "not giving up" is a trainable skill. "We ought to remember that when we think about Japanese competition in the international marketplace."

At five foot eleven, Campbell was a natural 180-pounder, but that was too light to compete on the international level in the open division. Realizing this, Campbell bulked up. He did it by eating six full meals a day and snacking on milkshakes and bananas. He also worked out with weights. Within three years he went from 180 pounds to more than 230, and he did it without the aid of drugs or steroids.

When Paul Maruyama, a Japanese American also training for the U.S. Olympic judo team, first met him, Campbell tipped the scales at about 240 pounds, and Maruyama still marvels at his gargantuan appetite. "Benny," as Maruyama always called him, "seemed to be constantly eating! It was so hot and the training so tough that I believe he felt he had to keep his weight up. Actually, 240 pounds was not that big. There were judo players well over six feet tall and 250 pounds, so lightweights like me had to work twice as hard just to survive!"

Since Campbell was a hard worker with a good sense of humor, he was well liked by the Japanese, who always called him "Canberu-san." In those days, Maruyama recalls, Campbell spoke pretty good Japanese. At

Meiji University he was considered a *senpai,* which means "one's senior," a highly regarded status, especially in an athletic team.

Being liked by the Japanese was important because foreign judo players at that time were looked upon as rivals rather than as disciples or apprentices. The reason for this is obvious: with judo now an Olympic sport and with the games to be held in Tokyo, the Japanese made winning all four of the gold medals in the judo competition a national goal. The challenge was heightened all the more in 1963, when a Dutchman named Anton Geesink had beaten everyone, including his Japanese opponents, to become world champion in the heavyweight division. Therefore, training their potential rivals for the Olympic gold did not sit well with many Japanese athletes. Usually too polite to make their feelings public, some chose to express their resentment on the training mats. As a result, Maruyama says, "you really had to be alert at all times, because you often had no idea whom you were working out with, and sometimes there were those whose objective was to injure you."

Training at Meiji in the heat of summer and the cold of winter is something none of them will easily forget. "We would begin each session with dry, fresh judo uniforms. Three hours later, at the end of the session, you could literally wring puddles of sweat out of the judo-gis. The uniforms would become so wet and slippery, we sometimes couldn't grab our workout partners." The workouts were so intense Campbell frequently lost ten pounds in one session.

After completing a session at Meiji, Campbell and Maruyama usually went to the Kodokan, about twenty minutes away, to work out some more. Here the training was less intense—it was a free workout and no one stood over the judoka with a bamboo stick to make him train to his utmost, as was done at Meiji. The Kodokan was and still is considered the mecca of judo. Campbell liked to work out there to meet competitors from all the different clubs and universities in Japan. Because of its reputation, all the world, national, and collegiate champions also came to the Kodokan at one time or another.

Maruyama admired Campbell's commitment to judo, but he considered him sometimes foolhardy in his willingness to take on any and all opponents. "For example, working out at the Kodokan is like going to a dance," Maruyama points out. "You must pick out someone you wish to work out with. Often it is a perfect stranger. You simply ask him to join you on the mat. You bow politely to each other, and then you proceed to beat the hell out of each other!" Since Campbell was a well-known champion, many Japanese wanted to work out with him in order to test their own skills. "Benny graciously took on all comers even though he often had no idea with whom he was competing. If the opponent's objective was to cause injury, a match could be career threatening."

Of the handful of Americans Campbell met in Japan, three—George Harris, his black nemesis on the AAU circuit, Jimmy Bregman, a Jew, and Paul Maruyama, a Japanese American—were to become his teammates on the first U.S. Olympic judo team. Together with Ben Campbell, then a closet Indian, the team was a multicultural phenomenon thirty years before the expression came into vogue.

The youngest member of the team was Maruyama, then a junior at Loyola University in Los Angeles. The son of a Japanese mother and a Japanese-American soldier stationed in Japan, Paul had studied judo in his homeland before coming to the United States in 1961. Although an American citizen, he sometimes had difficulty convincing doubting Europeans that he was a bona fide Yank.

At thirty-one, Harris, like Campbell, was approaching the end of his judo career. A sergeant in the Air Force, Harris got his start in sports as a Golden Gloves boxer in his hometown of Philadelphia. "I joined the Air Force rather than turn pro because too many of my friends were getting their brains scrambled." Harris was introduced to judo by Phil Porter, then a young navigator undergoing minor surgery at an Air Force hospital. Even then Porter was the judo fanatic he is today. "Judo?" Harris asked Porter. "What the hell is that?"

Campbell, of course, had come to know Harris before meeting him again in Japan. In fact, they had met several times in various AAU tournaments and, despite the spur of Harris's picture on his locker door, Campbell had lost each match. "This is the last time you'll beat me,"

Campbell had yelled in frustration after one loss, "because I'm going to Japan. When I get back, you'll never touch me."

Ironically, it was the last time Harris and Campbell met each other in a tournament. Rather than risk knocking each other out of the 1964 Olympics, they agreed to compete in different divisions. Thereafter, Harris fought as a heavyweight; Campbell competed in the open-weight division.

Their Jewish teammate, Jimmy Bregman of Arlington, Virginia, had been a severe asthmatic as a child. Although Bregman loved sports, especially football, whenever he played outside and got overheated and sweaty, he would be unable to breathe and fairly often would end up under a hospital oxygen tent. In his search for an indoor sport, Bregman tried gymnastics, tap dancing, even baton twirling, before he discovered judo. Once he started judo, the asthma attacks became less and less severe, and he got stronger and stronger.

By age fifteen he had earned a black belt; by twenty-one, he was best in the world outside of Japan at his weight. Only five foot seven, Bregman made up for lack of size by intense willpower. His favorite technique was the *uchimata*, which is an inner thigh throw.

Campbell was his hero. "I especially admired his quiet confidence and courage. When I was feeling really down and troubled and exhausted, he would just come and stand next to me." Ben did not have to say anything, just stand there. "With him next to me, I felt stronger. I felt that I could go on." Even when injured, Campbell continued to practice. That would give others around him the courage to continue practicing. "In the end," Bregman says, "I think the most valuable thing I learned from Ben was to have a lot of faith in yourself, to practice hard, and just never to give up. You can give out, but never give up. That was our motto: We may give out, but we will not give up. That kind of mentality is hard to defeat."

As luck would have it, Bregman was present the day Campbell appeared at a Meiji judo practice for the first time. "The introduction of a foreign judo player into a Japanese training session is really very brutal," Bregman declares. "No mercy is given; none is asked." The novice judoka is basically thrashed as each member of the team, in what is called a *randori* or free practice, challenges him to a match. No matter how good the player, he will eventually take a licking as he faces one fresh opponent after another. By the end of the session, it was all Campbell could do to crawl over to a corner and pull himself up by grasping a windowsill. Fighting for every breath, he gasped, "This is not going to happen to me again."

Getting beaten by one's teammates was only part of the training process. American judoists were also thrust into the rigid *senpai-kohai* system, which is the senior student–junior student relationship. Underclassmen, or *kohai,* have to work for the upperclassmen, or *senpai.* The junior student does what the senior student says to do out of strict obedience. "Go sit in the whirlpool!" and he goes. "Get me my towel!" and he gets the towel. Until a judoka is a third-year student, he is virtually nothing. This meant Campbell had to scrub toilets, wash floors, and do the laundry of the senior students. When a junior student lost a match he had to shave his head as an act of humiliation. If he failed to do it, the upperclassmen would do it for him.

Senior students also carried bamboo whips which they used on the junior students, if it appeared any of them were not training hard enough. This was one duty Campbell found difficult to enforce when he became a third-year student. In fact, one instructor once called Campbell aside and berated him for failing to use his switch vigorously enough during practice.

According to one foreign newsman, Campbell deserved "tremendous credit" for training at Meiji University. "No other American has had the technique or guts to do this," the newsman wrote. "In fact, most foreigners who go to Meiji for practice attend once or twice and then are afraid or physically incapable of returning again. This includes all of the foreigners, big and small, who train in Japan." His opinion is supported by Porter. "No one can fully appreciate the rigor of the Meiji judo program at that time," he declares. "Meiji is the toughest judo school in Japan, and Campbell is the only American who survived the whole three-year program."

Campbell would not disagree. "The training, in fact, was just absolutely brutal. My nose was broken a couple of times, I lost two teeth, and I guess I broke or dislocated virtually every finger and toe I've got and suffered any number of bruises, contusions, and swollen ears."

If left unattended a swollen ear will turn into what is called a cauliflower ear. To prevent that Campbell would have his ears drained, provoking all kinds of ridicule from his Japanese teammates, who continually teased him about it. Before practice, some would rub his ears and promise, "I'll fix those for you today." The Japanese took pride in their deformed ears and never had them drained. To do so was akin to hiding the visible symbol of their sport. If not drained immediately, however, a swollen ear will harden and then be impossible to correct later. Campbell actually saw judoists with ears so misshapen they closed off hearing. Such ears really looked like cauliflowers. To restore proper hearing required having a hole drilled through the cartilage. "It looked really strange, like someone had stuck a pencil through the tissue." To avoid this condition, Campbell would go right to the doctor when he injured an ear. "It was not easy to ignore because the ear would turn blue and throb like hell. When I explained to my Japanese teammates that a cauliflower ear is not much honored in the United States, most of them forgave my indiscretion at having them drained."

Swollen ears were a minor annoyance compared to the life-threatening injuries that are a fact of everyday life in the world of Japanese judo. Campbell, in fact, lost three teammates while enrolled at Meiji. Two suffered broken necks in judo falls and another ruptured his aorta.

Like any contact sport, Campbell explains, the higher the level of competition the rougher it gets and the more serious the injuries. As a rule of thumb, he could plan on being incapacitated by injury about one week out of every four. But risk was unavoidable because the only way to learn judo is to do it with another person.

During his four years in Japan, Campbell eked out a living by teaching English and acting in Japanese movies. He thought about teaching art, but gave up the idea when he realized he had nothing to offer the

Japanese in this field. "My God, they invented art." The fact that Ben had no acting ability mattered little. It was his foreign face the Japanese filmmakers wanted and there was always a market for foreign faces in Japanese movies. A friend named Johnny Yuseff, who had a casting agency for foreigners, got Campbell a number of bit parts. When too injured for judo training, he could go on location, stay for a few days, and get paid for it.

"None of us was rich," recalls Maruyama. "In America judo was a poor man's sport. We all had to support ourselves teaching English, tutoring, whatever." Ben and Jim Bregman got parts in the movies because Japanese filmmakers wanted American types. "No one looked twice at me or George."

Bregman still bemoans the financial aspect of his training experiences. "Because we all had limited funds, Japan was not a very hospitable place for us. I remember, in the wintertime particularly, Ben and I having barely enough money to buy baked sweet potatoes from a street vendor. The potatoes were very cheap, and we could make a meal out of two of them. In that way, we got by until we got paid from our next class, but we sure got damn tired of sweet potatoes!"

Of the four, Campbell had the roughest time in Japan. Bregman's parents provided some financial support in return for his promise to get a college education while there. Maruyama's family lived in Tokyo. Harris, on active duty with the Air Force, ate standard American chow in the mess hall three times a day when he was in Japan.

Campbell, on the other hand, lived off the economy and his dietary needs were staggering. While training he easily consumed upwards of sixty-five hundred calories a day. Much as he came to enjoy Japanese food, he found it almost impossible to satisfy his gnawing stomach.

Now American athletes can live in the Olympic village in Colorado Springs where their meals, medical care, insurance, and training are all free. They even receive a small stipend as well. But in 1964 American Olympic athletes were on their own. Those who trained in Japan were especially hard pressed. "We didn't even have enough money to buy bandages," Campbell gripes. "If you dislocated a knee, you wrapped it with a bicycle tube."

But it is his memories of hunger that grate most on Campbell. Even today he is bitter about the policy at the U.S. Embassy in Tokyo where tourists, but not American athletes in training, were welcome to an American meal on occasion. "It made me madder than hell."

Campbell got a measure of revenge after he was selected for the United States Olympic team. Upon the team's arrival in Tokyo, Ambassador Edwin Reischauer invited the athletes to a reception at his residence for a photo opportunity. Campbell went solely to give the ambassador a piece of his mind. "I damn sure told those bastards when I got there about the rotten treatment I got." Although he did not make his complaints public, a request from Olympic Committee officials that Campbell honored, he had no hesitation about telling the embassy staff what he thought of their behavior. "Now they wanted to stand around and take their pictures with us after we made the team, but they wouldn't even let us buy a meal in the cafeteria when we were over there training and starving for an American meal. Let's face it, sometimes we just had to get away from the rice and the fish."

Although Harris knew Campbell was suffering, Ben was too proud to accept overt charity. Nonetheless, he helped him as much as he could, like the Thanksgiving Day Harris found himself alone in Tokyo. Away from his wife and children and feeling particularly lonely, he decided to invite Ben and Elaine to the base for Thanksgiving dinner. He readily found Ben's number in the telephone directory, but getting him to accept the invitation was not as easy.

"Have you eaten dinner yet?" Harris asked.

"Yes, we have."

"Gee, that's too bad. It's Thanksgiving and I'm here alone. I thought it would be nice to get together, being Thanksgiving and all. Are you sure you've eaten?"

"Yeah, we already ate," Ben insisted.

"Are you sure? I was going to make it my treat. I was even going to pay your cab fare over here."

With that offer, Harris recalls, Ben's attitude immediately improved. "How long can you wait?" he asked.

"No rush," Harris replied. "I'll meet you at the gate, and we'll eat when you get here."

An hour later their cab screeched to a stop in front of the gate at Washington Heights, the U.S. military base in central Tokyo. As Ben and Elaine hopped out, Harris paid the driver 1,500 yen (at about 350 yen to the dollar), and then escorted his guests to the NCO club, where Ben proceeded to eat his way through the menu. First he gulped a chocolate malt. He washed that down with a vanilla malt and then savored a strawberry malt chaser before ordering dinner. After polishing off the turkey dinner, Ben proceeded to the ham dinner. "It really tickled me to see Ben wolf that food," Harris chuckles. "It was just like family. That was the night we started getting real close."

Harris then treated his guests to several cocktails in the club lounge, where singer Tony Bennett entertained them. At the end of a great evening Harris gave them a farewell present, a forty-ounce bottle of vodka which he tucked under Ben's arm. "By then," Harris recalls, "they were both feeling pretty mellow." He gave a cabby 2,000 yen with instructions to make sure they got properly tucked in and told him to keep the change for his trouble. "The whole evening didn't cost me more than twenty bucks or so, but I could see that it was a fortune to Ben."

Campbell never forgot this moment of kindness, and years later he had a chance to repay the favor. "I understand," he informed the U.S. Judo Association in April 1975, "that the board did George Harris and myself the great honor of promoting us to the 7th degree black belt, pending our acceptance. After careful consideration and discussion with judo leaders, I must honestly say that I do not feel worthy of this honor." Campbell wanted to see it go, instead, to Harris alone. "In all fields of endeavor in human effort and among the many who strive there, occasionally [there] are individuals who, by their actions and deeds rather than words, emerge as great leaders by the acclaim of their fellows. Such a man is George Harris, my lifelong friend. It is my opinion," Campbell wrote, "that George, above all American judoists, is worthy of the 7th degree black belt."

Campbell and his teammates owed much to American servicemen like Harris whom they met in Japan. Sometimes they snuck food to the judoists; sometimes they let the judoists sleep in the barracks for a few days. Particularly helpful to Campbell was Tom Jenny, a pilot with Flying Tigers Airlines, who spent a lot of time flying American "advisers" into Vietnam as the American presence there began building. Jenny, who also stayed at Tachekawa at the Washington Heights military base in downtown Tokyo, allowed Ben to use his room whenever he was out of town. Campbell then enjoyed base privileges including access to the dining hall. "I'd just act like a G.I. When I had to sign for things, I used my old Air Force serial number—AF19378620. No one questioned it."

When not training Campbell was competing. As a member of the U.S. judo team, he maintained an incredible schedule as he sought to compete against the best the world of judo had to offer. During his four years in Japan, he fought fifty tournament matches, losing only two, and those were to Japanese opponents. His finest moment as an athlete, in fact, was in the Pan American Games held in São Paulo, Brazil, in April 1963, where he earned the gold medal in the open-weight division. It was the first gold medal won by the United States and helped ease the pain of the 13-to-1 trouncing Fidel Castro's Cubans inflicted on the American baseball team.

São Paulo itself, however, was chaotic. Workers were still trying to complete the dormitories as the athletes moved in (the windows in Campbell's room, for example, lacked glass panes), there was insufficient food for the training table, and transportation and security were inadequate. In short, the Brazilians in 1963 were simply not prepared to conduct a world-class athletic tournament.

Security was especially important because the Brazilians take their sports seriously. At the Pan American Games, Campbell recalls, the authorities had installed machine guns at each of the gates to the stadium, not to intimidate terrorists but to control fans. Although forbidden to carry bottles into the arena, the Brazilians were able to buy frozen cups of ice cream and these made dandy missiles. A favorite target was American athletes who beat Brazilians. More than one frozen cup left its mark on Campbell, while Harris once had to take cover under the judo platform to avoid a hailstorm of ice cream. "The Brazilians are wild and mean compared to American sports fans, and those cups could raise real welts," Campbell grimaces in memory. "The police usually had to escort us in and out of the stadium. In fact, we had to worry more about the fans than the folks we competed against in many South American countries."

Following his success in the Pan American Games, Campbell returned to Japan, where he was among six hundred foreign athletes and officials, including a dozen or so world-record holders, who accepted the invitation to participate in what amounted to a dress rehearsal for the 1964 Olympics. Although Japanese officials preferred that the event—officially titled Tokyo International Sports Week—not be called a "pre-Olympics," that's exactly what it was, even to its opening exactly 365 days before the start of the XVIII Olympiad.

In this era before videotape, the Japanese, by inviting the top athletes in each event to the pre-Olympics, were able to study and film performances of their future opponents and thereby be better prepared to compete against them the following year. Nonetheless, five Americans accepted invitations to the Sports Week. Among them were Harris, Bregman, and Campbell, who was team captain.

A group of sixteen hundred athletes and officials paraded into the National Stadium in Tokyo on the afternoon of October 11 to open the six-day tournament, which featured twenty official Olympic events. Participating in the games were 120 foreigners who, like Campbell, had been living in Japan in hopes of enhancing their chances in the actual Olympic Games.

It was during Sports Week that Ben first experienced any real heckling, and the hecklers turned out to be tipsy American tourists. During the matches, Ben noticed three young men waving at him to come up into the stands. When he reached them, he got an earful of abuse: "You guys look awful! What the hell's wrong with you? Quit loafing!" they yelled, referring to the fact that the Japanese judoists appeared to be handling the Americans with relative ease.

"Those drunks made me so damn mad," Campbell remembers. "Get off your ass and come down to the mats, if you think this is so easy!" he challenged one. "If you can beat me, I'll give you my black belt and you can take my place in the tournament!"

When Campbell stormed back to his seat and told Harris and Bregman what had happened, they agreed to give the drunks a judo lesson, but the hecklers scooted from the arena before anyone could catch them. "We were going to beat the shit out of them, no doubt about that. The idea that fellow Americans would treat other Americans like that really pissed us off!"

Campbell could not have been unduly agitated because he pulled off the biggest upset of his career in the tournament by defeating the captain of the Meiji University team, Asada, one of the best in the country and a strong contender to make the Japanese Olympic team. Ben threw him with a move called *o guruma* (major hip wheel throw) that truly stunned the packed crowd and deprived Asada of his chance of ever again competing for Japan in a major international tournament. Campbell, to his credit, tempered his joy at such a major upset—no one would have ever dreamed that a foreigner would so cleanly throw Asada—by expressing complete empathy for Asada. "We all knew," writes Maruyama, "that the loss had effectively ended Asada's brilliant career. Losing to a foreigner, in the Japanese mind, put a stigma on him that could never be erased—or forgiven."

Campbell was outstanding in the pre-Olympic tournament. He fought eight matches against the best heavyweights in the world, earning the most points by a non-Japanese competitor—eight. During these contests no one threw him for a full point, whereas he scored one full point himself (against Asada), was held down once, drew once, and lost some close decisions. His performance inspired one journalist to write: "Campbell is easily the best judo player America has ever produced."

Although the best, Campbell still had to compete for a spot on the 1964 U.S. Olympic team. To qualify he first had to fight his way through the regional eliminations. His were held in Fresno, California, where he defeated, among others, his college teammate and pal Mel Augustine. From there Campbell joined some two hundred other judo Olympic hopefuls at the national trials, which were held on the grounds of the World's Fair in New York City, and it was here that Campbell's luck as a judoist began to run out. "To win in judo," Maruyama points out, "you need not only skill and strength, you need luck. In those days there were only four weight divisions. There was no such thing as an alternate. Winning first was the only thing that counted. Past records meant nothing."

With two hundred judoists competing, each of the four finalists fought against as many as a dozen opponents. Bregman, easily the best outside of Japan in his weight division, won with no difficulty, as did Paul Maruyama. For Harris and Campbell, however, it was a different story. Harris, now thirty-one and too old to expect another shot at the Olympics, lost one of his early matches. Not only did he have to fight his way back through an additional series of elimination matches, but also he went into his final match still trailing on points. The only way he could win a spot on the Olympic squad was to throw his opponent decisively, thereby scoring a full point. He did it in less than two minutes. Then, realizing his Olympic dream had finally come true, he broke into tears. "I thought I'd blown all those years of work and effort. I thought I'd lost my chance."

Although Campbell won all seven of his matches, five on falls and two on decisions, he had the misfortune to separate his right shoulder in his last match, against Robert Nishi of Hawaii. He, too, came close to losing his spot on the Olympic squad. "I went to throw my opponent and missed," he recalls. "We both went down and we both got injured, but only three minutes had elapsed." Since Campbell had a half-point lead before the injury, he was able to win the match "by kicking around for the remaining seven minutes and staying out of his reach."

After the trials, Ben went home to Weimar, where he was the talk of the town. No one before had gone to the Olympics from this rural community, and he basked in the limelight, regaling friends and reporters alike with "war" stories. "Despite the injury," he assured one newsman, "I am in good shape for the Olympics." When another asked him to describe his most exciting moment in judo, a question often asked him during his career, Campbell hesitated. "I cannot isolate one moment," he confessed, "because every time I compete I get the same thrill. I'm a greedy winner. In fact, every match I have ever won delighted me in the same way. When winning doesn't thrill me anymore, I'll quit competing." And that moment might not be far away, he realized. "After all, anything after the Olympics would be an anticlimax and fifteen years of competition is a long time. Also, it is about time I settle down."

While in Weimar Campbell resumed his training at a judo club in nearby Sacramento, where he was joined by Harris and Bregman, who had moved there so they could train together. The three remained in Sacramento the entire summer and then moved to San Jose State, the site of the judo training camp for the 1964 Olympics and where, finally, Paul Maruyama joined them. Instead of college dormitories, however, the future Olympians had rooms in the DeAnza Hotel, a rather posh place only two blocks from campus which also served as the quarters for the San Francisco Warriors professional basketball team in training camp at the same time.

For Campbell, training camp was a real déjà vu experience because the coach of the 1964 team was none other than Yosh Uchida, his former coach at San Jose State. Unfortunately, although an excellent college coach, Uchida was out of his league in training a team for the Olympics. He had no program other than to have the Olympians scrimmage constantly against a group of less skilled judoists he managed to round up as cannon fodder. That was precisely the wrong program; it is against inexperienced competitors that judoists are injured, and this is what happened to Campbell. He suffered what is known as an ACL, the tear of a crucial internal ligament in his right knee during a scrimmage when his opponent attacked him while he was off guard. In itself the injury was not serious and, with enough rest, would have mended nicely, but the Olympics were so close there was no time to let it heal. Ben merely shrugged it off and continued to train.

The XVIII Olympics opened in grandeur and style. The seventy-six thousand ecstatic spectators who thronged the National Stadium in Meiji Olympic Park witnessed an extraordinary spectacle that warm, sunny day in October. As the sixty-six hundred athletes and officials from about a hundred nations paraded around the oval track, ten thousand balloons and eight thousand doves competed with cascading fireworks for space above the stadium and temporarily blocked from view the five Olympic circles being etched against the bright blue sky by F-86 fighter jets. Throughout the ceremony could be heard the sound of gongs as temples and pagodas across Japan expressed their enthusiasm. "These sounds," it was explained, "are the symbols of the soul of the Japanese people being transmitted to the world."

In fact, symbolism permeated the opening ceremonies. Yoshinori Sakai, the nineteen-year-old college student who carried the Olympic torch into the stadium, had been born near Hiroshima on August 6, 1945, the day the bomb fell. The Olympic flag measured 49 feet, 10¾ inches in length, the precise distance covered by triple jumper Mikio Oda to win Japan's first gold medal in 1928 in Amsterdam.

Most of the symbolism was lost on the American athletes. Numbering some 550, they marched in behind their flag carrier, the great shot-putter Parry O'Brien, each wearing white bucks, blue blazers, white slacks, and each clinging to cowboy hats that threatened to blow away in the breeze. "The cowboy hats were the dumbest thing I ever saw," Campbell laughs. "Our uniforms were silly enough. They were more appropriate for yachtsmen, but then to wear cowboy hats in addition just made us look ridiculous, simply because President Lyndon Johnson wanted us to have them."

Wardrobe worries were secondary to the feelings of intense patriotism that washed over the athletes. "We took pride not only in ourselves for having reached the Olympics," Campbell recalls, "but in what we were fighting for, the honor of our country. Walking into that stadium behind our flag is something none of us will ever forget."

No one stood prouder than Emperor Hirohito, once a god to the Japanese people and still their venerated leader. Dignified, diminutive—

he was only five foot three and a half—the emperor bowed in gentle two-inch arcs about three times per minute as the athletes paraded before the reviewing stand, a task which, like everything else relating to the Olympics, had been rehearsed to the smallest detail in the preceding weeks. The emperor, as did everyone throughout this island country, hoped and prayed that the Olympics would be flawless.

As much as three billion dollars had been spent giving all of Tokyo a face-lift. The buildings necessary for hosting the games and the athletes alone cost more than three hundred million dollars. Nonetheless, it was obvious what mattered most to the Japanese. For the judo events, as befitting the national sport, the Japanese built a magnificent Budokan that resembled an ancient temple, its roof capped by a golden spire. The interior featured two judo mats in the center with steeply rising bleachers on all sides giving everyone an unobstructed view. The basketball arena, on the other hand, although equally new and aesthetically pleasing, could seat only four thousand spectators. As a result the dramatic confrontation between the American and Russian teams caused a frenzy of ticket scalping that made the postwar black market seem like a church bazaar.

For the athletes' living quarters the Japanese converted Washington Heights, the barracks-like U.S. military suburb where Harris had usually stayed when in Tokyo honing his judo skills. It became the Olympic Village, home to as many as eight thousand athletes and officials, some of them crammed seven to a room. In the women's quarters there was one shower for each eighteen athletes. For meals, the athletes could eat in the dining hall's Fuji and Sakura rooms, which featured dishes from across the world, although many of the athletes were able to eat foods prepared by their own cooks. The French, for example, took no chances that strange foods would hamper the performance of their athletes. According to *Newsweek,* the French team arrived with 500 kilograms of cheese, 12,000 bottles of mineral water, 32 bottles of cooking cognac, 2,850 liters of wine, and their own chef.

The athletes were free to eat in each other's dining halls, and Campbell took full advantage of the opportunity. No longer did he have to go hungry in Japan. One day he might eat with the French, the next day with the Russians. Soviet borscht, Japanese sukiyaki, or Korean roast beef were all savored. After having traveled so much during his judo career, he enjoyed foods from everywhere, even though many athletes were horrified at the thought. "Athletes who were acclimatized to a certain kind of food did not want to take a chance with other foods so they would only eat at their own dining hall, but we were allowed to eat anywhere and I did."

For entertainment, the athletes could visit the International Club, where they enjoyed free Ovaltine "for health and strength" along with milk and ice cream. Each night the club rocked with the popular disco music of the day—the frug, the surf, and the international favorite, the twist. "Everyone was doing the twist," Campbell recalls, "the French guys, the Argentine girls, the Americans, the Canadians, everyone, that is, but the Russians." One evening Campbell noticed Andre Medved, the Russian world champion light-heavyweight wrestler, in a dark corner behind a pillar trying to twist in time with the dancers on the floor. Since Medved could speak English, Campbell walked over to him and yelled, "Come on, Andre, get on the dance floor with the rest of us." Embarrassed and startled, the young man glanced furtively around, then said, "Oh no, I cannot. Our leaders have told us the twist is the dance of a decadent, dying society and we are forbidden to do it."

Except for a certain amount of camaraderie at mealtimes and in the discotheque, the sportsmanship and goodwill of the Olympic Games are overrated, Campbell believes. The judoists, for example, believed that the person who first offered to shake hands or acknowledge the other would lose the match when they met in competition. Perhaps team sports are different, he says, "but when it's one on one, there is a lot of meeting of the minds before a fight. You can be good friends afterward, but you must go into a match thinking you will tear your opponent apart. You must feel that way to have any hope of winning. The guys filled with love and kisses are losers. It is the ones who enter matches like damn animals who usually win. I ought to know; I was one."

Campbell strongly believes that psychology is a large part of athletic success. Certainly it was in his case. "There is no room in my mind for second best." This was confirmed to him by a sports psychologist who discovered that championship athletes have such self-confidence that in their dreams they think they can fly, like Superman. "There must be something to this," Campbell laughs, "because I'm here to tell you that I would fly all the time in my dreams. I still take off in my dreams once in a while. I just have more weight to worry about at liftoff."

No matter that scarcely an American face was to be seen among the fifteen thousand avid fans in the Budokan when judo events began at 1 P.M. on October 20, 1964. Early in life Campbell, Harris, Bregman, and Maruyama had committed themselves to a sport that few of their countrymen appreciated or understood. Each hoped to accomplish the unthinkable, wrest the coveted gold medals of judo from the Japanese on their home court.

To this day that moment is burned in their memories. A Jew, an Indian, a Japanese American, and an African American each striving for personal success and national glory. "It was really funny," Campbell recalls. A German reporter looked at the team and asked, "*Ja, gut,* but where are the *Americans?*" Bregman told himself, "This is what America is all about. We were a Cinderella team. Even now I get choked up thinking about it," he admits.

At that point their fate was in the hands of God and chance. They had done everything possible to make themselves the best, and they were good. On any given day any one of them could have beaten some of the best players in Japan, as Campbell had done a year earlier when he had defeated Asada in the pre-Olympics. Each of them had reached the highest level of judo on the basis of skill and technique. They were in that group of seven to ten in each weight division at the very top of the field.

Bregman, fighting in the middleweight division, made the best showing of the Americans. He reached the medal round by defeating three opponents—Gabriel Goldschmied of Mexico, Peter Paige of Australia, and Rudolfo Perez of Argentina—and could well have a won a silver medal but for incredibly inept officiating that could have left him with a crippling injury. His opponent was Wolfgang Hoffmann of Germany. Bregman scored first, gaining a half-point on Hoffmann with a left-hand shoulder throw, but the alert German countered with an armlock. Bregman tried to get out of it by lifting Hoffmann, who was still clinging to the arm, completely off the floor. The referee then called "*Mate*"—wait—but Hoffmann either could not hear the command or ignored it because he continued the lock. With his arm about to break, Bregman conceded. The official—"in one of the poorest displays of refereeing seen in a long time," according to Porter—then reversed his previous call and awarded a full point to Hoffmann. This gave the victory, gained after the whistle, to the German and cost Bregman his chance to compete for a gold medal.

Poor officiating in the heavyweight division also hurt George Harris, who easily beat his first opponent but lost by a half-point to Parnoaz Chikviladze of Russia. Chikviladze managed to flip Harris for a half-point loss midway through the match and then proceeded to retreat outside the mat every time Harris tried to grab him. Not until the final minute of the match did the referee finally warn Chikviladze to stay in bounds, but by then it was too late and Harris lost as time ran out.

As luck would have it, Maruyama drew Takehide Nakatani, the Japanese favorite, as his opponent in the second quarter-round of the lightweight division. It was no contest. Nakatani caught him with a foot sweep and dispatched him early in the match.

For the fifteen thousand spectators in the Budokan all of the action thus far had been merely an appetizer before the main course, the expected confrontation between Anton Geesink of the Netherlands and Akio Kaminaga of Japan in the open weight division. Since the winner of this division also became the world champion of judo, the Japanese considered these matches the most important of the entire Olympic Games. As a result, work throughout the country came to a standstill as people listened to their radios or watched the matches on television.

Campbell had no realistic hope of winning the gold, but he could dream. The year before, in the pre-Olympics, he had crushed Asada, the all-Japan collegiate champion, a person he had never been able to best in practice. Perhaps it could happen again.

By the time his turn came to take the mat, Campbell had become a raging bull. He bowed politely to his opponent, Thomas Ong of the

Philippines, and then rushed forward. Ong never had a chance. Campbell simply swept Ong's feet out from under him in a lightning move and the match was over—in less than six or seven seconds. "It was like Babe Ruth hitting a home run out of the stadium on the first pitch," Porter marveled. "A loud 'aaaaah' rose in the Budokan and then everyone cheered wildly."

Campbell's second opponent, Klaus Glahn of Germany, was no Thomas Ong. He was better and far heavier. As Campbell grappled with him, he felt his knee weakening. Once or twice it started to give as the match wore on and finally, about midway, it collapsed altogether as he tried to flip his heavier opponent. Campbell fell to the mat, unable to continue. "I realized there was no way that knee was going to hold up, so I had to forfeit."

Stunned, shocked, pain riveting his body, Campbell bowed to Glahn and hobbled to the edge of the mat. He sat down and fumbled with his sandals, trying to tie the straps through a glaze of tears. "I was crying, just kind of to myself, when some guy—I mean, this is how cold it is—yelled, 'Hey, buddy, get off the mat, will you? I can't see.' "

Campbell was not the only one weeping at that moment. At ringside were Phil Porter, his teammates, and a number of Japanese friends. "Oh God," Porter remembers, "there we were, with tears streaming down our faces, just gritting our teeth, knowing that a great career had come to an end. Had it not been for that knee, Ben would have chopped Glahn to pieces."

After getting his knee taped, Campbell returned to the Budokan floor to watch the featured match. Geesink, who outweighed his Japanese opponent by forty-five pounds, had already defeated Kaminaga once in the matches leading up to the final event. Since he had beaten him easily, most experienced observers knew what to expect. The Japanese, however, prayed for a miracle.

It was not to be. Geesink attacked throughout the match. Kaminaga managed to elude the giant for a few minutes, but a left-side foot block caught him for a half-point loss. Now desperate, Kaminaga tried without success to knock Geesink off his feet with several body drops before the Dutchman ended the match by smothering him in a rolling bear hug and pinning him to the mat. The victory gave Geesink the gold medal, confirmed him as world champion, and saddened all of Japan, although one Tokyo columnist later "humbly thanked" him for helping make judo a truly international sport.

Although the Japanese had performed as expected, garnering one silver and three gold medals, the team was disconsolate and many people in the audience wept openly. The Americans, on the other hand, had reason to rejoice because Bregman's bronze was a major coup for the United States. Not until 1976 did another U.S. team better that performance, despite the fact that the Olympic Committee expanded the competition to six weight divisions in 1972. In fact, with one or two breaks and a slightly better draw, each of the Americans might have won a medal in 1964.

The world press likened it to the equally astonishing victory in the 10,000-meter race by Billy Mills, a member of the Lakota tribe from Pine Ridge, South Dakota. Campbell and Mills, the only American Indians on the Olympic squad, are now good friends, but they did not know each other in 1964. Today, Mills is the Indian whose name springs to mind when talking about the 1964 Olympics, whereas few know Campbell even participated. Then Campbell was the international star, well known both to the press and to the Japanese. Mills, an obscure long-distance runner who barely qualified for the Olympics, was so anonymous that when he crossed the finish line in one of the greatest upsets in Olympic history an official asked him, "Who are you?" And the man he beat, Australian long-distance champion Ron Clarke, when asked if he had been worried about Mills, responded, "Worried about him? I never heard of him."

Not everyone was pleased with the showing of the American judo team. Porter, who covered the matches for *Black Belt Magazine* and was perhaps the most knowledgeable non-Japanese observer at the matches, directed heavy criticism at the refereeing and at the coaching of Yosh Uchida, blaming him for America's poor showing because he lacked a formal training program.

The United States may one day send a stronger judo team to the

Olympics, but it will never field a better group of young men in terms of integrity, dedication to the sport, and devotion to each other, says Porter, who has been part of their lives for the past three decades. "The character of those four people," he declares, "is unimpeachable, and their careers have been magnificent."

Each of those remarkable athletes on the Cinderella team of 1964 continued to lead enchanted lives after the Olympics. Each went on to make a genuine contribution to their families, their community, and their country. Harris retired from the Air Force as a master sergeant and is now a contracts specialist with the U.S. government. Married, he has three children and three grandchildren, lives in New Jersey, commutes to midtown Manhattan, and still works out with a local judo club. Maruyama reached the rank of lieutenant colonel in the U.S. Air Force and is enjoying a pleasant retirement in Colorado Springs. Bregman, who lives in Springfield, Virginia, is a computer specialist and senior executive with the Bureau of Indian Affairs.

Fourteen days after it began, the XVIII summer Olympics ended with the same style and flair with which it had opened. By all accounts, it had been the most impressive and best-administered summer Olympics ever held. Only the weather failed to cooperate. Indeed, except for the warmth and sunshine at the opening and a few pleasant interludes in between, the weather had been less than clement. But no drenching rain or threat of typhoon dampened the bonhomie of the games or taxed the marvelous patience and hospitality of the Japanese people. Even the Japanese pickpockets had been gracious. Of 194 arrested during the games, only four had tried to pinch foreign wallets.

For Campbell the closing ceremonies provided a special moment because he carried the American flag from the stadium. Swimmer Don Schollander, winner of four gold medals, carried the flag into the arena, but he had to leave early, thereby giving Campbell his opportunity. "My knee hurt like hell," he remembers, "but I was not about to let someone else have that flag." As luck would have it, Campbell found himself walking out of the stadium next to Leonid Zhabotinski, the gold medalist Russian weightlifter who was 330 pounds of iron. Zhabotinski held the

Russian flagpole stiffly at arm's length before him, as if it were a Popsicle. "Nobody can do this but these goddamn big bastards," Campbell laughs. "The Eastern bloc countries always give the flag to their heavyweight weightlifters. With my aching knee and that cold, gusting wind, I knew I couldn't match that act, so I edged forward to keep well away from him as we marched out of the stadium."

Campbell has never forgotten that moment. He remembered it clearly twenty-five years later when, as a member of Congress, he voted for the amendment to make desecrating the American flag a crime. "I got some heat from the liberals for that vote, but it made no difference to me. I told my colleagues on the House floor that I didn't fight in Korea or carry our flag in the Olympics so some fool could burn it."

Paul Maruyama has his own special memory of the closing ceremony and of Campbell. "Benny was into collecting posters and other paraphernalia of the Games as well as getting his picture taken with well-known athletes from all over the world. It seems to me he must have gone home with a pretty large collection of souvenir posters, flags, and pins. Since I was not very skillful at it, I'd hang around him as he traded, bartered, and posed with some of the most famous athletes of the day. He was good at charming people into giving him all kinds of souvenir items."

Preparing to leave the stadium at the closing ceremony, the U.S. team found itself lined up next to the Russian team, and Paul could not resist trying one more time to get one of their pins, which were very difficult to obtain because each Russian athlete received only one and would not trade it. While Maruyama was negotiating with a reluctant Russian athlete, Campbell decided to help. He brought over the huge silver medalist weightlifter, Yuri Vlasov, who could speak a little English. Ben explained the transaction to Vlasov, who facilitated the negotiations by yanking the pin out of his teammate's hand and giving it to Paul. Vlasov then took the belt buckle Paul had been offering as payment and kept it for himself. As soon as the unorthodox transaction was completed, Ben leaned over and whispered, "Now quick, disappear before the kid realizes what has happened!"

Maruyama remembers that Campbell did his own disappearing act the day a Japanese girl came into the Olympic Village looking for him with matrimony on her mind. Paul was resting on his bunk, when Ben banged through the door gasping, "Quick! Hide me!" The only place available was Paul's locker. "Somehow," Maruyama marvels, "all two hundred forty pounds of him squeezed into it."

Only moments later a young lady knocked on his door. "Do you know where I can find Canberu-san?" she asked. After chatting with her a few minutes, Maruyama convinced her that Campbell was not in the area and she left. With that Ben burst out of the locker, a picture of embarrassment and pain. The young woman, Ben explained rather sheepishly, had somehow confused words like "attraction" and "bed" with "love" and "marriage." Campbell had promised her the world before returning to the States for the Olympic trials, thinking she would not understand or remember what he said to her. "Unfortunately," Maruyama says, "the girl had fully understood most of what Benny had told her and she had been patiently awaiting his return to Japan. Campbell never dreamed she would come looking for him, especially into the security-tight Olympic Village."

As an athlete, Ben never lacked female companionship. It is a fringe benefit for any handsome, popular, and successful sports figure. Harris, for example, was followed around the world at her own expense by a beautiful, blue-eyed blonde who appeared at virtually every event in which he participated from Brazil to Tokyo. Campbell never had such a devoted groupie, but he seldom slept alone after international meets. With the fanfare and publicity that surrounded the American team in its travels, girls naturally flocked around the athletes. Most were good-looking young women who hoped to attract an American husband with their sexual charms. After a meet in Paris, for example, Ben and his teammate Mickey Tsuchida stopped for a few days in Geneva, where they met a friend who, it turned out, was a professional gigolo. "I didn't know this until later," Campbell says. One evening while putting on an exhibition at a judo club, Campbell noticed a number of pretty women in the stands. After the workout, the friend called Ben over and asked him to pick out his companion for the evening.

"You've got to be kidding," Campbell replied.

"No, no, I'm serious. Pick one."

"All right, I'll take that blonde over there."

The blonde was a sophisticated, cultivated woman, a White Russian whose parents had escaped to Switzerland during the revolution. She was a public relations officer for Standard Oil and spoke four languages. "That happens when you are on top in any sport," Campbell states matter-of-factly. At the time he never gave any thought to sexually transmitted disease, but he believes such a lifestyle will become a relic of the past because of herpes and AIDS.

Although Campbell ranked fourth in the world at the time he retired from active competition, he paid a stiff physical price for his success. "I think I've suffered every kind of pain except childbirth," he jokes. "For a while, it got to the point where I couldn't sleep nights unless I ached." He broke his nose nine times. He separated his shoulder twice and fractured seven ribs and all of his toes and fingers, some twice. He lost two teeth and pulled or tore more ligaments, tendons, and muscles than he cares to remember. "Who said judo means gentle way?"

Today his body continually reminds him of the abuse it suffered. Campbell must wear a brace to support a spine with two vertebrae out of line, and every morning he must coax aching muscles into behaving. Some mornings it is an ordeal simply to reach for his socks and shoes.

Sitting in his Capitol Hill office, Campbell now wonders if it was all worth it. "When I look back I don't know what I did it for. I wish I had gone into some sport that had a professional counterpart. If you do anything five hours a day for fifteen years like I did, you're going to get pretty good. Whether it's golf or swimming, playing checkers or playing the violin, you will get good at it. I got good at judo. But now, when I ache everywhere in the morning, when everything hurts, I think of the enormous amount of energy I expended and the torturous training I endured, and I wish I had done golf or tennis, something with a professional counterpart that I could have enjoyed for many more years and that would not have been so harmful to my body and that would have enabled me to provide for my family." Instead, Campbell received medals, ribbons, and trophies, hundreds of them. Most of them are meaningless dust collectors, for he has long forgotten the victories they represent. Those that break, he throws away as junk. "Not one of them is worth ten bucks, if I melted it down and tried to sell the metal."

If judo's disciples are left with a life of pain, if the sport provides them no opportunity to make a living, then what benefit do they derive from it? Judo, they claim, gives its devotees a will to succeed. It provides the inner strength to overcome adversity no matter how crushing it may appear. As Bregman likes to say, "We are survivors." Virtually nothing can make them give up before they give out. That is not always a healthy approach to everyday life. "Sometimes," Bregman realizes, "it's just better to surrender in a particular situation, lose that match and move on to something else. You don't have to fight every battle to the death, but I will push an issue or try to achieve an objective well beyond most people."

Campbell also values the sport's discipline. "The mechanical skill of throwing some guy on the floor may not help you feed your family, but judo teaches you to persevere, to never give up. That skill is transferable to business, to school, to politics. I am sure judo gave all of us intangible benefits."

What Campbell cannot explain as easily is where he gets his extreme competitiveness. Did judo give it to him, or did judo merely provide an acceptable outlet for something already present in his psyche? "Part of it has to come from my childhood, an orphan wanting to be as good as the next guy. I have always been a self-driver, I know that. I don't know why. I have never felt that I had to be the best, but I have always felt I should be the best I could be." Take the 1964 Olympics, for instance. "My body let me down. I know the gold medal was beyond my reach. Anton Geesink would have been too much for me. But I think to myself, even now, that I could have gotten a silver medal were it not for my knee." Whatever the explanation, judo prepared him well for life's battles, and nowhere was that preparation better served than in the decade after Campbell gave up competition and tried to make a living as a teacher and promoter of judo.

Although Campbell gave up competitive judo more than twenty

years ago, he got a chance to put his skills to good use in March 1991 as he was returning late one evening from a neighborhood grocery store to his home on Capitol Hill, less than two blocks away from his office. Campbell had just about reached his home when someone grabbed him from behind and spun him around. "Give me the money, man. This is a forty-five in my pocket." At that moment, Campbell remembers, a lot of crazy thoughts flashed through his mind. Not one of them involved giving up any money. One was the scene in the movie *Crocodile Dundee* when the youthful mugger shows his knife and Dundee pulls his own, which looks like a machete in comparison. "In Colorado," Campbell says, "I have a permit to carry a forty-five because I am often delivering expensive jewelry. When that guy claimed to have a gun, I wanted to step back and say 'No, man, that's not a forty-five, this is a forty-five.' It would have been perfect. Instead, in my best Humphrey Bogart impersonation, I said, 'Oh yeah? Show me the gun.'

"Maybe he didn't have a gun, or maybe he just didn't like the way I did Bogart because as soon as I said it he busted me in the mouth."

With that the fight was on. Campbell quickly got him down but could not keep him down. "I couldn't hold the son of a gun. He was a big guy, probably six two and very athletic. He took off running and I tried to give chase, but something wasn't working. I must have torn my ankle when I went off the curb with him, because I came up limping. Although he got away, maybe he'll give more thought when he decides to mug someone again. At least he learned that I don't easily give up my peanut butter and jelly. In fact, that was another of the crazy things that flashed across my mind. 'God,' I thought, 'if I chase him somebody is going to get my groceries.' What a thing to think about when you've just been mugged. Anyhow," Campbell laughed, as he discussed the episode over coffee the following morning with his crutches lying next to the table in the Longworth Building cafeteria and various colleagues coming by to congratulate him for his temerity in the face of danger, "I found out that I wasn't a twenty-year-old judo champ anymore. I'm nothing but a fifty-eight-year-old overweight congressman."

THREE

CAMP BUSHIDO

At thirty-one years of age, Campbell literally had to start life over again, having sacrificed just about everything of importance to him in pursuit of the Olympic gold. Despite his failure to win a medal, he returned to the United States a local hero, and he was by no means destitute. He had some cash, and he had an impressive collection of Japanese weapons, including several complete suits of samurai armor assembled over the many years of his intense interest in the history of martial arts. Throughout his stay in Japan, he had nurtured the idea of writing a master's thesis on the subject, and the collection seemed an appropriate research resource for the thesis, which still remains to be written. For a time he displayed the collection at his judo school in Sacramento, but eventually he sold the weapons to a wealthy collector in Oakland, California, when he wanted to buy a horse. Sadly, the collection burned in a fire some years later.

Campbell considers the period right after the 1964 Olympics one of the most enjoyable of his life. Having survived an austere and solitary, if not monastic, regimen in Japan, he made up for lost time by indulging in flashy women and even flashier cars. For four years running, he bought a new XKE Jaguar, a luxury he maintained by juggling a dozen or more credit cards.

When not driving flashy cars, however, Ben enjoyed tooling around the countryside on a motorcycle; it is a passion he has never outgrown. In fact, as a present for winning a seat in the U.S. Senate in 1992, his wife gave him a new black and red Harley Davidson 1380C softail, which brought him as much media attention as his senate victory.

His primary means of support was teaching. He had a job waiting for him in the Sacramento area thanks to a judo friend, Ken Santiago, who worked for the San Juan Unified Public School District. Ben had actually acquired the position as a physical education teacher in the district while in Sacramento training for the Olympics.

But for Campbell teaching was only a means to an end. Judo was still in his blood, and he saw no reason to leave the sport. Why should he? Judo had given his life purpose and direction, and it had given him fame and confidence.

With his career as a competitor now ended—even Campbell realized that—he could still remain active in the sport as a coach, administrator, or politician. He tried them all. Although no one had yet been able to make more than a modest living as a judo instructor, Campbell with his typical boldness thought he could beat the odds by transforming judo from a sport known only to a few aficionados to one of mass popularity. It was a dream he had cherished since his sophomore year in college when he surveyed California high schools to plumb the depths of interest that could be tapped by someone with charisma, imagination, enthusiasm, and energy—traits he possessed by the bucketful.

Although Campbell spent only the next eight years or so fully committed to judo, they were crucial years for the sport. Indeed, Campbell's longtime associate Phil Porter insists that the years Campbell devoted to the sport after the Tokyo Olympics were "tremendously important." He devised a new training method now used around the world; he caused the sport to expand exponentially; he helped found the U.S. Judo Association; and he produced a number of junior, senior, and collegiate gold medalists. "Ben's ideas," Porter says, "are still the basic secret, if you will, that will unlock the growth of American judo, and it was a tremendous loss to the sport when he left it to pursue his interests in jewelry and ranching."

Campbell, in fact, pursued a variety of activities, but judo was uppermost in his thoughts. First he reorganized and revitalized the Sacramento Judo Club. One of the oldest clubs in the country, it had been founded in the early 1930s by two young Japanese immigrants, Ted Ikemoto and Hiroshi Matsuda, who rented space in a Buddhist church in downtown Sacramento. Unfortunately, Ikemoto and Matsuda were swept up in the anti-Japanese hysteria of World War II and spent the duration of the war in an internment camp. Their club lay dormant until Campbell returned to California after the Korean War. In looking for a place to work out, Campbell went to the local YMCA, where he met Porter, who was also training there. They got to talking and became fast friends. Together they decided to revive the old club. They located some of the former Japanese members, including Ikemoto and Matsuda, whom they persuaded to come out of retirement and assist in the project. Quarters for the club were found in a dilapidated building in Sacramento's skid row section. "It was pretty much a shoestring affair," Campbell admits. "Our audience in those days was often equal parts of parents, hookers, and drunks. When we threw each other, plaster would fall from the ceiling and the floor would crack. We existed on the dues of the members. Everybody pooled their dues, and that's how we paid the rent. There was no money in judo in those days, and there still isn't."

When Campbell returned ten years later, he was delighted to see the club still in operation, but its prospects were gloomy. The club, which had only thirty or so members, still rented space in the same building, which, if possible, was even more dilapidated than Campbell remembered. The club desperately needed a boost and a face-lift if judo was ever to overcome its negative public image. Campbell's biggest problems, he recalls, were to persuade the members to think in terms of "building" as well as working out and teaching and to maintain enthusiasm in the club until more appropriate quarters could be found.

Campbell's big break came when he located an abandoned schoolhouse in the Perkins district of Sacramento, opposite a public golf course. Although the building had been condemned, the city of Sacramento agreed to let the club use the site for judo as long as the old steam boiler was removed. "We cut it apart with acetylene torches, threw away all the pieces, and turned the former school into the finest judo club in the country."

The new Sacramento Judo Club was in a fashionable neighborhood on a four-acre tract of land that included a baseball diamond, basketball and volleyball courts, and chinning bars. The outstanding feature of the complex was a seventeen-room building with seventy-five hundred feet of floor space. On the main floor were several spacious rooms that served as dojos or gymnasiums for judo practice and two smaller rooms on opposite sides of the building that Campbell used for teaching aikido and karate and other martial arts. Downstairs was a large weight room. In addition to shower facilities for both men and women, the club also boasted a training room, a sauna, and an "arms room," where Campbell displayed his collection of Japanese weapons.

The facility, palatial in comparison to the club's former quarters, offered its members just about everything one could expect in a judo club except air conditioning and heat, which, Campbell liked to say, was in keeping with his "toughening program." The absence of heat and air conditioning, he told the incredulous, made for ideal training conditions: judo, when properly taught, "is supposed to be applicable to all weather conditions this side of the North Pole."

Club members got all this for only seven dollars a month—six dollars for children, because Campbell believed in starting them young. Indeed, of the club's 150 members in May 1967, half were aged twelve and younger, six were just that, and a few claimed to be only five years old. The other members covered the age spectrum from adolescents to grandparents.

Although members were predominantly male, women were welcome. Campbell had only two requirements: good health and a fighting spirit. "It's the fight that separates the men from the boys," he informed a reporter for *Judo Illustrated*. His students also had to be willing to undergo a rugged regimen, because Campbell taught judo as the Japanese do, "with less talk and more practice, supplemented with modern training techniques for diet, conditioning, and treatment of injuries, and, above all, a hard attitude. By this," he told the reporter, "I mean no rest, no breaks, no drinking water, no coming in late." No matter that the beginner's class each year experienced a 50 percent dropout rate; those who remained were certain to have the proper fighting spirit. Because "the strong seek out the strong," Campbell's club continually attracted members from the twenty-five or so high school judo programs in the surrounding area as well as world-class competitors from around the country, including his Olympic teammate Paul Maruyama and Hayward Nishioka, the U.S. champion.

Tough, yes, but vicious, no. Campbell's program closely adhered to the Japanese principles of judo. "It is a mental as well as physical training designed to develop balance, effectiveness in action, inner and outer harmony, and relaxation," he told one reporter. Campbell's students learned that judo is an art that demands complete body control, delicate balance, and fast reflexes. The ideal, he would tell them, is to develop a sharp-reacting mind coordinated with a strong and disciplined body.

Campbell had little patience for those who came to judo merely for its self-defense or attack skills. "Judo," he told his students, "belongs in the gym." Anyone caught using it on the streets was automatically blackballed. They could take out their aggression in individual matches and in competition with other clubs.

Thanks to Campbell, there was no lack of opportunity for competition. "We placed a bunch of kids in the national championships and the national collegiates, as well as several on the U.S. Olympic team in 1972. We had a pretty good club," Campbell is willing to admit. That, says one of his star performers, John Vinson, is an understatement. "At that time, the Sacramento Judo Club was probably one of the strongest in the United States."

Campbell's energy, enthusiasm, and success brought him both regional and national attention. Not only was he elected president of the 2,000-member Northern California Blackbelt Association, but he also received the first Amateur Athletic Union U.S.A. All-American Judo Award. Almost singlehandedly, Campbell had turned Sacramento into the nation's leading judo center.

Although Campbell adhered quite closely to the format of the training he had received at Meiji University, his program differed in several key respects. The most important one was his concept of the "moving training drill." According to Don Savage, one of Campbell's premier students, who learned judo under this new system, the drills included a thrower and a receiver, but they were dynamic, not static. "You wouldn't stay in one place and just pull your partner in what we call *uchicomi*. The students moved up and down the mat continually attacking with, for example, a foot technique." The drills also gave students the ability to use defensive techniques—hip posturing, for example—to ward off being thrown or taken off balance. "These were very energetic, very dynamic drills," Savage explains. Perhaps more important, they reduced the risk of injury because they improved stamina for when the athletes did *randori*, or free-style fighting, where each person had to prove in actual combat what had been learned.

Campbell eventually wrote a book detailing his revolutionary training technique, *Championship Judo: Drill Training*. Still in print, the book was edited and published in Sacramento in 1974 by Porter.

To Savage and others who have followed Campbell's life since the 1960s, he is a Renaissance man in the true meaning of the word. Ben was always thinking about the sport, always promoting it and the people working in it with him. "No matter what he was doing, writing articles, writing books, whatever, he let us participate. A lot of us in the club are the people whose pictures are in the books demonstrating the moves. He got us on television programs. He brought sports reporters from the various stations to watch us compete. He always made sure that there was coverage of the sport: local newspaper coverage, local television coverage. We went down to Southern California and did a series of training tapes to be shown on public television. He was always involved, always looking for something to enhance the sport. To me," says Savage, "that is the mark of a Renaissance man, taking something to a level that nobody has ever taken it."

Judging by the galaxy of stars Campbell produced, his techniques worked. One of his most remarkable disciples is John Vinson, a successful investment broker in Phoenix with offices in Japan as well as the United States. As a teenager Vinson called Campbell and announced he wanted to quit school, move to California, and train under him. "No way," Campbell replied, "you finish high school first." Vinson did, in fact, complete high school—"he still couldn't spell a darn," Campbell laughs—before moving to Sacramento and living in the judo club. "I let him sleep in the basement, and I agreed to train him on the condition that he help keep the club clean and attend college." In residence with him at the club were two other aspiring judoists destined to become U.S. national champions, Doug Nelson and Harold Makimoto. "Our job," Vinson remembers, "was, basically, to keep the club clean by mopping the floors and vacuuming the mats. We also had to help teach the kids' classes."

The arrangement worked well most of the time, but occasionally Campbell felt that Vinson was neither as diligent with his chores nor as respectful as he should be. Matters came to a head one rainy evening.

"This floor is not clean," Campbell informed him.

"It's clean enough for me," Vinson retorted.

"You don't tell your teacher that!" Campbell yelled as he proceeded to give his student a lesson in manners before tossing him—bleeding, vomiting, and semiconscious—onto the rain-soaked driveway in back of the judo club. "I had been lying in the road in the rain and mud for about thirty minutes," Vinson recalls, "when some of my buddies sneaked around back to throw me in a car to get me out of there for a few days. Ben saw them, however, and told them to leave me alone." After a bit, covered with mud, blood, and vomit, and drenched to the skin, Vinson staggered back into the clubhouse.

"This floor is not clean," Campbell repeated.

"You're right," Vinson mumbled. "I'll get to it as soon as I take a shower."

Vinson also has more pleasant memories of his days with the Sacramento Judo Club. After their Friday night workouts, for example, the members would get a couple of cases of beer and sit around talking, usually about the Olympics. On more than one occasion parents bringing their youngsters to the club for Saturday morning lessons found their instructors still asleep on the mats.

His training techniques may sound brutal, Campbell admits, but it's all part of judo. "I had to shave my head when I lost a match at Meiji University, I had to wash the dirty judo-gis of upperclassmen, I had to scrub toilets, and I had to do all kinds of stuff as an act of self-discipline. What I did for John was just exactly what I went through in Japan. You discipline yourself, or somebody else will discipline you. That's judo training, and I swear it's one of the things that made him such a tough businessman. He's a multimillionaire today, and we are still good friends. He is kind of my pride and joy because he's been able to transfer judo training to other areas."

Vinson, who later spent four years studying judo in Japan, agrees. "Without the preparation Ben gave, I probably would not have been able to go through what I did in Japan. In fact, I think the three years or so I spent living with Ben along with the years I spent in Japan have helped more than anyone can imagine in my personal life and business career. A one-on-one sport like judo teaches a person tenacity." Lest he ever forget the lessons that he learned from judo, Vinson still retains a note Campbell wrote him. It is framed and hangs on the wall in his Phoenix office: "John, the bathroom is not clean yet. Clean it or I'll beat the hell out of you when I get home."

John Vinson is just one of dozens of youngsters Campbell influenced through judo. Another is Don Savage, who today is in his midforties and a captain on the Sacramento Police Force responsible for investigating narcotics gangs. A warrior in his own right, having received numerous commendations for valor in the line of duty, Savage—at six foot two and 220 pounds—exudes confidence and competence. Like Campbell, he also grew up on the streets. As a youngster, he knocked around foster homes in California and then served six years in the U.S. Army, where he was introduced to judo by a Hungarian freedom fighter who had enlisted as a way of gaining United States citizenship.

"One day in 1964," Savage recalls, "I was sitting in the barracks at Fort Lee, Virginia, watching the Olympic tryouts being held that year at the New York World's Fair and saw Ben Campbell for the first time. The announcer said he was from Sacramento, California. As I watched him fight I thought, 'Oh, I've got to go learn from that guy.' Immediately upon receiving his U.S. Army discharge in August that year, Savage went to Sacramento, where he spent a week or so getting settled before making his appearance at the judo club. Campbell had just returned from Japan and was living at the club, Savage remembers. "I walked in and they were all there—Campbell, Harris, Bregman, Maruyama, all the guys I had been reading about in *Black Belt Magazine*—and I was meeting them. It was just unreal."

Savage was smitten. He and Campbell became pals, and he became addicted to judo, attaining the rank of third-degree black belt, which he now holds. The high point of his competitive career was 1970, when he took fourth place nationally in the light-heavyweight division. To this day Savage treasures the black belt Campbell wore while competing in the Tokyo Olympics. "He told me to keep it because he expected me to be there one day."

Other success stories include a youngster named Jimmy Martin, who came to Campbell at nine years of age and lived with him at the Sacramento judo club on weekends. He eventually earned a place on four different U.S. international teams and won a half-dozen U.S. championships as an adult. Douglas Nelson, another star, was the only American ever to win a national championship while still in high school. He showed up at Campbell's door after having dropped out of school in order to train with him in California. Campbell accepted him on the condition that he attend and finish high school. Doug agreed to the challenge and earned his diploma while earning the plaudits of the world of judo. Campbell also lost some good athletes. One young man, the top high school judo competitor in the country at the time and a scholarship holder at San Jose State, got into drugs while in college and gave up the sport.

Almost simultaneously with revitalizing the Sacramento Judo Club, Campbell launched a summer training program for judo. Such a program had been very popular in Japan for a long time, but it had never been tried in the United States before he started what he called Camp Bushido, which means "the warrior spirit way" or "the warrior training way." Campbell established the first camp in Squaw Valley, California. It was so successful that the following year he established similar camps in Soda Springs, California; Davenport, Iowa; Middlefield, Connecticut; and Estes Park, Colorado. As a result, Campbell would spend his summers on the road going from camp to camp to train youngsters in competition judo.

John Vinson helped set up the first camp and worked with Campbell at the second, third, and fourth camps as well. "The setting could not have been better," he writes. "At Squaw Valley, the site of the 1960 Winter Olympics, the seven-thousand-foot elevation, tall pines, and cool weather made training perfect."

A reporter covering the camp for the *Sacramento Union* concurred. To her, "training camp" had always conjured up images of foul-smelling gyms frequented by cigar-smoking mobsters and their pug-ugly associates, but Camp Bushido seemed to be the antithesis of all that. Campbell's camp featured several former Olympic athletes as instructors and an assortment of clean-cut all-American-looking young men—and two fifteen-year-old girls—ranging in age from eight to twenty-six. For girls, Campbell told the reporter, judo instruction was largely defensive, and their training differed from that of the boys. That, she thought, had merit since she watched one of the boys, who seemed quite proficient at the sport, lose two front teeth "in an instant." The injury she witnessed, Campbell assured the reporter, had been the only one at the camp except for a broken arm suffered by one youngster in horseplay not connected with judo.

Although Camp Bushido is still going strong, Campbell disassociated himself from it long ago. "I got tired of the constant travel," he says. "Besides, I wanted to get into Indian art, and I could not do both." The camp is now the property of the National Judo Center in Colorado Springs, and Campbell's old friend Phil Porter is executive director. "I gave Phil the right to continue using the name when I got out of judo."

Another of Campbell's innovations for the sport was attempting to make judo a standard part of public school physical education. He returned from the Olympics convinced that he could make judo more popular in the United States by teaching it to youngsters on a massive scale in junior and senior high schools. "Judo," Campbell wrote in 1966, "is one of the most controversial and least understood sports in the United States. Its objectives—self-control, discipline, and moral responsibility—the cornerstones of competitive judo, probably appear far-fetched to the layman watching a rough-and-tumble match." A commonly asked question by people unacquainted with the sport, for example, is "Are judoists registered with the police?"

To help judo achieve a broader level of acceptance, to increase its practitioners from the relative handful of zealots then pursuing the sport, Campbell persuaded administrators of Carmichael's San Juan district, the second largest in the state of California with a potential pool of a hundred thousand judokas, to permit the introduction of judo into the curriculum for one year on a fully voluntary, experimental basis. Campbell chose that district for the experiment, he claimed, because it had "a young, progressive, and open-minded staff and administration, many of whom already participated in judo, including several who were holders of the black belt." The fact that Campbell was already teaching in the district must certainly have been a major factor in getting permission to conduct the experiment.

Although other high schools in the country had offered judo in the past, nowhere had it ever been attempted on the scale Campbell envisioned. The reason, in large part, was the lack of qualified instructors with the appropriate teaching credentials. "My idea," Campbell later explained, "was to try and teach coaches to become judomen rather than to get judomen into teaching."

Eight senior high schools in the San Juan district participated in the experimental program, which was conducted by Campbell and three assistants, including John Vinson and Kenny Santiago. A total of 1,107 boys enrolled in the judo classes, each of whom received fifteen class hours of instruction. Only the last two days were devoted to actual competition. In the classes, the students learned about the history and objectives of judo; falling, throwing, and pinning techniques; rules for competition and scoring; and the belt-rank system. Throughout the course, the instructors stressed judo's moral and mental training and its application to everyday life. "Surprisingly," Campbell later wrote, "it was this aspect that most impressed both educators and students alike."

Interesting a large number of boys in judo classes was relatively easy. More challenging was the task of interesting their physical education teachers, because the key to the program's success was to develop a cadre of qualified judo instructors who would commit themselves to continuing the sport as part of the school curriculum. Campbell eased the way by offering them the opportunity to earn two units of college credit and a chance to qualify for the brown-belt rank in judo for participating. Thanks to this attractive incentive, worked out with nearby Sacramento State College, forty-four junior and senior high physical education coaches enrolled in Campbell's class, entitled Techniques of Judo Teaching. Each day the coaches attended two classes. In the morning sessions, the coaches took notes and tried the movements themselves just as the students did. In the afternoon the coaches were the judo teachers, putting into practice what they had learned in the morning. Campbell and his assistants were present, but only as observers who offered nothing in the way of advice or criticism. This was to determine if students could learn as much from an inexperienced judoist who was a professional teacher as they could learn from an inexperienced teacher but an expert in the sport.

The results, Campbell later reported in *Black Belt Magazine,* were "noteworthy." The boys in the morning and afternoon classes learned at the same rate. This came as no real surprise because physical education teachers were already adept at handling large groups of boys. Admittedly, the experiment worked well with beginning students, but what remained to be determined was whether the outcome would hold true for students who progressed beyond the novice stage. "Perhaps over a longer period of time or at a higher level of competition there might be a noticeable difference between the two groups," Campbell suggested, but he assumed some of the coaches would want to continue to improve themselves in judo, and such individuals would be able to handle more advanced students.

Certainly, this seemed to be the case with the initial group of forty-four. In the spring, after little more than a semester of training, a team composed of five of the coaches entered the Northern California team championships and placed first in the novice division. "This," Campbell boasted, "proved they could practice what they preached." At the end of the two-credit course, the coaches each received a third-degree brown belt.

The students were equally pleased. Upon completing the course, each student filled out a standardized evaluation form that asked questions concerning likes and dislikes, continued interest, and so forth. Of the 1,036 students who completed the course, only 71 claimed they did not like it. One wrote, "It's a waste of good football time." Another noted simply, "It don't work."

More than 98 percent of the students, however, overwhelmingly endorsed the program. They not only liked judo, they wanted to see it in the permanent curriculum. "I liked judo," wrote one youngster, "because it has the potential to be a very popular high school sport." Wrote another: "Judo was the first activity I have done in school which I felt was exciting and fun. It was the first time I ever felt I had learned anything or had any success in physical education."

The few problems encountered were readily resolved. Since the experiment had a very limited budget, Campbell could not afford to buy uniforms for the students, so the boys attended class in swimming trunks or sweat suits. The instructors, as a result, did not teach any technique that required the judo-gi for gripping an opponent. Although the boys were at first disappointed at the lack of uniforms, the grumbling disappeared after the first lesson or two.

Because of the potential for injury, judo classes require strict teacher control. A good way of maintaining that control is to limit the size of the classes. In the first year, classes ranged in size from thirty to one hundred boys, but thirty to forty appeared to be ideal. Remarkably, only eight injuries requiring medical care were reported, a figure that even Campbell admitted was unrealistically low because actual contact had been limited to the last two class sessions. Statistically, judo injuries normally occur about as frequently as wrestling injuries, but four times more often than in track and field events and four times less often than in football.

Campbell preceded the program with considerable public relations work because of judo's negative image. Before launching the program, he and his associates demonstrated sport judo to PTA meetings, rallies, and coaching clinics. He also found it necessary to emphasize to his students the difference between sport judo and unarmed combat because many of the boys, it turned out, had fathers who had learned "neat ways to kill" while in military service.

For Campbell, the real mark of the program's success was the fact that twelve of the teachers—six senior high and six junior high—wished to teach judo the following fall and form judo teams. As a result, these schools formed the nation's first high school and junior high conferences, and member teams participated in sanctioned meets throughout the state. In the first year alone the new league introduced eight thousand students to the sport, one and a half times the number of high school students enrolled in AAU-sanctioned judo programs nationwide. Based on the results of the first year, Campbell looked forward to a full-fledged judo conference with regular competition between all ninety-eight schools in the San Juan district.

"That was the first time something like this was ever tried in the United States," Campbell says proudly, "and it worked great!" It worked so well, in fact, that at the end of the first year Campbell invited a Japanese high school team to a dual meet with the best of his high school judoists. "They beat the hell out of us," Campbell laughs, "but it was great even if it was unorthodox. We had a packed house, too."

The experiment is especially memorable to Campbell for another reason as well. Through it he met Linda Price, now his wife of more than twenty-five years. The beautiful, blond daughter of a rancher from Montrose, Colorado, was teaching in the San Juan district when Campbell started his high school judo program. How they met and married is a story in itself.

Linda Price is a small-town girl with traditional values and upbringing. Her maternal grandparents came to the United States from Sweden; her paternal grandmother crossed the Plains in a covered wagon and settled in Whitewater, where she met and married a fellow from North Carolina. The Prices were a close-knit family and very supportive of each other. Linda liked ranch life and fully expected to marry a rancher one day. Upon graduating from Western State College of Colorado in nearby Gunnison, she returned to Montrose, where she accepted a teaching position at her old high school, and settled down to wait until that certain rancher showed up and she could start her own family.

For Barbara Wear, her best friend and fellow teacher, however, Montrose was a bit too tame. "She always was a little fiery," Linda laughs. During the summer of 1964, Barbara went to California and got a job at Harrah's, a casino and resort at Lake Tahoe, and loved it. She, in turn, persuaded Linda to join her the following year. They quit their teaching jobs in Montrose at the end of the school year and drove directly to Lake Tahoe. "Barb had worked at Harrah's the summer before as a keno dealer, and the casinos always prefer to rehire rather than to train new personnel; so she had her job, but I didn't have one." At first Linda felt out of her element. "I was pretty naive," she admits. "I had never even been inside a bar before except a little place in Gunnison that sold 3.2 beer. I walked into Harrah's late on a Sunday night, and I didn't know where I was. Here were all these old women pulling these handles. It was just so unreal."

Reality found Linda the next morning in an employment line that stretched clear out into the parking lot. "First we had to stand in the line until we reached a central window, and then they moved us wherever. It was like a cattle drive, and the fellow at the window said the most awful things to people, things that no employer could ever say today."

"You have really bad acne," he brusquely informed one young man. "We'll have to put you back in the kitchen, out of the public eye."

The girl right in front of Linda was a little overweight. "Lose ten pounds, and then come back and talk to us," she was told.

"All the time, my heart was pounding, and I kept thinking, 'Wow, what are they going to say to me when I get there?' " But Linda did not have to worry. The interviewer took one look at her, smiled broadly, and said, "We'll put you in dealers' school."

Linda started the one-week course the next Monday. The first three days she spent learning craps and blackjack. The fourth day she watched the dealers at work. The fifth day she handled a table, and the instructor stood by and watched her.

"My folks," Linda admits, "were not excited about my new job. In fact, the whole family was real nervous about my going to Lake Tahoe. Every relative I had came out and visited me that summer, but when they saw I was all right, they relaxed."

For Linda, obviously wholesome, friendly, and fresh off the farm, it was great. "The people up there could not have been nicer to me," she reflects. "I guess they could tell I was pretty naive, because they really took care of me, like the time I got propositioned and didn't even know it." The mistake was easy to make, Linda explains, because players were always slipping tips to dealers they liked instead of putting the money into a pool for the entire staff to share. "This old guy had played at my table a long time and had won a lot. When I left for my break, he came up to me and said something I could not understand. All I could hear him say was 'one hundred dollars.' At first I thought he wanted to give me a hundred, but then I realized he was saying, 'How would you like to earn a hundred?' My mouth dropped open right then and there. 'What did you say?' I stammered. I was so shocked."

As luck would have it, Linda's pit boss happened to be standing behind her as this exchange occurred. "What did that guy say to you?" he asked. When she repeated the conversation, her boss said, "If he ever comes back to your table, call me and we'll kick him out of here." Fortunately, he never did, Linda remembers, but her boss visited her table three times that night to make sure. "That was how they treated me at Harrah's, just real protective, kind of fatherly."

As soon as Linda landed her job, she and Barb hurried on to Sacramento to see about teaching positions for the fall. Thanks to a tip from one of Barb's friends, they had already sent their applications to the big San Juan district. Both received contracts—Linda to teach physical education and Barbara to teach home economics—and both were assigned to La Sierra High School in Carmichael, a community outside of Sacramento, where they shared an apartment.

They worked at Harrah's every weekend. "After school on Friday, I would drive up to Tahoe, work three shifts, and then drive back down. I did that all school year. It was seventy miles one way, and I drove it in my little black Volkswagen. One tank of gas that cost four dollars would last all week long going back and forth to school and to Tahoe and back."

Almost immediately, Linda heard about Ben Campbell. "We were talking about guys, of course, and one of the teachers said, 'Oh, there is this one really neat bachelor here, he just got back from the Olympics and he drives a red Jaguar, but I don't know if he likes women.' "

Linda saw Ben from time to time because he was teaching adaptive physical education to the boys for the entire district, which involved ten schools, and he visited La Sierra the last period of the day. "I remember seeing him," she laughs, "because I remember the car. That red Jaguar was really neat. Sometimes I would see him in a red and white station wagon, which I found out later was his girlfriend's car. She was also a P.E. teacher, but I never did see her. All I know is that she was a really big-busted person."

Except for noticing his car Linda never thought much about Ben, but the other teachers did. At lunch one day the wrestling coach challenged her: "Why don't you ever go out with Ben?"

"Because he's never asked me, that's probably why," she retorted.

"Would you go if he asked you?"

"Oh, maybe," she said.

"So, don't you know," Linda recalls, "he goes right over to Ben and does him the same way."

"Why don't you ever take Linda out?" he asked.

"Oh, I don't know, I never thought much about it," he shrugged, giving her a casual glance.

That was the status of their relationship until the second semester when Campbell announced his innovative high school judo program. "Oh, let's take that judo class," Barbara urged. "Then when we go back to Montrose we can teach it there." Linda's reaction was less than enthusiastic. "I'd never even heard of judo before. It certainly wasn't an interest of mine."

Nonetheless, at the next district-wide physical education meeting, she sought Campbell out. "My roommate wants to know if she can take your judo class, since she is not in P.E."

"Oh, sure, no problem," Campbell told her.

Because Barbara really wanted to learn judo, Linda went to the first class even though she was still filled with misgivings. "Here were all these people, and I thought Well, I'll just go this first time, then if I don't like it, I won't go back. I didn't want to get obligated." As things turned out, she had little choice. The first thing Campbell did was hand out uniforms to the group. "Now," he announced, "if you are as big as Linda here, you'll take a size five."

"Excuse me," Linda choked.

"I mean as tall as Linda," Campbell corrected himself, which gave everyone another chuckle.

Then he announced that the students could pay for the uniforms at the next class. "After that, you are pretty obligated to go," Linda says, "so that's how it started." They had their first date after one of the classes.

What attracted Linda to Campbell was not his Jaguar, but, of all things, his feet. "I know this is really crazy," she laughs, "but he had the prettiest feet. They were long and he used them all the time in judo. He was so agile. I had never noticed anyone's feet before, and I certainly never did afterward."

After the second class, sometime in early February, Ben invited Linda to go out for coffee. Since they were dripping with perspiration, she suggested he pick her up at home so she could shower and change. He readily agreed, but when he arrived, he just sat down, chatted for a long time, and then announced that he needed to leave. "Don't you want that coffee?" Linda asked. "Oh yeah," he replied. "Let's go."

"So what does he do—" Linda shakes her head—"but take me to a bar. I guess he thought I was fast or something because I worked at Tahoe. Anyhow, when we got there, I ordered orange juice. I know that surprised him. I also remember he had a big key ring, and I kept messing with his keys. I was really pretty naive. Remember, I was only twenty-three, and he was about ten years older."

Linda had dated a lot all through college and during her time at Tahoe, but she had never been in love. "I liked guys until I knew they liked me; then I didn't like them anymore. It was really funny, but I didn't want them close to me. The challenge was in trying to attract them. Once I had them it wasn't fun any longer. It happened over and over. I'd gone out with a bunch of really neat guys before Ben, but they really turned me off. I kept thinking, as I went out with Ben, when is that going to happen? It never did. The reason it didn't, I guess, is that I never really knew where I stood with him. I still don't. Ben is a very private person. Once, after we had been dating only a month or so, he told me that I scared him."

"Me?" Linda responded in surprise. "How can that possibly be?"

"Well," he admitted, "I have a wall built around me and I don't let anyone inside. I feel that you are getting inside of that inner circle."

"I was really shocked by this admission," Linda remembers. "We came from such different backgrounds. I am so open and friendly. I've always had a lot of security from my friends and relatives, and he had none. I'll never forget him saying that to me. He only said it that once and never, ever brought it up again. But I do think he has a real fear of losing what he has, and that makes him very insecure. To this day," Linda admits, "I really don't know where I stand with him. He's not one to share his inner feelings with anyone. In fact, I don't think he has a close friend—lots of acquaintances but no close friends."

Linda also soon learned that Ben was very impulsive. She thought his red Jaguar coupe was very nice, but in chatting with him one day she offhandedly told him that, if given a choice, she would have gotten a black convertible. A few days later she bumped into him in the hallway at school, and he announced, "I've got a surprise for you tonight!"

"Golly," Linda exclaimed, thinking he had gotten her a diamond ring.

That evening, when she opened the door to his knock, she was startled, since it had been a warm spring day, to see Ben wearing a red plaid wool jacket and a stocking cap. "Come on, come on," he urged, "get your coat! I want you to see your surprise!"

"You guessed it," Linda laughs. "I walked out to the street and there was a new black Jaguar convertible."

Linda and Ben continued to see each other casually until the term ended, when she went back to working full-time at Lake Tahoe. "Ben came up a couple of times early in the summer," Linda says, "but didn't like what he saw. The pit bosses were really friendly, always talking to me. They weren't making passes, but he didn't like it and wanted me to quit. They hate it when people quit during the season, but I did it because I really liked him, even though we had never talked seriously about our relationship or anything. He never even hinted at marriage."

Since Linda now needed to find other employment, Ben suggested she help him with Camp Bushido, which was going strong at the time. "I asked her to come and work with the kids, be a counselor. We got little kids, sometimes six and seven years old, still wetting their pants. I didn't know how to handle some of the little devils, so Linda came up and worked at the camp."

Linda remembers it a bit differently. "I went to the camp all right, but I never got paid. He said he'd hire me, but he never did. He still tells people that I was a camp counselor, but that's a bunch of bull. I did all of the registration, all the clerical stuff, and never received a cent for it."

Campbell obviously had other plans for Linda. As she remembers it, he walked up to her one July day and "just out of the clear blue" said, "Let's get married." They had been dating only a few months. Startled, yet pleased, she simply blurted, "We can't unless you talk to my dad!"

"So I called up her dad," Campbell says. "I'd never seen him, never met him, nothing. I told him who I was and that we wanted to get married, and he said okay." They exchanged vows a week later, July 23, 1966.

"I swore I never wanted a church wedding," says Linda, "because my sister and a close friend got married a few months apart in Montrose, and for a whole year all I heard was weddings, weddings, weddings! I hated it, and I promised myself I would never go through something like that. Well, I didn't, but I'm not sure what I went through was any better."

"It was a very impromptu thing," Campbell admits, "so we had a hired wedding." Linda and Ben went to Reno with Phil Porter and his current girlfriend, a military officer named Yvonne Capoiullez, whom they all called Captain Jo. Phil was the best man; Captain Jo was the maid of honor; and somewhere Ben bought a ring. Everything else he rented. "It was the funniest thing I ever experienced," Campbell claims. "The preacher was like an actor who can play the part of a drunk beautifully, only this guy wasn't acting. He was soused, and he had wine stains all over his rumpled white shirt."

When asked about the size of service they wanted, Porter and Campbell selected the most elaborate one being offered, something on the order of $27.50. "For that," Campbell claims, "the minister drummed a few guys off the street who came in, sat through the ceremony, waved, clapped, threw rice on us, and did all the stuff you do at weddings. We got to laughing and couldn't stop. It was just torture, it was so damn funny. Then the preacher got mad because we were laughing so much. When it was over I began to wonder if it was even legal. The best thing about it, we never missed a day of training."

Linda did not get her honeymoon until the following summer, when Ben arranged a trip outside California through Operation Champ, a program set up during the Kennedy administration by the President's Council on Physical Fitness and then administered by Vice President Hubert Humphrey. The program presented sports clinics to inner-city youngsters across the country, and a number of well-known athletes participated, including Joe Louis, Johnny Unitas, Rocky Marciano, and Stan Musial. Their goal was to encourage ghetto kids to channel their energies through sports and make something of their lives.

Many of the athletes involved in Operation Champ, like Campbell himself, had grown up in broken homes and had experienced life on the streets. "It was felt at the time that those of us who had come up the hard way would have something in common with these kids that we were dealing with in the ghettos. To some degree," Campbell believes, "the program was successful, and some kids probably recognized that through sports they could have an opportunity to straighten out their lives and work toward a goal within the realm of social acceptance. I certainly would like to think we did some good."

Operation Champ required Campbell to travel a good deal during the summers of 1967, 1968, and 1969. Although Linda usually remained in California, Ben thought it would be nice to use one of the trips as the honeymoon they never had, so he arranged for her to accompany him to St. Louis. There he and Kenny Santiago were to give judo demonstrations at the Pruitt-Igoe housing project. "If I ever came close to losing my life in combat," Campbell insists, "it was not in Korea but in St. Louis on that trip."

The night before the scheduled demonstration, Ben and Ken went to an all-black judo club to work out. There they were warned by some of their black judo friends to be very careful, because the people who lived in Pruitt-Igoe were angry, hostile, and violent. This was a surprise because they had been assured there would be no problems.

The next morning, deciding to take no chances, Ben and Ken insisted that Linda remain in their locked car on the street while they went into the middle of a large grass playing field where someone had placed several judo mats. With them was another white athlete, who was to teach the kids wrestling holds. As they approached the demonstration Campbell was surprised and pleased to see several of the black judoists from the night before. "They said they were interested in watching, but I suspected they were there to help us if there was any trouble."

By the time the demonstrations began, several dozen black kids had assembled and were watching in rapt attention. Campbell, meanwhile, had noticed that a large group of young blacks involved in a baseball game at the other end of the field were now slowly drifting toward the mats, and many of them were carrying their bats. "I took that as a bad sign," Campbell says with typical restraint.

Although Campbell and his associates continued with the demonstrations and tried to ignore the newcomers, it did no good. Some began to heckle them and shout obscenities; others cursed them for being in an all-black neighborhood. Suddenly, one heckler charged the wrestler with a knife in hand. The wrestler managed to grab and toss the assailant, who lost his knife when he hit the mat, but that only served to incite the crowd even more. "In an instant, we were in the middle of a full-scale riot. I mean, everybody was on the mat, including our black judo friends who were trying to keep us from being killed. And we would have been killed.

It was just a melee. All I could see were fists and dust and bats. It was a hell of a fight." Somehow the three of them managed to break free of the crowd and dash for the car. Linda had the motor running by the time they got there. They jumped in and sped from the neighborhood, thankful to escape with just a few cuts and scrapes. "I didn't see any of those black judoists for four years, and I always felt guilty that we didn't stick around to help them or to thank them. They risked their lives to help us out of a very dangerous situation. When I finally bumped into some of them at a national championship meet, I apologized for leaving them like that. They understood and were real nice about it."

Campbell remained active in judo until 1972. During that time he was secretary of the United States Olympic judo team for a few years and the president of the Northern California Judo Association as well as one of the leading judo coaches in the country. Under his tutelage the Sacramento Judo Club produced a U.S. collegiate champion, a U.S. high school champion, several U.S. open champions, and several champions of different age groups of young teenagers. His crowning achievement, however, was the 1972 Olympic Games in Munich because three of the four members of the United States judo team—John Watts, Douglas Nelson, and James Wooley—were athletes he had trained.

The 1972 Olympics also marked Campbell's departure from the sport. In brief, he had expected to be named coach of the Olympic team but was deprived of that honor by the politicians who controlled judo on the national level. Bitter and disheartened, Campbell simply walked away from the sport he loved. "Having averaged five hours a day for fifteen years on the mats," Campbell says, "I think I was simply emotionally exhausted."

Today, Campbell's place in the history of American judo is remembered by just a handful of his former students. Even the Sacramento Judo Club has tried to erase his memory, says Savage. No better example is needed than the club's fiftieth anniversary in 1985. "We had a big dinner and everything," Savage recalls. "The mayor even gave the club a resolution from the city. Some of the older Japanese guys were there, people who had always been back behind the curtain, so to speak, as the governing body of the judo club, but you never saw them. No one mentioned Campbell! Not one mention of him, not one, in recapping the history of that club, was given to Ben Campbell! I was furious, as were many of the people there, especially those my age and younger. To us Campbell *was* the Sacramento Judo Club. To us he was *sensei* Campbell, our teacher. For him to be completely overlooked was unconscionable, but it shows the depth of feelings that still prevails about the changes he tried to bring about in the world of judo." Savage believes the traditionalists misunderstood what Campbell had done to judo. He changed some of the training techniques, but he never tampered with the ancient aspects of the art. "He incorporated a lot of drills and programs that expedited training, one's ability to excel in the art, yet he kept in a lot of the etiquette and the Japanese way—I don't want to say the zen part of it—the bushido attitude, the warrior training that they consider so fundamental to judo."

After four years in California, Linda began to yearn for Colorado, so in June 1969 the Campbells resigned their teaching positions at the San Juan school district and moved to Montrose. Ben helped his father-in-law with the ranch for a while and then accepted an appointment as athletic director of Colorado Western, a newly established private liberal arts college in Montrose where he also taught physical education. Unfortunately, the college could not make a go of it financially. "The damn college folded as soon as I got the job. It survived only four or five years total and I was there the last year."

As a result, Campbell returned to California in September 1970 in hopes of picking up where he left off the year before. San Juan had no openings so he began making the rounds of other school districts in the Sacramento area, seeking a position in physical education. Things looked pretty bleak until he met James Fales, the principal of William Daylor High in the Elk Grove Unified School District.

"What do you know about shop?" Fales asked.

"Well," Campbell shrugged, "that's not my training, I'm in the P.E. business, in art, but I've been around shops all my life."

"Can you set up a shop for me?" Fales asked. "We are just setting up a school for kids who have been bounced out of regular schools, very tough kids. I mean guns, drugs, the whole damn thing. Could you handle something like that?"

"Hell, yes," Campbell told him.

"Then you're hired."

And that, Campbell laughs, is how he became an industrial arts teacher. According to Fales, California's continuation schools, which average only three hundred students in size, were developed for divergent youths who would not, or could not, function well in regular high schools. Classes are small and courses are structured to give students the tools for performing as contributing members of society. "Ben was ideal for the program," Fales recalls. "He developed new and meaningful programs designed to accommodate these special students." In industrial arts, for example, Campbell individualized the instructional tasks and got to know many of the students on a personal level. After about three years Fales approached him about starting a jewelry-making class for Indians within the adult education curriculum. "It was then, I believe, he developed his intense interest in his Indian heritage," Fales says. "He produced in the classroom some of the most outstanding Indian artwork I have ever seen."

Fales's sentiments are echoed by Donald Stanfield, who took Campbell's Indian jewelry-making classes at Daylor High. "Ben never interfered with a person's creativity and was always there to help with the techniques. There were some wonderful things going on in that class," Stanfield remembers.

Another person at Daylor High with fond memories of Campbell is Roberta Hall, who was Fales's secretary. "Ben was a competent, skillful teacher," she recalls, "who worked well with students. He could get them interested in different projects by the example of doing rather than ordering. He was knowledgeable in many fields and could help in any field of interest. He also did not mind giving his opinion on any subject."

Campbell, she recalls, had a full life and a tight schedule. "Ben typically would come to me with his typing needs—a thesis, an article on judo with the U.S. Olympic team, an article on training horses, a résumé of his career for special needs." He had time for only the occasional judo class. The school day ended at 2 P.M., and Ben would often be the first one out of the parking lot on his way to his other activities. "His interests at that time were quarter horses, specifically one named Sailor's Night, and working with the sheriff's mounted division," Hall remembers. She also remembers Campbell's pride in being Indian. "He always made it known that he was part Indian and that he was proud of his heritage."

Like everything else in Campbell's life, his involvement with police work came about accidentally yet naturally, considering his police training in the Air Force and his original plan to study police science at San Jose State. Campbell finally got his chance to try his hand at police work because two fathers of youngsters taking lessons from Campbell at the Sacramento Judo Club happened to be policemen: Richard Phillips and Duane Lowe, who is currently head of the California State Police. They befriended Campbell who, in turn, supported them when they decided to run for office—Lowe for sheriff and Phillips for deputy sheriff. "I helped them with their campaign in the Japanese community, because I had a lot of Japanese friends, and they won."

Shortly after taking office, Sheriff Lowe decided to establish a mounted police unit for Sacramento. Its primary jurisdiction was to be along the American River, where there is an extensive network of hiking, jogging, and bridle paths that wind through marshy areas heavily overgrown with sedge, willows, and brush. "Because the place was so secluded," Campbell declares, "it was notorious for all sorts of problems, from guys jumping out of the brush and exposing themselves to girls to more heavy-duty stuff like rape and drug sales. It was pretty rough at one time."

Although a mounted unit made sense, Lowe's department could not afford one, so the sheriff created a semivolunteer patrol by persuading friends with police training and horses to work for him on a part-time basis. "That is how I started," says Campbell. "He deputized us but we provided our own horses, our own trucks, and our own trailers to get to work. We kind of volunteered our services that way. It was supposed to be only for a summer or two, to help him get going, but I worked for him about six years on a part-time basis."

Campbell's police career was uneventful, other than finding a dead body along the river and making a few arrests. Nonetheless, in typical Campbell fashion, he left his mark on the Sacramento Police Department by writing the manual for the mounted patrol. "It was published under Sheriff Lowe's name, but I wrote the thing, every word, and I did all the research. It's all original from the standpoint that I wrote it, but some of it is what other police departments were already doing." The manual, which was printed in 1975 and is 117 pages long, includes a bibliography as well as a chronology of the history of mounted policemen—the first recorded unit was established in Durban, South Africa, in 1668—and features all manner of useful information, from selecting the appropriate horse to training, doctoring, and working with it.

Campbell wrote the manual as a way to keep busy during the winters when the mounted police unit was disbanded. "Nobody uses those trails in the wintertime," he explains, "so there was no need for the horse unit, but because of my teaching credentials and judo skills, I was asked to work for them year round." Summer months he spent either on patrol or training horses at a ring he built by the bomb pit and gunnery range. The rest of the time he spent at the police academy teaching arrest and take-down techniques, grading papers, and doing whatever else was needed, such as researching and writing the mounted patrol manual. "It was an interesting experience, and I did enjoy it," Campbell admits. "We had the first all-women's class, and we shared facilities with the California Highway Patrol—the speed track, the gunnery range, and all that stuff. Since I had already taken a few police classes in college, I took as many as I could in one of the local colleges and little by little I got enough credits for a minor in police science."

It was at the police academy that Campbell and his former judo student Don Savage renewed acquaintance. Savage had left Sacramento in 1966 to seek fame and fortune in the field of marine biology but soon discovered that most marine biologists were starving to death. "Unless you were aboard the *Calypso* or had a job at the Scripps Institute, you'd better know how to dive so you could get food off the bottom. You sure weren't going to make a living otherwise." Thinking that life was passing him by—"I was like a firehouse dog; every time there were problems or I saw a police unit going by, red lights and sirens, I wanted to be where the action was"—Savage obtained a degree in police science. Eventually, he returned to Sacramento where, in 1974, he entered the police academy and ran into Campbell. "He was our nighttime baby-sitter," Savage chuckles. "He made sure nobody snuck off the academy grounds or visited the female cadets. Ben's office was set up in the women's barracks, I think, so we couldn't sneak in there. If his office had been in our barracks, see, it would have been easy for us to sneak out and visit the women, but no one was going to try that with him sitting by the front door grading our notebooks from the day before."

During this period Campbell survived on an average of four hours of sleep a day. Besides working the shift from midnight to eight at the academy, he still taught school and had begun raising horses. Something had to give, and it was Campbell. He began to suffer dizzy spells and blackouts, once at his desk in the police academy. "I don't remember passing out, but I do remember waking up. I was on the floor." A doctor finally convinced him to quit working at the academy even though he enjoyed it so much. "You cannot keep up that schedule without ruining your health," the doctor told him. When Campbell left the sheriff's department, Lowe let him keep his badge. It now hangs in his office on Capitol Hill along with a photograph of his colleagues in the mounted police unit.

As if this workload was not enough to crush an elephant, Campbell somehow found time in this period to work as a counselor with American Indians who happened to be on the wrong side of the law. He not only visited inmates at Folsom Penitentiary and at Vacaville, a medium-security prison, each about thirty or so miles from Sacramento, but he was also active in Sacramento with a halfway house for Indians.

The goal of the halfway house was to obtain early releases for Indian convicts and then help them return to society as productive citizens. "We would get them jobs and help them get their life together." In order to qualify for public funding, state law required the halfway house to have someone in law enforcement on its board of directors, a stipulation also mandated by the organization's bylaws and constitution. Since Campbell was both an Indian and working part-time for the sheriff's department, he was asked to serve on the board and, before he knew what happened, found himself its chairman. "Those two things happened at almost the same time," Campbell recalls. "I just started going into prisons, talking to some of the guys we were trying to get releases for. Some we could help, but there were others—just as in the rest of society—who were just absolute critters. In no way could they ever be released."

Campbell was introduced to counseling by an Indian friend named Leo Kamp, who used to run an alcoholic recovery center for Indians called the Turquoise Lodge, a program in which Campbell's own father participated from time to time. Leo had been going into Folsom for quite some time and he persuaded Ben to volunteer.

Ben was involved in this program for three years. At Folsom he averaged one Monday afternoon visit every three weeks. Although he did not teach classes in the prisons, he did bring the inmates books and craft materials, including wood and turquoise for jewelry making.

Counseling could be a bittersweet experience, Campbell discovered. Most of the inmates, he recalls, were sincerely appreciative for any interest shown them, but a few had short memories. "Once they hit the bricks—once you got them out—some of them forgot how grateful they had been. We also lost some. They'd end up back in prison or dead."

A Creek Indian named Elliot Narcomi, an ex-rodeo cowboy, was one they lost. "Elliot was a cousin of the famous Indian artist Jerome Tiger and had a lot going for him," Campbell says. "He was big, strong, handsome, artistically talented, and very popular. Somehow he had killed his first wife, but we got him out and he held together pretty well for a while. We got him back to the rodeo as an announcer, and we got him a job at the Indian Center in Sacramento. He eventually met and married a California Indian girl and things looked real good, but then he fell off the wagon. His marriage broke up, and one bad thing led to another until he got stabbed to death in a fight."

Campbell's most unusual experience inside Folsom concerned not the inmates but some visitors. "I was in the prison one day and watched a show put on for the inmates by a group called 'The Hell's Angels Rock and Roll Band.' I don't know if they were really part of the motorcycle gang, but that is what they called themselves, and they were all dressed in black leather jackets and motorcycle apparel. Anyhow, during the show as the girls were dancing and singing, the convicts started yelling, 'Take it off! Take it off!' and these girls started doing a strip. I mean, they got right down to nothing except their panties, particularly this one girl. I just knew that had to be against prison regulations, but nobody did anything about it."

During his next visit, Campbell questioned one of the guards. "You know," Campbell told him, "I was up here last week and I saw the girls with the Hell's Angels band disrobe right up there in front of all those inmates. Isn't that against regulations?"

"You're goddamn right it is," the guard fired back, "but who do you think was going to get up in front of fourteen hundred cons and tell those girls to put their clothes back on?"

ROOTS

After judo, the most dominant force in Ben Campbell's life is his identity as an Indian. Comparing the Campbell of today to the Campbell of his youth, however, is sometimes an interesting exercise for those who have known him since childhood, when most people had no idea he was part Indian. His explanation for this is simple and straightforward: "My father insisted we keep our Indian background a secret."

Ben himself cannot recall when he learned the truth about his father's ancestry, but it was early in his youth and it was not a positive experience. "Don't worry about it, we were told. Just keep your mouth shut. It doesn't mean anything; don't have anything to do with it; don't do anything about it."

When pressed about his reasons for leaving the Cheyenne reservation, his father would cut the discussion short with a curt "I was tired of being hungry, that's why." More likely it was a sense of shame in being Indian. Albert Campbell grew to manhood in an era of severe stress for America's Indian people. Their lands were shrinking at a startling rate, tuberculosis and other diseases were ravaging tribal populations at a pace far greater than average, and all aspects of their traditional culture, including religion, languages, and crafts, were under continued assault as undesirable vestiges of an unprogressive past.

Sadly, many Indians came to believe that they were foreigners in their own land and tried to embrace the mythic American melting pot. They packed away the buckskins and beadwork reminiscent of another era; they struggled to learn English; some even changed their names to Smith, Jones, and other equally mainstream examples. A great watershed for Indian men was World War I. Thousands volunteered to fight in the Great War, and when they returned they were no longer content to accept the prewar status quo.

Albert Valdez Campbell fits this profile perfectly. An Army veteran with an anglo name, he apparently decided to "pass" into white society and leave the shame and ignominy of his Indian background behind him. One can imagine how such a decision, and the guilt and ambivalence associated with it, contributed to his lifelong struggle with alcoholism.

Because of his father's reticence about his past—no doubt complicated by Ben's emotional distance from his family as an adolescent—the search for Ben Campbell's roots was, to put it modestly, an archival challenge. The only documentary genealogical evidence in Campbell's possession is a badly tattered copy of his father's Army discharge. Even that is missing a crucial corner. According to this document, Albert B. Campbell—someone later replaced the B with a V—was honorably discharged from the Army in August 1922, having served three years and four days, mainly in China. At the time of his discharge at Fort William McKinley in the Philippine Islands, Private Campbell, serial number 6412140, was twenty-one and described as being five feet five and a half inches tall and having a "ruddy complexion," dark brown eyes, black hair, and an "excellent" character. He chose to draw travel pay to his place of enlistment: Sheridan, Wyoming.

Normally, a military service record is a genealogical gold mine, but not in Albert's case. His entire military service record, along with those of millions of other servicemen from World Wars I and II, was lost in the catastrophic fire at the National Personnel Records Center in St. Louis in 1973.

Since birth cerificates, diaries, newspaper clippings, scrapbooks, photographs, and other potentially useful documents that might shed light on Albert's background were nonexistent, the only information available with which to reconstruct Ben Campbell's family history was his recollection of stories told by his father. Fortunately, archival records buttressed key elements of these stories. Albert thought he had been born around 1900 in either Pagosa Springs, Colorado, or Chama, New Mexico, and that his mother—Ben had never known his grandmother's name—was a Cheyenne related to the Black Horse family on the Northern Cheyenne Reservation in Montana. Albert claimed that his mother died when he was around ten years old, so he ran away. Somehow he reached Montana, enrolled in the school on the adjoining Crow reservation, and supported himself by wrangling horses on various ranches in the area until enlisting in the Army soon after the First World War.

Albert had no idea when or how the family got the surname Campbell. Ben had always assumed it had come either from the family for which Campbell County, Wyoming, is named, or from some family named Campbell on the Northern Plains that had presumably adopted his Cheyenne grandmother. That was as plausible an explanation as any, if his father's story was valid.

The first step in unraveling the mystery, it appeared, was to find a family named Campbell with a ten-year-old boy named Albert on the 1910 federal census for either Pagosa Springs or Chama, and that is exactly what happened. The schedule for Pagosa Springs lists the large extended family of Alexander C. Campbell, who was born in New Mexico, and his wife, a woman named Ramoncita, also of New Mexico. In addition to two minor children and a married daughter and her children, the family included an eleven-year-old boy named Alexander Valdez and his younger sister named Refugo, age four, who are listed as the grandchildren of Alexander and Ramoncita Campbell. Neither a father nor a mother for the Valdez children is mentioned. A visit to the Pagosa Springs Public Health Office later produced a birth certificate dated July 12, 1900, for "Albert" Valdez, who had been born to Fortunata Campbell and Ben Valdez. Armed only with this evidence and the wonderful assistance of archivists in Colorado and New Mexico, it was possible to trace the family history with remarkable completeness. The fascinating story that unfolded proved once again that truth is stranger than fiction.

The family name comes from Richard Campbell, a Virginia fur trapper who in 1827 led a party of seventeen men from New Orleans to San Francisco by way of New Mexico and Arizona. He is believed to be the first American to reach California by way of Arizona. Campbell later trapped with Albert Pike and then opened a trading post in Taos, New Mexico, where he remained the rest of his life. Richard Campbell married a woman of Taos Pueblo, Rosa Grijalva, by whom he had several children including a daughter named Petra. At the time of his death in 1860, Campbell was obviously a person of some distinction in the community. Besides operating his trading post, he had served for a time as a sheriff and as the first presiding judge of the probate court in Dona Ana County. He also had a large extended family that, according to the 1860 federal census, included one person listed as an Indian, a fourteen-year-old boy named Jose Campbell.

Living with the Campbells for a time and evidently a business associate was a man named Parry Cochrane from Arkansas who, according to the 1850 census, was twenty-five. Cochrane married Campbell's daughter Petra, by whom he fathered a son that the couple named Alexander. The family was together a very short time; in fact, Petra may have died in childbirth. As for Cochrane, he left for California in 1852, never to be heard from again. Presumably he joined the thousands of other young men flocking to the California gold fields in that era. In any case, he left his son in the care of Petra's elder sister, Peregrina Campbell, in whose household Alexander Cochrane subsequently appears, according to various documents in the New Mexico State Archives. In time, Alexander Cochrane took Campbell as his surname, identifying himself thereafter as Alexander C. Campbell. On January 30, 1879, Alexander Cochrane married Maria Ramona Mestas of San Juan Pueblo. Their first child, Fortunata, was born almost nine months later, on October 15, 1879. Fortunata is Ben Nighthorse Campbell's paternal grandmother.

Fortunata is obviously part Indian, but it appears that she is a Pueblo Indian, not a Cheyenne. At first blush, therefore, it would seem that Albert Campbell's brief version of his family history is somewhat fanciful. Further research, however, indicates otherwise. The key person in Albert's story, in fact, is not Fortunata but her mother—Ben's great-grandmother—Ramona or Ramoncita Campbell, who suddenly appears as a fully grown woman in San Juan Pueblo at the time of her marriage at approximately age twenty-five, which was determined by her entry in the 1880 federal census for New Mexico. No birth or baptismal records can be located for her nor, for that matter, can any other documentation be found in the New Mexico State Archives. "Where Ramona came from is a mystery," writes a New Mexico state archivist. "She may very well be *genizaro*."

Beginning in the late seventeenth century, Spanish settlers in New Mexico began buying captive Indian children to serve as laborers, work as domestics, and assist in the defense of the frontier from Indian marauders, the very tribes that had kidnapped them in the first place. These captives became known as *genizaros*, a class of people in American history unique to the Spanish Southwest. Most of the children came from tribes that lived in and around New Mexico—Navajo, Ute, Apache, Kiowa, Comanche, Cheyenne, Arapaho, and Pueblo—but captives from as far away as Montana, including at least one Flathead, are documented in New Mexico archival records. The children sometimes were taken in war, but most of them were bought or bartered from their Indian captors, primarily the Kiowa and Comanche, who scourged the Spanish borderlands until finally restricted to reservations in the late nineteenth century.

The Spanish had several motives for adopting Indian children. Besides having the benefit of their labor, the settlers could also bring the children into the Catholic faith and offer them a better fate, presumably, than letting them remain with their captors. For example, in 1694 a Navajo war party immediately beheaded a group of captive children when Spanish officials refused to ransom them. Shocked by this atrocity, the Spanish king authorized the use of royal funds to redeem such unfortunates and thus unwittingly spawned a thriving business.

Whatever the rationalization, the Spanish quickly assembled a large group of detribalized Indians. Although the number of these genizaros was substantial, only recently have historians paid them much attention, largely because they are so difficult to research in Spanish and state records. Genizaros at best were people of low status who earned their livelihood as laborers, farmers, and shepherds. These individuals were ethnically Indian but culturally Spanish. Most genizaros adopted Spanish customs and surnames, and many of them were settled along the northern border of New Mexico in the little communities that are integral to Campbell's family history—Chama, Ensenada, Los Ojos, and Rio Arriba.

Interestingly, Taos Pueblo was a major center for the sale of Indian captives. At an annual fair held there each July or August, Spanish settlers could buy or trade Indian children. Especially desirable were girls between the ages of twelve and twenty, who could be had for two horses; males were worth half as much. Since Richard Campbell's wife came from Taos, she may well have been a genizaro herself.

Equally interesting, one of the more prominent genizaros was a Ute named Manuel Mestas who worked as an interpreter along the New Mexico frontier in the early nineteenth century. Whether Ramona was a member of this family or some other Mestas family is not known, but the absence of documentary evidence or information about her origins, coupled with her grandson's claim, argues that she was, in fact, a Cheyenne girl who was adopted by a genizaro family living at San Juan Pueblo.

The fact that Alexander Cochrane Campbell may himself have been part genizaro could explain why he married a genizaro Indian woman. His daughter Fortunata, whose name belied her short and troubled life, also married a genizaro, it appears. This was a young farmer named Venceslado Valdez from Ensenada, a small community outside the Jicarilla Apache Reservation in northen New Mexico, a few miles below the Colorado state line. Fortunata and Venceslado were wed in Tierra Amarilla, New Mexico, on Novemner 24, 1894. She was only fifteen; he was no more than seventeen or eighteen. For the first decade of their married life they lived in Tierra Amarilla, where three children were born: two sons, Alexander and Luis, and a daughter whose name appears as Ruben in some records and as Rube in others. After ten years in Tierra Amarilla, the family moved to Pagosa Junction, Colorado, about sixty miles to the north.

Inexplicably, Alexander's birth was not officially recorded until 1947. At that time, his birth was cited as Pagosa Springs, Colorado, not Tierra Amarilla, New Mexico. There are also certain other discrepancies. One is the date of birth, which is recorded as July 12, 1900. The date has to be July 12, 1899, however, because Alexandro Valdez was baptized in San Jose Catholic Church of Rio Ojos on July 21, 1899. The final discrepancy is the name. On the baptismal record it is Alexander; on the birth certificate it is Albert. By the time the birth was recorded, Ben's father had long since changed his name from Alexander to Albert and from Valdez to Campbell, the name he used upon enlisting in the Army.

According to the testimony that Fortunata presented at her divorce proceedings in 1905, her years with Venceslado were a living hell. From their first year of marriage, she insisted, "by his inhuman treatment he . . . made life a burden to her and their children." Not only had he repeatedly threatened to kill her and her parents, but he beat her so frequently and so viciously—choking her, tearing her hair, and striking her—that she feared for her life. Once he had tried to shoot her with his carbine, and most recently—on the Fourth of July, 1905—he had tried to choke her to death with his neckerchief. She deserved none of this, Fortunata told the court, because "all during their married life [she] . . . demeaned herself [to him] . . . as a dutiful wife." The judge, in granting her a divorce, also issued an injunction against Venceslado Valdez that prevented him from troubling or interfering with his former wife in any way or manner "at your peril." As part of the divorce, Fortunata's maiden name was restored.

Venceslado returned to Tierra Amarilla, where he remarried. Fortunata—now Fortunata Campbell—and her children moved to Pagosa Springs, where her parents lived. It was there, little more than four years later, that she was murdered. The cause of death according to the coroner was a gunshot wound to the chest. At the time of death she was pregnant with her sixth child. Two other children had been born since her divorce.

Although certain delicacies of the day prevented the press from detailing the circumstances surrounding Fortunata's death, she apparently at times supported herself after her divorce through prostitution. Her killer was Jose Benedito Martinez, a member of a prominent Pagosa Springs family. Martinez, married and the father of several children, was a violent and lawless person who had killed at least two other people before shooting Fortunata on the evening of January 15, 1910.

His motive, evidently, was jealousy. A few days earlier, Martinez had showed a large-caliber pistol to a friend and told him that he had been "laying up with a woman over the river" in Pagosa Springs who he

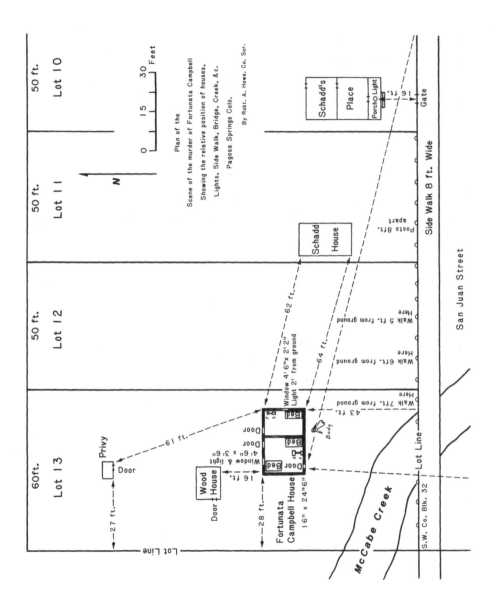

Plan of the
Scene of the murder of Fortunata Campbell
Showing the relative position of houses,
Lights, Side Walk, Bridge, Creek, &c.
Pagosa Springs Colo.

By Robt. A. Howe. Co. Sur.

suspected was not being "true" to him. Martinez promised to shoot "the son of a bitch" if he found out.

About midnight on Saturday, during a driving snowstorm, Martinez went to Fortunata's two-room house on San Juan Street near Schadd's Saloon, where she lived with an older woman of equally questionable moral character. Upon looking in the lighted window, Martinez evidently did not like what he saw, because he yelled for Fortunata to come outside. When she did, he shot at her three times. One bullet grazed her face; another struck her in the chest. Apparently Martinez had seen Fortunata with a customer, who slipped out the back door during the commotion, because the sheriff found a man's coat and vest in her bedroom after the shooting.

The case against Martinez was fairly complete. Fortunata's house-mate claimed to have recognized the killer when he looked in the window, and the authorities were able to follow his tracks in the snow. The people of Pagosa Springs were so convinced of his guilt that his trial had to be held in another county because an impartial jury would have been difficult to find. Even with a change of venue, however, Martinez was readily convicted and received a ten-year sentence for second-degree murder. Little more than a year later, however, he was released on bail pending a new trial on grounds that the first one had been conducted improperly. The second trial was never held.

Shortly after Fortunata's death, various people came forward to claim her children. One was Venceslado Valdez, who tried but failed to get custody of his own three children. According to an article in the *Pagosa New Era* for January 29, 1910, families from Tierra Amarilla adopted three of the children: Roque Ulibarri adopted Luis Valdez, age seven; and a family named Chavez adopted Rube Valdez, a girl twelve years old, and Eloie, a boy less than two.

The remaining children lived for at least a short while with their grandparents because they appear as members of Alexander Campbell's household on the 1910 federal census, which was enumerated in Pagosa Springs on April 22 of that year. Living with Alexander and Ramona at that time were a daughter named Simona Gallegos, age twenty-eight, and her two children, Lina and Manuel; another daughter, Petrita, nineteen; a son Paulin, fifteen; and the two grandchildren, Alexander, eleven, and Refugo Valdez, four.

The family situation apparently remained unchanged until April 5, 1911, when Alexander Campbell died. According to the death certificate he was a Mexican who died of the complications of alcoholism. For occupation the attending physician wrote: "If any a school teacher." Perhaps it was a macabre joke, perhaps it was someone's way of paying him a parting tribute, but in an election for city trustees held the day he died, Alexander Campbell received one write-in vote, according to the *Pagosa Springs Sun*.

What then became of Ramona Campbell, who died in Denver in 1924, and the rest of the Campbell clan is unknown. No members of the family appear in the 1920 census for Pagosa Springs. Presumably, the various family members scattered, which supports Albert's claim that he ran away after his mother died. Albert was now nearly twelve years old and, conceivably, he could have found his way to Montana by himself, but it is far more likely that someone in the family took him.

In either case, in December 1916 a fifteen-year-old boy named Albert Baldez popped up on the Crow Reservation, which adjoins the Northern Cheyenne Reservation in southeastern Montana. According to information supplied to the Bureau of Indian Affairs by Even W. Estep, superintendent of the Crow Reservation, the principal of the Crow Agency Boarding School had enrolled "one Albert Baldez, who claims to be an Apache Indian. This boy has no living relatives that he knows of, and is not sure of the reservation on which he belongs, but thinks it is the Jicarilla of New Mexico." Estep asked the Commissioner of Indian Affairs for permission to continue paying the boy's school expenses. Although Commissioner Cato Sells authorized the expenditure of federal monies for the boy's education, he urged Estep to verify his story because the information available thus far appeared "very meager."

Less than three months later, Albert Baldez, half Apache, was dropped from the rolls of the Crow Agency Boarding School. The reason listed was desertion. Perhaps inquiries into his past had made him nervous and he chose to run away. Perhaps, like any typical teenager, he did not care for the boarding school regimen. Whatever the reason, Albert Baldez disappeared from official records for two years. On July 10, 1919, he enlisted in the U.S. Army in Sheridan, Wyoming, as Albert B. Campbell. Since Sheridan is the nearest large community outside the boundaries of the Northern Cheyenne Reservation, there is no reason to doubt that he lived on or near the reservation until then, working as a ranch hand, as he had told his children.

How Albert Campbell got to Montana, however, remains a mystery. It may well have been his grandmother, Ramona, who either escorted him personally or arranged for him to find his Cheyenne relatives. Although it is unlikely that so young a child could have made his way across Colorado and Wyoming to Montana at that time, it would not have been impossible. But why go to all that trouble except to find relatives on the Northern Cheyenne Reservation? After all, his immediate family, including several siblings and his natural father, were in Tierra Amarilla, just a few miles from Pagosa Springs. His natural father was evidently of Jicarilla Apache descent; otherwise why, upon entering the Indian school at Crow Agency, would the boy claim to be half Jicarilla Apache? Given his unhappy home life, it is easy to understand why he would later shut out the memory of his dysfunctional family—an alcoholic grandfather, an abusive father, a murdered mother whose death certificate lists her occupation as "washer woman" (a well-known euphemism for a prostitute on the American frontier)—and tell his own children only of the Northern Cheyenne relationship. Even so, Albert Campbell did his best to shut out that memory as well.

According to the available evidence, Albert Campbell was part Apache and part Pueblo Indian and, most likely, part Cheyenne, and he lived for a time with members of the Black Horse family on the Lame Deer reservation. Sometime during this period, however, he made two critical decisions: he decided to enlist in the U.S. Army and, at the same time, to turn his back on his Indian ancestry. That is why, when pressed by his son about the family's Indian background, Albert Campbell, who understandably had at best a very muddled knowledge of his own heritage, gave him the only solid bit of evidence he had, a Cheyenne family named Black Horse.

How tragic that our nation compounded a double tragedy on our Indian peoples. We not only crushed them physically while following what we perceived to be our manifest destiny, but then we also crushed their spirit to the point that a person like Albert Valdez Campbell would turn his back on his heritage and seek to erase his Indian identity from his memory. Certainly, he had reason to be proud of his Cheyenne ancestors, for they were a warrior people who, like Ben Campbell's judo associates, "gave out, but never gave up."

Ruben Black Horse was such a warrior. Born sometime in the mid-1850s, he grew to manhood during a period of traumatic change for all the tribes of the Northern Plains. From the Civil War until 1880 warfare with the white man was a fact of everyday life for the Cheyennes and their Sioux and Arapaho neighbors. Rather than submit to a demeaning life on reservations as wards of the government, they chose to resist as long as humanly possible, and some Cheyennes even managed the impossible.

Black Horse was of this group. He enters the historical record in 1875 as a young warrior, approximately nineteen years of age, who surrendered with a band of Southern Cheyennes at Darlington Agency in present-day Oklahoma. Shortly afterward, the government decided to select about thirty leaders and others guilty of having committed depredations against whites and imprison them at Fort Marion, Florida. Among those selected was Black Horse, accused of being a "ringleader," which meant no specific charge could be found against him.

Guilty or not, on April 6, 1875, he was taken from the guardhouse to the agency blacksmith to be fitted with a ball and chain to ensure his safe arrival at Fort Marion. As the despondent warriors waited in line for their irons, a group of Cheyenne women watching the public humiliation of their loved ones began singing battle songs to lift their spirits and inspire them to resist.

This was all the encouragement Black Horse needed. Just as the blacksmith leaned over to fit a bracelet around his ankle, the angry young man kicked him in the chin and dashed across the compound, hoping to seek shelter among the tepees on the other side of a nearby creek. He never made it. The guards, although caught by surprise, recovered quickly enough to fire a barrage of bullets in his direction. One caught him in the side and knocked him off his feet.

Meanwhile, the gunfire caused panic among the other Cheyennes, who had been fearful of Army treachery and thought the shooting was a prelude to a full-fledged attack on their camps. Within minutes a state of war existed at Darlington, with some two hundred Cheyennes—men, women, and children—rushing to nearby sandhills to recover guns and ammunition hidden for just such an emergency, and three companies of soldiers hard on their heels in hot pursuit. During the bedlam several of the men still waiting to be ironed rushed over to Black Horse and carried him to safety.

For the rest of the day and well into the evening, a terrific battle ensued, but the Cheyennes refused to surrender even though the Army brought up a Gatling gun in an attempt to dislodge the frightened Indians from their trenches. During the night, as the Army prepared for an all-out assault the following morning, the Cheyennes managed to slip away.

Although most of the Southern Cheyennes involved in the needless incident eventually returned to the agency, a large group of warriors and a few women decided to break away and join their northern relatives. Among them was Black Horse. Although officially counted among the dead that day, Black Horse recovered fully from his wound and eventually found his way to Montana. There he joined the bands of Dull Knife and Little Wolf and with them answered the call of the Sioux spiritual leader Sitting Bull, who chose to resist a government order that all free-roaming bands of the Northern Plains tribes move onto reservations. The result of this ill-advised and unwarranted order was the battle of the Little Bighorn. On June 25, 1876, a combined force of Cheyenne, Sioux, and Arapaho warriors annihilated the proudest military force in the United States, the Seventh Cavalry led by the impetuous and bold George Armstrong Custer.

Black Horse and his Cheyenne companions acquitted themselves well that fateful day, but their victory only delayed the inevitable. Within a few months a vengeful Army, embarrassed in the centennial year of the United States, had completely crushed the last of the northern tribes. Particularly brutal was the treatment accorded Dull Knife's village, which was attacked by the cavalry in its camp on the Powder River the winter following the Custer fight. Although most of the villagers managed to escape, their camp was destroyed, and they suffered terribly from exposure before obtaining sanctuary with Crazy Horse, the famous Sioux leader. The following spring, Dull Knife and his followers decided to surrender rather than risk obliteration.

To their surprise, however, the government did not place them on a reservation in the northern country to which they were accustomed. Instead, the Bureau of Indian Affairs transferred the entire village, some 937 men, women, and children, to the Cheyenne and Arapaho Agency at Darlington. With them was the luckless Black Horse, for whom the memory of Darlington was particularly unpleasant.

Black Horse was not the only one disheartened by the outrageous decision. Unable to adapt to the intense heat in their new home, demoralized, and despondent, the Northen Cheyennes sickened and died in appalling numbers. After a year of suffering and rejection of their pleas for permission to return to the Powder River country, several of Dull Knife's followers began urging their leaders to seize the initiative and simply sneak away from Darlington and make their own way north. No matter that it was a journey of more than a thousand miles. No matter that they lacked weapons, horses, and equipment. It was better to die in battle as befitted Cheyennes, they reasoned, than to waste away by inches without dignity and pride.

Ironically, Black Horse helped precipitate action, as he admitted years afterward in a conversation with the noted anthropologist George Bird Grinnell. One day in the late summer of 1878, after more than a year in exile, Black Horse and two other young Cheyennes, Mad Hearted Wolf and Whetstone, decided to return home by themselves and rejoin other Northern Cheyenne bands that had been allowed to remain in the north country. After their unauthorized departure, the Indian agent at Darlington ordered Dull Knife to bring the three men back to the agency.

Knowing this would be impossible and fearful that the cavalry would punish them for this transgression, a large group of Dull Knife's band decided to follow the lead of the three young men and return home as well. Borrowing horses and weapons from their Southern Cheyenne kinsmen at Darlington, some three hundred Northern Cheyennes—fewer than ninety of them warriors—under the leadership of two principal chiefs, Dull Knife and Little Wolf, packed their few belongings and, on September 9, 1878, set out on one of the most remarkable odysseys in American history.

To make pursuit more difficult, the runaways split up into several groups, each wending its separate way toward the Tongue River in present-day Montana. Eventually, the various groups—including Black Horse and his two companions—came together. Although the chiefs had asked their people to cause no harm to any of the whites they encountered along the way, violent incidents were inevitable since it was necessary to steal horses from farmers and ranchers on the route.

It was in this role that Black Horse excelled. As the main party traveled through the sandhills of northern Nebraska, Black Horse would take two or three companions and search for horses. Sometimes they would start out on foot; sometimes they would ride worn-out horses and replace them with the fresh mounts they managed to steal.

One reason Black Horse so willingly took these risks, he later told Grinnell, was to atone for the harm he and his companions had caused by running away from Darlington. They blamed themselves for compelling the main body of Northern Cheyennes to return home. As one of Black Horse's companions pointed out, "We three had better go to war. We shall have to bear the blame of everything that has happened along the way, for we three were the first ones to leave the Southern agency to come up here. We are in for it, and we may as well carry it out. We may as well do as much as we can before we are caught."

Accordingly, even though the leaders had counseled against violence, Black Horse and his two companions sought white men to fight, to count coup upon, and to kill. In one raid, for example, they first encountered two riders. Without hesitation the three Cheyennes charged the white men and counted coup on them by hitting them with their quirts as they tried to outrace the Indians. Whetstone killed one of the men; Mad Hearted Bull killed the other. Meanwhile, Black Horse had spotted a third white man some distance away and went in pursuit. As this man rushed for the safety of a nearby cabin, Black Horse knocked him off his horse with a long-distance rifle shot, but he got inside before the warrior could overtake him.

After continuing on their way for some distance, the warriors came upon a ranch house with three herds of horses grazing nearby. While Mad Hearted Bull watched from a hill, Black Horse and Whetstone—keeping out of sight of the ranch house—rounded up one of the horse herds consisting of fifteen head and returned with it to Mad Hearted Bull.

"This is enough," Whetstone said. "Let's go back to camp with this bunch."

"No," Black Horse replied. "We have taken these and we may as well get more. Hold these horses while I go and get some from the next bunch."

Black Horse rode back to the next herd by himself, cut out the best-looking horses, and then drove them to where his companions waited with the others. He was pleased to see that he had also gotten fifteen head. Now, he believed, they had enough to last for a while, and the elated young men returned to the main camp where they divided the animals among those people whose own horses were exhausted.

As the band neared the North Platte, Black Horse again "went to war," as he called it. This time three other warriors joined him. On their first night out, a snowstorm covered them as they slept. At a ranch the next afternoon, while two of the men watched the house, the two others took horses out of the barn and adjoining corral and got away before anyone noticed what had happened.

As the war party continued on its way, the decision was made to cross the North Platte, but the floating ice and snow so frightened the horses they refused to enter the water. Black Horse then volunteered to cross the river on foot, leading one of the horses, which would then encourage the others to follow. He pulled off his leggings and went across, but the river was so wide and the water so cold he almost perished. As he collapsed on the other shore, he shouted to his companions that he was freezing to death. Upon hearing his cries for help, the others rushed across and began rubbing his body until he was warm again.

On this side of the river there were many small ranches, and the raiders soon assembled a large herd. As they were returning to the main camp, Black Horse noticed a white man coming their way. "One of our 'friends' is coming," he told the others. "Let's surprise him." The four warriors knelt in ambush as the unsuspecting white man approached. All four fired at once knocking down both the man and his horse, which pinned the rider to the ground. The warriors then rushed forward, counted coup on their hapless victim, and then killed him.

The four young men now dashed for the main camp, having completed one of the most successful raids during the flight. All told they had captured some one hundred head of horses, enough to provide fresh mounts for everyone who needed one. They surged into camp with their splendid herd, raising everyone's spirits and letting them forget for a moment their terrible peril.

The next day Black Horse's luck left him. As the main group continued on its way north, scouts reported seeing two white men watching them from a nearby hill. Black Horse and several other young men went in pursuit and came upon a house just in time to see a white man mounting a horse tied near the front door. Black Horse lifted his rifle and fired a shot at the man, who turned and ran back inside. The Indians quickly surrounded the house. Black Horse went around back, tied his horse, and entered the stable, then heard some shooting at the front of the house; one of the Indians was shooting at several saddled horses, hoping to scare them away. After yelling to his friend to stop shooting, Black Horse and several other Indians rushed toward the house on foot. Black Horse crawled into bushes where he could watch the house and yet remain out of sight. Before long he saw the face of a white man at one of the windows. Lifting his rifle, he fired a shot through the glass and shouted, "I have killed the man who went into the house."

Hearing that, two of the Cheyennes ran to the front of the house to take the horses tied to the rail. As they did so, someone in the house broke a window and stuck a rifle out as if to shoot at them. "Run," one of the Indians yelled. "The white man is still alive."

This time Black Horse decided to take charge. "I am going into the house," he called to his companions as he ran to the front door and kicked it open. Peering inside, he shouted, "I did not kill the man I thought I had killed." Looking back at his friends, he urged them to come forward and help him. "Why do you stand there?" he yelled. "This is just what I have been looking for, for years. If I did not want to meet with something like this, I would have stayed in camp. I have found what I was after. This is my last day on earth. Often I have thought of my dead father and have wondered how I could get to him. Now I see the way."

When no one stepped forward to help him, Black Horse walked inside alone, but the light was so dim he could see very little. Then he noticed several sacks of flour piled up under a table and two rifle barrels pointed at him. Although he jumped aside as soon as he saw the guns, he was not quick enough. Both bullets hit him. One opened a large gash in his side; the other shattered his left thigh and lodged in his right. The force of the bullets hurled him backward so hard that he was knocked unconscious when his head hit the floor. After what must have been only a few moments, he awoke to excruciating pain in his legs and felt certain he would soon die. Slowly his senses and courage returned, and he decided to escape by sliding his body toward the door. It was slow and painful work, for his legs were useless and he had to pull himself forward with his hands. At any moment he expected the white men would shoot him again, but they never did. When he finally made it through the door, two of his friends grabbed him under the arms and dragged him to one side. The war party then set fire to the house and killed the two white men when they tried to escape.

Although his left leg was terribly mangled, Black Horse tried to ride his horse back to camp. He managed to stay in his saddle for about a mile, but his legs became so swollen and the pain so intense that finally he pleaded to be left behind. "I was looking for this and found it," he told his companions. "Leave me here to die." This they refused to do. Instead, they cut poles and made a travois for carrying him back to camp. When they got there, however, a discussion ensued about the wisdom of taking him along. He was, in fact, very badly wounded, and caring for him might jeopardize the welfare of the others. Nonsense, said Buffalo Wallowing Woman. "I will not leave my nephew," she announced. "I will stay and die with him, if necessary." Thanks to his aunt's stubbornness, Black Horse was allowed to continue with the main party, but it was Buffalo Wallowing Woman's horse that pulled his travois.

Upon crossing the North Platte River, the Northern Cheyennes made a fateful and, for most of them, a tragic decision. Thinking they were at last safe, Dull Knife decided to separate from Little Wolf and go to Fort Robinson, which was the headquarters for the Sioux reservations in South Dakota, so he could rejoin his Sioux friends and relatives. With Dull Knife went almost two-thirds of the Cheyenne camp. Cold, hungry, and anxious to stop running, they felt certain the authorities at Fort Robinson would give them food and shelter and let them remain in their beloved north country. Instead, they were ordered to return to Oklahoma. The Cheyennes chose death instead. On a bitter cold night in January, most of them were either killed or wounded in a desperate attempt to escape from the fort.

The Cheyennes who chose to remain with Little Wolf fared much better. This group, including Black Horse, hid in the sandhills until March and then, when the weather improved, continued north. Upon entering present-day Montana they met several Northern Cheyennes working as scouts for the United States cavalry operating out of Fort Keogh. One of these scouts was Wolf-Voice, a Gros Ventre who married into the Cheyenne tribe. He told the refugees that Lieutenant W. P. Clark, known as White Hat to the Cheyennes and a friend of Little Wolf's, hoped the runaways would surrender without a fight. If they did so, Clark thought he could prevail on the federal government to let them stay in the north country. Little Wolf accepted the offer, and the next day the Cheyennes met with Lieutenant Clark, one of the minority of soldiers on the western frontier at that time sympathetic to the plight of the American Indians. With Clark was an Army doctor who attended to the sick and injured Cheyennes, including Black Horse.

Except for sporadic incidents, such as the well-known massacre at Wounded Knee, South Dakota, in 1890, the capitulation of Little Wolf and his followers ended the Indian wars on the Northern Plains. With Little Wolf when he surrendered on March 3, 1879, were 33 men, 43 women, and 38 children, a pitiful remnant of the 336 Northern Cheyennes who had left Darlington the previous October.

Lieutenant Clark, who was himself to die tragically at Sioux hands in 1890 during the height of the Ghost Dance troubles, kept his word. Little Wolf's people were allowed to remain in their northern homeland. In fact, most of the men—among them Black Horse, whose shattered leg left him lame for the rest of his life—enlisted as scouts in the U.S. cavalry under Clark. Shortly thereafter, the Northern Cheyennes, which included Dull Knife and the remnants who survived the breakout at Fort Robinson as well as several other bands that had not been sent to Oklahoma, were given a reservation in the rolling hills and rich grasslands near the Tongue River. The Northern Cheyenne Reservation is often called Lame Deer, after its principal town, which is named for a Sioux chief who died there in a fight with the U.S. cavalry. It was there that Black Horse lived out the rest of his life, a respected veteran of the Indian wars. It was there that he told his story to George Bird Grinnell, who in his classic work *The Cheyenne Indians* of 1923 wrote of him: "Black Horse, an elderly and crippled warrior, . . . was a great fighter in the decade between 1870 and 1880." It was there, too, that his son Alexander befriended a troubled young man from California searching for his roots.

Although Ben Campbell does not have many fond memories of his father today, he can understand his decision to minimize his Indian background. "Let's face it," Campbell shrugs. "You're being told your people are rotten, you don't want to be one of those anymore. Indians have been hearing that for two hundred years. You can see why some of them just left the reservation, hid their identity, had nothing to do with their past. It was just too tough, too emotional. Blacks used to use the word 'pass.' If you were light-complected enough, you would pass as something else. I think that is exactly what my dad decided to do."

Campbell no longer faults his father for that decision, because he has found it to have been a common experience in many Indian families. "It's certainly not a point of shame or embarrassment at all. I think that we, as Indian people, almost all know someone in our own families who chose that route."

Janine Pease Windy Boy, president of the Little Big Horn Community College on the Crow Reservation, confirms what Campbell says. "Almost all Indian families are picking up the pieces of their past," Windy Boy points out. "It is a result of the incredible repression they endured for so many years, when there were no rewards for being Indian. There were restrictions placed on religion, on assembly, even family gatherings. Among tribes in our area at least, there is a generation of Indians when the government did its level best to abolish their culture and language. Obviously," she continues, "it wasn't totally relegated to invisibility or meaninglessness. Ben Nighthorse is an example, and there are many others. He's certainly proof of the fact that it still meant something to be Indian; it meant a great deal, even if his father made every attempt to bury it. If his father had been successful, I don't think there would be a Ben Nighthorse Campbell today."

Campbell himself did not come to grips with his Indian identity until after the Tokyo Olympics, when he was in his early thirties. The reason for this, he thinks, was curiosity. He felt a need to know who he was and where he came from. He was always fascinated by Indians and by nature. "I really tuned in to nature. I used to love it. I used to camp out alone a lot, and I felt very comfortable out in the woods, even in the winter in the snow by myself."

Yosh Uchida, his college judo instructor, however, believes that it was Campbell's stay in Japan that inspired the quest for his American Indian roots. "I believe the time he spent there was a period where he learned a great deal more about himself as an American and as a Native

American, because only when confronted with another culture do you truly begin to question and appreciate your own heritage. Ben taught English to earn enough to pay for his room and board and so," Uchida believes, "had an opportunity to get to know the Japanese people and their culture. I think that experience not only helped him technically as an athlete, but it helped to broaden his perspective as an individual."

Exposure to Japanese culture was probably only partially responsible, because Campbell returned to the United States during a period of tremendous social and political unrest. The 1960s was a decade of social change, and Ben's quest for his roots coincided with an exuberant and exciting period of cultural resurgence among American Indians. The takeover of Alcatraz Island in 1969 and the beginning of the Red Power movement changed—and charged—the lives of many Indian peoples across the United States.

Ben Campbell was just one of hundreds of young men and women who sought to salvage their Indian heritage. "When I finally decided to try and track my roots, I asked my dad who I should go talk to. He told me we were related to the Black Horse family on the Northern Cheyenne Reservation in Montana. That's all he could tell me." With that information, Campbell in the summer of 1966 began to make inquiries. Officials at the tribal headquarters in the town of Lame Deer told him that the patriarch of the Black Horse family was an old man named Alec Black Horse who lived in a cabin along Lame Deer Creek near the home of Grover Wolf-Voice. By a remarkable coincidence, at a flea market in California that very summer, Campbell saw an old photograph of an Indian in traditional dress. Recognizing the designs on his moccasins as Cheyenne, Campbell asked the owner if he could take the picture out of the frame and examine it. On the back was written: "Wolf-Voice, Miles City, Montana, 1882." Ironically, this was the scout who had directed Black Horse with the rest of Little Wolf's band to Lieutenant Clark.

"You know," Campbell said, "I think there's still a Cheyenne family named Wolf-Voice living on the Northern Cheyenne Reservation. Can I make a copy of this?"

After getting the photograph reproduced, Campbell paid Grover

Wolf-Voice a visit. He found the old man living in a log cabin on the Lame Deer reservation. Looking through the open door of the two-room cabin, Campbell could see two or three women and several dogs. "Is Wolf-Voice around?" he asked. "Yeah," one of the women responded. "He's in the other room working on a bonnet."

Grover Wolf-Voice, an old man in his eighties who wore thick glasses and a perpetual smile that warmed his seamed and leathery face, turned out to be the son of the man in the photograph. After Campbell explained the purpose for his visit, the old man did not say anything for a very long time. When he finally broke the silence, he spoke in fractured English.

"You half white man?"

"Yeah," Campbell admitted. Again Wolf-Voice did not speak for a long time. Instead, he seemed intent on watching three little children romping on the floor. Two of them were obviously full-bloods; one was obviously a mixed-blood, the offspring of a granddaughter who had run off with a white man only to return pregnant and alone. Wolf-Voice stared at his little half-blood grandchild and then at Campbell.

"It okay," the old man said at last. "Him half white man, too."

Wolf-Voice and Campbell got to be good friends before the old man died at age eighty-nine. With Grover's passing, the tribe lost an important cultural resource, for he was one of the last traditional flute makers as well as leader of one of the dance clans. Wolf-Voice told Campbell that Alec Black Horse and his wife, Mary, lived in a similar cabin just a short distance away along the same creek.

Leaving Wolf-Voice, Campbell hurried over to the Black Horse cabin and knocked on the door. After introducing himself, Campbell eagerly explained his reason for disturbing them: "My dad told me that in some way I am related to you through your older half sister."

Black Horse's reaction was similar to that of Wolf-Voice. He listened intently as Campbell blurted out what little he knew of his family history. The old man did not interrupt and he asked no questions. When Campbell finished, Alec Black Horse smiled and said, "I'm glad you came. I needed another son."

Campbell still marvels at the reception he received. "Isn't that the nicest thing. I mean open, just open. Come in, you're my family. That's the way it happened."

The meeting occurred in the summer of 1968. Thereafter, Campbell started visiting Lame Deer on a regular basis—at least once a year, sometimes twice and even three times. Usually he came laden with gifts. "I would bring food and clothing, whatever I could scrape together. I was working for the sheriff's department then, and for a few years I ran a clothing and food drive. A lot of the deputies would bring things in and leave them for me. Then, when I had enough for a load, I would hire a big U-Haul truck and bring it all to Lame Deer." Once Campbell gave a shipment to the St. Labre Indian Mission, but instead of distributing the clothes and canned goods, the staff sold it all and put the money in a fund. "That's not what I wanted. I wanted to give it directly to people. Maybe the mission needed the money, but that's not what I wanted done with the stuff." After that, he let his cousins on the reservation handle the distributions.

Campbell believes his generosity facilitated his ready acceptance by the Northern Cheyennes. "I have never wanted anything from them except their friendship. I don't want their coal, I don't want anything. You know, they've been burned by so many people from the outside. Somehow everyone who goes up to Lame Deer has a hidden agenda; they want something. I'm probably one of the few people who ever come up here to just give them what I can and leave."

The fact that Campbell is now a U.S. senator appears to mean little to the Cheyennes with regard to their acceptance of him. They had made the decision long ago, when he was a novice jeweler and struggling schoolteacher. What matters to the Cheyennes, as well as other Indian peoples, are values other than political power or material wealth. "In the white world," Campbell points out, "status is a big house, nice car, salary, power, position, authority, title, but not to Indians." None of that heightens status in the Indian world. "There you are measured by how much you've given to people, how much you help people. You can be poor as a church mouse on the reservation and yet have the highest status within the tribe; you can be in rags and barefoot and still have the most respect. It's just topsy-turvy from mainstream society.

"The traditional Indian value system is akin to Confucianism or Taoism and Buddhism," Campbell says. "Perhaps that is why I related so well to oriental philosophies when I was in judo. I must have seen the connection to the way Indians think with regard to the world around them and their role in it."

From Alec Black Horse, Campbell learned about his Indian family. "He told me mostly about my father's mother, at least who he thought was my grandmother. Alec thought my father's mother was his older half sister. Who the hell knows? All Indians attach great importance to the oral tradition and to the knowledge of the tribal historians and storytellers. I don't have any way of knowing the real story."

According to Alec Black Horse, sometime in the late nineteenth century, after the Northern Cheyennes had moved to their present reservation and the tribal census rolls were established, Black Horse chose or was given the first name Ruben and was thereafter known as Ruben Black Horse on all official records. Black Horse had at least three wives, two of whom were from the northern branch of the tribe and one from the southern branch. By these wives Ruben is known to have had several children, including Alec, who was in his sixties when Campbell met him. Alec believed that Ben's grandmother was an older half sister, who lived with the southern branch of the tribe in Oklahoma.

This belief is supported by other Northern Cheyennes living on Lame Deer today. They claim that the wife of Black Horse who lived with the Southern Cheyennes was a daughter of Chief Black Kettle named Yellow Woman. She remained with the Southern Cheyennes and never joined her husband in the north. On the other hand, according to Alec, his father frequently visited Oklahoma and told his northern family that he had a wife and children with the Southern Cheyennes. "Over the years I have heard stories about several different wives," Campbell says. "Some people say these were liaisons, some say they were marriages. Who knows now?"

Although it is widely believed that one of the children from this relationship was Ben's grandmother, archival records dispute this. More likely, a blood relationship to Black Horse can only exist through Ramona, Campbell's great-grandmother, who could have been Black Horse's sister since they were very close in age. What is especially intriguing is that Black Horse's given name was Ruben, which is strikingly similar to Rube, the name of one of Ramona's granddaughters, and that Black Horse named one of his children Alexander, the name of Ramona's husband. Furthermore, according to the 1911 Northern Cheyenne Tribal Census, Ruben's wife at the time was named Lena, which is similar to Lina, the name of another of Ramona's granddaughters.

Perhaps all this is only a remarkable coincidence, perhaps not, but proving any of it at this late day is probably impossible, because any potentially useful tribal records at Lame Deer burned in a fire in 1958. Regardless, in 1974 Campbell began asking questions about his family among the Southern Cheyennes, whom he found to be equally interested in helping him trace his roots. That summer a large delegation of Southern Cheyennes came to Lame Deer as part of an effort to restore the various warrior societies and the chiefs' council that had existed in the pre-reservation days. As a gesture of support for the effort to revitalize traditional Cheyenne culture, Campbell made a handsome ceremonial pipe for the occasion. Richly inlaid with stones and silver and decorated with beads and feathers, the pipe is now on display at the visitors' center at Bear Butte State Park in South Dakota. Bear Butte is the tribe's most important religious site because it was there that the prophet Sweet Medicine gave the People, as the Cheyennes refer to themselves, a sacred medicine bundle. Cheyenne men still go there for vision quests and fasts.

During the meetings, Campbell made a few inquiries. "I asked them if anybody knew anything about my ancestors—particularly great-grandmothers. I could kind of track Ruben, I told them, but I couldn't track the female side of the family." One of the Southern Cheyennes, a man named Jasper Red Hat, promised to ask around.

The subject came up again the following summer when another group of Southern Cheyennes came to Lame Deer from Oklahoma for the

Fourth of July celebration. As they were chatting with Campbell, Jasper leaned over and said, "Oh, by the way, we think we've tracked your great-grandmother. She was killed at Sand Creek."

The notorious Sand Creek Massacre was the bloody work of Colonel John M. Chivington, a former clergyman whose compassion for his fellow man did not extend to Indians. In November 1864 the Cheyennes with Black Kettle were camped, at the direction of the U.S. Army, on Sand Creek, a small tributary of the Arkansas River in eastern Colorado. Chivington led his Third Colorado Volunteer Cavalry in a dawn attack against the sleeping and peaceful village, slaughtering more than two hundred Cheyennes, most of them women and children. It remains one of the most blatant atrocities in American history.

But perhaps Campbells's great-grandmother was not among the mutilated and murdered but instead among the widely scattered survivors, a young girl separated from her family, taken up by strangers, who fifteen years later emerged in New Mexico as Ramona Mestas, *genizaro*. Campbell himself has no way of knowing. "Indians have their own ways of putting things together, and I've just sort of accepted it."

So did Alec and Mary Black Horse. "They accepted me," Campbell says, "and I accepted them. That was good enough. They didn't want anything, and I didn't want anything. They were wonderful people, Alec and Mary."

In addition to their home near Lame Deer, the Black Horses had a little cabin in the Wolf Mountains several miles away. Here they stayed each summer, returning to their cabin near the agency when the weather turned cold. But their idea of cold was not Ben's. "I remember going out to their mountain cabin one time, and it was already colder than the devil outside. The cabin had only one window, and that had no glass. To keep out the cold they hung a blanket over the window. In the cabin they had a big leg of beef hanging on a nail and it was frozen as solid as a rock. When they wanted to eat, they just chopped off a chunk with an ax and boiled it. That was it."

Ben asked the old man, "Hey, why don't you get a piece of glass for the window?"

"What for?" he said. "We're comfortable."

"They probably were comfortable," Campbell chuckles. "Remember, these were people who thought nothing of trudging fifty or sixty yards through snow to reach their outhouse in the wintertime."

Alec and Mary had two children, Francis and Annie. Francis had died some years ago, but Annie, who was fifty-eight in 1992, still lives in Lame Deer, using her married name of Annie Limberhand. No one in the family objected when on their own initiative, Alec and Mary added Ben to the Black Horse family. They went to the tribal council and testified that Ben was related to the family. He was duly enrolled in 1980.

Although Campbell readily affirmed his Indian identity, that was not true of Linda and their children, Colin and Shanan. At first Linda gamely tried to become part of life at Lame Deer with her husband, but she has never quite been able to make the transition. The Cheyennes, nonetheless, love her and welcome her as Ben's wife no matter how uncomfortable her relationship with them might be. "You know," Ben says, "Linda finds it hard to relate to some of my Indian kinfolk because they do things a little differently from the world in which she was raised, like skinning and boning a freshly killed deer in your living room while visiting with friends."

As a result, Linda's visits to the reservation have become more infrequent. Although she does not try to curtail Ben's participation in Indian life, members of his congressional staff believe they can sense a tension in their relationship with Linda when Campbell is visiting Lame Deer. As she candidly admits, when they first met she would have guessed Ben was Japanese because of his intense interest in judo and his passion for their culture. "I knew nothing about his being Indian, that's for sure."

Campbell has been more concerned with how their children relate to their Indian heritage. When Colin was younger, he frequently accompanied his father on visits to Lame Deer, and he received an Indian name in a traditional naming ceremony conducted by Alec Black Horse.

Shanan, on the other hand, preferred staying at home with Linda to traveling to Montana with her brother and father. In fact, until she was nineteen, she had never even visited Lame Deer. To Ben's great satisfaction, however, Shanan started to express an interest in her Indian background and eventually accepted an Indian name. What sparked her change of attitude, he believes, was working at the Toh-atin Gallery in Durango while attending Fort Lewis College. "There," Campbell says, "she learned more about the beauty and the beliefs of Indian America and decided she wanted to go home, as we called the Northern Cheyenne Reservation."

Shanan received her name in a ceremony at the Ashland Powwow Grounds at the 1990 Labor Day Powwow and Celebration. Annie Limberhand, Alec Black Horse's daughter, prepared the feast; Joe Little Coyote, leader of one the warrior societies, arranged the honoring songs and supervised the protocol; his wife, Brenda, was Shanan's tutor and adviser during the ceremony; and Austin Two Moons, the Cheyenne spiritual leader, conducted the ceremony itself. "No one but the person who conducts the ceremony knows what a recipient's Indian name is going to be," Campbell explains, "so it was a very pleasant surprise when Austin, at the conclusion of the ceremony, which included a blessing, an honoring dance, a formal giveaway, a feast, and a camp announcement, announced that Shanan's name would be Sweet Medicine Woman, which is Mo-ze-yo-ne in Cheyenne. It is a wonderful name, since Sweet Medicine was the Cheyenne prophet who descended from the sacred mountain of Bear Butte with what is called the Holy Bundle that is still so revered by the Cheyennes."

As part of the research effort for this biography, I accompanied Campbell to Lame Deer in May 1991. The trip shed little light on his genealogy, but it demonstrated how completely the Northern Cheyennes had accepted him. Our host and escort for the visit was Dennis Limberhand, whose great-grandfather—Limberbones—was one of the six Cheyennes killed in the battle of the Little Bighorn. Today he is a personnel officer for the Montana Power Company, the largest employer of Northern Cheyennes living on the reservation. The utility's operations are on the northern edge of the reservation, and its headquarters are in Colstrip, a company town located along a two-lane highway about twenty miles from Lame Deer.

Dennis Limberhand is also Campbell's brother—in the Indian way, as the Cheyennes like to say. Dennis had an older brother, also named Ben, who was one of Campbell's friends on the reservation. When Ben Limberhand died unexpectedly of a heart attack, his grief-stricken mother wanted to replace him with an adopted son, which is still a traditional practice among Indians of the Northern Plains. The person she selected was Ben Campbell. "From the standpoint of the Northern Cheyennes," Campbell says, "she is now my mother, and she is referred to as my mother, and Dennis is my brother." It is practices such as this, of course, that make it so difficult for anyone to trace actual blood relatives in an Indian community.

During the four days Campbell spent on the Cheyenne reservation, people continually wanted to shake his hand, ask a favor, and have him say a few words. Since this was Memorial Day weekend, there were many social events, and Campbell was expected to be at all of them. He spoke at a meeting of the Sand Creek Survivors Association; at a luncheon and giveaway in a large hall in Lame Deer, where he signed and distributed dozens of copies of his colorful poster featuring him and his wonderful spotted horse—Black Warbonnet—in Cheyenne regalia; and at the Lame Deer Cemetery for the annual ceremony honoring deceased Cheyenne war veterans, including those like Dull Knife and Little Wolf, whose exploits were on fields of valor in opposition to the United States. Also buried in this cemetery are Ruben Black Horse and other Cheyenne veterans of the Indian wars who lived into the reservation era. Campbell also managed to squeeze in a dinner at the home of tribal chairman Ed Dahle and a tour of Dull Knife Memorial College, all in addition to the ostensible purpose for our visit, seeking out information about his Cheyenne ancestry.

The most symbolic event in which Campbell participated was the honor ceremony for a young man named Ron Big Back, who had just returned to the reservation from Operation Desert Storm. The ceremony confirmed the revival and continuation of centuries-old traditions in which war heroes received the praise and plaudits of friends and relatives. At the ceremony, Ron first underwent a purification with the incense of sage to cleanse him of any evil spirits that lingered around him as a result of his combat experience; then he was given a new name, Charging Eagle, in honor of his bravery in the face of a Scud missile attack that occurred one evening while he was on sentry duty. According to his commanding officer, who informed Ron's family of his heroism and whose letter was read at the ceremony, Charging Eagle had alerted his sleeping comrades to the incoming missile with a Cheyenne war cry, thereby awakening the camp.

Campbell also participated in a special meeting of chiefs and warrior society leaders. The Cheyennes, as part of the effort to revitalize traditional ways, have restored four of the old warrior societies—the Dog Soldiers or Crazy Dogs, the Elk Men, the Kit Foxes, and the Bowstrings—and the Council of Forty-four Chiefs, which inducted Campbell in 1982. Because of the problems that beset the Cheyennes today, problems that are endemic on Indian reservations throughout America, such as unemployment, alcoholism, suicide, and school dropouts, tribal leaders felt a need to restore old values. The tradition of warrior societies was especially important; in the pre-reservation days the societies were responsible for the well-being of the People.

The meeting was held in a large tepee erected at the home of Johnny Russell. As the members chatted in the tepee, their wives prepared a buffet supper while dogs howled outside and a score of children roughhoused and otherwise contributed to the general bedlam in the Russell backyard.

In the large drafty canvas tepee that blustery and damp afternoon were seventeen men, ranging in age from their midthirties to midseventies, who sat on cushions and discussed matters of tribal importance much as Indian leaders have done since time immemorial. The seventeen included nine chiefs, one of whom was Campbell, seven warrior society members, and Austin Two Moons, the spiritual adviser to the societies.

Austin delivered an impassioned speech in which he discussed current concerns of the Cheyenne including the suicide of a high school senior, which had occurred the day before our arrival and had cast a pall over the entire reservation. The young man had learned that he would not be graduating with his class, and as a result his girlfriend had broken up with him. Despondent, the boy shot himself through the chest with a high-powered rifle. Austin had gone immediately to the boy's grandmother. "Sometimes you have to cry. I have cried many times in my life," he said, "and I cried with that grandmother for her son—her grandson—and we prayed together." The boy, Austin reported, was the great-grandson of Kills-Enemy, a great chief. All his surviving brothers—Martin, John, and William—were members of the council of chiefs, yet this young man, from a family of leaders, had killed himself. "That's why," Austin explained in a strained voice to his hushed listeners, "it's so important that the chiefs in this newly restored society work together for the betterment of our people. God put Cheyennes on this earth. The Cheyennes were once a powerful people. They have to work together now to stay together, so that there will be Cheyennes in the future."

At one point in his remarks, Two Moons turned to Campbell. "You, too, are now a Cheyenne chief. Because you are a chief and because of where you are, in Washington, D.C., you are now the leader of our people, and we all follow you. You have to stand up for our rights. You have to speak out for your people. You are in a position to help us, and we are grateful for your help."

"Austin," Campbell replied, "just because we're in Washington doesn't mean we have all the answers. We, too, seek leadership from many directions and from all sources. Every day the Congress opens with a prayer, and we ask people to pray to God their own way."

No more telling example can be found of the difficulties the Cheyennes face in trying to restore the pride and dignity that once made them lords of the Plains than Jim Town, a notorious bar on the road between Lame Deer and Colstrip, the community built for its employees by the Montana Power Company. Jim Town is in the middle of nowhere, but it is located precisely at the reservation's northern boundary, and its sole reason for being is to furnish liquor to Indians, who cannot buy alcohol legally on either the Cheyenne or Crow reservation. Jim Town's major claim to fame, besides being responsible for dozens of Indian deaths, is a mountain of empty beer cans out back that is considerably higher than the building itself. The beer cans accumulate over a period of several years. Then a bulldozer flattens and buries the pile so the process can start all over again. "It was pictured in *National Geographic* magazine," one of the Cheyennes noted with pride.

Jim Town is no place for the weak of heart. Bullet holes pockmark the walls, broken knife blades protrude from table tops, and tree stumps—since bar stools and chairs are too readily broken in fights—serve as seats.

Stories about Jim Town are legion. Dennis Limberhand's favorite concerns a group of local rednecks who dropped by one evening and decided to have a little fun at Cheyenne expense. One of the white boys had on a chain a vicious Doberman pinscher that would lunge at unsuspecting Indians as they entered the bar. The chain jerked the dog off its feet just short of the startled patrons. The rednecks thought it was a great joke to see the dog scare the hell out of Indians, but they finally pulled the trick on the wrong one. As the Doberman went through its antics, one young man quietly left the bar only to return to few moments later. "Is that your dog?" he said to one of the rednecks. "Yeah, what of it," the man smirked. The Cheyenne pulled out a pistol, pointed it at the dog, and shot it between the eyes. "You need to get it outta here, that's what."

Since the bar is on the road between Colstrip and the reservation, strangers often make the mistake of stopping in for local color and a drink. One Saturday morning a Seattle attorney helping the tribe negotiate a coal lease stopped at Jim Town with Dennis Limberhand and the tribal chairman. As the well-dressed attorney entered the bar, the bartender, a big, burly fellow about six foot four, took an instant dislike to him. Dennis and the tribal chairman ordered a beer; the attorney ordered a martini, which displeased the bartender even more. "He got this sour look on his face," Dennis recalls. "Listen here, mister," the bartender snarled. "I don't know who the fuck you are, but if you don't order wine, whiskey, or beer, get the hell out of here!"

Once word got around that Campbell had brought an expert from Washington, D.C., to help him trace his Cheyenne ancestry, we were overwhelmed with advice and suggestions. Although no one knew anything of importance—everyone encouraged us to chat with some knowledgeable relative who was sure to have all the needed information—it was wonderful to experience the openness of the elderly Cheyennes, who wanted so desperately to help Campbell establish his roots.

Most obliging was Mildred Red Cherries, a young woman who had been working for some time helping Northern Cheyenne families establish their genealogies so descendants could prove their relationship to the Cheyennes massacred at Sand Creek. Even now, more than a century after that dreadful moment in American history, the Cheyennes hope a sympathetic Congress will one day enact legislation to compensate the descendants as an atonement for this atrocity. In their minds, reparations are just and due; many Indian tribes traditionally believed wrongful deaths could be expiated by material goods.

Red Cherries, who works with the Sand Creek Survivors Association, was well read and eager to help. She took us to her house to see her files—a cardboard box completely crammed with papers of all shapes and sizes—and shared with us the genealogy charts that had been submitted by various tribal members related in some way to Black Horse and, presumably, Campbell. She made her most meaningful comment, which may explain the willingness of the Cheyennes to help Campbell establish his ancestry, as we examined the contents of the box. While we were standing in the muddy driveway in the back of her weatherbeaten tract house, a curious neighbor woman walked over and started to chat. They exchanged a few words in Cheyenne, their native language, before Red Cherries introduced us. After the neighbor went along her way, Red Cherries remarked sadly, "Some people are cursed. That lady's got no parents or grandparents. She don't know who she's descended from."

Our most hopeful visit was to the tidy home of Grandma Kinsel, reputedly—at near one hundred—the oldest person on the Northern Cheyenne Reservation. Her cabin, constructed of clapboard and logs with a white-washed interior nicely decorated with prints and religious objects, was as warm and cheerful as Grandma herself, a wisp of a woman who was obviously Cheyenne in name only. In the house when we got there were a dozen or so relatives, each curious about the quest for information about Black Horse and excited about the company of a congressman.

The family tried hard to elicit helpful information from the old lady, who did her best as well, but Grandma Kinsel—who died later that year—was nearly deaf and had a great deal of difficulty determining what we were asking.

"Grandma," her daughter shouted into one ear. "Do you remember Ruben Black Horse?"

"Of course I remember him," she shouted back. "He was crippled and went everywhere in a wagon. He would come visit me every once in a while."

That was about the most helpful information we obtained from Grandma Kinsel, because most of her responses were slightly skewed. Her answer to the question "Do you remember Black Horse's wife?" for example, was an emphatic and impatient "Of course he was married!"

More useful was our conversation with Annie Black Horse Limberhand, Alec's daughter. According to Annie, her grandfather Ruben traveled frequently to Oklahoma and told the family that he had a daughter among the Southern Cheyennes. Since he was a messenger for the cavalry and made a number of trips to Oklahoma as part of his official duties, the family had no reason to question his story. Other than that Annie could shed little light on Campbell's Cheyenne ancestry. "Black Horse had too many relatives," she confessed. "Some were down south in Oklahoma. He's got relatives in South Dakota among the Sioux. He's got relatives it seems all over. I don't even know half of them." Although Black Horse is known to have many descendants, few are at Lame Deer, which is one reason Annie so readily accepted Campbell as a member of the family when he came seeking Black Horse descendants. Annie was delighted to find another Black Horse, and the other members of the tribe were happy for her as well. "They were happy for me," she said, "because my only brother had died some years back of a heart attack. Ben is the only immediate member of the family I have left now that my dad and my mother are dead."

As for Campbell, establishing a technically pristine paper trail was never a high priority. He believed he had found the right family back in the late 1960s, and that was all that mattered to him and the Northern Cheyennes. Indeed, once he met Alec Black Horse a great weight had been lifted off his mind, and he became more and more involved in Indian life. "It was a good time for me," he recalls. "I began singing with an Indian drum whenever I could, and several of my newly found Cheyenne cousins put together an Indian straight-dance outfit for me. I began dancing in Northern Plains style, and I began enjoying powwows and going to the art shows. Later I was running the tribal horse training center for the Southern Utes. It was a time that I look back on with fond memories."

Particularly memorable to Campbell for several reasons was the hundredth anniversary commemoration of the battle of the Little Bighorn in 1976, an event that attracted a thousand or more people, most of them members of the three main allied tribes that had defeated Custer a century earlier—the Sioux, Cheyenne, and Arapaho. "First of all," he explains, "there was still a great deal of fear and distrust toward Indian people in Montana in 1976. Our camp at Austin Two Moons' ranch, about twenty miles or so from the battlefield, was under scrutiny by the Montana National Guard, which had been alerted for a possible Indian uprising. Their helicopters flying over our camp were a nuisance, and their armed surveillance jeeps parked on faraway hills were a constant reminder of the mistrust that still prevailed in Indian country."

These were minor irritants, however, to what occurred on the morning of June 25, 1976. When the Indians went to pray at the battlefield, they were told they could not do so without a police escort. "I was truly offended," says Campbell, who still gets upset thinking about it. "I felt that was an invasion of my privacy and an infringement on my rights as a citizen. In addition, our cars—only the Indian cars, by the way—were searched and their license plates recorded while we were in prayer. That was a clear violation of our constitutional rights as well, but it was nothing new to a people who have had their rights stripped away so many times before."

The commemoration lasted for four days, as do many Indian events because the number four is sacred. During that time, the participants held a number of special ceremonies, including the pipe ceremony, the ground blessing ceremony, purification sweats, the feast, the giveaway, and a "victory dance," which Alec Black Horse led as a member of the Dog Soldier Society.

Despite being relatively new to Cheyenne ceremonial life, Campbell participated as fully as possible and contributed uniquely to the event's success. He not only made the lance and drum Alec used in the victory dance—the drum he donated to the Dog Soldier Society; the lance he still owns—but he also designed and donated fifty handcrafted commemorative medals to Cheyenne organizers of the event, which they presented to selected friends and certain tribal members deserving special recognition, such as the Sun Dance priests. Two non-Cheyennes who received medals were actors Iron Eyes Cody and Ned Romero; both had portrayed Indians in movies and on television with great dignity.

Although the event took place without any untoward incidents or mishaps, two things occurred which Campbell still has difficulty rationalizing. "To me, a detribalized Indian awakening to my heritage, they were—and remain—a source of interest and question."

One involved an elder named Jim Little Bird, who, the Cheyennes claimed, could change the weather through prayer and got the chance to prove it. After almost two days of continual downpour that threatened to cancel the event, worried Cheyenne leaders on the morning of June 24 asked Little Bird to stop the rain. "I have no idea what ceremony Jim Little Bird and the other elders and spiritual advisers did that morning," Campbell admits, "but it was one that I had never heard of before. I know Indians often are kidded about doing so-called rain dances, but this was the first ceremony I ever heard of to make rain go away." Whatever he did, it worked. At the conclusion of the ceremony Little Bird announced that the rain would end by noon. "Sure enough," Campbell marvels, "by noon the clouds began to break up, and the sun began to shine through. It shone brightly for the remaining two days and dried out the camp. To the white people who witnessed what happened it may have seemed like a coincidence, but it was certainly no coincidence to those among us who still have faith in the old tribal ways."

The second event might also have been a coincidence, but Campbell doubts it. One evening tribal police informed a young man that his father had been seriously injured in an automobile accident and had been taken to the hospital at Crow Agency, about twenty-five miles away. According to the person who drove the young man to the hospital and then told Campbell what had occurred, a large, white owl suddenly flashed in front of their car as it sped through the darkness along the narrow two-lane road between Busby and Crow Agency. Twice more the owl appeared. The third time, however, it flew ahead of the car and then landed on the road in full view of their onrushing headlights. "Slow down," the young man said when he saw the owl in the road. "We don't have to rush anymore. My father has died." When they got to the hospital a few minutes later, they learned that the boy's father had in fact died just a short time before.

For Campbell, the events of 1976 helped crystallize his thinking about American Indian issues. He became more closely identified with his newly found relatives and he determined to embrace them and their concerns as ardently as he once had embraced the world of judo. The American warrior had, indeed, come home.

Of all the people on the Cheyenne reservation with whom Campbell identifies, the person most important to him is Austin Two Moons, grandson of Chief Two Moon, who participated in the battle of the Little Bighorn. Austin is a tall, spare, elderly Cheyenne with classic Indian features and long gray hair. His ranch lies on the road between Crow Agency and Lame Deer. Like many Indian men of his generation, he has survived periods of alcoholism and has known considerable personal anguish. One of his sons is currently in prison for having killed a Crow man after a drinking spree. Today Austin is not only a respected religious leader among his people, he is also an apostle of peace, preaching brotherhood and friendship to people the world over. Thanks to Campbell, Austin once opened a congressional fellowship meeting in the Capitol with an Indian prayer.

Two Moons is an important force in Campbell's life. In fact, when Campbell considered running for Congress, he sought Austin's guidance. Austin advised him to run because of the importance it would be to Indian people to have one of their own in Washington.

That is why Campbell, as we were saying our good-byes and Austin admired his ring, did not hesitate to remove it from his finger and give it to him. "Take it, it's yours," Ben said. It was a magnificent gold ring, bulky and heavy, with the symbol of the Cheyenne morning star inlaid in blue coral.

"How long did you wear that ring set?" I later asked. "Ten years or so," Campbell replied.

As we were leaving the reservation driving west toward Billings, we entered the town of Busby, where a dance was being held in a high school gymnasium. Ben pulled into the crowded parking lot and we slipped into the gym in time to watch the judging of the five young girls who were finalists in the shawl dance contest. "Number 585 will be the winner," Campbell predicted confidently. "She carried herself very well. She had poise." Sure enough, she won. "No doubt about it," Ben smiled.

After watching the dancing and visiting with various friends for another hour or so, it was time to leave so we could catch our flight back to Washington. As we walked through the parking lot toward our car, the sound of the drums and singing in the dance hall kept us company. Campbell remained quiet for quite some time and then said, half to me and half to himself, "God, how I love these people."

AT HOME ON THE RANGE

Afrer judo Campbell turned his competitive energies toward quarter horses—not just any quarter horses, of course, but the Anton Geesink of quarter horses. Never one to be satisfied with second place, he set out to have the best quarter horses possible and—in typical Campbell fashion—he succeeded.

In 1969 Ben and Linda bought a registered quarter horse named Sailor's Night. After eleven years of training—two of them spent helping the horse recover from a broken leg—Campbell had his champion, and what a champion he was! In the relatively short history of quarter-horse breeding, 3.1 million have been registered, yet only 44 achieved the status of supreme champion before the American Quarter Horse Association stopped awarding that classification in 1991. Sailor's Night was one of that select group. "It's the highest award a quarter horse can get," Campbell beams. "It means he has won on the track, looks great, and behaves beautifully."

Quarter horses as a distinct breed date only from the late 1800s, although their characteristics can be found in bloodlines that go back for centuries. To work cattle, the western ranching industry needed horses that combined brains, brawn, quickness, sprinting speed, and, above all, cow-sense. Ranchers began seeking and breeding horses that possessed these attributes. The result was the quarter horse, a superb animal that owes much to the quarter race horse popular in pre-Revolutionary America. Because many village greens were little more than a quarter mile in length, this soon became a standard racing distance, so gentleman farmers bred for horses that could reach top speed in a short distance.

The quarter race horse against which all others are measured is a remarkable chestnut stallion named Janus. Foaled in England in 1746 and imported into the colonies in 1752, Janus remains the prototypical quarter horse. According to Edgar's *American Race-Turf Register* (1833), Janus possessed great bone and muscle, was round, compact, with large quarters and speed, and reputedly reproduced replicas of himself with amazing regularity. Janus lived to age thirty-four, and the finest American quarter horses carry his bloodline, according to the American Quarter Horse Association, established in 1939, which maintains the registry for this popular breed.

Although Campbell had owned and ridden horses since childhood—"The outside of a horse is good for the inside of a man" is one of his credos—it was Linda who got the family into the business. "Coming from a ranch family, she wanted to have a horse," Campbell says, "so we just went down and bought her a little riding horse. One thing about horses, though, you always try to get a better one, to upgrade, like cars—get a fancier one or a faster one or something. Another thing about horses—and everybody who owns them gets into this—you get one and it's not enough. You gotta have two, so you can ride with a friend. Then, I don't know how in the hell it happens, but two always turn into thirty. They multiply like rats," he chuckles. "You tend to breed them and fool with them and so on, and the next thing you know, you're horse poor. You've got more goddamned horses than you know what to do with after a while!"

Linda's explanation about how they got into the horse business differs somewhat. She wanted a horse, she says, as a diversion from judo. At the time they married, the sport still dominated Ben's life. Indeed, their first home was a house trailer parked behind the Sacramento Judo Club. "It was really ridiculous, judo six and even seven days a week," she declares. "Our entire life revolved around it. If you know Ben, everything he does, he does two hundred percent. When he was in judo, everything was totally judo."

Linda needed an outlet. She thought first about skiing, but horseback riding won out. "Since I was raised on a ranch, and since I loved to ride, I got a horse." Keeping it in Sacramento was no obstacle because the judo club featured a large grassy lot out back.

Then Linda's problem became one of having an opportunity to ride. Since she taught school, the best time to ride was on weekends, but weekends invariably found them on the road attending judo meets. "Every single weekend we went to a judo tournament," Linda groans, "and I got sick of them. You would think these were times when Ben and I could be alone and enjoy each other's company, but that was seldom the case. Have you ever been around a coach? All the way to an event Ben would be into his mind, thinking about how his kids would do in the competition. He would be tense and preoccupied. He wouldn't talk. Then, on the way back it would be the same thing. He would be thinking about how they did. Just silence, nothing but silence."

One day she exploded. "We were on our way home from a tournament, and I shouted, 'If you bought me a trailer, just a beat-up old trailer, then I could at least ride my horse while you are watching your tournaments!' So what does he do?" Linda sighs. "He goes out and buys me this brand-new black truck. It was a beautiful horse trailer with a living room and everything." Since then she has learned to think carefully before asking him for anything. "He will always overdo."

Like all else in Campbell's life, horses became a big thing. "I just wanted a nice trail horse that we both could have and enjoy," Linda says, "but we couldn't just have a nice horse, we had to have the best. It was Ben who made sure."

"That's true," Ben admits. "I just can't do a little bit of something. I don't know what's wrong with me, but I've got to do the best. Anyhow, it all started with Linda wanting a little riding horse, and she got this great horse. It wasn't registered, it was just an ordinary horse. Then I got the opportunity to get a registered racehorse real cheap, a mare named Kahlidor, who was a quarter horse–thoroughbred cross. We raced her for a while, but she wasn't very good, won a couple of seconds, that's all, so we got rid of her and bought another mare."

The Campbells, meanwhile, continued to live at the Sacramento Judo Club and kept the horses out back. As Ben's interest in horses intensified, however, his interest in judo began to wane—"Ben's life seems to go in ten-year cycles," Linda laughs—and the couple decided to move to Montrose, Colorado, so they could be near Linda's family and have a place to raise horses.

The move, which took place in 1969, was ill fated. Ben got a job teaching gymnastics and art at Colorado Western College, a little private school outside of Montrose, but it closed during his first year there and he could not find another job. As a result, he ended up back in California, where he accepted two jobs. During the day he taught crafts and industrial arts at Daylor High School, and at night he worked for the Sacramento Sheriff's Department, where he had earlier helped form the mounted police unit. By the time Linda rejoined him about a year later, he had saved enough money for the down payment on a thirteen-acre ranch with a barn and arena near Elk Grove, about fifteen miles south of Sacramento toward Stockton.

It was then that the Campbells got into the horse business in earnest. The key was finding Sailor's Night. "What happened," Campbell says, "is that I just kept buying better horses until I found the right one. I wanted to buy a quarter-horse stallion that tried to win. I wanted one that could be a supreme champion." He sold his Japanese weapons collection for five thousand dollars and with the money began looking for his champion quarter horse.

This quest was not as foolhardy as it sounds, however, because Campbell enlisted the help of two competent horse trainers—Bobby Ingersoll and Duane Pettibone. Campbell had befriended them through his work with the mounted police unit, and they got him interested in becoming a horse trainer himself. "What little I know about training," Campbell says modestly, "I know because I watched them carefully and rode with them a little bit and tried to learn. They can do things with horses you wouldn't think a horse could do, and I don't mean by hurting them either. I mean through knowing horse language. And there's really something to that. You spend time with horses. You've got to have patience and do it at their speed, that's all. See, if you've got some idea you're going to force them or make them go faster than they can go or push their training past their ability to learn, forget it! All you're going to do is blow them out and get hurt; that's what you're going to do. Horses make you slow down to a calmer, more paced lifestyle. You know, horses are not real high on the ladder of intelligence like pigs and dogs. I think they're down there about number seven. They're not real smart, but Jesus! They've been here for millions of years, they must have done something right. They can do things man damn sure can't do. How'd you like to be able to run that fast, fight off everybody that gets in your way, and take care of thirty wives all at the same time? A stallion stands for everything a man in his subconscious would like to be—strong, powerful, a lover, the whole works."

Campbell began to haunt the local horse auctions, usually with Pettibone or Ingersoll in tow. He saw several likely-looking animals and, in fact, bought one stallion that did not work out. Campbell started to get discouraged when, after several weeks of searching, he heard about a dispersal sale at Seven Bar Ranch in Oakdale, California, that was going to feature some good-looking horses with athletic ability that were just coming off the track. Campbell called Pettibone, rushed to the sale, which was held on September 29, 1969, and found Sailor's Night. It was love at first sight. "He was a nice horse," Campbell says matter-of-factly.

Nice horse? Sailor's Night was the horse of a lifetime. The sale price was forty-three hundred dollars but the Campbells rejected an offer of ten thousand dollars as soon as they got him home. The brown seal stallion was large, standing sixteen hands high, and on his sire's side went back to Bold Venture, the 1936 Kentucky Derby winner. In twenty-one starts, Sailor's Night had taken three firsts, one second, and two thirds.

Once the Campbells got him, however, he never raced again. "I got him when he came off the track as a three-year-old, but we rebroke him and trained him for the show ring," says Campbell. "I showed him that fall, but in the spring he had to come home and work, you know, because we bred him. We stood him as a public stallion. So he really paid for himself. He made his own wages, so to speak. I mean, we'd book him to maybe a dozen mares at five hundred dollars each and make enough from the mare breedings at least to keep him in training the rest of the year."

It was not all sex and fun. Sailor's Night also had to train hard to earn his ranking of supreme. He was on the road throughout Canada and the United States for seven years straight. The Campbells did part of this work. "I used to show him at halter and Linda did, too." When Ben or Linda couldn't go, then he went with a trainer. "You contract with a trainer that's taking several horses, so you can share the expenses. He's pulling a trailer with four horses and showing four horses; he divides up the mileage between the four owners. It's a little cheaper that way."

But Ben and Linda did their share. "We've towed horses all over this country—Oklahoma, Montana, Colorado. It's no big deal. I used to love to go with them," Campbell says, "and I didn't do the fancy motel thing. I used to take my sleeping bag and sleep in the stall with the horses, then shower at a KOA campground. I would keep my horses in the local fairgrounds when I was on the road."

Campbell slept with his horses for two reasons. "It was one of the few times when I could camp out. Otherwise I was too busy. I used to enjoy that." More important, sleeping with the horses is a good way to protect them. "Those horses were valuable, and I worried about them on the road. It's pretty easy to steal horses, and recovering them is difficult because show horses aren't branded. It ruins their looks." Usually show horses are identified by tattoos inside their lips. Sometimes a "freeze brand" is applied under their manes where it is not obvious, but the burn brand is not recommended for show horses.

Theft is not the only concern for horse owners. Horses can easily injure or kill themselves even in the safety of their own stalls or paddocks. "They can get upside down in the stall while rolling around scratching themselves, and they can die there. They end up upside down with their legs against the wall. They can't stand up, and when their guts twist—it's called "cast"—they die. We have had that happen to horses worth fifty or sixty thousand dollars. You have to watch them all the time. One little scratch and there goes not only the show, but the potential for breeding."

During his active life Sailor's Night had to work with several trainers because each one is a specialist. To get the best out of a horse in the categories necessary to qualify for a supreme ranking, someone competent in the various classes such as showmanship, halter training, racing, performance as a working cow horse, was essential. In other words, if a quarter horse is being prepared for the race track, then a racing trainer is hired until the horse finishes his racing career. For cutting and roping, a different trainer is required. No single trainer is broadly skilled enough to make a horse into a supreme champion. Trainer Bob Kozlowski, for example, helped Sailor's Night win the show points needed to qualify for the supreme championship. The sleek stallion had great eye appeal and easily won the aged-stallion class at shows in Woodland and Gridley, California. Throughout two seasons he was among the top ten in stallion halter points for the Pacific Coast and was the 1972 Pacific Coast champion. After that victory, in fact, the Campbells received—and rejected—a thirty-thousand-dollar offer for him. Sailor's Night earned his roping points with the talented trainer Smoky Pritchett of Cottonwood, California. Together they won three Class A roping tournaments. The final halter points needed for Sailor's elite standing, which the American Quarter Horse Association awarded him on August 13, 1977, were garnered under trainer Jack Brizendine of Rosedale, California.

Notwithstanding the spectacular success they had with Sailor's Night, raising stallions is always risky, Campbell says. "The only way you can handle a stud is to be a little more stud yourself. They're not women's horses. They're unpredictable, even the ones that are kind and sweet, like Sailor's Night. He was the most gentle-dispositioned stud you'd ever want to meet," retorts Linda. "He was the gentlest horse I ever rode."

Gentle or not, stallions are unpredictable, Campbell insists. "One will be as sweet as everythng for ten years and suddenly just take a chunk out of your hide one day. Horses can really bite. I mean, they take meat right out of you when they bite. Stallions will also kick you, or drag you, and even corner you in a stall and kick the hell out of you. It's been known to happen by horses that everybody thought were so sweet. Stallions are not good to own unless you're making money on them. They're just a macho thing if you're not making money. Who needs them? That's why so many are gelded. Geldings are reliable. They haven't got sex on their mind. All they do is eat and sleep. Stallions, on the other hand, think about nothing but sex and food, in that order."

It was sex, in fact, that almost led to Sailor's early demise. Although the Campbells kept him in a supposedly safe paddock made of pipe, he got so excited when Linda walked a mare past him one afternoon that he somehow laced his hind legs through the rungs of his fence, fracturing a hock. He did not panic, Linda says. He just stood there as she frantically tried to spring his legs loose. When finally freed, he could not walk. Fortunately, it wasn't a bad break, just a bone chip and a hairline fracture, but it required constant care for him to recover. "I doctored him. I soaked it and wrapped it every day. Ben never went out there. It bothered him so much, he never went near the horse until he recovered enough to continue his training and was ready to show. And then he got his supreme rating. This is typical of Ben. He is the pusher, the innovator, but all the details are left for me to take care of."

Despite the hazards of keeping a stud, the primary reason the Campbells sold Sailor's Night was because they left California for Colorado. Sailor's Night was too valuable a property to turn out to pasture. As a retired supreme champion he commanded significant stud fees, but there were not enough quality mares in Colorado for him to service. Duane Pettibone had warned the Campbells this would happen. "You're moving to a place that's probably fifteen years behind the rest of the country for high-powered horseflesh," he told them. "You're probably going to have trouble there getting good mares to him because that Four Corners area where you're going to live is so far out of the way." Pettibone was right, Campbell declares. "During the breeding season after he'd won a supreme championship and retired, even with all these titles and awards, Sailor was only getting maybe twenty, twenty-five mares a year, which is nothing for a really famous stud. We were in the wrong place; too far to pull the good mares from Texas and nothing nearby to breed to him at all—a lot of heads but no good horseflesh." As a result the Campbells sold Sailor's Night, although they retained breeding rights to him. "The Sailor was a good stud," Campbell says. "He made about a hundred thousand dollars a year in breeding fees for the syndicate—about one hundred mares at a thousand bucks a mare." Nice horse, indeed.

The last time Campbell saw his prize horse was in Edmond, Oklahoma, in 1986. Colin Campbell was competing in a horse show nearby in Oklahoma City, so father and son took a day to renew acquaintances with their old friend. By then Sailor was about twenty and looking his age. "He'd never been what's called pasture-bred—just turned out with the mares—so he didn't know anything about protecting himself from cranky mares that kick and bite and raise every kind of hell, just like cranky women, I guess. When we had him he was always hand-bred. Controlled breeding keeps horses from getting kicked or hurt. A horse gets so valuable he can't even have sex—that's pretty bad, isn't it? We controlled all the breeding on our ranch, but the later owners just turned him out to pasture with some mares, and he got the crap beat out of him." Indeed, Campbell was appalled at the grand old horse's condition. "He had bite and hoof marks all over him. He didn't know any better. He'd just run up to a mare and—wham—she'd kick the hell out of him and teach him some manners."

The Campbells' decision to leave California had nothing to do with horses but rather with health and climate. "I had a touch of asthma that I'd always had as a youngster," Ben says, "and that damp air in the valley around Sacramento was really starting to bother me," and Colin was having asthma trouble, too. Colorado seemed as good a dry place as any. Linda had been born there, and so had Ben Campbell's father.

Campbell's first choice, actually, was not Colorado but Wyoming, especially the area around Cody. "I always liked Cody. I had friends there, and it was only about three hours by car from the Northern Cheyenne Reservation. Living in Cody would have enabled me to participate in the tribal ceremonies on a regular basis, yet I could stay close to the western art market, since I had begun working as a jeweler by that time as well."

The year of decision was 1977. "We agreed that I could go on the road with my jewelry business and start looking for a place to live at the same time. Linda, meanwhile, would stay in California with the children until I found the right place. When I did, Linda would sell the ranch and join me." To keep themselves afloat financially, Linda took Ben's teaching position with the Elk Grove School District.

Ironically, Campbell never got the opportunity to look around Cody for a place to settle. The year he made the decision to move, he had committed himself to two, virtually back-to-back jewelry shows in New Mexico: the Gallup Intertribal Indian Ceremonial and the Santa Fe Indian Market. With only a week between shows, however, it made no sense for him to drive all the way to Cody. He needed to set up shop closer to New Mexico, and the perfect spot was suggested to him by Jimmy King, a Navajo friend who lived on the Southern Ute Reservation near Ignacio, Colorado. King invited Campbell to spend the week with him and his wife. Not only would it save a long and tiring haul across Wyoming, but Campbell could use the time he saved to make more jewelry.

Campbell was nothing if not flexible, since his jewelry shop was a converted house trailer that he pulled behind a pickup truck fitted with a camper. "With my little trailer shop I could set up camp anywhere, so I had a great time making my jewelry and just enjoying my life."

Campbell enjoyed his visit with the Kings so much that he returned to Ignacio after the Santa Fe market. One week passed into another until he realized he no longer wanted to leave. Meanwhile, in taking notice of his surroundings, he discovered that the Utes owned a state-of-the-art horse training facility. The Utes, in turn, discovered that Campbell knew something about training horses. "How about giving us a hand with the place?" asked a tribal member one day. "Okay," Campbell said, thereby initiating still another change of direction in his life.

Leaving his patient wife to wind up affairs in California, Campbell started to work for the Southern Ute Indian tribe in late 1978. For three years he ran their horse training center. During that time he not only sponsored rodeos, horse shows, and 4-H fairs, but he also managed to raise federal money to expand the program and improve the buildings for what is now called the Ute High Altitude Horse Training Center.

A whole year passed before the Campbell family was reunited. First to join Ben was Colin, then about eight years old. He attended school at Ignacio and lived in the trailer with his father for the six months or so it took Linda to complete the sale of the ranch in California, pack all their belongings, and organize the move to Colorado.

151

Only after Linda and Shanan arrived did Ben start looking for a place to live. Eventually, they found a wonderful tract of land on the mesa overlooking the Pine River Valley opposite the Southern Ute tribal buildings. It is a beautiful little mesa abounding with wildlife. Deer and elk play in the pastures, while hawks and owls nest in the trees. Golden eagles and bald eagles, which like to hunt along the river below the mesa, are also year-round visitors. Often they come floating up over the top of the valley and fly over the Campbell house at treetop level.

Little by little the Campbell ranch began to take shape. First they built their log home, then they began putting up fences and building pens so they could resume raising horses. Eventually, they built their own arena for showing horses. Their pastoral idyll was short-lived, however. "Linda wasn't there more than about three weeks," Campbell claims, "before the supervisor from the local school district came and offered her a teaching job." Since the school needed someone desperately, she accepted it. "While Linda was teaching school, I resumed my jewelry business, but my primary income came from running the Ute equestrian center."

Although the Utes owned the arena, they seldom used it and instead rented it out. One of the center's main sources of revenue was "jackpot" steer and calf roping contests, a form of high-stakes gambling that attracts young cowboys who pit their skill at riding and roping against all comers. "We put on jackpot ropings two times a week there," says Campbell. "One was a practice night, the other was a competition that drew some hundred or hundred and fifty ropers from across the Southwest. Those boys were serious ropers. I mean, they would bet the farm. Some, in fact, did end up losing their homes and everything else, although a few good ones made money."

Roping from horseback requires balance, dexterity, strength, precision timing, complete trust between horse and rider, and a ten gallon hat's worth of luck. A touch of lunacy is also helpful. For a while Campbell dabbled at it, but his interest in the sport faded fast. "Sooner or later," he realized, "you're going to get hurt, because you're dealing with big, powerful animals." In one night, Campbell watched as a steer put a horn through a cowboy's foot and two other ropers lost fingers. One was holding his hand too far out in front of him, and when he tossed his rope over the steer's horns, a loop closed over his thumb just as his horse put on the brakes. "I saw his thumb go. *Bing!* The tip just flew off into the muck on the arena floor. Once that happens you can't risk trying to reattach it." The other cowboy lost a finger during the dally event—a finger got in the way as he looped his rope around the saddle horn and was chopped off. "Oh, boy, I better give this up, if I hope to remain a jeweler," Campbell concluded.

Another source of revenue was rodeos, a sport that is probably rougher on the animals than it is on the riders. "God!" Campbell exclaims. "I used to see horses get killed. To make them buck, for example, sometimes they give horses a 'hot shot' with an electrical cattle prod. It gets them to buck out of the chutes. If a horse doesn't want to move, they startle or stab him with one of those hot shots. You shouldn't use those things on a horse. It blows them up. I saw one fall over backward and hit his head on a steel girder, killing himself right in the chutes. They just dragged him out of there. You see enough of that and it sours you on rodeos. I like to go to rodeos, but the fact is some people in the rodeo crowd use animals instead of working with them."

The danger of being around horses was brought home to the Campbells in dramatic fashion. Colin, like any eight-year-old, loved being around the horses and cowboys. In fact, he began to learn roping thanks to a kindly old cowboy who gave Colin a twenty-year-old gelding that had been a great roping horse in his day. But Colin's enthusiasm did not last very long.

One evening as the cowboys were gathering up the roping steers in a pasture across the river for a practice rodeo, Ben allowed Colin to go with them. His mount was a young, cranky mare that happened to be handy. As the riders began moving the steers through the brush, Colin's horse spooked. She pitched him into the air and then kicked him in the head on his way down, causing a severe concussion. Colin remained in a coma for three days, and for a while it appeared he would not make it.

Although the youngster suffered no permanent physical damage, the accident left him with such a fear of horses that Ben finally sought advice from his Cheyenne relatives, for whom horses remain essential to their psychological if not physical well-being. What resulted is something Campbell has difficulty explaining. To most non-Indians what happened was a series of remarkable coincidences, but to Indians such occurrences reinforce their belief that humans and animals can communicate with each other. Indians have traditionally believed that the human and animal worlds can interact, even talk to each other, through visions and dreams, since they all come from the same Creator. "My experience certainly made a believer out of me," Campbell admits.

The strange sequence of events began with Colin's naming ceremony, conducted about two years after the accident by Alec Black Horse during the annual Fourth of July powwow on the Northern Cheyenne Reservation. Alec, then about eighty-seven years old, gave Colin a spiritually powerful name—Takes Arrows—which is traditionally the name of the keeper of the Cheyennes' sacred arrows.

That evening, as Takes Arrows lay fast asleep in his sleeping bag and the Black Horse family enjoyed a few quiet moments around a flickering campfire in their large, canvas tepee, Ben shared his concerns about Colin with Alec. With them sitting cross-legged near the back of the tepee were a cousin named Francis and Alec's wife, Mary, who was laying out patterns for a new pair of moccasins. When Campbell finished describing Colin's withdrawn attitude and fear of horses, Alec remained silent a few moments and then told Ben to take heart. "There is a prophecy in the Black Horse family that you should know," the old man said. "I heard it from my father who first heard it when he was only a young man himself, no more than seventeen or eighteen years old, but it goes back to time immemorial among the Cheyenne people. The prophecy is about an eagle and a horse, and it may give you some comfort." Everyone in the tent fell silent. The only sounds were of the wood crackling in the fire and the throb of a drum coming from the dance arbor about two hundred yards away as Alec began to speak:

Many years ago several Cheyenne families were camped north of the Bighorn Mountains near the Tongue River. It was a favored winter camp close to firewood and water. Here hunters could usually find enough winter game to feed their families when the meat dried from last summer's buffalo kill grew short, but not this winter. This year the winter was long and hard. There was much snow and fog, and when the hunters went looking for game they found nothing. Everyone in the little village was worried that the children and old people would die of starvation before spring. Finally, one young man, an ancestor of Black Horse, vowed that he would find food on the first clear day.

Several days later, the sun broke through and the morning fog burned off. The young man set out with the other hunters in the village, who spread out in all directions in their search for food. He chose to hunt by himself and went east. With him he carried only his bow and arrows and knife because he needed to travel lightly and quickly. The decision not to take food was not his, of course; there simply was nothing left to take. The villagers had already been reduced to making soup by boiling water with scraps of fat or threads of meat that could be scraped from old hides and skins, but Cheyenne women were very efficient, and there was little fat or meat to be found.

As the young warrior hurried along, he spotted several rabbits and birds, but each time they were too far away for him to hit with an arrow. Eventually, he crossed a creek frozen so hard that he did not need stepping stones, and then he began to wind up a slope and through a clump of aspen trees barren of leaves. In a windblown meadow he saw a shape half covered by snow and on it, crouching and tearing at the frozen form, perched an eagle.

How the young man's heart bounded at the thought of fresh meat! In a glance he saw the eagle was tearing, not at the dead animal, but at his own leg, which was held fast in a snare that had been set on the carcass of an elk. As the young man drew his hunting knife and moved forward to kill the eagle, a strange sensation came over him and caused him to pause. He had killed eagles before, but only by hiding in a pit covered with branches and using a dead rabbit as a lure. When the bird tried to pick up the rabbit, he would reach up through the cover and grab the unsuspecting eagle. Afterward he had undergone the purification ceremonies and said his prayers of thanks to the Creator for giving him the feathers he needed for a warbonnet to be made in the traditional manner. But this was different. The Cheyennes call these great birds the Keepers of the Mother Earth, and he had never before had time to look into an eagle's face before he killed it. Even more unnerving, the great bird seemed unafraid, as though it were judging him.

"Brother, I do not wish to harm you," the young man apologized. "I have no need for your feathers, even though they are a fine set, but I am hungry. Although our Creator has told me we are brothers, I must kill you to live. You are fastened to the ground as surely as are our warriors who wear the bear belt into battle so that they may stake themselves to the Earth. It is a great honor to die in battle while staked to Mother Earth, and it shall be your honor to die in that way so I may live myself."

As the warrior lifted his knife to strike, the eagle spoke to him. "It need not be so," the eagle announced in a clear voice. "I know you well. Many times while circling your camp I have witnessed your kindness to those less fortunate than you. I have often seen you share food with the old ones who have no sons. I have seen you give honor to those less brave when the honor was yours. You know me as the Keeper of the Mother Earth and witness to all things, both past and future. As I look into your future I see a young warrior riding like the wind itself on a great horse whose color matches my own. The black and white horse will carry you to honor in battle and you will bear his name as proudly as he bears you on his back. Though his wounds in battle will be many, his heart will be good and his strength unending. He will come to you in the spring when the chokecherries ripen. He will be yours and all that I say will happen to you on one condition: You must set me free and share with me this meat given us by our brother, the elk. I must grow strong again so that I can search the land for this great horse and carry to him the message that you need and await him."

The young man slowly lowered his knife. "Brother," he told the eagle, "I believe your words and I know you carry them from our Creator. I shall give you your freedom and share this meat so that you may grow strong. The elk is large. He will sustain my people until the hunting becomes good again."

And so it was done. The young man freed the eagle, and they shared the meat. As strength returned to the eagle, he vaulted into the air. The young man watched him circle and gain speed as he soared on the thermal air currents and once again became the master of the skies. Finally, with a distant cry and a backward glance he disappeared over the rim of the valley.

Soon the spring thaw appeared, and all things that lived began to reawaken. Little by little the days became warmer and the berry bushes began to bloom. Each morning, upon awakening, the young man gave thanks to the Creator, for that is the way Cheyennes start each new day, and each morning he also wondered if a great horse would appear as the eagle had promised.

That spring an uncle invited the young man to become a member of the Dog Soldier Society. It was a great honor because dog soldiers were renowned throughout the land for their courage and valor. Many young warriors coveted such an invitation, but only a lucky few were inducted into the society each year. To prepare himself, the young man needed a vision that would give him his medicine, or spiritual power, his war shield design, and his spirit helper.

After proper instruction from his uncle and his father, the young man journeyed to the sacred mountain from which it is said the Cheyenne prophet Sweet Medicine brought forth the sacred bundle still kept in the lone tepee by the Northern Cheyenne. This mountain, which is in South Dakota, is today called Bear Butte, because its silhouette is the shape of a sleeping bear.

Taking only tobacco, a straight pipe, and a blanket, the young man ascended the mountain until he found a place that suited his purpose, a small clearing on a ledge surrounded by rocks and facing the East. His mission, as it was for many young men before him, was to stay companionless for four days without food or water. He had listened intently to his advisers, because he knew that visions of meaning and power came only to one who followed the instructions of his teachers with great care.

The hours were torturously slow. As day faded into night, hunger began to scream for attention as did thirst and heat and cold. By the end of his second day on the ledge, the young man began to feel pain in every sensory part of his body. An afternoon thunderstorm on the third day brought slight relief as it cooled the scorching rocks upon which he lay, but now strange dreams began to disturb his sleep. He could not later recall exactly when it happened, but suddenly the words of the eagle came to him amidst a swirl of fantasy. He began to see the eagle circling down from the sky bringing his message. The young man's body was twisting on the ground as his vision began to appear. The eagle circled lower and finally folded its wings and dove down toward the ground. Faster and faster it plummeted until, an instant before crashing, the eagle pulled out of its dive and flashed low across the ground. As it did so, the eagle seemed to transform himself into a great black and white horse galloping at full speed across the meadow below.

The young man jerked upright, frightened and confused.

He was drenched with perspiration and shaking uncontrollably. It was the morning of the fourth day. He did not understand his dream, but at least he could return to his village and ask the spiritual masters to interpret his vision. Although he had seen no war shield design nor had he obtained any special power, the great black and white horse, surely, was meant to be the spirit helper promised him by the eagle.

The young man hurried back to camp as quickly as his weakened body would allow. As he slowly made his way across the meadow and into the trees beneath his ledge that now towered high above him, however, he realized he was not alone, for as he rounded the edge of a huge boulder he heard the soft nickering of a horse. His first thought was of enemies, and he glanced about nervously for a way to escape or to defend himself. Upon hearing the horse nicker again, however, he realized it was not the sound of a horse in fear or pursuit; it was a horse calling to a friend.

Although still afraid, the young man was also overcome by curiosity. Cautiously, he parted the underbrush and peered through in the direction of the nicker. Before him stood the great black and white horse he had seen in the vision. The horse's legs were corded with muscle; his chest was deep and full; his long, graceful neck, capped by a black mane, was swanlike. His wide forehead revealed intelligence and alertness. The horse's large brown eyes showed no fear, and his quick ears moved constantly to pick up sounds in the trees. His large nostrils, indicating an ability to take in great quantities of air while running at full speed, were constantly testing the breeze. Here was a horse of which warriors could only dream. It was the eagle himself.

The young man looked lovingly at the horse for a long time. When he did approach, the great horse showed no fear. The warrior stroked its satin neck and passed his hand over the rippling muscles of the horse's legs. He then took the horse's

159

muzzle, held it between his hands, and blew into its nostrils. The old ones called this "sharing breath," and once it was done a horse could sense if a man were to be trusted. It was no trouble to swing up onto the horse's broad back, although the young man had not the faintest idea if he had ever been ridden. The horse accepted the young man and within a short period of time, the warrior was convinced that either the horse had been trained by a master or he was still dreaming, because he knew all the cues Cheyennes used in guiding horses. For example, it was important to keep one's hands free to hunt or fight, so all good Indian ponies were trained to respond to the rider's legs. So enthralled was the young man with his newfound gift that he forgot about his hunger. This horse would be his brother and his friend.

Thereafter, the great horse and the young warrior were seldom apart. For endless hours they practiced the skills needed on the hunt and in battle. The young man was the envy of all of his companions. Many times he turned down offers to trade or to gamble his great horse at the hand games. When he slept, people noticed that he always tied one end of a leather thong to his wrist and the other end to the great horse's ankle. No one could ever win, buy, or steal his horse. Together they survived many battles and won many honors. The young man lived to become a great chief among his people, and his horse became a legend about which many stories have been told to this day.

It was almost morning by the time the old man finished his story. "I was mesmerized," Campbell says. As Alec closed, he leaned forward and told Campbell, "In the Black Horse family, we have always believed that when we are in need of help that horse will come again."

Unfortunately, the real world intruded too soon. Campbell rousted Colin out of his sleeping bag, packed his truck, and father and son were soon on their way back to Colorado. "Home," Campbell thought to himself, "is only about five hundred miles in distance, but it is light-years away in time."

The following March, the cry of an eagle caught Campbell's attention as he rode his horse one morning along the river that runs through the Ute tribal fairgrounds at Ignacio. "I stopped to look at him. He was a great golden, and he was perched on the snag of a branch a short distance away. As he watched me down below, I swear he spoke to me just as the elders used to say." The eagle peered first at Campbell, then at a horse and rider on the tribal racetrack about a quarter of a mile away.

Campbell rode over to get a closer look at the horse. "It was a large black and white gelding, about two years old, and he had all the marks of mistreatment. He was about two hundred pounds underweight for his height, which I judged to be about sixteen hands. Although he was a very big, fine horse, his coat was torn and dull and flecks of blood speckled his muzzle. His rider was obviously drunk and beating him unmercifully." Upon seeing this, Campbell galloped up and yanked the man from his horse, throwing him to the ground. "If I catch you mistreating that horse again, I'll kick the shit out of you!" Campbell growled.

As the rider got up and began knocking the dust off, he retorted, "If you like the son of a bitch so much why don't you buy him?"

"I'll do just that."

It turned out the drunk did not own the horse. He was the so-called trainer, and he was attempting to beat the young gelding into becoming a racehorse. Campbell called the owner, who happened to live near Montrose, and bought the gelding for three thousand dollars. He took him home the same day. "Having been around pretty good horses all my life," Campbell says, "even with the mud and the blood I could see that the youngster was truly a beautiful animal. He was a black and white, Tobiano paint, whose registered name with the Paint Association was Highlight Scamp. We kept that name, but I always call him Black Warbonnet because, when I look at him," Campbell admits, "all I can think about is the eagle's prophecy."

Scamp responded to food and kindness, and by spring he was a thing of beauty. "When he ran proud and free out in the fields, it was like watching the wind itself." Even more wonderful to behold, however, was the bond that began to form between Scamp and Colin. The young horse that had been mistreated by a man and the young boy who had been mistreated by a horse formed an inseparable friendship. When Campbell saw Scamp and Colin flying across a field one morning, he felt certain that Black Horse's prophecy had come true.

Since Colin and Scamp were spending so much time together, the Campbells decided to take the relationship a step further. They hired a trainer named Sherry Palmer, who taught Colin and Scamp how to compete in the show ring. Before long the two of them were winning every prize in sight. From the local county fairs, they progressed up the ranks through the various 4-H shows and other events in the Four Corners circuit to the Colorado State Fair, which they won two years in a row.

The capstone to their remarkable career was to be the world paint championship in Oklahoma City, which they entered in the summer of 1986 when Campbell was running for Congress. Because Colin was very nervous during the warm-ups, Ben heeded some advice once given him by Alec Black Horse and slipped a bit of eagle feather fluff under Scamp's saddle blanket. "I hoped to give Black Horse's prophecy a little boost," Campbell says.

The eagle feather did not help. Colin and Scamp finished sixth. It was a terrible disappointment to the young man, who had entered the show confident that he and his splendid horse would win. "I tried to console him with the fact he was the youngest person in the competition and up against professional trainers, but he found it of little comfort." To make matters worse, Campbell discovered that the eagle feather had fallen to the ground during the competition. "That is a bad omen in the Indian world."

Campbell gave little thought to the feather at the time. That fall Colin went to school, and Scamp went to pasture for a little rest and recreation before attempting to win the world paint championship the following year. Disaster struck when a loose horse from a neighbor's ranch got into the Campbell pasture intent upon flirting with their young fillies. Scamp challenged him, provoking a terrible fight with teeth and hooves. As they struggled, the horses went through a barbed wire fence and Scamp suffered a grievous injury when a stake and wire tore a huge chunk of muscle and part of the tendon out of his left leg above the hock, leaving a hole the size of a softball.

When the Campbells reached Scamp, their wonderful horse could no longer lift his hind leg, and the veterinarian who later examined him confirmed their worst fears. The horse would probably be crippled for life. At best, Scamp would never walk again without a limp.

Despite the awful verdict, the Campbells elected not to destroy Scamp. "We wanted to keep him because we loved him and because of Colin." With Ben running for Congress, the task of doctoring Scamp fell to Linda. She treated that horrible wound twice a day throughout that long winter and spring—first in a small stall that kept him from moving about, then in a small paddock. Ever so slowly the great gaping hole began to fill, and as it did, Scamp began to put more of his body weight on his injured leg. After six months of treatment he was able to walk about the pasture, but he winced noticeably whenever he put his full weight on that leg. By June he was again trotting and loping with Colin or Shanan on his back, but his leg was obviously stiff and his stride unsure. Finally, with the 1987 championship less then eight weeks away, the Campbells decided to let Scamp try once more to fulfill the Black Horse destiny that they had all now come to believe was theirs.

The problem, in a nutshell, was to somehow squeeze the 90 to 120 days normally needed to bring an uninjured horse into competitive condition into fewer than 60. With Colin in Europe on a summer tour before entering college, Scamp began an accelerated training program with Sherry in Farmington, New Mexico. Scamp trained an hour a day for the first two weeks, two hours a day the second two weeks, and three hours a day the final two weeks. It was much too fast a pace for a horse recovering from such a serious injury, but there was no alternative. All anyone could do was hope and pray that Scamp, with his great heart and courage, would not buckle. Each day ended with extensive massaging of the bad leg.

Less than a month into the training schedule, the Campbells decided to test Scamp's progress by entering him in a registered paint show in Albuquerque. On the outcome hung his future show career. Scamp entered ten classes during the three-day event, which was a grueling schedule even for a horse in excellent condition. Scamp passed his test with flying colors, winning nine firsts and one second and proving once again that he was a special horse indeed.

Even with the accelerated training schedule, the 1987 National Paint Championship in Albuquerque came all too soon for Scamp. The Campbells had a difficult decision. Should they enter Scamp or not? Scamp and Colin had been inseparable for almost seven years. The horse had transformed the boy from a timid child with no self-confidence to a bold teenager for whom no obstacle was too great; and Colin, who had been watching Scamp's recovery from the sidelines thus far, very much wanted to participate. Win or lose, he wanted to finish their show career together. And what about Scamp? His destiny, according to Black Horse's prophecy, was only half fulfilled. Since the entrance fees were already paid and everyone had worked so hard for the past two months to get Scamp ready, it seemed foolish to back out now.

Western Riding, where each horse and rider performs one at a time, was the first event. Colin and Scamp were the eighth of nine entries. "As each horse entered the arena, going through and closing the gate, I began to score them mentally," says Campbell, for whom the day is indelibly etched in memory. "I looked for the same almost indiscernible flaws that a judge would look for in a field of almost perfect equine athletes. Number one, I remember, ticked a log in his step over. Number two was slow changing a hind lead. My attention was distracted for Number three's turn, but I wondered if it was a perfect ride. Number four was nondescript. Number five looked good. He was not quite so smooth in his flying changes, but the rest of his performance looked very nice. Number six, who ringed his tail as he loped, worried me a little bit." Campbell can remember nothing about Number seven; he was already looking ahead to Scamp and Colin, who were next.

The big horse moved sideways through the gate and around the obstacle course with an effortless grace acquired only after endless practice. Colin latched the gate and Scamp walked briskly to the first log barrier. Once over that, he was supposed to break into a controlled jog, but he broke before his hind legs cleared the log. "I could see first place slipping away," confesses Campbell, whose heart was in his throat the entire time.

At the end of the first cone in an eight-cone course, Colin led Scamp into a lope. They went around the second cone with the quiet, smooth flying change for which Scamp had become famous and then moved flawlessly through the serpentine pattern. Experienced horsemen near Campbell on the rail nodded approvingly as Scamp and Colin maneuvered through the crossover part of the pattern and smoothly crossed over the log without breaking stride, ending with a final lead change around the last cone. Scamp came to a smooth stop and then took several straight backing steps with his nose tucked. It was a near perfect performance.

With only one horse left to perform, Campbell had already convinced himself that Colin and Scamp had won. "Obviously, I was prejudiced, but I could see few flaws in their performance. My only fear now was how Number nine would do." Nine failed to arrive in time and was scratched. With the event now over, all that remained was the official announcements. "My heart was pounding loud enough for me to hear it," Campbell confesses. "I wanted so badly to hear: First place and new world champ, Highlight Scamp ridden by Colin Campbell of Ignacio." But that did not happen. Colin and Scamp placed fourth.

Although everyone was understandably disappointed, they had reason for happiness as well. Colin and Scamp had finished their show careers in commendable style. Scamp had fully recovered from his injury, and Colin had proven once again the equal of the finest horsemen in the world of western riding. Perhaps Black Horse's prophecy had come true.

The great horse and the young warrior had proven themselves time and again on fields of glory. The horse had even triumphed over wounds received in battle that would have been fatal to most. It was, after all, not victory that mattered most; what mattered was having the courage to do battle in the face of great odds and obstacles. Here Colin and Scamp had proven themselves worthy of any challenge. Alec Black Horse would have been proud.

Prophecies aside, it was Linda who involved the family in showing horses. She did so largely because she dislikes the more violent aspects of western horse life, like rodeos and roping. "Linda," her husband notes, "always had a real problem with people misusing animals, so she encouraged the kids not to rodeo but to show instead. Show people are much more sensitive to the welfare of horses than rodeo folks, who just knock their ponies around. You would not believe how tough some of those rodeo folks are on their animals."

Needless to say, Linda has no use for bullfights either, as King Juan Carlos of Spain learned when the Campbells visited Madrid in October 1991 as part of the United States delegation to the North Atlantic Assembly. During the visit Ben unwisely decided to introduce Linda to bullfighting, but the spectacle so upset her that she stormed out of the arena, with her husband in tow. Campbell half expected her reaction to the bullfight, but he was wholly unprepared when, at a palace reception the following day, Linda gave the king her unsolicited opinion on the subject. To their surprise, Juan Carlos not only confessed his own dislike of bullfights but also admitted that the queen flatly refused to attend them. "With that revelation," says Campbell, "I heaved a sigh of relief that we had not infringed on international protocol by upbraiding royalty."

As a result of their mother's strong feelings about animal welfare, both Shanan and Colin spent a goodly portion of their childhood years in the show ring. Both became expert riders, and both came to share their parents' love of horses. In fact, Campbell was surprised that neither one chose to become a trainer when they reached maturity. "They could very easily have done so," he says, "because they had a natural, good, free-flowing understanding of horses. But when they got to college, horses under the hood got to be more important than horses under the saddle, and the horse world lost them both."

Perhaps Campbell's own fiercely competitive nature is partly to blame. Although rightfully proud of his children, he was also very hard on them as he was on everyone around him, including Linda. "The kids hated it when Ben went to the horse shows with them," Linda claims. "It wasn't fun when he would go. He is so goal-oriented that he insists everything be just right. He wanted them to be the best and they were. They were the best of any of the kids they showed against. They won the state fair, local fairs, everything. But he put so much pressure on them that he made them nervous. Then, if they didn't do everything perfectly, he would get mad and leave. When the kids and I went to shows it was different. We would have a good time. We'd cook hamburgers, we'd laugh and joke. They would win and we would have fun. Life can be fun, if you relax."

Linda tells a story that she thinks reveals a lot of the inner person in her complex husband. When they still lived in California and the children were toddlers, Linda and a girlfriend entered a horse show. "We were late and barely got saddled in time to make our class. When you go into a show with a cold horse you don't do very well, and I lost the first class. Ben," she says, "got so angry and disgusted, he grabbed the kids and left. After the first class, however, we did really well and finished on top. I was so excited, I could hardly wait to tell Ben."

"Golly," Linda beamed as she bounced into the house, "you should have stayed around. I won the next two classes."

"You didn't win," he snapped. "The horse was the winner."

"I was so hurt, but he meant it. That is his approach to life. In order to be a winner, he believes, you have to put everything into it, and he does. When he got back into jewelry, he put everything he had into it, and now he is the best in the country. But he could not do that without having someone like me to take care of everything else. I have always ridden horses. I do it for fun, and I consider myself a good rider. I practice, but not eight or nine hours a day. I simply don't have the time. I teach school,

I clean, I cook. I run the ranch, feed the cows, do the irrigating, keep the books. Ben can do jewelry or politics because everything at home is taken care of, even the taxes. I can do anything, but nothing really great. For Ben it has to be great."

Indeed so. Ben is the showman, the politician, the person in the limelight, but it is Linda who makes it all work. She does it quietly and effectively. In many ways they are in stark contrast to each other. He is big and burly; she is petite and graceful. He is loud and flamboyant; she is quiet and dignified. He is dark-haired, a reflection of his Portuguese and American Indian forebears; she is a blonde whose ancestors came from Sweden. Both, however, are tough, determined, and forceful.

Perhaps an appropriate metaphor for their relationship can be found in a story about horses that Ben tells on himself. Years ago in California, the Campbells lived down the street from a retired Air Force colonel named Dick Unger, whose hobby was building wagons. His pride was a marvelous replica—"wheels, spokes, the works"—of a Concord stage. After building the wagons, he got the concession at the California State Fair to provide stagecoach and covered wagon rides to the visitors. "You know, pay a dollar and ride in a wagon." To pull the stagecoach he had a six-up set of matched leopard appaloosas. "It was the wildest-colored thing you ever saw."

Since Campbell had always wanted to learn how to hook up and drive a hitch, he asked Unger for lessons one day. "Swell," Dick replied, so the next four or five mornings Ben helped him hitch up the team. The morning he was to drive, Linda came along. "After I got them hooked up," Campbell continued, "the three of us got on top of that stagecoach. The seat on a stagecoach, you know, is way up there, about ten feet or so off the ground. You sit way above the horses. Anyhow, Dick started them out and then gave me the reins—six in each hand, I guess, with six horses—but I mean to tell you, it wasn't two minutes before I had them pretty badly tangled. I had those horses going backward and forward and climbing over the top of each other. I couldn't control those suckers for nothing."

As calamity stared them in the face, Linda leaned over. "Let me see those things," she muttered, grabbing the reins out of Ben's hands. In a moment, she got all six horses straightened out and away they went.

The same could be said for her role in their married life. When they met, Ben carried maximum balances on something like a dozen credit cards, he drove expensive sports cars that he bought new each year, and he was floundering. After their marriage, Linda took away his credit cards, persuaded him to trade his Jaguar for a Volkswagen bus, and helped him channel his energies.

Perhaps she was too successful. "Ben always has goals," Linda says with a note of exasperation. "He's always thinking ten years ahead. Sometimes I like to enjoy today, but for Ben that is impossible. I don't think he's a happy man, that's why he always sets these goals that seem impossible. Yet he often reaches them. I don't know how to explain that."

Ben can. "Coach Uchida always told us there were three kinds of people in this world—winners, losers, and spectators. I want to be a winner. I hate second place, but I'd rather come in second than not reach for the brass ring at all."

Although Linda credits—or blames—Ben for overdoing it when it came to raising horses, she was a willing accomplice. The fact is, she is the animal-lover in the family. Indeed, once they pared down their investment in horses, Linda began to raise cattle. In May 1992, when Ben began his race for the Senate, she had a herd of seventy-eight Brangus cattle, including twenty-three mother cows, nineteen calves, and eleven heifers. They are her responsibility and, Ben says, her pets. "You should see her walk up to a two-thousand-pound bull and scratch it behind the ears. And when it comes time to send some of her animals to the stockyards, she gets all depressed and mopey."

At its peak the Campbell stable had ten mares and two stallions, all good horses. Some of their brood mares, in fact, rivaled Sailor's Night in form and performance. According to the American Quarter Horse Association, only five mares out of the more than three million registered horses in the history of the breed ever got the title Supreme Champion and the Campbells owned two of them—Destiny Jagetta and Desto Bar. In addition, the Campbells' brood mare band boasted eight AQHA champions. "We had a really good horse farm," Ben says with justifiable pride. "Some we bought after they had won all their championships; a few we trained ourselves. We competed with them on the road until they proved themselves."

Only one brass ring in the world of quarter horses eluded Campbell. This was his dream of developing a supreme champion out of two supreme champions, but even that was within his reach. Of the five foals ever born out of a supreme sire and a supreme dam, he had two. One received a puncture wound and died; her full sister is growing old gracefully on their ranch in Colorado. "Once I got into politics," Campbell sighs, "I no longer had the time to take her to the track and train her properly. I never got to do it, and to this day no one else has done it. Politics killed that dream."

It was also politics that forced the Campbells out of the horse business. As of December 1992, they were down to three horses. Two were Sailor's—one out of a supreme champion mare and one out of an AQHA champion mare. The rest they sold. "We made some money raising horses," Campbell claims, "but we did not do it for that. We did it for the challenge and because we like horses."

SIX

BEN NIGHTHORSE, JEWELER

To an entire generation of collectors of Indian art, Ben Campbell is known only as Ben Nighthorse, the name he uses in his role as one of America's most creative designers of Native American jewelry. Indeed, he added a new dimension to Indian art, for he brings to the traditional world of silver and turquoise a brilliant combination of metals and stones. His designs reflect the mosaic pattern of his life, combining symbolism and techniques borrowed from Japan and Europe as well as his Native American origins. He has developed a unique style of jewelry that places him far beyond traditional American Indian craftsmen. His designer jewelry sells for upward of ten thousand dollars, and he is represented in galleries from coast to coast and border to border. At the peak of his production, he was earning $150,000 annually and, in fact, took a severe economic loss to enter politics.

Campbell may have had to drive himself beyond normal bounds to attain the pinnacle of world judo, but art came naturally. "The key to success is to learn what your gift is," Campbell once told a reporter, and to him that gift is art, which has been a part of his life since childhood. "I cannot remember a time when I had no interest in crafts. Even as a child, I loved to draw and carve," he declares. "Since we were too poor for me to buy materials, I would scavenge trash heaps and local dumps. With found materials I would copy traditional Indian crafts. I sewed clothes from leather, tanned skins, carved bows, and made arrows. Doing things like that occupied much of my time as a child and, I believe, provided a kind of escape for me."

Campbell credits his father with inspiring him to work with his hands. "When my father was home, he would make our toys, including snow sleds in winter and scooters in summer. He also made jewelry, a skill he claimed to have learned from Navajo friends who lived in California. Our small two-room cabin with no plumbing or electricity was the only place my dad had to work on crafts. He would carve in horn and bone as well as wood, soapstone, and serpentine, which were plentiful around Weimar. These were free," Campbell points out, "unlike the materials needed to make jewelry." For that his father used coins and copper obtained from cast-off electrical wires as well as the tops of chewing tobacco cans. "I think he made pieces now and then to trade for food, but he never sold any jewelry that I know of, nor did he sign any of it. In those days nobody signed their work, nobody followed anybody as an individual craftsman as they do now. That all really started in the 1950s and '60s."

Albert's tools were old files, drill bits, and saw blades. These he annealed by heating red hot and then burying in sand to cool slowly. The design filed into the metal was then tested by stamping on soft copper (sometimes pennies). A piece of discarded railroad track served as his anvil. If the design was suitable, the die stamp was reheated with a blowtorch or at a blacksmith friend's forge. When the tool was cherry red, Albert retempered it by plunging it into cold water or oil. These handmade stamps—some of which Campbell still owns—along with a straight-edged cold chisel, a coping saw, several files, a hammer, some pumice for sanding, and a blowtorch formed his father's entire tool kit except for an old tree stump with depressions burned into the top, which he used to form conchas, half beads, and other shapes. Bracelets were formed around different-sized limbs sawed from oak trees.

"I learned a lot by watching," Campbell says. "I even made my own things out of coins, mostly pennies, nickels, quarters. I also did some carving in bone and wood, but I rarely carved Indian designs. Like most children, I was influenced by machinery. I still have a model P51 Mustang, a futuristic car, and a small horse as well as a bone letter-opener, all done in the years 1940 to 1945."

Although local postmaster Vic Roberts and Ben's uncle Frank Vicrra, a gifted sketch artist who lived across the road in Weimar, both encouraged the obviously talented youngster to pursue art as a career, Campbell displayed little interest in the few art and shop classes he took before dropping out of high school and enlisting in the Air Force. No matter. He might have tried to run from his past, but he could not hide from his talent. The Air Force soon recognized—and capitalized upon—the young man's considerable artistic skills: it assigned him after basic training to the model-making shop at Lackland Air Force Base in San Antonio.

Ever competitive, Campbell could not resist entering a base-wide carving contest designed to identify enlisted men adept at carving models of people, vehicles, planes, and buildings that Air Force personnel could use at job fairs to show potential recruits the opportunities available in an Air Force career. Working primarily with balsa wood, Campbell and his fellow craftsmen carved military equipment and buildings to scale from blueprints and plans, while the human figures—usually two or three inches tall—they rendered freehand. "I did this for about eight months, but I finally got burned out," Campbell remarks. "It was no fun carving nothing but models for six or seven hours a day, week after week."

At his request, the Air Force reluctantly reassigned him to Air Police School in Florida and, ultimately, to Korea, where Campbell found time not only to practice judo but also to pass his GED high school equivalency exam. One of his correspondence courses was an art class, which got him interested in cartooning. By the time he left Korea few bulletin boards on base were without his work. He continued this interest by drawing illustrations and cartoons for the newspaper at San Jose City College, where he enrolled after his discharge from the Air Force.

While in college, Campbell maintained a modest interest in art by taking a few classes as electives, including two in jewelry making. One was for beginners, the other was a class in advanced casting. "I was not an art major, but I enjoyed the classes enough to qualify for a minor. I also needed the easy As," he grins. The jewelry classes also enabled him to make a little pocket money by knocking out simple rings and pins, which he sold to fellow students for fifteen or twenty dollars. Again, his talent did not go unnoticed. One of his art teachers bluntly told him he was wasting his time in physical education and urged him to major in art. "In retrospect, he was right," Campbell admits, "but as usual I was too stubborn to heed anyone's advice."

Nonetheless, Campbell was not above using his artistic skills to support his obsession with judo. During the two years between his graduation from college and his move to Japan, he taught art and shop to grades K through 8 at the Cypress Street Elementary School in the Campbell Unified School District near San Jose. There he painted, drew, made jewelry, did some woodworking, and even tried his hand at mosaics.

The most profound impact on his later development as an artist resulted from his four years in Japan. Through his reading, Campbell had learned that two of his heroes in the history of jewelry making—nineteenth-century French master Frédéric Boucheron and Peter Carl Fabergé, the Russian goldsmith acclaimed for his decorated eggs—had been influenced by Japanese craftsmanship during their careers. This knowledge reinforced his conviction that he could combine traditional Native American and Japanese styles, which he greatly admired, and create a distinctive style that would honor the finest artistic expressions of both cultures. As time permitted, he visited a number of Japanese crafts-men, especially sword makers, to watch them work. "The Japanese," Campbell explains, "make samurai sword blades by laminating together hundreds of wafer-thin pieces of metal of different carbon content and sometimes different color so they can create a pattern right in the metal. The surface is flush, but the differences are discernible to the naked eye. The process is called *mokume,* which means 'wood grain,' and it fascinat-ed me, because I believed that style, which required few tools, could easily be adapted to Indian designs."

Some techniques the Japanese craftsmen would show him; others were family secrets never shared with outsiders. Nonetheless, he learned enough from his Japanese counterparts to enable him, years later when his judo days had ended, to create a new style of Native American jewelry. According to Campbell, he began to experiment with combined metals following the Japanese example. "I may not have been the first

American to do this," he says, "but I am the first American Indian. Over a period of months I taught myself how to use sterling silver, gold, brass, German silver, copper, and red brass as colors for design elements for an all-metal jewelry form."

The contrast of colors in Campbell's finished pieces looked so natural, much like multicolored sand paintings, that his Navajo friends called the process "sandpainting in silver." This seemed so apt that Campbell named the style Painted Mesa, after the natural colors of the mesas around the Four Corners area of the American Southwest, where his home in Colorado is located. Ben not only still makes Painted Mesa jewelry, but he also has had the satisfaction of seeing it acclaimed as a milestone in the continuing evolution of American Indian jewelry.

Jewelry, of course, remained a secondary interest until Campbell was well into his thirties, when he finally left the world of judo. It was Jim Fales, the principal of Daylor High School, where Campbell had been working as a shop teacher while trying to make a go of his judo club, who gets credit for turning him toward jewelry. Fales knew that Campbell made jewelry and, one day, chatting over coffee in the school cafeteria, asked him the question that marked another transition in his life: "What do you think of trying to teach a jewelry-making class targeted to unemployed Indians in the adult education program? The goal would be to show them how to make a living at it."

Over the four or five years that Campbell ran this innovative program, he taught more than one hundred people how to make jewelry. Most of his students were Indians, and many became full-time jewelers. One was Edith Edika, who was in her late sixties when she enrolled in the class. "She was just an old girl everybody had given up on," Campbell recalls. "She had been told that she was untrainable, too old, didn't have the skills to learn anything. She came to that class anyway. The fact is," Campbell chuckles, "when I finally got her going, her stuff was not really of high quality, but it caught on as being made by an 'Indian primitive.' My God, she sold that stuff as fast as she could crank it out. It didn't look good, but people loved it anyway. This little old lady made it as a real original Indian primitive. She did great, and now her daughter works as a jeweler."

His most talented student was probably Victor Gabriel, who is half Washo, a small tribe located in the mountains around Lake Tahoe. Today Gabriel is a very successful jeweler whom Campbell occasionally meets at art shows. "When I do, I like to tease him: 'I should never have taught you,' I tell him. 'Now you are getting all the ribbons!' "

Gabriel had been attending college at the University of California at Davis when a friend told him about Campbell's jewelry-making class at Daylor High. "I was the first person he admitted to the class, which he funded through the California adult education department. With the money he bought grinding equipment so he could cut stones, soldering equipment, and a lot of hand tools. I had always been interested in jewelry making," Victor says, "and there I found myself. I arranged my college classes so that I could have more time to go to Ben's class. At first my wife was packing me a lunch, but in a matter of months, she was packing me lunch and dinner. I was staying there so much that Ben finally just gave me a key to the shop and said, 'When you are through, return everything and lock up.' "

Gabriel studied with Campbell for about a year and a half. During this time, Victor recalls, Ben started making a name for himself as a jeweler. "Because of his unique designs, he was getting invitations to quite a few shows, and many of them overlapped. Sometimes when he couldn't attend a show, he would send me in his place. It forced me to get out, meet people, and learn how to sell. That is what really got me started. I was shy and afraid to talk to people. Ben told me what to say and how to act. As I got out into the circuit, he introduced me to people, to promoters. But he has always been my teacher. Even now, whenever I see him at an art show, he looks at my pieces. If he doesn't critique something, I will ask him about a technique. I don't think there's ever been a time when I've seen Ben that I haven't learned something from him. He is always very generous with information and advice. Although he was a little selective about who he accepted into his class, he always made room for any Indians who wanted to get into the program. I know

The Vierra family shortly after arriving in the United States. Ben's mother, Mary, is seated in the center of the group. (Courtesy Ben Nighthorse Campbell)

Mary Vierra and her mother in 1937. (Courtesy Joseph Vierra)

Ben and his sister, Alberta, as young-sters. (Family album)

Ben and his sister as teenagers. (Family album)

The entire student body of the New England Mills Elementary School in Weimar. Ben is standing far right, in the third row. Alberta is seated far left, in the second row. (Courtesy Jeanne Dickow Rood, *who is in the second row, fifth from left*)

Ben astride the obstreperous Redwing. (Family album)

Airman Ben Campbell. (Family album)

Ben, just returned from Korea, with his childhood buddy Lowell Heimbach, who was on leave from the Marines, standing in front of Ben's 1952 MG. (Courtesy Jeanne Dickow Rood)

Ruben Black Horse. The old man's
crippled leg can be clearly seen in this
detail from an undated photograph
taken at a reunion of Northern
Cheyenne cavalry scouts at Fort
Keogh, Montana. (Courtesy James
King, Lame Deer, Montana)

Albert Campbell, Ben's father, with
his ever-present cigar, in front of the
family grocery store in Weimar.
(Family album)

Lena Black Horse, Ruben's wife, with dog travois. Photograph taken at Lame
Deer Agency about 1921 by T. M. Galey, who later gave it to Mathew Stirling of
the Bureau of American Ethnology. Galey took the photograph at the time he
asked Ruben and Lena to make two dog and two pony travois from him. "[They
were] real old-time Cheyennes who were in the war," Galey informed Stirling.
Although Galey paid them forty dollars for the travois, "they were annoyed," he
claimed, "because I insisted the ties be made with thongs when bail wire was
handy." (Courtesy National Anthropological Archives, Smithsonian Institution)

Pagosa Springs, Colorado, as it looked at the time of Fortunata Campbell's murder in 1910. (Courtesy Denver Public Library, Western History Department)

Campbell (on top), during one of his championship bouts, scoring a full point on Hayward Nishiokha. (Courtesy Ben Nighthorse Campbell)

Campbell is dwarfed by Anton Geesink, "The Dutch Giant," who stunned the Japanese fans by winning the gold medal in their national sport at the 1964 Olympic Games in Tokyo. (Courtesy Phil Porter)

Coach Josh Uchida with the 1964 U.S. Olympic team: Harris, Campbell, Bregman, and Maruyama. (Courtesy Phil Porter)

Campbell competing in the medal round against Klaus Glahn of West Germany. (Courtesy Phil Porter)

Campbell's injured knee finally collapsed on him during the match against Glahn, giving the bronze medal to Glahn by default. (Courtesy Phil Porter)

Campbell conducting a class at the Sacramento Judo Club. (Family album)

Campbell and members of the Sacramento Judo Club after a successful tournament. (Family album)

Ben and Linda on their wedding day. (Family album)

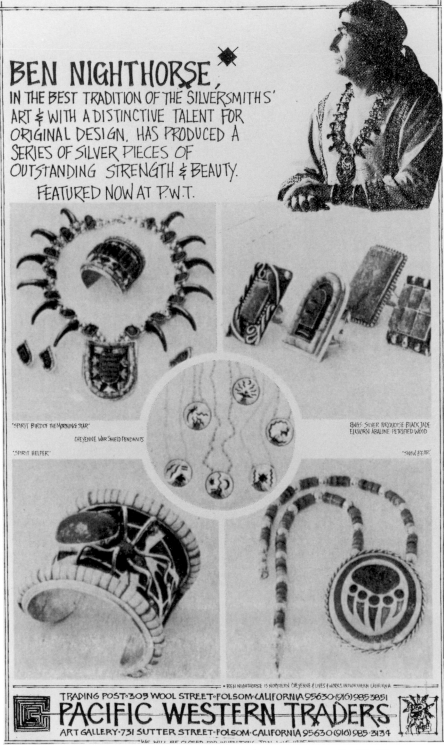

Advertisement promoting the sale of Ben Nighthorse jewelry at Pacific Western Traders. (Courtesy Herb and Peggy Puffer, Pacific Western Traders)

Campbell with the buffalo skull inlaid with precious corals that he gave to the Dull Knife Memorial College. At the height of his jewelry career, he wore shoulder-length hair and dressed accordingly. (Courtesy Leon Hodge, Gallery of the West)

Campbell at his jeweler's bench. (Photograph by Dudley Smith, 1982; courtesy Denver Museum of Natural History)

Victor Gabriel and Leon Hodge in 1992. (Photograph by Herman Viola)

The necklace that won first place in the California State Fair and launched Ben Nighthorse's jewelry career. (Courtesy Herb and Peggy Puffer, Pacific Western Traders)

An informal family portrait taken in 1979: Colin, Shanan, Linda, and Ben at their ranch in Ignacio, Colorado. (Family album)

Ben and Linda at the Democratic caucus in Denver. The caucus, which Campbell won by a narrow margin, was his first step on the road to winning a seat in the U.S. Senate in 1992. The caucus victory meant that Campbell's name would be listed first on the ballot for the Democratic primary to be held later in the year. That morning Linda had learned that she needed immediate surgery to correct a congenital heart defect. (Photograph by Herman Viola)

Campbell and Cristóbal Colón, Duke of Veragua, leaving Tournament House after a morning session with the media prior to their appearance in the Tournament of Roses Parade, New Year's Day, 1992. (Courtesy Mel Melcon)

One of Campbell's first goals upon being elected to the Colorado legislature was to have a sign erected on the site of the Sand Creek Massacre. (Courtesy Ben Nighthorse Campbell)

View, from "Last Stand Hill," of the visitor center and surrounding countryside at the recently renamed Little Big Horn Battlefield National Monument. Situated on the Crow Indian Reservation in Montana, the battlefield attracts some 300,000 visitors a year, making it one of the most popular historical attractions in the West. (Courtesy U.S. Park Service)

Austin Two Moons (holding the eagle wing fan once owned by Chief Red Cloud), former Little Big Horn Park Superintendent Barbara Booher, and the newly elected senator share a special moment at the victory celebration held at Lame Deer in honor of Campbell's successful election campaign. (Photograph by John Warner, Lame Deer, Montana)

Campbell holding a symbolic coup stick and blessing one of the youngsters attending part of the victory celebration held at the Lame Deer elementary school. (Photograph by Herman Viola)

Campbell waving to the Northern Cheyenne delegation that came to cheer his appearance in the Clinton Inaugural Parade on January 20, 1993. The rider in front of Campbell is the actor Rodney A. Grant; the rider behind him is Gilbert Little Wolf, grandson of Chief Little Wolf. (Photograph by Herman Viola)

that people always walked away after meeting Ben feeling better and with more information than when they came."

Less successful were Campbell's efforts to help Indians in Folsom Penitentiary, a high-security prison located near Sacramento. "When I was counseling at Folsom Prison I met some really talented guys, but I could not actually help them make jewelry. Sharp tools, saws, and files, needless to say, were strictly forbidden. About the only method they could use in prison was casting. I used to take them turquoise and other materials when I got a good buy on inexpensive stones, but that was about the extent of my help to them. What few things they made, they could try to sell to the public through the prison arts and crafts shop."

Campbell ran his unique program until he moved to Colorado the second time. Linda kept it going another year, until she could sell their ranch and join Ben. The program folded soon afterward, a victim of Proposition 13, which, according to Campbell, "just cut the guts out of all the adult education programs in California."

Campbell not only taught jewelry making, he provided his students with an outlet for their work. He accomplished this by opening and operating an Indian arts and crafts store in the historic district of Sacramento. His partner in the enterprise was Dee Rouse, a young woman who owned and operated another jewelry store in town but who also shared Campbell's vision for assisting urban Indians to find employment and dignity at the same time. Together they rented a small store—less than four hundred square feet—in Old Sacramento, spruced it up, installed display cases, and opened for business. Dee named it Nighthorse Studios in Campbell's honor. "Indian people could bring their work to us, and we would sell it on consignment for them, deducting twenty percent, which we put into a kitty that paid the rent, clerks, and the other things needed to keep us in business. We did that for two or three years," Ben says, "but the truth is I didn't much like being a shopkeeper."

No wonder Campbell relishes the day Leon Hodge walked into his life. Hodge had been in business in Gallup and now wanted to open a place in Sacramento. "My wife needed a city that had a college nearby so she could get her degree, and I wanted to live in Northern California,"

Hodge explains. "We looked in the Bay area and in Auburn, but we finally settled on Sacramento and Ben's shop was ideal. It was small and had almost no inventory, but Ben had such a fine reputation at that point, as an up-and-coming craftsman, I wanted to be associated with him. It simply made sense for me to buy his shop instead of another one in town."

"What would you think," Hodge told Campbell one February day in 1977, "if I bought your cases and the stuff here and did the same thing you are doing? I would have Indian people bring their things in, consign them, but carry a bigger inventory."

"Mister," Campbell responded, "you just got yourself a store."

Hodge got his store, which is now on K Street in Old Sacramento, and local Indian jewelers still have an outlet for their work. The new owner at first called it the Sacramento Indian Jewelry Gallery, but now it is known as the Gallery of the West. Hodge employed two of Campbell's students: Jeannette Duncan, a Shoshone woman, who worked in the shop for twelve years and still does repair work for him out of her home, and Victor Gabriel. "Ben recommended I hire him, and he has been with me for fourteen of the sixteen years I have owned the store." The business has grown considerably in that time. Hodge now serves three thousand collectors in the Northern California area who come to him because of the high-quality artists he represents, including Gabriel and Campbell, who still sends his work to the gallery.

Leon Hodge is second in Campbell's heart only to Herb and Peggy Puffer, who own and operate the Pacific Western Trading Post in the town of Folsom, near the prison. "We first met Ben in 1974, during the peak of the Indian jewelry business," recall the Puffers, a middle-aged couple whose shop is crammed with the work of dozens of local artists representing every creative endeavor from basketry to jewelry. "He came into the store, looked around, and said, 'I make jewelry.' We asked to see his work, so he brought a piece in. It was very interesting because it wasn't run of the mill. It was not the very best of all that we had seen, but it was different."

"Well," Peggy told him, "this is really good. To me it looks like about $450," an incredible price considering the fact that the Puffers had been paying only $150 for Navajo-style squash blossom necklaces at that time. "That first piece went as fast as we took it into the store," Peggy remembers. "It sold the next weekend to a person from Southern California. We told Ben to bring us more."

"I was absolutely astounded!" Campbell admits. "I had no idea my jewelry could be worth so much. I suddenly found out that a hobby could become a way to make a living if people liked your work." Equally startling to Campbell was the Puffers' request that he sign his pieces, something he had never done before. "We still have the first one he ever signed Nighthorse," says Herb, who has devoted a lifetime to helping Indian artists like Campbell.

As easily as that, Campbell became a professional jeweler. "I would make jewelry and Peggy would price and sell it for me. She was like my agent and she gave me a great split, something like seventy-thirty. For four or five years the Puffers bought everything I made, beginning with that first necklace. We had a great relationship!"

The Puffers paid him more than Campbell had expected, they say, because his pieces were so unusual. "He didn't follow old patterns. His technique was quite different from Southwest stuff. It was inlaid in rows, not simply a big chunk of turquoise with a bezel around it. Besides," Peggy told him, "if you price your work cheap, then all you have is cheap jewelry."

The Puffers also got Campbell to enter juried shows, beginning with the California State Fair. "That was quite a step for someone who had never shown a piece," Ben declares. "The California State Fair is a damn big show." For it he crafted a piece based on a dream he had of an Indian hunter who shot a bear and made a necklace from its claws. Campbell's necklace featured black beads—"I cut all the beads out of jade, which is a very tough stone to cut"—interlaced with coral, sterling silver claws, and a large shadow-box pendant, also of silver, embellished with two bear tracks and turquoise stones to give it color. "Peggy entered that thing and

it won first place! I just honestly couldn't believe it. There were thirty-five ·
hundred entries that year."

That victory was important to Campbell in more ways than one.
Suddenly and unexpectedly, he had found another outlet for the competitive fires that still raged within him. These fires had only been banked,
not snuffed out, by his retirement from judo. Campbell now pursued
awards on the art and jewelry circuit as avidly and with as much success
as he had formerly earned judo trophies and ribbons.

Of all the recognition accorded him as a Native American jeweler,
Campbell especially relishes the "Most Popular" award he was voted by
visitors to the California State Fair the year after his initial victory for a
buffalo skull he inlaid with turquoise, coral, jade, and mother of pearl.
This spectacular piece now belongs to the Northern Cheyenne tribe and is
on display at Dull Knife Memorial College in Lame Deer.

Once awakened to the world of juried art, Campbell helped pave the
way for other aspiring Indian artists. "Since I was older than a lot of them
and I had been around, I showed a number of young Indian artists how to
enter shows, how to get into juried competitions, how to set up booths.
One of the guys I helped is Navajo artist Ray Tracey, who has won more
awards than anyone can count. He now has something like forty Indian
craftsmen working in his shop in Gallup, New Mexico, doing a sort of
production-line jewelry business. A few pieces he makes totally himself to
enter into juried competitions, which his employees then reproduce. He is
one of the best."

Another talented and successful artist Campbell befriended is Gibson
Nez, a former rodeo rider. "When I first met him, Nez was just a Navajo
cowboy trying to hook it around the rodeos. To keep body and soul
together he made leather chaps, which he sold to the other cowboys." To
enter his first art shows, Nez had to hitchhike cross-country to get there.
At night he would sleep in culverts under the road. "Now," says Campbell, "Nez goes in style."

Campbell's closest friend in the Indian jewelry field was a Paiute
artist named Delmar Adams, whose family had been part of the government's relocation program in the 1950s. As a result, Delmar was born

in Burns, Oregon, but he married a girl named Ruth from Jemez Pueblo in New Mexico. "They had three children and were active in the powwow circuit. In fact," Campbell recalls, "I met them at a powwow in Oakland, California. Del and I got to be best friends and began to travel together. We were almost inseparable for the next four or five years." Once Ben got into state politics, however, he could no longer travel as before and they grew apart. Delmar eventually returned to his Oregon reservation, where he died of cancer in 1990. "Ruth and the family lost a wonderful husband and father; I lost my best friend in the art world," Campbell says. "Since those days I have never again traveled with anyone else but my family."

The one show Campbell never misses, even today, is the Santa Fe Indian Market held each year in August. For ten years running he rented a booth in the square from the Southwest Association on Indian Affairs, but now he prefers gallery shows because too many people have come to know he is a politician. "I would be in a booth trying to show someone a bracelet," he grumbles, "and invariably someone else would come along and say, 'Hey, aren't you that congressman? I want to talk to you. Why did you vote on such and such a bill a certain way? Why aren't you supporting this? How did you support that?' Man, oh man, does that blow me up. I had to quit getting a booth about five or six years ago. Now I just do gallery shows. That way Linda can watch the jewelry and I can smile, shake a few hands, and leave if someone gets on my case about something."

Campbell's career as a jeweler got a big boost in 1979, the year *Arizona Highways,* an internationally read art and travel magazine, ran a series of articles for collectors of American Indian art. The editors published issues on Indian rugs, pottery, and traditional jewelry before finally deciding to do one on what they called "the new look in Indian jewelry."

When the issue appeared Ben Nighthorse found himself in the heady company of such giants and pioneers in the field of contemporary Indian jewelry as Charles Loloma and Preston Monongye, as well as Gibson Nez and Delmar Adams who, like Campbell himself, were just emerging from their starving-artist days. Their work, which was published as only *Ari-*

zona Highways could do it in those days, was entrusted to Jerry Jacka of Phoenix, considered even now one of the truly great photographers of western and Indian art. Jacka took several hundred photographs, most of them posed on Indian models and set in the Monument Valley on the Navajo Reservation, which he then turned over to the editors for selection. "Talk about luck," exclaims Campbell, who still gets excited thinking about that special time in his artistic career. "The editors picked sixteen of my pieces—more than any other jeweler—including three they featured on the inside front cover. That issue more than any other single thing helped launch my career." Indeed so, laughs Leon Hodge. "I had been out for a show in May 1979, the month after that issue came out, and we sold every piece of his jewelry we had." Other magazine stories, news articles, and television specials followed, and these reinforced his reputation as an artist, "but," Campbell declares, "Arizona Highways was my first big break."

It was a big break in more ways than one. "For years," Campbell explains, "a few of us, beginning with Loloma and Monongye, the first to break away from traditional styles, had been experimenting with gold, pearls, and faceted stones—diamonds, rubies, and the other valuable cut gems—as well as with the so-called traditional jewelry materials such as turquoise, coral, ivory, wood, and shell. Although any number of Indian jewelers now work in these materials, those of us who did so in the early days were all subtly penalized for it. Because our work was so different from the stereotyped image of a Hopi piece, or a Navajo piece, or a Zuni piece, the people who screened the entries for the jewelry shows kept us out. Even the most noted experts in juried competition discriminated against us simply because there was no division for contemporary jewelry or because they refused to recognize it as Indian."

Campbell, for instance, is still piqued at Clara Lee Tanner, a celebrated authority on Indian art in the 1970s, who did not recognize one of his concha belts as being sand-cast by hand and disqualified it not once but twice: at the Tanner show in Scottsdale in 1976 and at the Casa Grande show held the following year. "I had gained a special effect by random-chiseling the mold and thereby hiding the telltale grain of the sandstone. She did not disqualify it out of malice, of course; she simply did not see that I had made an innovative change to the traditional way of casting, but the verdict was no easier to accept. Today works that are considered unusual, creative, or ahead of their time are judged in separate divisions."

Ironically, Campbell and his innovative colleagues are now enjoying the last laugh. "Today," he claims, "we are doing better financially than we did years ago. The fact is, a lot of the old designs have been so overworked and worn out from copying and recopying that the real market is now in unusual contemporary things." *Arizona Highways,* therefore, did more than give much needed exposure to the artisans of the "new look" in Indian jewelry; it helped establish their credibility.

The magazine also helped collectors realize that jewelry making is pan-Indian and not limited to a handful of southwestern tribes. "It is really interesting to me, being part Cheyenne," Campbell says, "that a lot of people for years thought jewelry was made only by the Navajo, Zuni, and Hopi Indians, the three main tribes that have the reputation as being jewelers. The fact is, some northeastern Indians learned how to make jewelry long before they did in the southwestern United States. The Cheyenne, for example, began making simple stamped jewelry when they lived near the Great Lakes before getting the horse and moving onto the Plains. They got metal ornaments from traders who, in turn, got them from colonial tinkers, who made hair ornaments, barrettes, and trinkets for the fur trade."

The Puffers, however, largely credit Campbell's class at Daylor High with shifting the focus of jewelry making away from the Southwest. "Through that class," they claim, "he taught jewelry making to a lot of the California people. As a result, Ben played a big part in promoting Indian jewelry making in the state. Before teaching his class, Indian jewelry was only known as Southwest jewelry."

Another pleasant benefit of the *Arizona Highways* publicity was Campbell's discovery that he no longer needed to teach school and work nights as a policeman to support himself and his family. As a result, he could spend more time making jewelry and, in so doing, continue to stretch the boundaries of Indian art. "I began to experiment with faceted stones, including diamonds, rubies, peridot, topaz, emeralds, and sapphires as well as ivory, wood, and a variety of materials not normally associated with traditional jewelry." Campbell also switched from fourteen- to eighteen-karat gold, which he found appealed more to overseas collectors. Still another milestone was reached when prominent figures from the entertainment world began buying his work. Suddenly, as if by magic, Campbell had more orders than inventory. For the first time in his artistic career, he found himself backlogged with orders from galleries across the nation.

Campbell knew he had made it when, in the early 1980s, the Franklin Mint in Philadelphia asked him to handcraft a gold pendant for reproduction and sale. "I made one based on an old Cheyenne men's society design called Red Shields. It incorporated design elements of lightning, a bear track, a buffalo tail, and three coup counts and was strung on turquoise beads." The Franklin Mint promptly renamed the piece Pendant of the Winding Waters—"which did not fit the design at all," Campbell insists. The company nevertheless sold the entire issue of eighteen hundred pendants at $1,500 each, grossing $2.7 million in the process.

Campbell also created a ring for QVC National Telemarketing under the same conditions—trading a piece of jewelry for a small price but getting massive publicity from it—with astounding results: QVC sold fifteen hundred rings over national television in seven minutes.

Success and popularity have their downside as well. One is off-the-wall commissions—which Campbell usually rejects—like the request from a New Yorker to put turquoise on the hubcaps of his Cadillac or the grieving son who asked Campbell to design jewelry incorporating his dead mother's teeth! Another downer is appeals for donated jewelry to be used as fundraisers for assorted professional and nonprofit groups as well as political candidates, requests which by 1990 were totaling six to eight a week. The Campbells at first tried to honor most of them, but they no longer do so for several reasons: only the cost of the materials are tax deductible, not the actual retail value of donated pieces; they could not keep up with the demand; and—particularly insulting—the jewelry was sometimes given as door prizes rather than used to raise funds. "Now," Campbell declares, "we have become very selective about donated pieces and limit them to ten or twelve a year."

Campbell attributes much of his success as a jeweler to Linda. "She has a terrific head for business, and she managed our finances extremely well during our growth years. Then, after my election to Congress in 1986, she formed a family corporation to satisfy the Ethics Committee restrictions on outside earned income. She also copyrighted the name 'Nighthorse' to cut down some of the blatant design thefts or knockoffs that occur in the jewelry world. She even gave me a few design ideas when I was fumbling for a new piece. There is no question in my mind that if not for Linda's organizational skills I would not have made nearly the progress I have as a businessman and artist. Many fine artists have trouble supporting themselves because they either lack marketing skills or do not have someone to act as their business manager. I was lucky."

The Campbells joke that Ben is the "engine" and Linda is the "brakes" of the family corporation. "I'm kind of impulsive, and she's very measured," he admits. "I know how to make money, I just don't know how to spend it well. I don't know anything about the business. I just make the jewelry. When I'm done with it, I put it in the safe. I have no idea where she sends it. She also gives me the orders. She puts notes on my workbench—'Make one of my horses,' 'Make one of these smaller,' 'We need more rings.' She's the boss. I just work there. Remember, she owns the name Nighthorse."

"Actually," Ben smiles, "it's an ideal system. Artists are too emotionally involved with their creations. It becomes a love-hate relationship. Some pieces you don't want to sell for any price, others you would give away just to get rid of them. People who aren't emotionally involved have a much better feeling about what to charge. Artists are the worst people to market their own work."

One thing Linda did for Ben was raise the prices placed on his work. The price of his jewelry is determined in part by the cost of the materials in a piece and in part by what the consumer is willing to pay for it. "Years ago," Campbell shrugs, "I would simply sell my stuff to a store, accept what the owner offered me. How was I to know what it was worth?" He learned its value by asking the people who bought it. "You know, I made that," he would tell perfect strangers he encountered wearing a piece of his jewelry. Startled and yet flattered to meet the artist, they would invariably respond with something like, "Oh, I just think it is wonderful, and I only paid a thousand dollars for it."

"How nice," Campbell would reply, all the while thinking, A thousand bucks and I only got a hundred for that thing. "If there's that much of a markup in the stores, Linda decided, by golly somebody must think my jewelry is worth a lot, so we started raising the prices."

To cut down on the time he spent on the road, Campbell took up flying—"It was something I had always wanted to do." His first airplane was a Varga, a little two-seater made in Phoenix. After getting his private pilot's license, he acquired a high-performance single-engine Mooney, in which he became instrument-rated. "Whenever I would get orders from California or Texas or just about anywhere in the West, I would deliver the jewelry personally. In that way I could write off both the plane and the trips."

Campbell had only one awkward experience as a pilot. Soon after earning his license he agreed to present a one-artist show at the Museum of the Southern Plains Indian in Anadarko, Oklahoma, and decided to test his skills by flying there solo. About two hours out of Durango, however, Campbell realized he was hopelessly lost and out of contact with any airport. Since he had a full fuel tank and knew he was heading generally in the right direction, he decided to decrease altitude, find a road, follow it to the first town, and then try to locate himself on a map. As luck would have it, he soon reached a little crossroads community with a dirt airstrip on which stood a pilot refueling his Ag-Cat, a popular crop duster made by Schweizer Aircraft Corporation. Campbell circled once, landed nicely on the dirt runway, taxied smoothly to the Ag-Cat, cut his engine, and then strolled over to the pilot.

"Say, buddy," Campbell asked with an air of nonchalance that he hoped would mask his keen embarrassment, "what part of Oklahoma is this?"

"Well, mister," replied the crop duster without so much as an upward glance, "we like to call this part of Oklahoma Texas."

"You knew I was lost?" Campbell croaked.

"Oh, heck, son, you're not the first one that's been lost," laughed the crop duster, who then gave him directions even a novice pilot could follow without getting lost: "Take off and fly north. Find the first paved road to the right and then follow the power lines. Eventually you will end up in Anadarko."

These were good years for Campbell. "I was making it as an Indian artist and enjoying the freedom that normally goes along with a successful artist's lifestyle," he says with a touch of nostalgia. His only regret was no longer having time to teach school.

After he moved to Colorado he was approached by administrators at Fort Lewis College in Durango, which is near his ranch in Ignacio, to teach a class on Indian jewelry making as a means of encouraging Indian students to stay in school. Because Fort Lewis College offers free tuition to Indian students, a condition of its charter, it has a fairly high Indian enrollment, roughly 10 percent of a student body of forty-five hundred. Unfortunately, something like 50 percent of the Indian students drop out their first year. "Many of the kids are right off the reservation," Campbell points out, "they haven't been away from home before, and they're not very well equipped to handle the competitive conditions. The college hoped Indian instructors might help keep the Indian kids in school, give them somebody to talk to, somebody to identify with, and somebody to be responsive to them."

Always willing to help, Campbell taught classes in painting and jewelry making at Fort Lewis College twice a week for two years, with mixed results. "I had many young Navajos who had a great deal of experience. For them it was a rather easy class. But a lot of non-Indian students wanted to learn Indian jewelry making, and they would fill up the classes and keep Indian kids out. As a result," Campbell says, "I'm not sure if it worked as well as the college would have liked. I, for one, really enjoyed it. I learned how much I missed working with young people in a teaching environment."

About the only teaching Campbell has time for these days is for Colin and Shanan and an occasional apprentice or two. "I noticed early on that both of my children had artistic talents. My son Colin, in fact, started working in my shop when he was only nine or ten. He would make small rings, which he sold for ten dollars each at the Southern Ute tribal crafts shop, but his interest as well as his sister's ebbed and flowed."

Shanan eventually decided she would rather market art than make it, but Colin remembers his childhood loss of interest in jewelry making a little differently. "I was getting pretty cocky as a little kid," he says. "I was making good money for a ten-year-old, and I began to act like the shop belonged to me. One day my dad had enough. He kicked me out of his shop, and I stayed out for several years."

Campbell's shop, which bears the elegant name Nighthorse Studio, is a squat log cabin, formerly a garage, which sits a few steps away from the front porch of the ranch house. The gallery is clean and bright and functional. In one corner is a wonderful old safe, which the Campbells keep more for effect than necessity since most pieces of jewelry are shipped out as soon as they are finished.

Because Campbell's Congressional responsibilities allow him to be only a part-time jeweler these days, he has had to turn over more and more of the work to apprentices. Besides Colin, these include members of the Southern Ute tribe. From time to time he also employs a part-Cherokee friend, Bruce Phillips, who helps with the casting. The Campbells also get occasional help from Indian craftsmen who are in alcohol treatment programs at Peaceful Spirit, the Southern Ute recovery home, which is near the ranch.

Although the Nighthorse jewelry business appears to be thriving and prosperous, it also operates with a high overhead. "Virtually every dime we have made in jewelry over the years," Campbell explains, "has been put into shop expansion, materials, promotion, and better tools. High-speed diamond cutters are really expensive and so are the materials we work with, especially the gold and gems."

The secret of success, Campbell is quick to argue, is not the materials used or the craftsmanship, but the design. "Quality craftsmanship is important, of course, but it is only one of the factors that sell a piece. The key element, I believe, is the design. Unusual, different, creative designs are the real secret, just like they are in any other art."

Having said that, Campbell then readily admits he seldom designs a piece before beginning work on it. "If I am sitting on an airplane or something, or I am traveling around and can't get to work on a piece for two or three days, then sometimes I will make a little quick sketch and stick it in my pocket to keep it fresh in my mind. But most of the things I make, I just go in cold and start on them. Sometimes during the night I will wake up thinking about a dream; then I will get up and either lay out a piece of jewelry before it fades out of my mind or at least draw a quick sketch so I won't forget it in the morning. The fact is, a jeweler, just like a painter or sculptor, doesn't have to go looking for things to do. There is normally so much in your head, you can't begin to get it all down. I bet I haven't made one-fourth of the things that I have thought up. Ideas come and go fast. Sometimes they come back to mind and sometimes they don't. If I am working on ten pieces already and I suddenly get an idea for two or three more, I can't drop everything to sketch out the new ideas, so they will probably fade from memory before I can get to them." This, Linda laughs, is no exaggeration. "If someone ever splits Ben's head open, I'll bet they will find it filled with rings."

Campbell's style of jewelry may have changed over the years, but not his philosophy of art. "I believe that it should be spontaneous and bold. To keep my spontaneity fresh, I usually work on three or four different pieces at the same time and switch from piece to piece as I go along. I still enjoy early morning work the best, when my surroundings are quiet and everything smells clean and fresh. At the ranch, I usually start between five and six A.M. so I can see the sunrise as I work and then, about noon, I will ride my horse or do chores before returning to my shop for the afternoon. I know craftsmen who spend sixteen-hour days at their bench, but I burn out when I try that."

When Campbell is in Washington, his schedule differs somewhat. "I work early mornings and evenings, sometimes late into the night. Because of the time crunch on Capitol Hill, I will often do the layout and preliminary shaping of several pieces and then, when I return to Colorado, give the uncompleted pieces to my apprentices for finishing."

According to Campbell, these are difficult times for Indian jewelers. "Store owners tell me that Indian sales in the last few years have been awful, just awful." For this Campbell blames market saturation. "I mean, you can go into any jewelry store and see the same damn thing in terms of design. Everyone is doing traditional designs, and the public is getting bored with them. Contemporary Indian jewelry, on the other hand, not only is a much warmer and more personal form of jewelry, but also the buyer is guaranteed that there are not ten thousand other pieces just like it on the market. Whoever buys a piece of my jewelry," he insists, "knows that only one or perhaps two pieces look just like that. Nobody wants to buy something that everybody else in town's got, whether it is a dress or a bracelet. Most people like something a little unusual, a little different, a personal statement, so to speak."

As the only Indian and one of only two professional artists in the House (the other, interestingly, was also a Coloradan, Republican Joel Hefley), Campbell stood in a unique position with regard to legislation affecting both groups. He walked a tight line to avoid conflicts of interest, yet he was able to provide a perspective on certain issues that no one else in Congress could offer. Consider, for example, the questions surrounding the sale of "authentic" Indian art, an issue that Campbell addressed soon after taking office. Over the years six western states had passed different laws intended to protect both the Indian artist and the unsuspecting buyer. According to the Commerce Department, by 1990 Indian art had become an industry worth four hundred million dollars a year, yet about forty million dollars of those sales were fraudulent, that is, not made by Indians. Since 1936, when the original Indian Arts and

Crafts Act was passed, no one had ever been prosecuted for selling fake Indian art even though the law was clear in its intent.

"Reviewing the original law was long overdue," Campbell points out, "but because of my special status, I could not take on the job until the House Ethics Committee assured me that it would not be a conflict of interest. Once I got that in writing, I proceeded, with Congressman Jon Kyl of Arizona, to rewrite and upgrade a federal statute that would apply equally to all Indian artists across the nation. Our challenge," Campbell claims, "was to write a bill that protected the unsuspecting buyer, the nonenrolled artist of provable ancestry, and tribal sovereignty."

After holding hearings in Washington and Santa Fe during Indian Market days, a bill was drafted, passed, and signed into law by President Bush. "All in all," Campbell is proud to say, "the bill has been acclaimed by tribes and the vast majority of Indian artists. Only a few so-called Cherokees who could not prove ancestry have complained that it is unfair." In essence, the law required a person who markets his work as Indian either to be an enrolled member of some tribe or to prove that he or she has tribal approval. "In other words," Campbell explains, "if someone is going to market himself as a Navajo artist then he needs proof that he is, indeed, Navajo." Even at that, the law left up to the tribes how they, as sovereign nations, should validate those artists wanting to use their tribal names as a marketing device. "My position was very clear," Campbell declares. "If an artist is proud of advertising that he is a specific kind of Indian, then he should have no problem tracing his background, even if he is not enrolled. On the other hand, if he cares so little about his heritage that he never has anything to do with the tribe from which he claims to have descended except to use it as a marketing ploy, or if the only way he can get his work sold is by advertising that he is an Indian, then he should not be validated. There are a great many artists out there doing Indian art, but good art should be able to stand on its own merits and not need the words 'Indian-made' to prop it up."

Before long other jewelry-related issues were in Campbell's lap, issues such as the proposal to include a prohibition on the importation of diamonds in the sanctions against South Africa, the increase in the surtax on luxury items, including jewelry, and the effects of the end of the Cold War on the international gold market. Having to confront such issues soon brought Campbell into contact with "the real heavyweights" of the jewelry business. First was Bert Foer, president of Melart jewelers, a family-owned chain prominent in the Washington metropolitan area. Foer, in turn, introduced Campbell to Lloyd Jaffe, of the Diamond Institute in New York City; to Mike Roman, director of the 25,000-member National Jewelers Association; and to a host of other people who belonged to the prestigious New York Diamond Club or were executives of major jewelry corporations, among them Leo Shakter, the largest U.S. importer of cut diamonds.

Because of these contacts, Campbell became increasingly interested in diamonds. "For years," he declares, "I had thought diamonds were too 'cold' in appearance for my type of jewelry, but after attending several national jewelry shows in New York City, I learned that the 'ice' in diamonds can also reflect 'fire,' if used right. After some practice, I could do most of my own diamond settings, but I still send my complicated designs to experts or get their advice before trying to set them myself. I did find out one thing rather quickly," Campbell smiles. "When executing a gold and diamond bracelet, it is not difficult at all to get into four or five thousand dollars in material costs alone."

It was only a matter of time, of course, before Campbell got the urge to show his own designer jewelry in the East. "I had always sold in art galleries, museums, specialty boutiques, and trading posts, but I had never attempted to place my stuff in regular jewelry stores, and Bert Foer gave me the opportunity. Unfortunately, neither Melart show did well, so I went back to my old standby outlets."

By the mid-1980s, after twenty years as a jeweler, Campbell began to contemplate his future and what he wanted to do with the years that might be left to him. "I was now relatively well known in the art world, my pieces were in the hands of some of America's most famous people, and my family's future seemed secure, yet I felt I was missing something,"

Campbell confesses. "I began to think that I should start planning for the time when I would no longer be here. At midlife, I knew I had twenty-five or so productive years left and I did not want my jewelry to die when I did. In reading about some of the great jewelers of the past, including Tiffany, Cellini, and Tillander as well as my two favorites, Boucheron and Fabergé, I began to see a pattern. Each of those artists had coupled craftsmanship and design with the building of name recognition through marketing. They documented their work and, in so doing, enabled their sons or daughters to carry on their art."

Because his own children were finally becoming interested in jewelry, Campbell determined the time had come to start saving his designs as well. He does this by keeping the original model of each new piece he makes. "In this manner," he explains, "even after I am gone, anyone who apprenticed with me would be able to look at the original model and craft another. Each succeeding piece could be unique, yet it would be based on the original model. The original models—and I have accumulated several hundred thus far—are stored in a bank vault in a totally different location where they will be safe if a fire or other calamity destroys my shop. Although I had begun to photograph my better pieces, I considered this a much better way of passing my style of jewelry on to my descendants. By the time I came to this decision, many of the great and creative Indian jewelers who had befriended me over the years—Charles Loloma, Preston Monongye, Ted Charvese, and my own dear friend, Delmar Adams—had either retired or passed away. At most all they left the younger generations in their families were their tools and, perhaps, an interest in pursuing jewelry. Not one to my knowledge has left what I want to leave."

SEVEN

BUCKSKINS VS. BROOKS BROTHERS

Ben Campbell's entrance into politics is a real-life story that sounds as though it had been scripted for a television movie. As Ben tells it, he was minding his own business—flying his airplane, playing with his horses, spending quality time with his family, and generally enjoying a successful career as a jeweler and artist—when fate intervened. On May 22, 1980, intending to deliver some of his jewelry to a dealer in San Francisco, he went to the La Plata County Airport just a few miles from his ranch in Ignacio, only to learn about a severe storm between Colorado and California: "Although I considered myself a pretty proficient pilot," he says, "I had no desire to fight that storm in a single-engine airplane, so I shut down and went into the terminal to kill some time by reading our local newspaper, the *Durango Herald*. Almost immediately I spotted a notice about a political meeting being held that day in downtown Durango. All registered Democrats were welcome.

"I was a Democrat, I guess, because my mom had been. I had never been active in politics. I voted pretty regularly, but I didn't think of myself as a conservative or a liberal or a single-issue person or anything. In fact, I didn't even consider myself very knowledgeable about the political process."

What attracted Campbell to the meeting was the discovery that Al Brown, one of his college classmates who had been a police major at San Jose State, would be nominated to run for sheriff of La Plata County. "Well," Campbell recalls, "since I hadn't seen Al for ages, I decided to go down to this political meeting to see if someone was needed to speak on Al's behalf."

Campbell rather enjoyed the meeting. The local Democrats nominated candidates to run for the different offices—county commissioner, sheriff, and so on. When Al Brown's name was put in nomination,

Campbell got the opportunity to say a few words on behalf of his old college chum who did, in fact, later win the race for sheriff.

"Then," Campbell recalls, "came the nominations for Democratic representative in the state legislature for House District 59, where I lived, which is known as the Four Corners area, consisting of four counties on the Western Slope." The Republican candidate, Dr. Don Whalen, had already announced, and he was a fine person, very well known in the community. "Don had coached basketball at Fort Lewis College for a number of years and had all the attributes of a candidate who should be able to win," Campbell says. "He was tall and he was handsome and he dressed impeccably and he had a lot of friends. He had been very active in the community on many different boards and commissions in the Four Corners area and really had paid his dues."

Depending on one's point of view, Campbell happened to have either the misfortune or good fortune to be in the right place at the right time. The Democrats were having difficulty in finding a candidate to oppose Whalen. "I was just sitting on the end of the bench listening as one nominee after another declined to run, each one with a good excuse. One person, I remember, was not feeling well; another person was too busy. In the end, nobody could or would do it. By default more than anything else, I guess, everyone started looking at me. "Would you be interested?" someone asked.

"Well," Campbell replied, "I really wouldn't know what to do. How could I learn everything in such short time?"

"Don't worry about that," someone else said. "We can tell you everything you need to know."

"Well, does it take much time?" he asked.

"No, no, it doesn't take much time," everyone assured him.

"Does it cost very much money?"

"Oh no, it doesn't cost very much money. Besides, we have funds to cover most of the costs."

"Of course," Campbell laughs, "they were wrong on all three counts." But he did not learn that until later. "Well, okay," he said, "I think I would be interested in doing it."

And that is how Ben Nighthorse, jeweler, started on the road to becoming Senator Ben Campbell. The race for the state legislature proved to be a six-month, sixteen-hour-a-day ordeal that took him across ten thousand miles of mountain and desert highway and cost some twenty-three thousand dollars, thirteen thousand of it his own money. In the process he wore out a set of tires, a pair of boots, and himself, but he managed to enlist the aid of three hundred volunteers for his campaign.

Although Campbell did, in fact, receive the unqualified support of the Democrats gathered that day, he did not find out until later that he was expected to be just a Democratic name on the ballot. "Nobody," he learned, "expected me to win. Certainly I didn't know enough to have any expectations whatsoever. What I later learned is that no party ever wants to let another party's candidate run unopposed, because there are always hard-core party supporters who will vote for whoever is on the ballot, and you never know what will happen during a political campaign." Nonetheless, the fact of the matter is that no one in that room gave Campbell a snowball's chance in hell of defeating Don Whalen. "Can you imagine what those Democrats were thinking of me at the time? In those days, I wore my hair in a ponytail clear down to the middle of my back."

As Campbell stood in the middle of the room accepting the congratulations of those who were so blithely feeding him to the lions, Sam Maynes, a long-time party patron from La Plata County, strolled over and stuck out his hand. Maynes had been active in Democratic affairs for years and years, and Campbell respected his political horse sense. "Do you think I have a chance of winning? " Campbell asked.

"Oh, I think you have two chances," Sam replied. "You have little, and you have none."

"That was all I needed," Campbell remembers. "My old Olympic competitive drive began to rise up inside of me, and I thought to myself, 'Well, we'll just see.' At that moment, I knew I was going to give politics my best shot."

The hardest part of accepting the nomination, Campbell recalls, was breaking the news to Linda and the kids. At the time Colin and Shanan were still in elementary school. "Here they were, thinking I had gone to California. Instead, I went to a political meeting and had agreed to run for the Colorado legislature." As Campbell pulled into the driveway, Linda was mowing the lawn and Colin and Shanan were roughhousing with one of the dogs. "Guess what?" Campbell told them. "It looks like I'm going to run for office."

Linda's reaction was, to put it mildly, less than enthusiastic, "Oh, shit," she snapped. "What did you get yourself into now?" Colin said simply, "Now are you going to have to learn to lie and all that stuff?"

"And that," Campbell recalls, "is how I started my political career." As he sat home that afternoon wondering what he was supposed to do next, he got a telephone call from a woman in Durango who identified herself as Ann Brown, a person he knew about but had never met. "Do you know what you're doing?" she asked.

"No," Campbell admitted, "I don't have a clue."

"If you want some help," she told him, "then you had better come down here and talk to me."

That afternoon Campbell drove back to Durango, about twenty miles away, and met Ann and her husband, Donny, thereby beginning a friendship that remains solid to this day. "To me," Campbell marvels, "they have been like a brother and sister." Ann, it turned out, really did have a lot of political experience. She herself had run for office several times and eventually became mayor of Durango. Her family had deep roots in the Four Corners area of Colorado, and through her Campbell learned the political process. "She told me what to do and where to go." That very night Campbell went to Pagosa Springs, about forty-five miles east of Durango, to attend a Democratic meeting and announce his candidacy.

Ann's first advice concerned his ponytail. Since Campbell refused to cut it off, she gave him the names of people who could help him deal with what would be negative perceptions by folks in the 59th District, which was composed largely of ranchers, farmers, and blue-collar workers. At the head of her list was a man named Jimmy Suckla, a rancher in southern Colorado who was a former president of the Colorado Cattlemen's

Association and a well-respected and well-connected member of the agricultural community. Suckla ran a livestock sale barn in Cortez where, every Wednesday, cowboys, ranchers, and other stockmen bought and sold sheep, pigs, goats, horses, and cattle.

The very first Wednesday after accepting the nomination, Campbell went to Cortez for his first face-to-face meeting with Jimmy Suckla. They chatted over coffee in the little restaurant attached to the sale barn. Suckla wasn't very talkative at first, Campbell recalls. "He just kind of looked me over rather carefully as I told him about myself." Finally he said, "You're going to run for office, huh?"

"Yes, I'm going to run for state legislature."

Jim gave him a hard look and then said, "Well, are you going to cut that hair?"

"No," Campbell told him. "What folks see is what they get. I'm not going to cut my hair. I'm afraid if I try to change my image, it would bode very bad for me. Besides, Indian people would not respect me very much if I did that."

Jim mused for a bit. "Well, okay," he shrugged. "Even if you're going to keep your hair long, we can give it a try. I'll support you anyway."

With that Campbell followed Jim into the sale barn, where some hundred or hundred fifty hard-eyed, weather-beaten ranchers were intently bidding on a likely batch of white-faced beef cattle. Although Ben knew a few of them, these were largely Linda's kind of people—tough, hardworking folks, politically conservative and just the sort to have trouble accepting a politician with a ponytail.

Suckla wasted no time with formalities. He grabbed the mike and stopped the sale in order to introduce Ben to the crowd. "Ladies and gentlemen," he announced. "This is Ben Nighthorse Campbell. Ben's going to run for the state legislature and he's here to say a few words. I'm going to support him." Having said that much, Suckla then seemed to go absolutely blank. Considering that he just met Campbell for the first time only a few minutes before, it is not surprising that he could think of nothing more to say about him that would sound good to his sunburned, tobacco-chewing friends. He stuttered and stammered a few moments and then, looking at Ben, suddenly brightened: "Now, I don't want you to mind that long hair of his. He's an Indian, he's got a right to it." Then, again at a loss for words, he blurted out, "He's got a right; he ain't no damn hippie."

Campbell learned some valuable lessons in the initial weeks of his first political campaign. To start with, he learned the importance of meeting as many people as possible and getting to know them on a first-name, personal basis. He accomplished this by walking a lot of streets and knocking on a lot of doors. Campbell obtained maps of every community in his four-county district and then systematically walked every single street. "I would drive into a town and park on one of the streets and just simply walk along knocking on doors until that street ran out and then work my way back along the other side. Then I would get back in the car and come home that night dead tired. I did that for almost six months straight, but I managed to meet most of the voters in my district." Campbell also worked himself into a sickbed. His last debate with Don Whalen, held the day before the election, Campbell conducted from his bedside.

Stumping the streets was not without its hazards, Campbell soon learned. One irate fellow thought Campbell had come to repossess his furniture. Ben was knocking on his door, when the man pulled up and jumped out of his car clutching a tire iron. "You're not taking my furniture," he yelled. "Hey, mister," Campbell assured him. "I'm not here to take any furniture. I'm just campaigning for an office." After the fellow calmed down a bit, they had a friendly chat. "By the time I left," Campbell laughs, "he agreed that I was the candidate he'd want to support, when just a few minutes before he was going to bash my head with a tire iron." Another time, he recalls, " a very vampy-looking lady invited me into her home. That scared the devil out of me, in part because I was afraid of her and in part because I feared it might have been a setup by someone trying to derail my campaign."

Campbell also learned that voters make many of their decisions very personally on what they think a candidate will do for them. "A lot of people have no civic spirit," he claims. "They couldn't care less what is good for the majority. They care about what is good for them. If you can tell them what you're going to do for them personally—help them provide a living for their youngsters, or make sure that their family has a nice, clean environment, things of that nature—then they can relate to you and support you."

As Campbell talked to his future constituents, he found that he had much to offer them. In many ways he could relate to his voters on many levels. "Having been a teacher, having been a policeman, having been a truck driver, having been a laborer, having been a kid on the streets, having identified with minorities and the many other facets of my life, I guess I had some kind of bridge to virtually everyone I talked to. I think that's what really helped me win that first election."

Another valuable lesson Campbell learned in his maiden campaign is that, like it or not, an announced candidate makes instant enemies as well as friends. "You inherit some enemies that you don't even know and didn't do anything to. They simply form opinions of you based on reasoning that doesn't exactly fit you. It's because they read something detrimental about an issue or person, and if you identify with that issue or person, suddenly you're the enemy. Or they dislike somebody that happens to like you and automatically assume you are not to be trusted. On the other hand, people you never heard of work night and day to support you."

Campbell's Indian ancestry became of point of conversation in many meetings. "With the exception of the towns of Aspen and Durango, western Colorado is really about as conservative a place as any in America, and the voters generally associate long hair with hippies or crazy artists or antiestablishment types. But I was not any of those; I was just very independent. Fortunately, since I had been a member of the Cattlemen's Association and the Farm Bureau and the Farmers Union, they were willing to overlook the long hair that ranchers normally would have viewed with skepticism. Although a good number of people claimed they would not vote for me if I did not cut my hair, I knew Indian people would be terribly hurt if I tried to change my image for political gain, so I was determined to stick to my decision.

"And I guess that's another great lesson I learned in politics; people will support you if you stand for something and stick by it, even if it is widely criticized. More and more people began to tell me they would vote for me because I had the courage to stick by my beliefs. And so the ponytail became a trademark long before the New York designers in the 1990s made it a yuppie emblem."

Looking back on that campaign, Campbell realizes how much credit for his surprising victory should go to Ann Brown. For one thing, she knew how to anticipate and defuse problems, like the ponytail, before they caused any serious damage. "For instance," Campbell remembers, "she taught me not to wear dark glasses when campaigning, because people like to see your eyes; they're suspicious if you wear dark glasses when you're talking to them." Another bit of good advice concerned posture. Don't stand in a crowd with your arms folded, she warned him, because it projects a standoffish manner; you should stand with an open-armed attitude so people recognize you as a friendly, open person. "This," Campbell says, "is what is known as image marketing. As a candidate you have to learn hundreds of little things like this, besides selling yourself on your knowledge of the issues and your ability to handle them, which requires a great deal of reading and thinking."

It wasn't long before the campaign became known in Denver as the "buckskins vs. Brooks Brothers" race. "I guess because I was wearing long hair and had come right off the reservation and Dr. Whalen had portrayed the image of such a well-mannered and well-manicured person. Through hard work I managed to win that race. Of all the races I have run for the legislature and for Congress too, I can honestly say that was the most upstanding, upbeat, and fair campaign. An awful lot of political races degenerate into yelling and screaming and distorted accusations and downright muddy battles. Don Whalen was a very fine, outstanding, gentle, good human being, and of the opponents I've run against and beaten, I consider Don to be the greatest gentleman. Late on election night he came over and congratulated me, and he's been a good friend of mine ever since. We often joke about that campaign. He likes to say that I didn't win, I lost. He says this every time he tells me he's going fishing with his kids on Saturday or he's going off on a vacation in Mazatlán or doing something that's really fun and interesting, and I have to put in another eighty-hour week dealing with problems I did not create and for which I have no answers. Here I'm about to tear my hair out; I'm under tremendous stress and pressure, and he's going fishing. Sometimes I think to myself, maybe Don was right."

One thing Campbell knows for certain. If elected, Whalen would have done a good job. "I won, I think, because I simply outworked him, and people saw and liked that hard work. Besides, I couldn't stand the humiliation of public rejection two times."

Two years earlier the Southern Ute tribe had recommended Campbell to fill a seat on the local school board in Ignacio, which had been vacated in midterm. The school board president at the time, Robert Hott, flatly rejected the recommendation even though Campbell had been a teacher and had credentials as well as considerable experience in public education. "Very simply," Campbell says, "I was 'home towned' in favor of a white rancher with half my qualifications. I never held it against anyone; I simply recognized it as a fact of life. My experience, I am sure, is all too familiar to other members of minorities across the country. If you want equal treatment, it's not free. You have to be willing to work twice as hard as the nonminority and not carry a chip on your shoulder while you are doing it. Frankly, I look back on it as merely an interesting footnote to my career. Here, I wasn't good enough to serve on the school board in my own home town, but four years later I was good enough to serve in the United States Congress."

His victory certainly stunned the political pundits. Campbell won about 57 percent of the vote, including a 15 percent crossover of registered Republicans. He shocked the experts, who predicted Don Whalen would be a shoo-in. "I've got the bumblebee syndrome," Campbell joked, as he tried to explain his upset victory to the press. "You know scientists say there is no way aerodynamically that a bumblebee can fly. But he doesn't know it and works real hard until he goes ahead and flies." Linda, for one, was not surprised that he won. "Ben," she told a reporter, "doesn't like to lose. If, for instance, he ever decides to run for governor of Colorado, well, he'll be governor of Colorado."

One person who was pleased with Ben's victory was Colorado Senator Gary Hart, whom Campbell grew to admire and later supported for president. "Congratulations on your victory," Hart wrote. "You ran a great race and I will look forward to working with you on issues of concern to southwestern Coloradans. Please keep in touch."

Even before Campbell arrived in Denver and learned that his victory entitled him to a free license plate and a parking space, people were predicting a great political future for him, perhaps even the governorship. Certainly everyone who met him succumbed to his charm, even the Republicans. "I hear you're sending us an Indian," House Speaker Carl Bledsoe mentioned in a telephone conversation after the election to a Durango Republican. "That's right," replied the Republican, "and you ought to listen to him when he gets there because he is an honorable man." Gushed Governor Richard Lamm, a fellow Democrat whom Campbell later was to defeat in his bid for a Senate seat: "He's such a unique individual. My God! He just sings depth and commitment."

Now Campbell could add politics to all the other things he liked to do, such as creating jewelry, raising horses, and flying. It proved the greatest learning experience of all, because, as he confesses with a tinge of guilt, he had never set foot in the Colorado State Capitol Building before he took the oath of office. "I went to Denver and became a politician," he admits, "but I didn't know anything about the job. I just came blowing into town, I guess you might say, trying to figure it out as I went."

Campbell quickly found that "the public doesn't care about your family, your future, or your preferences. Once elected, somehow you miraculously inherit a magic wand to fix all of their personal problems, and your own simply have to fall by the wayside. In later years when I was representing literally thousands of people in the United States Congress, I often thought about it this way: most people probably never, ever call an elected official; they just get on with their lives. Some call when they need help once in a great while. But there are a few that simply complain all the time and expect cradle-to-grave attention from their public servants."

Campbell's first task in Denver was to take his assigned seats on the Agriculture and the Business committees. "I felt relatively comfortable on the Agriculture Committee, because I knew a little bit about agriculture, and since I was in business for myself, I assumed that I would understand the problems that business people faced."

His euphoria at being a freshman legislator was relatively short-lived. "I got some terrific shocks and began to have second thoughts about whether I really ought to be there." One serious concern was his family. His children were quite young, and Linda now had the entire burden of running both the ranch and the jewelry business and maintaining the family while Ben was trying to squeeze in the ceaseless demands of his far-flung legislative district. "I did have problems dealing with my family obligations," Campbell admits. "It was very difficult to keep us together because I had to spend so much time on the road. When I wasn't dealing with constituents on the local level, I had to be in Denver for sessions of the state legislature."

Another casualty was his driving record. He accumulated three speeding tickets in one year and lost his driver's license for six months. A third casualty was his bank account. "Our income took a severe nosedive because my salary in the Colorado legislature came nowhere near what I had been earning as a jeweler." His legislator's salary of fourteen thousand dollars barely paid his travel expenses, which included at least five hundred dollars a month for gasoline alone. "I enjoy the job," he told a reporter from the *Denver Post*. "I like the challenge. I like the education. I enjoy meeting people, but I don't like going broke. I'll have to take a look to see if I can afford to seek reelection."

The problem was the enormous drain on his time that being a legislator entailed. "If I don't design, I can't sell. Whoever told me the job did not take up much time certainly did not know what he was talking about," Campbell grumbled. "We are working twelve hours a day. There is no paid staff, and I average a hundred letters a week. That's where my nights go—answering letters and phone calls and reading bills. You have to answer the letters and calls, or your constituents think you don't care."

Certainly, while the Colorado legislature was in session, Campbell had little free time. His "official" day began with breakfast, usually provided by one lobby group or another. From breakfast he went to his seat in the House and then could plan on spending at least four hours in committee hearings, where the real legislative work occurred. Each day was closed by a dinner that invariably involved a political function of some sort. "I am lucky to be home three or four weekends when the legislature is in session," he lamented to a reporter for the *Durango Herald*.

Campbell, however, did have the good fortune of being seated on the House floor right next to an old-time politician by the name of Bob Shoemaker. A one-eyed Marine veteran of World War II, Shoemaker took an instant liking to Campbell and served as his legislative mentor. "Shoemaker," Ben recalls, "came from Canyon City, Colorado, where he had ranched for years and years. After losing his eye in combat, he had turned to politics. He did not have any academic credentials, never having gone to college, but he had more common sense than most people I ever met in public office. I served with Bob for four years. He was about as western as they come, but I sure learned a lot from him."

Typical of the homespun wisdom Shoemaker shared with Campbell was his assessment of a bill that seemed to make no sense to the freshman legislator. "You know, Bob, I'm having trouble thinking through this bill. I don't understand the reasons that are being offered to support it or to oppose it. If I don't understand it, how can I vote on it?"

"My gosh, Ben." The canny old lawmaker feigned shocked disbelief. "Reason? What does reason have to do with anything? You will soon learn that most of the stuff we face up here is based on just three things: turf, money, or emotion."

And learn Ben did. "As I moved further and further into politics," he admits, "I began to recognize that Shoemaker, unfortunately, had been right. Too many people who deal with the legislative process want to manipulate public policy for their own purposes. They're certainly not working for what is good for Colorado, or for America, or for the majority of people. Their angle on legislation generally is based on what they stand to gain or lose in terms of money or spheres of influence and control. Then too, on bills dealing with such topics as the handicapped, the sick, education, and religion, the legislature could get embroiled in very emotional debates."

One bill Campbell would like to forget concerned raising the liability limits in negligence cases affecting parents whose children had been injured or killed in accidents. The proponents of the bill wanted victims to have the right to sue for any amount of money a jury might award. Backing them were trial attorneys, whose incomes, of course, are based on the awards their clients can collect.

The sponsors of that bill, Campbell remembers, used every trick in the book in their attempt to gain passage. One clever stunt was to invite members of the Colorado press to attend the hearings on the bill, a rather obvious effort to intimidate the lawmakers who presumably would be reluctant to vote against such a seemingly popular bill with news reporters in the gallery.

One trick that certainly backfired as far as Campbell was concerned was to mail photographs of dead youngsters to the wives of Colorado's legislators. "This one really made me angry, so I challenged them. Why send pictures of dead children to my wife when, in fact, I was the elected representative?" Their answer? "They hoped my wife would appeal to my emotions and thereby persuade me to vote for the bill." The whole business repelled Campbell so much that he voted against it.

Equally controversial was a bill concerning the right to die with dignity. The bill proposed allowing doctors to unplug medical apparatus if a person being kept alive by machine was clinically dead. The main opponents of that bill, Campbell claims, could not have cared less about whether patients lived or died. They were the manufacturers of the life-support systems, who anticipated plummeting sales of their equipment if the bill passed. Although hundreds of millions of dollars were at stake, they cloaked their testimony before the Colorado legislature in pious and emotional terms regarding the sanctity of human life.

Campbell, of course, had a few lighter moments as a legislator. Always good for a hearty chuckle were the demands from the "crazies," the folks who have such obviously self-aggrandizing requests that no one can take them seriously, like the one Campbell received from a man who wanted to change the state song to one written by his brother. Another constituent urged passage of a bill requiring people to be kinder to chickens. One fool recommended that all Colorado's prison inmates be blinded—they would be easier to control and less likely to escape. He claimed the nerves could be reconnected, when it was time to let them out of jail! And Ben still shakes his head over the manufacturer of wooden butterflies who wanted him to introduce a bill that would have made the butterfly the Colorado state symbol.

Hearings could also be occasions for relaxed, homespun humor as reported by Carl Hilliard of the Associated Press, who sat in one day on the deliberations of the agriculture committee. "House Ag," he noted, "is a favorite among lobbyists, not just because of its honesty, but because of its entertainment factor." Committee members like Bob Shoemaker and Ben Nighthorse Campbell, he wrote, had a knack for making witnesses feel at ease. They had been farmers and had an earthy, self-deprecating sense of humor that made their hearings a delight to cover. "Last week," he reported, "they joshed a farmer from Romeo who had come to testify before the committee."

"Is it true," asked one of the committee members, "that because of the town's name, its male population has a great, healthy sex life?"

"Not true," the farmer replied. "The town is healthy because its residents have no bad habits. Romeo is so small, it can't afford a town drunk, so we all have to take turns."

Campbell found "lobbyists" everywhere, even in the room where legislators took their breaks. Early one morning as he stood in line for a cup of coffee, he was confronted by a bag lady who haunted the capitol halls. "What are you doing to feed the poor people of China?" she challenged, poking him in the ribs to get his attention. "It's only seven A.M.," Campbell pleaded. But as he turned to face her, she had expertly shoved ahead of him to get at the free coffee.

Less humorous were the occasional confrontations and angry debates with special interest groups. These, he says, are inevitable in political life. One particularly disagreeable episode concerned his support of House Bill 1172 and the Animas–La Plata water project, a major public works program that would have, among other things, provided drinking water to a part of the Ute Indian tribe.

Animas–La Plata was just one component of a vast reclamation program to manage the water resources of the Colorado River drainage basin. Its construction had been authorized by the U.S. Congress in 1968, when the influential Wayne Aspinall held the seat representing the Western Slope later occupied by Campbell. But Animas–La Plata had never been funded, and there was longstanding opposition to its construction. Nevertheless, the project was very important to the Utes. Tribal water rights went back to the nineteenth-century treaties that established their reservations and were further assured by the Winter Doctrine of 1912. But the Ute Mountain Utes, who live south of Cortez, even as late as 1990 still had no fresh drinking water other than that supplied by truck. Their only domestic water supply was an open ditch with a gravel backwash filter system.

House Bill 1172 was introduced in 1981 by majority leader Chris Paulson to validate the water conservancy boards in Colorado and to mute pending litigation by opponents of the Animas–La Plata project. A group from Durango called TAR—Taxpayers Against the Referendum—filed a suit against the La Plata Water Conservation District. The members of TAR claimed that the water districts in Colorado had been formed without public input and questioned their assessment authority, but their real motive was to block construction of the project.

Although Campbell did not sponsor the legislation, he did support it and, for so doing, was immediately attacked by the anti-Animas group by means of the telephone, letters to the editor, and personal visits. "The people opposed to that bill," Campbell remembers, "were willing to go to any length to try to get that project killed. They didn't kill it, but it was not for lack of trying." They were so desperate, in fact, that they once managed to hide a tape recorder under his desk in a meeting with him and then tried to manipulate the conversation to make it look as if he had done something illegal or unethical in his efforts to promote passage of the bill. "My gosh, were they rabid! It was my first experience with a group of single-issue extremists and one of my most unpleasant experiences in politics. After that test by fire, my indoctrination to politics was pretty well complete."

Political extremists—no matter which side of the political spectrum they represent—are people for whom Campbell has little tolerance. "I learned early on that the more extreme their position or ideology, the less they have in common with the majority of the electorate. Although I had never questioned my beliefs or tried to fit them on some philosophical scale between liberal and conservative," Campbell says, "I did soon find out that I didn't agree with either extreme and considered the right-wing nuts just as dangerous to the American way of life as the left-wing nuts. Throughout my political life I have taken a great deal of verbal abuse and derogatory correspondence from both extremes; I figure I must be doing something right if I get hammered from both sides."

From the right he was attacked by John Birchers, the Posse Comaradus, and white supremacists, each of whom would cloak virtually every issue in phrases of national security. From the left he received angry letters from Earth First and the Socialist Party. "Extremists are absolutely no fun," says Campbell, who finally got to the point where he simply wrote them off. "I got so disgusted with them that I answered their letters with everything I could think of in four-letter words. I also told them to run for public office themselves if they wanted things fixed only on their terms."

Some of his biggest headaches, however, have come from single-issue activists—those who are either for or against firearms, for or against abortion, for or against any one of a dozen controversies that become the cause of the day. "These people," Campbell says, "reduce everthing in America to a single issue. They do not judge a legislator on total performance, on what that representative is doing for everybody. They are concerned only with what a legislator does for them on that one single issue."

At the time Campbell served in the Colorado House, he was but one of a hundred legislators. At the same time the state had 410 registered lobbyists, each one representing some special interest group. "That meant," he likes to point out, "we were outnumbered about four to one, and that's when I learned about the grading system." The grading system is based on a legislator's voting record on selected issues. It is not unusual to have voted as many as six hundred times in a year, since bills can go through several stages in the legislative process—committee hearings, readings on the floor, sometimes conferences—before passage. Each one of those special interest groups—whether it is the teachers or the teamsters, a labor group or a gun group, an antiabortion group or a business group or an envirommental group—picks out only three or four or five votes and then judges a legislator's total performance based on that sample. Campbell, for example, received a rating of 83 percent from a lobby group representing senior citizens. This score was compiled from his voting record on seventeen bills related to policies and programs affecting the elderly that were introduced into the Colorado legislature during his second term.

"Obviously," Campbell explains, "you can't get a very good score from every group, because some are diametrically opposed in their beliefs. That means, if I got a hundred percent for, say, mining and timber, I could be assured of a zero from the Sierra Club or an environmental group. If I got a hundred from an environmental group, you can be damned well sure I would score a zero from the extractive industries. It fascinated me to discover that I could be wonderful in the eyes of some and godawful in the eyes of others, when to my own way of thinking I was basically trying to do what was best for the majority of people. My score fluctuated wildly because I am very independent and do not respond positively to what I call single-issue manipulative legislation."

Little wonder, then, that Campbell did battle with virtually everyone during his first term, including people in his own party. This occurred because he happened to befriend several Republicans and that, he soon learned, was a dangerous thing to do. "After two terms in the Colorado state legislature, I knew for sure that I liked people better than I liked parties. If you seem too friendly with members of the other party, you're often the object of a lot of antagonism from your own. The fact is, I've made some lifelong friends on both sides of the aisle, and I just cannot and will not ever bring myself to abandon them for partisan goals. I might be faulted by my Democratic colleagues for disloyalty, but I know for a fact that it is considered a strength by the electorate. Many people simply do not want partisan mudslinging from their elected officials."

Although Campbell sees his ability to draw cross-party and unaffiliated voters as a strength, the "party," be it Democrat or Republican, usually sees things differently. The party finds most appealing those candidates who cater to the ideologues or special interest groups within their ranks. "Unfortunately," Campbell says, "these individuals are also the least likely to approach their office with a fair and balanced view of public policy for all the people."

Campbell admits that he had a rather strained relationship with Democratic leaders in Colorado. "I simply found it uncomfortable and even childish to continually ridicule the other party. Democrats are supposed to blame everything that goes wrong on the Republicans, and Republicans, of course, are expected to behave the same way. But these, it seems to me, are the wrong priorities for someone in public office." Campbell blames the news media for some of this. The media, he points out, know that political confrontation and conflict bring high ratings. The juicier the story, the better.

One of Campbell's cross-party friends was Scott McInnis, a legislator elected the same year. "For some reason we hit it off and became close friends," says Campbell. "Besides, we served on the same committee— Agriculture and Natural Resources—so it was only logical that we would spend time together. But it really bothered some people, who often saw us at lunch or dinner together. I certainly saw nothing wrong; our friendship did not change my perspective on key issues. In fact, we sometimes got into heated debates on the floor. Interestingly enough, however, we agreed on more issues than not. Our friendship evidently did not hurt Scott. He has had a great and distinguished career." McInnis became majority leader of the House of Representatives in Colorado and in 1992 won the Third District congressional seat Campbell vacated.

Although freshmen legislators are usually seen and not heard, Campbell wasted little time in making his presence known. Ron Tollefson, a reporter with the *Denver Post,* for one, noticed him. Tollefson was covering discussions of the state budget the day Campbell marched to the microphone to introduce an amendment. "It was another assured loser of an amendment," Tollefson reported the next day. When Campbell noticed no one was paying any attention to him, however, he got indignant. "Are you awake out there?" Campbell challenged his colleagues. "That," retorted Republican John Hamlin, who was presiding over the session, "is not one of the requirements for members of this House."

Obviously taken with the earnest new legislator, Tollefson found Campbell to be "the most fascinating mix of humanity since ex-Princeton polo captain Mike Strang brought his Bull Durham fixin's, cowboy boots, rodeo-competitor scars and investment bank portfolio to the House from Carbondale in the early 1970s." Ironically, it was the same Mike Strang whom Campbell was later to defeat for the U.S. House of Representatives.

No one can ever suggest Campbell was put together by a political consultant, yet despite his rough edges, the people of Colorado quickly took a liking to their independent, down-to-earth, blunt-talking Indian artist-turned-politician. Campbell manages to put a humorous twist on even serious matters. A colleague in the legislature once attempted to describe how Colorado's water policy evolved from "the wild West."

"It didn't get wild until you white guys showed up," Campbell retorted.

Coloradans also like Campbell, who is known for his concern for consumer welfare, because he dares to do what most of us only wish we could do. One story, which he readily confirms, features his response to the owner of a health spa who was planning to close down operations without refunding the deposits of his patrons. "I don't know about the others involved, but the owner and I reached an agreement about my deposit," Campbell says. "He agreed to give me my money back, and I agreed to take my hands off his throat."

Tales about his independence and lack of predictability are also legion in his district. Although Campbell claims the story is not true—he did not do it deliberately—he reputedly defied an order by the Colorado House speaker to be present for a vote to raise the Colorado gasoline tax. The speaker, in turn, ordered the state police to fetch Campbell, who voted against the bill anyway. That, remarked one of his colleagues to writer C. R. Hilliard, was typical of Campbell's bullheadedness. "If he doesn't want to do something, there's no damned way you can get him to do it."

Outspoken, candid, independent—whatever the adjective one chooses to describe Campbell—it makes no difference to his constituents, who returned him to office with ever-increasing margins of victory.

"I did not really sponsor any significant legislation when I was in the state legislature," Campbell admits. "Being in the minority party limits you, but I did a few things that I thought were good." He cosponsored three bills related to Olympic training. One enabled Colorado colleges to give state-resident tuition rates to Olympic athletes training in the state. "As a former Olympian," says Campbell, "I had always been concerned about the difficulty youngsters had in keeping body and soul together while trying to make an Olympic team and getting a college education at the same time." Another bill allowed physicians to practice medicine at the Olympic camp without a Colorado license. The third bill allowed Colorado taxpayers to designate one dollar of their yearly state income tax to support the Olympics. Although several groups that already had in-state check-offs opposed the idea, Campbell saw no reason why Olympians should not have equal access to such discretionary funding. The result has meant hundreds of thousands of dollars of extra revenue for the U.S. Olympic Committee.

One bill popular with the constituents in District 59 was House Bill 1538, which required pipeline companies to post bond and to restore the land after crossing private property. Not only were pipe layers notorious in their disregard of property rights, but they often caused serious environmental damage to the fragile terrain in Campbell's district, damage that did not heal easily through natural processes. Having had firsthand and unpleasant experience with pipe layers on his own ranch, Campbell sponsored the bill and saw it through to law. Jim Earl, a member of the La Plata County Land Protection Association, who dubbed the bill a "truth in pipe laying" measure, gave Campbell much of the credit for its passage. "Ben did a terrific job, that's why it went through," Earl told a reporter from the *Durango Herald*. "I think he's done a hell of a job. He had it all pretty well organized."

Campbell also worked actively with the Colorado Historical Society on a project of personal importance to him, upgrading the monument at the Sand Creek Massacre site, which is near Eads, a little town in southeastern Colorado. "Since several of my Cheyenne ancestors died there," Campbell says, "I had always thought one thing I should do as a member of the Colorado legislature was to keep the memory of that terrible tragedy alive. As it is, the land is in private hands and the cheapskate owner charges admission for people to visit the massacre site." With Barbara Sudler, who was then the head of the Colorado Historical Society, Campbell succeeded in having the State Highway Commission place a memorial sign on the road along the tract of land that contains Black Kettle's campground.

Except for this work on the Sand Creek memorial, Campbell's first term in the Colorado legislature was marked by an absence of Indian-related issues. "Indian people knew I was in office," he says, "but for the most part they left me alone, not because they didn't like me, but because Indian people historically have not been very active in the political process."

Unaware of this when he first decided to run for office, Campbell naturally assumed he would receive the wholehearted support of the Ute Indians, since their reservations were in his district. He met with leaders of both the Ute Mountain Utes, whose reservation is near Towaoc, Colorado, and the Southern Utes, many of whom are his neighbors at Ignacio. Campbell still laughs when he remembers what one elderly woman on the Ute Mountain Ute Reservation said when he asked her for help in getting elected: "What are you going to pay?"

"Hell," I said, "I'm not going to pay anything for either your help or your vote!"

She looked surprised at that and then said, "Why not? That's how our tribal council gets elected."

Campbell had a somewhat different but equally disconcerting experience with the Southern Utes. At Ignacio he approached Sunshine Smith, a delightful old lady and a good friend, who promised her personal support but also warned him: "You know, Ben, if Indian people help you too much we're going to hurt you."

"I didn't quite understand her then," Campbell admits, "but as I spent more time in politics I began to recognize the racial prejudice and bigotry that sometimes lies just under the surface. I already had a couple of strikes against me," he knew. "I was an Indian running in an area that did not have very many Indian voters, and I had long hair. Sunshine was probably right—the more overt Indian help I received, the more likely that I would have experienced some kind of white backlash, at least from some of the radical right wing, which had a very strong hold in southwest Colorado at that time."

Nonetheless, Indians helped Campbell as much as they could, giving him what few votes they could muster. But they also helped him in more intangible and perhaps, in the end, more effective ways. "I know for a fact that some of the older people, those who had no money, who were reluctant to participate in the electoral process, prayed for me, or went to the sweat lodges, or performed ceremonies on my behalf. That in itself is a form of support, and I'll be forever indebted to them for it."

As it turned out, Campbell is only the second American Indian ever elected to the Colorado State Legislature. He had been preceded by Ted Bryant, a Choctaw, who had spent three terms in the legislature in the 1970s. Bryant, in fact, had been hung in effigy by angry Indian militants, who thought he acted more white than red. Campbell, therefore, was not breaking new ground by getting elected, but his arrival coincided with a widespread reawakening of ethnic pride among Indians across the state.

Bryant, for one, certainly wished him well. "He may become frustrated," Bryant told a reporter, "but when you think of it, a half-breed is one of the few people who can walk that middle line."

The significance of his election within the Indian community was brought home to Campbell shortly after his victory. At a reception in his honor sponsored by the Denver Indian Center, he met a woman who came over to him with tears welling in her eyes. "Finally," she sighed, as she hugged and kissed him warmly on the cheek, "we have one of our own in the legislature, too." Her perception, Campbell realized, was "that I was elected by Indians and for Indians. I didn't have the heart to tell her that I was elected for all people, not just Indians."

As his first term drew to a close, Campbell had reason to feel satisfied with his performance. His name had been linked to several popular pieces of legislation, and he had won the admiration of many of his constituents. In fact, the Colorado Bankers Association voted him one of the state's four outstanding legislators, while the La Plata Farm Bureau named him Man of the Year for his work on the pipeline bill.

Little wonder, then, that the Republicans had trouble finding an opponent to run against him when it came time for reelection. "I had proven to be pretty much of a moderate," he explains. "I was pragmatic and not an ideologue, and I had gained a lot of cross-party support." Eventually the Republicans persuaded a woman named Patsy Hart, a realtor from Cortez, to enter the race as his opponent. Although Campbell suffered briefly from freshman jitters regarding his chances for reelection, he had worried needlessly for he easily won a humdrum campaign marked by his opponent's withdrawal a few weeks before election day. Nonetheless, despite dropping out of the race, Hart still managed to get 39 percent of the vote, prompting this rebuke by Gary Henry, in the newspaper *Today:* "Even allowing for mistakes and protests at least one of three people was either uninformed, uninterested, or unconscious."

"If you can't lick 'em, join 'em" became Republican strategy after the election: Campbell's second term began with overtures by his Republican friends in the legislature to switch parties. "My voting record and independence had distanced me from the liberal Democratic leadership, and the Colorado press often described me as a Republican in a Democrat's clothes." Although that image has created a lot of discussion throughout Campbell's career, he never did switch parties. "One of the primary reasons," he admits, "is that both parties have problems with the extremists among them. The extremists always try to set the agenda for their party. As a result, I feel I can be just as effective within the Democratic Party as I would be within the Republican. If anything I am an independent at heart."

Interestingly, when Campbell later took his seat in the federal Congress, he noticed that his political beliefs were quite similar to those Southern Democrats often referred to as "Boll Weevils"—conservatives who had very little in common with the liberal philosophy that dominated the Democratic party in the 1980s. "Although I considered myself socially a liberal," Campbell says, "when it came to money, I was as fiscally conservative as any rock-ribbed Republican. I had been too poor as a youngster to give away someone else's money."

No legislation of any note marked Campbell's second term in the Colorado House. Although he introduced a bill to enable counties to levy a head tax on goods in order to promote tourism, it did not pass. "It simply was too good an idea for the Republican leaders to allow the Democrats to get credit for it," Campbell declares. "Thus, my bill was summarily killed only to be brought up again the following term under Republican sponsorship, when it easily passed."

The most memorable decision in Campbell's second term had nothing to do with the affairs of state. Rather, it was the decision to cut his hair. "By then, I had worn my hair long for over ten years, and it reached well down the middle of my back. Usually, I wore it in a ponytail, but sometimes, when I attended powwows or participated in Indian ceremonies, I braided it. But long hair is hard to care for. I had to shampoo it constantly because I worked with horses so much and it kept getting dusty, dirty, and tangled. Besides, Linda had never liked it."

After three years in the state legislature, Campbell thought the time had come when he could cut his hair and no one would notice. "How wrong I was," he laughs. Like everything else in Campbell's life, even a simple decision to get a haircut became a story. It all began with the suggestion by a friend that he could turn the decision to political advantage by making a big deal of it. "If you're going to cut your hair anyway, why don't you hold a raffle and turn it into a fundraiser by selling tickets. The person with the winning ticket can snip off your ponytail."

The idea appealed to Campbell, and it appealed to the folks in his district, who promptly bought four thousand dollars worth of raffle tickets. Unfortunately, the publicity brought the raffle to the attention of Natalie Meyer, Colorado's secretary of state, who advised Campbell that his raffle violated state laws because he had failed to get a license. "That," he grumbles, "was the first time I ever heard someone would need a license for a haircut. It sure was a silly rule." Evidently the *National Law Journal* thought so as well, because it featured the ruling in an article on the infringement of personal rights through licensing.

Silly or not, rules are rules, so Campbell had to refund all the money he had collected, but he still went through the public shearing. Those who witnessed the event were asked to make a donation toward his campaign expenses, but the potential fundraiser turned into a fundloser. The proceeds failed to cover the costs of advertising, printing the tickets, hiring the required professional beautician, and renting the hall.

To make matters worse, he offended many of his Indian constituents, to whom long hair is a matter of ethnic pride and religious belief. Many traditional Indians still believe that long hair should only be cut as an act of mourning for the death of a relative or loved one. To hold a raffle and use it as a fundraiser was viewed by them as an unwise, if not immoral, act.

Several Indian friends, in fact, tried to talk him out of it as soon as they heard about the public haircut, but Campbell is not easily dissuaded from any action once he has made a decision. "It will come back on you in the Indian way," warned Joe Locust, a young militant who had been active in the American Indian Movement. His concern was echoed by an old Ute woman who lived near the Campbells at Ignacio. "She was literally terrified at the idea," Campbell recalls. She not only scolded him for ignoring traditional beliefs, but she also warned of potentially harmful consequences. "I guess I should have listened to her," he now says. "Instead, I told her the plans were set, and that I was going ahead with it."

Although the actual haircut was uneventful, the foreboding of his Indian friends came back to him with a rush one afternoon about three weeks later. "I was riding a young and very nervous colt, who was the half brother to our big paint Highlight Scamp. Although he was pretty wild and spooky, I had the colt under control until our two dogs suddenly jumped out from behind the barn and frightened him. The colt bolted, crashing through a five-rung steel-panel fence, and then fell on top of me, breaking two ribs and my left arm in three places. I'd been hurt in sports many times, but during all my years on the mats I don't believe I ever got hurt this bad. The fall left me pretty much of a mess." Although Campbell managed to crawl out of the dirt, his troubles were far from over, because he was alone on the ranch.

Instead of trying to call for help, he struggled to his car and drove himself twenty-two miles to Mercy Medical Center in Durango, where he checked into the emergency room. There the staff immediately put his arm into a temporary splint to keep it from shifting and tried to put him through a CAT scan to determine the extent of his injuries. "Unfortunately, when they began to slide me through the CAT scan on this little rail car like they have, my arm wouldn't fit through the opening and in trying to make it fit, one of the orderlies pushed a little bit too hard. I felt something inside tear or break," he remembers. "You'd better pull me back out," he yelled. "Something has gone wrong." The "something" turned out to be one of his broken ribs piercing a lung.

Later that day as he lay in intensive care—with needles in his veins, oxygen tubes in his nose, his arm in a cast, and his body throbbing with pain—Campbell reflected on the warnings he had received. "Perhaps it had come back on me as the Indian people say."

Even at that, however, the ordeal was far from over. As he lay there, he says, "just having a terrible time and feeling pretty sorry for myself," he received a telephone call from one of his friends in the Durango business community. As luck would have it, Campbell had committed himself to being the grand marshal of the Navajo Trails Fiesta Parade in Durango, to be held just three days later. "Representative Campbell," he said, his voice almost breathless with anxiety, "we're really worried about you, but we're also really concerned about this parade. You are still going to be the grand marshal, aren't you? I mean, after all, we've already painted the sign and everything."

Three days later Campbell hauled himself out of the hospital and showed up for the parade. Instead of riding his horse, as he normally does, Campbell accepted a seat in the back of an open convertible, hiding his broken arm with a strategically draped blanket. As he rode along the parade route smiling weakly at the good people of Durango, he kept thinking about the parade organizers and their concern about the cost of a sign.

Then, to salt the wound, a few days later Campbell met the old Ute lady who had tried to warn him about the hazards of cutting his hair. "You see, I told you so," she reminded him.

To this day, Campbell wonders who was right. "Maybe those Indians knew what they were talking about. I mean, after all, the things that one believes are the things that are real. She believed very strongly in that old traditional way, and maybe I made too light of it. I often wonder if cutting my hair really caused that terrible horse accident. On the other hand," he laughs, "I also ask myself how come I got bucked off so many times when my hair was long."

Among the many cards and letters Campbell received as news of his mishap got around was one from Colorado Governor Richard Lamm, a person blessed with a wry sense of humor: "Dear Ben, I'm so glad to learn that you're out of the hospital and starting to move around again. I trust that the horse and dogs have been properly remorseful about the damage they did you."

In 1984, Campbell decided to call it quits. "I had been in public office long enough, I believed. Besides, I had never intended to make politics a career. I missed my family, and I was anxious to get back to making jewelry. In fact, I had spent much of my time recuperating from my horse accident by making a concha belt that won the 1983 Handy and Harmon Most Creative Metalsmith Award at the granddaddy of all the Indian shows, the Gallup Intertribal Ceremonial. I got a great deal of satisfaction from that, and I felt it was time to get back to the things that interested me, so I announced that I would not be running for reelection."

As a farewell present, perhaps, Campbell's colleagues accorded him a signal honor by voting him one of the ten best legislators in Colorado. Their plaudits were echoed by the press and officials throughout the state: "He has developed an excellent ability to work closely with the majority party on issues important to rural Colorado," reported the *Denver Post*; "A man of great integrity who too soon grew disenchanted with the system," said one state official; "We are sorry to lose him," added another.

If the flurry of recognition was a going-away present, it proved premature because, as events transpired, Campbell did not terminate his political career after all. Two years earlier, in January 1984, Ray Kogovsek, then the U.S. representative for Colorado's Third Congressional District, which encompassed the Western Slope, unexpectedly announced his retirement. The decision caused a furor and caught the Democrats unawares. The Republicans immediately found two strong candidates— former state legislator Michael Strang, a businessman and rancher from Carbondale, and James Clingsmith, an attorney. After the shock wore off, the Democrats mustered two candidates as well. One was a millionaire businessman named W. Mitchell. "He never used his name," Campbell marvels. "He just used W." The other Democratic hopeful was State Senator Richard Soash.

Although Campbell at first gave some thought to entering the Democratic primary, he decided against it, thanks largely to one of his campaign managers, Ann Brown, who felt convinced the party leaders would favor Mitchell. Campbell also felt he should give his constituents in the 59th District his full attention throughout his term. Besides, Linda and the children were opposed to the idea of a move to Washington.

Whatever the reason for standing back, it was a wise decision. Soash and Mitchell ran a mutually destructive primary, which Mitchell won.

His victory prompted a number of the conservative ranchers to bolt the Democratic party and support Strang, the Republican primary winner, who took the House seat. This marked the first time in more than a decade that the Democrats had lost the Third Congressional District, and that is why, when Campbell announced his decision not to run for a third time for the Colorado legislature, party leaders asked him to forgo retirement and help them try to regain the seat from the Republicans in 1986.

EIGHT

CONGRESSMAN BEN NIGHTHORSE CAMPBELL

Campbell's election to the U.S. House of Representatives is one of the great stories of modern Colorado political history. His opponent was Mike Strang, a first-term Republican from the Western Slope who had made very successful inroads into the predominantly Democratic part of the district, Pueblo County east of the Divide. All things considered, Strang, as the incumbent, should have won the election. He had far more money to spend than Campbell and, in fact, did outspend him by some $170,000. He was personable, engaging, polite; he had done a decent job during his first term; and he had the support of the media except for a few small local newspapers.

Then why did Strang lose? According to Ken Lane, who joined Campbell's team as his campaign treasurer and was later chief of staff of his congressional office, "Ben won because of his strong, effective campaign. He was an easy candidate for voters to identify with—he appealed to them. In all honesty," says Lane, "Strang failed to take Ben seriously enough until it was too late."

Although Campbell had been sincere in his desire to retire from politics, the thought of national office fired his imagination. It was another contest to win, and Ben Campbell thrives on challenges. He is not happy unless he is competing for something, and the idea of running for Congress charged his competitive nature. His Cheyenne background made the idea even more appealing because only a handful of Indians have served in the United States Congress—perhaps six in the House and three in the Senate. The last senator before Campbell was Charles Curtis, a Kaw-Osage from Oklahoma who had also served in the House of Representatives and then closed his career as vice president under Herbert Hoover. The last Indian to serve in Congress before Campbell's election was Ben Reifel, a Rosebud Sioux who left after the 1970 session, which meant that Indians had had no voice on Capitol Hill during one of the most crucial periods in their cultural resurgence.

This time, before making a decision to run, Campbell did discuss it with his family. Reluctant to face the rigors of what everyone knew would be an arduous and difficult campaign that offered little prospect for success, Linda and the children agreed even while secretly crossing their fingers that it would not become a reality. For a time the race did appear unlikely. Ben had agreed to run only on condition that there be no Democratic primary, yet two men had already announced their intention to seek Strang's seat. Although one of the would-be candidates withdrew his name as soon as party officials requested it, the other congressional aspirant seemed intent on running regardless of party wishes. This gave Linda some hope, but it was not to be. After a few days of indecision, the holdout called Ben and told him he would also withdraw.

Campbell nonetheless was not yet completely decided. He felt the need to consult with someone outside the family about the decision. "Everyone," he says, "has someone special they talk to in times of great emotional strain." For Campbell it was Austin Two Moons, the Northern Cheyenne religious leader, whom he visited at his home in Busby, Montana. "Austin is wise beyond his years. He is a man of such knowledge and spiritual power that he is well respected throughout Indian America. I stayed with Austin many hours telling him all that had happened to me and how unsure I was about trying for Congress." Two Moons urged Campbell to run, but he added a note of caution: "Just remember to do all you can for all people, not just Indians. That will make Indian people the most proud of you."

Having made the decision to run, Campbell next turned to putting a campaign team together. The first person he enlisted was Sherrie Wolff, the executive director of the Colorado Democratic party. Sherrie, who was preparing to take a leave of absence, needed little persuading to head up Ben's election effort. "Sherrie," Ben raves, "was a terrific worker and politically one of the brightest strategists I'd ever known."

Little by little, Campbell's campaign began to attract staff and volunteers, but it was tough going at first. "It was a cash-and-carry campaign," he jokes. "In fact, I was so exasperated at getting no help from my fellow Democrats at the State Assembly, I threatened to drop out if they didn't start helping raise some money for the campaign. It must have worked, because we gradually began building a bank account, and both Sherrie and I could start paying off our personal credit cards."

Campbell's meager war chest is confirmed by campaign treasurer Lane. "We constantly ran on a shoestring budget, never running up a debt. That was Ben's cardinal rule and, despite inclinations to go into debt at times, I agreed not to write any checks or permit any debt operations without knowledge that money was on the way to cover them. Sherrie always humored me about this, but the fact is we always knew money was forthcoming before we committed it."

Lane's darkest moment came early in the campaign, at the Third District convention in Denver in late May, the day Campbell was to accept officially the Democratic nomination. The campaign treasury boasted no more than one hundred dollars, "just enough," Lane admits, "to pay the pathetic three-man band we had hired to parade around the convention room upon Ben's acceptance." Yet, moments before making his speech, Campbell shocked his team by declaring his intention to announce that unless his campaign could raise one hundred thousand dollars by the end of June, little more than thirty days away, he would make no more than a token effort; he refused to mortgage his family and his life for public office.

"Imagine my depression," Lane says, "given the fact that Ben was a Democratic challenger from a small state running against a Republican incumbent with all the power and resources of the mighty National Republican Congressional Committee behind him." To make matters worse, Lane knew that Campbell meant what he said: "It's his hallmark as a politician." As extraordinary as it sounds, however, by the time June 30 rolled around, funds were close enough to the target to mount a credible campaign. "The race was on, and we never looked back."

As events turned out, Sherrie had been an excellent choice. In fact, everyone involved with the campaign, including Linda and Ben himself, gives her credit for the victory. "Sherrie," says Lane, "was tough as nails."

She had to be tough because she faced a daunting task. Colorado's mountainous Third District was 53,000 square miles in extent, at the time the eighth largest in the United States. It featured three major population centers, with one-fourth of the people—about 120,000 in 1986—clustered in Pueblo County. The rest of the population was scattered across the immense district in small rural communities. The district was neither Democratic nor Republican but rather was shared fairly equally by both parties and independents. The district was also strikingly diverse. It included pockets of the desperately poor and the super rich, many of whom were neo-liberal ideologues, with large dollops of blue-collar, union-supporting Democrats thrown in for good measure, while mining, ranching, agriculture, and tourism were its chief industries. To make matters worse for aspirants to public office, the district has a strong tradition of independence with regard to its voting history. "In other words," Lane explains, "running for office in the Third is like walking a political tightrope—if you lean too far one way or the other, you can get into serious trouble. We had little margin for error given the fact that we were in a race between a relatively unknown challenger and a well-heeled incumbent."

A key and, as it proved, shrewd decision Sherrie made was to play down Ben's Indian heritage with one important exception: the use of the name Nighthorse. Sherrie insisted that everyone involved in the campaign, from paid staff to volunteers, refer to their candidate as Ben Nighthorse Campbell. The name was simply too colorful to waste. One of the hardest things for a person running for public office to achieve is name recognition, and Ben's was ideal for this purpose. Soon the man on the street was saying things like "How's the Nighthorse doing?" or "I'm going to vote for the Nighthorse."

Fear of a white backlash was the overriding factor in the decision not to play up Campbell's Indian heritage. Indians made up less than 2 percent of the Third District's population and far fewer of the voters. The district was, in fact, predominantly white, western, and rural with scattered urban pockets. To have Ben run as an Indian for Indians would have been fatal. To charm the voters with his Indian background was another matter, however. "There was no question," Lane admits, "that being part-Indian gave Ben an air of novelty, a refreshing breeze in the political landscape, especially compared to his white-bread opponent."

The media certainly saw it that way. Fascinated by Ben's Indianness, it portrayed the race as "cowboy versus Indian." Lane, for one, found this characterization amusing, since both candidates were really cowboys at heart. Both were ranchers who identified with cattlemen and for whom cowboys hats were de rigueur. Of the two, Strang was more comfortable in a suit, while Campbell favored western-style clothes. Sherrie, in fact, early in the campaign tried to get Ben to change his dress habits, to wear a tie instead of a bolo and to forsake polyester for cotton. That, everyone now agrees, was a mistake. Nonetheless, the very first campaign picture, one still used by some of the smaller newspapers in the Third District, shows him in a clip-on tie, the closest they could get him to wearing a real one.

Rather than portray Campbell as an Indian, Sherrie chose to portray him as a "Renaissance man." The idea was to get the voters to identify with Ben as one of them, and this was easy to do because of his wide experience—semiorphan, high school dropout, Korean war veteran, small businessman, Olympic athlete, artist, truck driver, teacher, rancher, and admired state legislator. The combination was "positively explosive," Lane says. Each component of Campbell's unique background appealed to a different set of voters and contrasted sharply with Strang's, which seemed largely one-dimensional in comparison. "He simply could not compete with Ben in terms of personality, excitement, and appeal."

But Campbell's campaign depended upon more than image. It hit hard on several key issues. One was Strang's financial problems; another was his support of a controversial court decision allowing the sale of hundreds of square miles of oil-shale land, much of it located in the Third District, for only $2.50 an acre. Since Campbell had already come out strongly for the responsible development of natural resources, attacking the court decision was fairly safe for him. Strang, on the other hand, endorsed the court decision by actively working in the waning months of his term to prevent House consideration of measures designed to prevent the sale. On this issue, however, Strang misread his constituents. Western Coloradans traditionally had favored development of public lands, but watching the rich oil shales go to speculators for ridiculously low prices because of the anachronistic 1872 mining law outraged Western Slope residents, who felt they were being unfairly exploited.

The decision to make Strang's financial problems a campaign issue, which struck some as hitting below the belt, was hotly debated in the Campbell camp. In brief, Strang had taken out a very large loan for his ranch from a federal Farm Credit System bank and had failed to make any payments on the interest even though his personal income while in Congress had exceeded two hundred thousand dollars. As Campbell says, "Since he had, in effect, borrowed taxpayers' money, I thought it was unfair of him not to attempt to repay his loan, and I made a point of it." The "attack" was a very brief radio ad that played only a few days and was never aired again, but it did the job. Although the media, which favored Strang, criticized Campbell for making his opponent's finances an issue, it also began to ask the Republican rancher why he had failed to make payments on the loan. Strang at first ignored the question, but the public did not. Then, when he did attempt to make a payment, he did it secretly, which damaged him even more in the public eye. "That single issue," Campbell believes, "probably accounts for my upset victory over Mike."

Throughout much of the campaign Strang enjoyed a distinct press advantage. "I learned a very important lesson," Campbell admits: "Newspaper editorials generally go with the incumbent." He took a beating from several of the local papers in the Third District, with the *Durango Herald,* the one closest to home, being the most opposed. At the same time, Campbell found out to his relief that "most people pay little attention to such editorials, recognizing them for what they are—biased opinions of one or two individuals who usually don't have the courage to sign their work."

Although Campbell had run a good campaign, he remained several percentage points behind in all the opinion polls—his own as well the media's—going into the election. Only Ben seemed unrealistically optimistic and he remained so throughout that long and stressful November day, even in the face of continued media reports that Strang had the lead. These reports, although disheartening, were also perplexing, because Campbell staffers throughout the district were reporting their own tallies, and these numbers indicated Ben was holding his own where he had to and doing better than projected in other precincts. Regardless, around midnight, the various networks announced Strang the winner. Even then, the Campbell camp did not despair because Sherrie had noticed a crucial error in the official tallies—Rio Blanco County was credited with giving Strang fifteen thousand votes, when in fact there were not that many residents in the entire county (the number should have been fifteen hundred). Although the media failed to catch the mistake, Strang's people certainly did because his Pueblo campaign headquarters closed early. This only served to confirm what Campbell's backers had already known, albeit unofficially, and his headquarters started going wild with joy. "What a moment!" Lane recalls. "Those of us who had put so much into the campaign were overcome with fatigue but also with incredible happiness—the impossible had been achieved. That night remains one of the proudest moments of my life!"

Nonetheless, the majority of Coloradans went to bed convinced Strang had won. Only a few of the more savvy Western Slope reporters suspected that Campbell had pulled off a monumental upset and delayed submitting their stories for the following day's editions. One was Carol Knight, editor of the *Delta County Independent*. "That was a big year for Democrats," remembers Carol, who later became Campbell's Washington press secretary. "Tim Wirth beat Ken Kramer in the U.S. Senate race, which made us all real happy, and we had some other good successes on the Western Slope and in Delta County, so we were sorry to learn that Ben had lost." When the *Independent* reporter called Mike Strang's headquarters, however, he thought something did not seem right, so he told Carol it was real quiet over there. "What the hell is going on?" Carol asked herself. When her reporter called Campbell's headquarters in Pueblo, and hooting and hollering could be heard over the phone, Carol suspected the truth, and so her paper got the story right. "There were some big newspapers that didn't," she says with rightful pride. "My little paper got a great coup, but more important, we got Ben—we really wanted that seat—and we got the Senate seat as well. We were thrilled."

It was a narrow victory—52 percent to 48 percent—but what a victory! Campbell was one of only six challengers nationwide to beat an incumbent in the House to enter the 100th Congress.

Most of the core campaign staff remained with Campbell after the election. Sherrie Wolff became his chief of staff, Ken Lane his legislative assistant. Ann Brown, who had been so instrumental in Campbell's first political campaign and who had played an active role as a volunteer in this congressional race, took charge of his Durango office. In fact, six of the eight core members of his campaign team remained with Campbell throughout his six years in the House. This low turnover, very unusual in congressional offices, is one of the underlying reasons for his continuing success.

Nevertheless, it was not all peaches and cream for the campaign team. Few things are as stressful as running for political office. These are high-stakes events with little time for simple courtesies. Feelings get hurt, friends become strangers, enemies are made, old sores become open wounds. Campbell's campaign was no different.

One area of stress concerned his effort to enlist American Indian support. The person who agreed to do this for Campbell was Lucille Echohawk, a dynamic, politically astute woman of Pawnee descent who worked for the Council of Energy Resource Tribes in Denver. Lucille formed a committee called American Indians for Ben Nighthorse Campbell for Congress and enlisted the support of such Native American notables as Olympic gold medalist Billy Mills and actor Will Sampson, famous for his role in the award-winning movie *One Flew Over the Cuckoo's Nest*.

Although Echohawk eventually raised almost nineteen thousand dollars for Campbell, proving that American Indians could band together nationwide to help a candidate, her assistance was a mixed blessing that led to considerable friction within the campaign committee. As a fundraiser, she felt entitled to be a decision maker as well, but the campaign committee did not see it that way. "In my opinion," Lane declares, "to have allowed Lucille to become involved in determining how to run the campaign would have been counterproductive. She was very strong-willed, and she had no experience in Third District politics." Because of her close friendship with Campbell, however, she continued her separate efforts, which caused confusion and conflict for a time, but the bruises healed and she remained a good friend, ally, and fundraiser. In fact, she later helped raise one hundred thousand dollars from Indian sources for Campbell's Senate campaign.

Except for this unfortunate misunderstanding, the Campbell team had run a virtually trouble-free campaign and had achieved what many shrewd political analysts considered impossible, and it did it without incurring a campaign debt. Campbell won even though then President Ronald Reagan, former President Gerald Ford, and three cabinet secretaries all actively campaigned in Colorado against him. "All we had," Campbell beams, "was people, but they sure did come through."

Thanks to this charisma, Campbell once again found himself packing his suitcase and leaving home, this time for Washington, D.C. He arrived in early January 1987 and immediately began setting up his office, which was on the seventh floor of the Longworth House Office Building. "My gosh," he kept asking himself, "what's a poor boy like me doing here?"

The full import of this question came home to him at the swearing-in ceremony on January 6. "I was almost transfixed," Campbell recalls. "I imagined the interesting conversations my mother and father must have had, she having come to this country as a young girl thinking she had reached the end of the rainbow and then meeting my dad, a person as wild and free as the wind, who also tried to capture a piece of the American dream. And I thought about myself, a person probably no different than most Americans—a part of this country and a part of another, yet never really understanding our nation, just kind of taking it for granted." Campbell also thought—with a touch of chagrin, he admits—"about the many times that I had made fun of the political process, criticizing our elected officials and generally holding all government in pretty low esteem."

That morning Campbell found himself between two men of whom he had often heard. To his left stood Joseph Kennedy, son of the late Robert F. Kennedy, member of a family with a long history of public service whose very name evokes an image of power and wealth, of magic and dreams come true. To Campbell's right stood John Lewis, son of a black Georgia sharecropper. "If the Kennedys were dreams come true," Campbell thought, "then John Lewis's family certainly were dreams denied. Their only respite from the scorching sun and fourteen-hour workdays in the fields was reading the Bible on Sunday." John Lewis fulfilled his dream by working with Martin Luther King, Jr., in the civil rights movement during the 1960s. Together they had walked the streets of Atlanta, Birmingham, and Selma. Lewis had been jailed and beaten more than forty times; his body bore scars inflicted by police dogs and fire hoses that had tossed him across the ground like a rag doll. At times, he has told Campbell, he felt as though he were an enemy in his own country. "If anyone had been tested by the fires of social change, it was John Lewis."

The first order of business for congressional freshmen is to receive committee assignments. Historically the representatives from Colorado's Third District have served on the Interior Committee because many Western Slope issues are related to public lands. On the other hand, no one from Colorado had served on the Agriculture Committee in more than a decade. Since Campbell was interested in these two committees, the House Democratic Steering and Policy Committee, which makes the assignments, saw fit to place him on both and then added a third, Small Business. Campbell considered himself fortunate in his assignments; he greatly admired Morris Udall, chairman of the Interior and Insular Affairs Committee, who was well known for his wit when faced with difficult problems, and "Kika" de la Garza, chairman of the Agriculture Committee. Both men took a liking to Campbell and became his mentors.

Membership on the three full committees involved seats on five subcommittees—Mining, Water and Power, Tourism, Forests, and Livestock, Dairy and Poultry. Among these assignments Campbell figured to have all the bases covered for his district, but he also had more than a full plate. "I soon discovered that I had never before taken on a job that required more hours, was more stressful, was tougher on my family, or, in fact, was more thankless than being a member of Congress. All work weeks are eighty hours or more, and the logistics alone of keeping up with the demands of the public is like being in the Colorado legislature by pi squared."

Meetings gobbled up an enormous amount of time. "I've had as many as twenty-nine meetings in one day, every fifteen minutes for almost ten hours straight," Campbell groans. "New group, new problem. The first group says the sky is falling and if you don't fix it by tomorrow the world will come to an end! The next bunch doesn't care what the last one said—theirs is the important issue."

Any time left over was consumed by public appearances and speeches. Requests for these, Campbell says, averaged about fifteen per day, which meant a goodly number got rejected and he sometimes had hard choices. On the other hand, some—like hospital appearances—were almost impossible to get on his agenda. "Ben balks at requests to visit hospitals," admits Jane Wilson, his scheduler. "I guess it is a result of his childhood association of hospitals with his mother's tuberculosis and the time he spent with his family when they were sick. Ben's a great supporter of health care legislation, but he will do almost anything to avoid going to hospitals for ceremonial functions like ribbon cuttings or visiting patients. Do you have any idea how many hospitals there are in his district and how many requests like that we get in a year? We have to be pretty creative in our turndowns."

Creative or not, refusal is not easy for some folks to accept. John Horvath of Hesperus, Colorado, for one, vented his displeasure at Campbell for failing to accept an invitation to attend the annual dinner of the La Plata County Rocky Mountain Farmers Union. "Why, with your large staff of Washington types, do you have only one scheduler?" Horvath wanted to know. Campbell wrote back that the number of schedulers had nothing to do with the declined invitation. "My office receives several hundred requests a month for appearances at this or that event, and it is not possible to have more than one person handling these requests without complete chaos reigning." Campbell could not attend the La Plata dinner because he was already committed to attending the statewide dinner of the Farmers Union, and several other chapters had also requested his presence at their functions. As for his staff, all but one were from Colorado. "They would find it not only odd but offensive to be labeled 'Washington types,' since their homes and families are in Colorado, and they made the sacrifice of moving to D.C. to assist me and the residents of their home state."

Because Campbell's district was so vast and because he was expected to visit each community on a regular basis, it was not unusual for him to be away from home for long periods of time, living out of airplanes and suitcases. "You just can't do it all," he complains. "You never see your family and you never have a life of your own. You can't go anywhere into your district without people wanting to talk to you about something. I almost never can take my wife out for dinner in Durango, for example, because people will come right up to the table and say, 'Hey, I don't want to bother you during dinner, but I want to tell you . . .' and then they launch right into it. You can have your fork at your mouth, and they're telling you that their Social Security check didn't come on time. People have even come up to me in the movies. 'Hey man,' they'll whisper, 'I need to talk to you about something.' "

To serve his sprawling district effectively, Campbell found it necessary to open three regional offices—in Durango, Grand Junction, and Pueblo—besides the one in Washington. All told these offices handled more than five hundred contacts per day from mail, phone calls, and personal visits. In the Washington office alone, a week's mail stacked vertically averaged seven feet.

Few of the visitors were folks simply interested in saying hello. "Most want you to start something, stop something, change something, or fix something, and that something usually is to their personal or corporate advantage and someone else's personal or corporate disadvantage. No wonder the average citizen so often feels that politics are kind of a dirty business that ignores the needs of the common man."

Congress, Campbell soon discovered, is besieged by thousands of special interest political action groups and tens of thousands of professional lobbyists—known on Capitol Hill as "hired guns"—far more than the number with which he had to contend on the state level. "Lobbyists have us outnumbered on the Hill by sixty-eight to one, and what they want is not best for the country, but what's best for their special interest. In fact," he growls, "the double standard of many of the people who come to see me is something to behold. In one breath they tell me to balance the budget, lower their taxes, and get them ten million more dollars for some special project." That, he insists, is almost a daily demand. "In my heart, I like to believe that somewhere out there is the so-called silent majority, the people in our country who still believe in the virtues of hard work, loyalty, national commitment, and fairness, the virtues that Americans have always stood for, but I guarantee you they aren't the ones usually found hanging around congressional offices in Washington."

Campbell's complaints are echoed by his press secretary, Carol Knight. Job satisfaction? Forget it. "Nowadays," Knight says, "we exchange computer-generated letters with our constituents. We now have machines talking to machines. Who can take pride in saying that last month we sent out two hundred computer-generated letters?"

Not all outgoing correspondence, by a long shot, was computer generated. Campbell and his staff took pride in providing specific responses to specific questions or complaints. Correspondents soon learned, however, that their congressman could be as brash, blunt, and brusque on paper as he was in person. He was especially impatient with ax-grinders like Tillie, a visitor from Walsenburg, Colorado, who stormed into the Washington office one summer day looking for an excuse to get upset, found it, and then left promising to inform Campbell about the shoddy treatment she had received from his staff: "The receptionist was not friendly, in fact she was rude," Tillie complained to

Campbell in a letter, keeping her promise. "She did not even get up to greet me when I told her I was from Colorado and your district. I told her I thought that when people come in they were given the 'red carpet' treatment." The Colorado Senate staff did much better by her, she claimed. "You couldn't compare the treatment I got there. They showed me around and also gave me a pass to the Capitol to visit the Rep & Senate Chambers. (Your office gave me one too but no explanations.)" Then, perhaps hoping to finish with a flourish, she instead sabotaged her own argument: "I did tell your staff that I did not vote for you in the last election because I did not see anything you have done for us in Huerfano County. Perhaps this turned them off."

Perhaps so, Campbell responded, but that did not prevent them from doing their job. "You certainly made an impression upon my office! That half my Washington staff remembered your visit in detail is remarkable in and of itself, given the fact that so many visitors stop by my office every day, particularly in the summer. As three staff members remember it, you . . . made an unfriendly comment about me, then said you did not vote for me, and that, in fact, you 'didn't like the man at all.' Some introduction! You must admit that such statements are rather surprising ones to make, since even simple courtesy would generally preclude comments like that. They're fine in a political setting, but very rare when one is visiting an office as a visitor or tourist."

Tillie got off easily. Not so Roberta from Forest Grove, Oregon, who took exception to an item in the Sunday *Oregonian* in which Campbell aired his standard complaints about the electorate—citizens who do not vote, who are single-issue oriented, who fail to realize how stressful it is to be in public office. "You were quoted!" she huffed. "I resent being lumped into the general category of taxpayers you are dissatisfied with. You want respect? . . . It must be earned. It is a two-way street. In order to get it, you have to give it."

"I call 'em as I see 'em," Campbell huffed back. "I have a right to express my opinion on the state of our society just as you have a right to. I did not give up that right to speak out when I was elected to office. I'm sorry if you think all politicians should say only soothing things. I don't operate that way, and will not. If the truth hurts, I'm sorry. Isn't democracy great?"

Like the mail in any Capitol Hill office, letters to Campbell reflected the issues of the moment. The deficit, government waste, unemployment, Desert Storm, even the Clarence Thomas–Anita Hill hearings in the Senate unleashed torrents of mail on Campbell's beleaguered staff, yet few issues inspired constituents to vent their displeasure as much as the so-called congressional perks. Although Campbell personally was not involved in any of the scandals that surfaced in the 102d Congress and ruined so many political careers, he was deeply hurt by the furor for, like Roberta, he resented being lumped with the transgressors.

For once Campbell appeared defensive. To Jack of Pueblo—"I feel I have been doing a good job . . ."; to Jacob of Avon—"I have never bounced a check at the House bank nor do I owe money to the private contractor who provided food service to members, thank goodness . . .";to Ralph of Pueblo—"I didn't bounce any checks. . . ." It was a tiring, degrading, and demoralizing effort to rise above the mire and muck without appearing to hurt colleagues who were swept up in what became a media feeding frenzy at congressional expense. "It's not just Congress you need to be concerned about," Campbell cautioned one correspondent. "It's the whole atmosphere of society . . . picking apart every single event, trivial or otherwise, without attention to matters equally or more important. It's the obsession of partisan politics on every single issue, driven by special interest groups on the left and the right." To Carlos of Golden: "Free gasoline? That's pure bull-you-know-what. Subsidized meals? I didn't know a $1.75 hamburger, with no fries, constitutes a subsidized meal. By the way, I see no discussion [in all the media coverage] about the President's private tennis courts, his putting green on the White House lawn and other recreational facilities available only to the President. Why?"

With some, like Shirley of Pueblo—who wrote "I am livid in that we elect people sending them to Washington to represent us . . . [who] catch the career politician fever and feast like jackals at the public trough" and get "special banking privileges, free restaurant food, pharmacy, day care,

franking privileges, $25,000 discretionary fund per individual"—
Campbell's patience wore thin. The franking privilege an abuse? Come
on. "It's paying for this response. Is that not a legitimate use of taxpayers'
money?" As for Shirley's other gripes, "What nonsense," he retorted. "I
don't disagree there are problems in Congress . . . but please don't paint
every person who is a member of Congress with the same brush; and
gather the facts before making such accusations."

"The gentleman doth protest too much, methinks," Shirley fired
back, claiming she had not accused Campbell, personally, of any abuses.
"Nevertheless, you are a member of this elite congressional club. We . . .
are taxed more and more while our congressional members upgrade their
life style, plus fund every social scheme that comes along as well as such
scams as the National Endowment for the Arts' obscene and offensive
garbage." Besides, "your voting record closely parallels that of the big
spender [from Colorado] Pat Schroeder."

"Unfortunately, you miss the point of my first reply," answered
Campbell, once again. Instead of defending the perks, he had attempted
to point out the misinformation she harbored. "Incidentally, did you
happen to see the recent news story on the obscene perks and privileges of
the Executive branch? Talk about an elitist class! Or do those 'privileges'
not bother you?"

Another popular criticism was the "pork barrel," the appropriation
of federal funds for seemingly frivolous projects. "Great fodder for head-
lines, right? Congress dithering away money on studying the sex life of
screwworms." Even silly-sounding appropriations, Campbell assured one
concerned constituent, usually have a valid basis. This one had profound
implications. It provided the means to determine how to eradicate the
screwworm, a pest that caused untold damage to livestock and cost
consumers millions every year. Based on its successful extermination in
the United States, world health officials now predict its imminent eradica-
tion in Africa as well. "All this from a silly little 'pork barrel' appropriation."

When called to task by Norma of Lafayette for his voting record,
Campbell retorted: "Yes, I do on occasion vote against the party line, and

I will continue to do so." Nonetheless, he assured her, his voting record is solidly Democratic at least three-fourths of the time. In fact, he pointed out, he had been more consistent than his "good, liberal friend, Pat Schroeder, who has the reputation of being the Party's most partisan member from Colorado." In 1990, for example, out of 263 votes Campbell rated a 76 percent in terms of party support; Schroeder was close behind at 73 percent. In 1987 the difference had been more significant, 82 percent and 73 percent.

Although Campbell personally wrote relatively few of the letters his office generated, he did prepare his own speeches, even for events like graduations or Chamber of Commerce meetings. He is so comfortable at public speaking that he frequently outlines his remarks on a scrap of paper while waiting for his turn at the microphone. What enables him to do this, Carol Knight believes, is his remarkable memory. "He'll read something in *Newsweek,* for example, and all of a sudden I'll hear him talking about it at a town meeting. He'll announce a figure—something like '750,000 acres of timber are going to Japan'—and I'll think to myself, Where in the hell did he get that? He'll be right, of course. He just has this incredible memory. If he sees a figure, he retains it and later inserts it in the right place. He's good at that."

Typically, Campbell wasted little time in making his presence known when he got to Capitol Hill. First he tackled the congressional dress code, which requires its members to wear a coat and tie on the House floor. It is a regulation that is sometimes followed to absurd lengths: congressmen caught unawares in the gym have been known to rush onto the House floor to vote wearing sneakers and sweatpants as well as the mandatory coat and tie.

Campbell has no problem with suit jackets, but he avoids neckties because of a lingering judo injury. "I get hoarse easily if I wear anything too tight around my neck like a tie." Accordingly, on his first day in Congress, Campbell sought out House Speaker Jim Wright and showed him the scarf and clasp he preferred to wear. "I thought the timing was right—they were all western people in the House leadership," he later explained to a reporter. "If there was ever a time that the leadership would understand western dress, this was it." Besides, he quipped, neither George Washington nor Thomas Jefferson wore neckties. "What's good enough for the Founding Fathers of our country is certainly good enough for me."

Just to keep the record straight, Campbell was not the only boat-rocker in recent memory with respect to the House dress code. Hats are prohibited, but that never daunted Representative Bella Abzug, who was known for her outlandish headgear. Once, when legendary House Door-keeper William "Fishbait" Miller tried to keep her from the floor while she was wearing one of her hats, she told him—reported the congressional newspaper *Roll Call*—"to perform an impossible sex act."

Next to go was a painting by artist Seth Eastman that hung in the House Interior Committee Room. Entitled *War Whoop,* the painting was one of a group of seven western scenes commissioned by Congress in 1868 to grace the Capitol. Although the others in the set were pleasant pastoral scenes, this one depicted an Indian warrior holding aloft the scalp of his white victim in one hand, while in the other he brandished his still bloody ax.

Without hesitation, committee chairman Morris Udall removed the offensive picture at Campbell's suggestion. "The painting is not only grotesque," Campbell informed an inquisitive reporter from Grand Junction, "but it is also out of sync with modern-day sensitivities. If we have to keep a painting about scalping in government, then send it to the Internal Revenue Service. They scalp us all."

Legislative victories were harder to come by, although Campbell enjoyed unusual success for a freshman. Indeed, of all the frustrations that confront Congress, perhaps nothing equals the legislative process. "Don't think for a minute that we can say, 'Gee, oh, good! What we're doing matters!' " grumbles Carol Knight. "Congress never passes the best bill. We simply pass the best bill we can pass—and there's a big difference. To some, a bill will be not liberal enough, while to others it will not be conservative enough. What usually passes is the best version of a bill that we can get a majority of people to vote for. That's frustrating!"

And for Campbell, nothing was more frustrating than HR 2642, officially named the Colorado Ute Indian Water Rights Settlement Act and in actuality the implementing legislation for the construction of the Animas–La Plata water project. The bill ratified a compromise worked out over several years by thirteen different affected jurisdictions, such as the states of Colorado and New Mexico, various Indian tribes, and agencies of the Justice and Interior departments. The bill was opposed by environmentalists, a couple of key members of Congress, and President Reagan's Office of Management and Budget.

Even today, Campbell gets angry when talking about the furor over passage of the Animas–La Plata bill. Much of the noise, he insists, was generated by people benefiting from water Coloradans had a right to use. "Those who complained the loudest about protecting water, in fact, were Californians who did not like to see any storage projects that would stop Colorado water from reaching them."

The person Campbell most holds responsible for his difficulties with the bill is Democratic Congressman George Miller of San Francisco, who at the time was chairman of the water and power subcommittee. Campbell's bitterness toward Miller dates back to the days when he was in the midst of his campaign against Strang and happened to meet the California congressman at the Democratic National Club in Washington. Campbell seized the opportunity to tell him whom he was running against, outlined his plans for Animas–La Plata, and asked for his help if elected to Congress. "You know," Miller replied, "I think Animas–La Plata sucks, but if you get elected I'm going to help you get it." When Campbell later reminded him of the promise, however, Miller went the other way. "Not only wouldn't he help," Campbell remembers, "he tried to get the thing killed."

In the end Miller's opposition did not matter, because others came to Campbell's aid. Particularly invaluable was Ray Kogovsek, the former congressman from the Third District of Colorado, who had been working as a lobbyist for both the Ute Indians and the water conservancy districts to get the bill passed. "He did a terrific job of getting original cosponsors to help me with the bill," Campbell declares. Also crucial were Mo Udall and House Speaker Jim Wright, Colorado senators Tim Wirth and Bill

Armstrong who sponsored the bill in the Senate, and Daniel Inouye, chairman of the Senate Select Committee on Indian Affairs. "Without them," Campbell admits, "I probably would have lost the bill, because it took us two years, a complete term of Congress, to generate the support to get it passed into law."

Here Campbell learned the importance of behind-the-scenes negotiating. During the crucial Interior Committee vote, their staffs sent in all the proxies of the absent members. Miller, who was determined to do his best to kill the bill, had his motion fail on a tie vote. Not until weeks later did Campbell learn that Chairman Udall had not counted one proxy vote, which he had later found in his pocket. "By mistake or intent, my bill was saved in committee."

In the floor debates on Animas–La Plata, the bill's most vocal supporters were Republicans John Rhodes of Arizona and Larry Craig of Idaho, although it had the wholehearted backing of the entire Colorado delegation. "I think that John and Larry, both being Republicans, were crucial to its passage," Campbell says. "They were not only terrific debaters, but they were also much more experienced than me in the trench warfare that I was facing on the floor from the environmental community."

The rancor over Animas–La Plata also taught Campbell another lesson. Although his voting record in the Colorado legislature had earned an 88 percent approval rating from environmentalists, they showed him no mercy for former favors. "I found out then and there that people driven by ideologies, regardless of the issue, are rarely willing to compromise. No way did my strong voting record save me from attack when I decided to stand up for something they opposed."

After bitter debate on the House floor—for which Campbell blames Miller—the bill passed quite easily. But in the Senate Bill Bradley put a hold on it. (A hold is a parliamentary procedure unique to the Senate to keep a bill off the floor and away from debate.) The senator did this, Campbell believes, because of a turf issue; Colorado Senator Wirth had routed the bill around Bradley's water and power subcommittee. "Let me tell you," Campbell claims, "to get Bradley to withdraw that hold took a great deal of pleading on my part and that of a great many other individuals and organizations including the Operating Engineers union of the AFL-CIO, which had a great number of members in Bradley's home state of New Jersey. The engineers, of course, wanted the jobs that the Animas–La Plata dam project would generate."

Even with the hold lifted, the bill faced further obstacles. In the end it took personal telephone calls from House Speaker Jim Wright to break the bill out of the Senate and get it moving again. Finally, with a few minor changes agreed to by the House, the bill passed and went to the president for his signature. "And that," Campbell beams, "was the first major accomplishment of my first term in Congress." Indeed so. Dan McAuliffe, now his legislative director, insists it was that bill alone that got Campbell reelected so easily.

Campbell had reason to be proud. By the end of his first term, he had recorded the highest percentage of bills introduced and passed into law— including a resolution naming January 7 National Ski Day—among the eight-member Colorado delegation, according to a *Denver Post* survey. *Westward,* a small Denver-based newspaper, also named him Best Colorado Legislator that year.

Campbell even had the satisfaction of helping suspend the sale of oil-shale lands to speculators. The measure to curtail further sales passed by a three-to-one margin. To those of his colleagues who claimed it was unfair to change the rules in the middle of the game, Campbell responded, "If rules aren't changed to fit the social needs of the times, then women might still not have the right to vote!"

During his first year in Washington Campbell also got a chance to experience congressional government at its most byzantine. The milieu was the complicated budget process, and the specific issue was the controversial congressional pay raise, which Ben strongly opposed, contrary to Democratic party policy. Ronald Reagan initially proposed a 16 percent hike from $77,400 to $89,500 for members of the House and Senate in his budget for the 1988 fiscal year, a 2,247-page document sent to Congress on January 5, 1987. The pay proposal, once noticed, sparked a storm of protest. Congressional salaries were already reflecting, since

January 1, a 3 percent cost-of-living increase voted by the previous Congress. But the real clincher was a governing provision stipulating that any pay raise recommended by a president in an annual budget would take effect in thirty days unless disallowed by both chambers. The House passed the resolution rejecting the increase on February 4, one day too late.

Unbelievably, in Campbell's view, this was not the end of the matter, nor the end of parliamentary machinations and bitter partisan wrangling. Later in the year a further 3 percent cost-of-living increase in salaries of federal employees was included in two related measures, the fiscal 1988 budget reconciliation and the continuing resolution bills. This would have lifted congressional pay from $89,500 to $96,600 and to $100,000 after three years. Because of his opposition to the raise, Campbell says, "I endured some heavy-duty arm twisting and witnessed the worst guerrilla warfare I've seen since Korea." Twice he broke ranks and voted with the Republicans. In the end he voted for the massive and complex reconciliation bill because otherwise automatic budget cuts would have devastated Colorado. Eventually the Democratic leadership bowed to the pressure, and members of Congress were exempted from the federal pay raise appropriated in the continuing resolution. The two final measures cleared the House on December 22, the last day of the session and almost three months after the 1988 fiscal year had begun.

To confirm his disapproval of the congressional pay raise and at the same time demonstrate his strong support for education, Campbell divided his increase of approximately $5,000 (after taxes) among the five colleges in his district. "My own parents never went beyond the eighth grade," he admitted to a reporter when announcing the gifts.

Campbell found he could be effective as a congressman even though he is fiercely independent and pretty much of a loner. He did not socialize with his colleagues on Capitol Hill. "I don't go golfing with them. I don't go to nightclubs with them. I don't do any of those things they do together. That doesn't mean," Campbell insists, "that I am standoffish. I've got a lot of friends on the Hill; I just don't go to the parties. My aversion to that kind of social life goes back to my childhood memories of alcohol. Most Washington parties are full of liquor. I go to the receptions to say hello when people from Colorado are coming, but if I've got free time, I'd rather work on my jewelry or be with my family."

And being with his family meant being in Colorado, because Linda chose life on the ranch over life on the Hill. Her visits to Washington were few and far between, although she did attend regularly the annual White House barbecue for congressmen and their families. As a result, Campbell spent a great deal of time in airplanes between D.C. and Colorado. "I fly in on Monday. I do my job, and I leave on Thursday."

Campbell preferred one-on-one work with his associates—at lunch, in the gymnasium, in the hallways. "Then," he says, "you have an opportunity to talk where the press isn't always hanging over every word. Also, a lot of the guys on the Hill are a little posture-conscious, but in the gymnasium when they're down to their shorts and tennis shoes, they look like anybody else. They don't have to worry about their image. There they don't have to worry about that Mr. Chairman bullshit. I can say, 'Hey, Bruce, come on, I need a little help on this, so how about giving me a break,' or I can ask, 'How about scheduling that hearing in Montana that I need?' It's easier to talk about things like that away from the structured environment of the offices. I can get down to the nitty-gritty of the problem better if it's not a situation where our staffs are hanging all over us and where we have to keep up appearances. Then I say, 'Okay, listen. Let my staff call your staff so they can put the thing together.' It works all the time."

Campbell did not worry that his aloof style would one day cost him his job, because he had no intention of making it permanent. "I'm sure," he declares, "that there have been others like me who don't look at Congress as a place where the sun rises and sets, but not in my lifetime. I think a real problem on the Hill is that people get addicted to the lifestyle. Then you become part of the problem and you never find part of the solution." Campbell, in fact, believes strongly in term limits. In 1990 he supported a Colorado initiative limiting the terms of U.S. senators and representatives to twelve years.

Since Campbell finished his first term with such flying colors, he decided to go another round. To his surprise, however, Mike Strang, the expected opponent for his House seat, did not run. Instead, the Republican Party selected Jim Zartman, an outspoken conservative from Montrose whose campaign strategy consisted of little more than trying to paint his opponent as a left-wing liberal. The result was a landslide victory for Campbell, who won with 78 percent of the vote, the widest margin for any elected official in Colorado that year. "Zartman never did call to concede, but I didn't hold it against him," Campbell laughs. "I think he was still angry at me for threatening to punch him in the nose during one of our televised debates. He accused me of not being patriotic, and I didn't take very kindly to that from a person I considered to be a right-wing nut, and I told him so."

Zartman found out, as have many others before and since, that Campbell has a quick temper. Yet he is just as quick to calm down. Carol Knight, for one, will never forget her first interview with Campbell, which she conducted for the *Delta County Independent* during his first congressional campaign. "I asked him a question about the oil-shale issue, and he became a wild man. He jumped up and started waving his arms around, and I thought he had gotten angry at me. 'What's gotten into him? How does anyone work for him?' I asked myself. Only later did I realize that it was the oil-shale business that had set him off, not my question. I had no idea how much the oil-shale business pissed him off. After a bit he sat down and it was all over. He was simply passionate about this oil-shale thing. He was ticked off that the government gave hundreds of thousands of acres to people for $2.50 an acre. That set him off."

Knight thinks Campbell gets mad when he is frustrated and, naturally, this reaction is reflected in his interviews with reporters who do not know him well. "I've had reporters tell me 'Campbell angrily said this or that when he wasn't angry at all. Once they get to know him, they realize that he isn't popping off at them, but you do have to know him. He gets angry at individuals, too, and yells at them; but again, he gets over it pretty quick. He's just not terribly patient."

No one knows that better than Campbell. "I gotta control myself," he tells himself in reflective moments. On the other hand, he enjoys a good fight and nothing stirs him up more than having people hurl insults at him. "Once they go beyond what I call the rules of civility," he admits, "once they start swearing at me, or threatening me, or yelling at me— 'We'll get you, you son of a bitch. You vote it that way and we'll throw you out'—when they say things like that to me, then the fight is on. Goddamn it! I got elected as a public official, not a public doormat, and I don't intend to be one. I just won't stay in office if those are the conditions. I tell them back, man. I've told people more than once, if they don't like it, run for office themselves. They can fix it the way they want when they're elected. I remember one guy at a town meeting who was yelling at me about how much money we congressmen waste, that we're no good, that we're living on them—all that kind of bullshit. Well, according to the Congressional Research Service, our salaries only cost the average taxpayer two cents, so I gave the bastard his two cents back and told him to shut up."

Campbell likes to view himself as a person of passion, not anger. "I mean, if I really support or oppose something, I get passionately involved." That, he rationalizes, is not the same thing as anger. "Losing your temper means you lose control. In sports, getting mad enabled me to fight harder, but that's not losing control. I like to think there is such a thing as controlled anger. I've never felt," he insists, "that I've been out of control in a public situation, like a debate. The last guy I ran against [in 1990], for example, accused me of being weak at protecting Colorado water. I lit into him. 'Where the hell have you been for ten years?' I told him. 'Where were you when I got the money for the Animas–La Plata project? What have you been doing all this time? And now you're suddenly the big authority on water.' Afterward a reporter said to me, 'Geez, you really blew up.' I didn't think so. They've never seen me blow up. In my opinion, I was just telling him what I thought, but I was telling him passionately."

Passionate or angry, Campbell has no intention of changing his ways. In fact, he thinks more public figures ought to follow his example. One who would have benefited from this advice, he is convinced, was

Michael Dukakis, the Democratic presidential hopeful in 1988: "I tried to tell him to get a little fire in his belly, to quit wallowing around with his damn platitudes, to show some passion." The perfect time, Campbell thinks, would have been during the debate with Bush when he was asked "What would you do if your wife was raped in the street?" Instead of saying, "I'd kill the son of a bitch, or something like that," his answer, Campbell groans, "was so weak, sterile, and wimpy that he lost about half the men in the United States."

Although Campbell's charisma has continued to serve him well with his own constituents, it did not rub off on the candidates he supported for president in 1988. His first choice for president was his colleague from Colorado, Gary Hart. "I thought he had generated a spirit in America almost to the degree that John F. Kennedy had. He captured the imagination of our country's young people, and that's tough to do. Anybody can deal with issues and give numbers, regurgitate the stuff that staffs put in candidates' heads, but there aren't many people who can capture your imagination, who can really motivate you to work and do something better than you normally do, to rise above yourself. Kennedy had that ability, and I think Gary Hart did too."

To help Hart raise money for his campaign, Campbell came up with the idea of designing a commemorative belt buckle to be produced in a limited edition—one for Hart and one for each state—to be raffled off by the Democratic Congressional Campaign Committee. Anticipating that the auction would raise at least five hundred thousand dollars for the Hart campaign, Campbell produced a beautiful buckle design known as the Band of Eagles. Hart's buckle was made of eighteen-karat gold; the other fifty were sterling silver. Unfortunately, just as Campbell completed the group, Hart's campaign collapsed as a result of the infamous *Monkey Business* affair.

"We gave him fifty-one belt buckles and he still couldn't keep his pants on," quipped Carol Knight in what she thought was a private conversation. The quip, to her dismay, immediately found its way into *Newsweek,* making a sad episode even sadder. "I never meant that comment to become public; I didn't want to embarrass Hart. Then I became afraid that I would lose my job over it. The last thing Campbell needed," she says, "was to have a smarty-pants aide making such a flippant remark. It only goes to show that the walls do have ears."

Campbell can laugh about the buckles now, but that is about the only thing he can find humorous. "I was disappointed with the whole Hart situation," he admits. "I think he was a loser for his indiscretions, but the whole country was a loser—we lost the best candidate."

The buckles were not a total loss, however. Campbell donated the original buckle and its mold to the Colorado Historical Society. The rest went to Hart's presidential committee to help defray his campaign debts.

Evidently getting burned once was not enough for Campbell. As soon as Hart withdrew from the race, he announced his support for Tennessee Senator Albert Gore, a moderate whose father had also been a U.S. senator. Unfortunately for Campbell, however, Gore quickly met the same fate as the other "moderates" in the Democratic primaries and withdrew, leaving the field to Dukakis. This prompted a reporter to ask Campbell if he had any other endorsements to announce. "Yes," he snapped. "I am now working on a plot to stop the Republicans by endorsing George Bush for president."

In some respects Campbell's second and third terms seemed almost anticlimactic compared to his first. His bills, for one thing, were less successful, prompting John Andrews, director of the conservative Independence Institute in Golden, Colorado, to describe Ben as a "lackluster legislator."

He was by no means idle, however. Instead, the years were absorbed by committee work, speechmaking, and an increased role in national American Indian affairs. During his second term he sponsored six economic development seminars, five congressional hearings, and twenty-five town meetings in his district. Campbell retained his assignments on the Interior and Agriculture committees, dropping Small Business but picking up a seat on Interior's National Parks and Public Lands Subcommittee. In addition, he became active in a number of congressional caucuses. He joined the Arts Caucus, the Steel Caucus, the Beef Caucus, the Competitive Caucus, the Hispanic Caucus, and—he jokes—"I was the only congressman west of Texas invited to become a member of the steering committee for the Conservative Democratic Forum, which, in the old days, was called the Boll Weevil Caucus."

Campbell also found time to form a new caucus—for the U.S. Olympic team. As he started his second term, he concluded that the team did not enjoy the stature in Washington that it should, so he took it upon himself to rectify the situation. With him on Capitol Hill at the time were two other former Olympians, both of whom had been basketball players: Senator Bill Bradley of New Jersey and Representative Tom McMillen of Maryland. At Campbell's request, they agreed to be cosponsors of a fledgling Congressional Olympic Caucus whose goal was to raise awareness and support for the U.S. Olympic team. All told, about fifty congressmen and senators joined as charter members and helped sponsor a number of "Meet your Olympic athlete" receptions in Washington.

Campbell also spent considerable effort on environmental issues. He prepared legislation to upgrade the Black Canyon National Monument near Montrose to the Black Canyon National Park, and he tried to find a compromise between Colorado's senators on a new wilderness bill for the state. In his first term, Campbell had put together a committee in Montrose to work on changing the status of Black Canyon. Then, after three years of rather intense negotiation, Campbell was able to introduce a bill that would have renamed the monument while preserving an area for multiple use to be administered by the Bureau of Land Management. Unfortunately, Campbell ran out of time as the 101st Congress came to a close, so he had to reintroduce the bill at the start of the 102d.

Less satisfactory was the resolution of the wilderness question, as diametrically opposed special interest groups, none of which represented the needs of the majority of people in Colorado, virtually flogged the two Colorado senators. At one extreme was the Sierra Club, which demanded that the legislation mandate a wilderness area of more than 1.5 million acres, with water rights reserved to the federal government. At the other extreme was the Farm Bureau—and its allies—which did not want any more land at all to be designated as wilderness. Failing that, the Farm

Bureau insisted on explicit language denying a federal water rights reserve.

After months of effort on behalf of the more moderate people in Colorado, Campbell and his staff put together a compromise proposal that offered a means for getting both senators to the bargaining table. The proposal, as expected, met with resistance from both extremes: the agricultural groups said it went too far; the environmental groups complained it did not go far enough. Campbell, determined to resolve the dispute, introduced his own Colorado wilderness bill at the beginning of the 102d Congress in 1991. It intentionally left the question of water rights neutral, since Campbell believed that the courts could best determine the question. But the bill stalled, a victim of opposition by Miller, who had replaced Udall as chairman of the Interior Committee. Miller would not support it without the federal water rights reserve.

Meanwhile, Campbell's career almost took another turn, when Colorado Senator Bill Armstrong announced in 1989 that he would not seek reelection in 1990. At the urging of party leaders and close friends, Campbell formed an exploratory committee to determine his prospects should he seek that seat, even though he still felt uneasy about making such a long-term political commitment. Two Republicans were considering a run for Armstrong's seat. One was Congressman Hank Brown from Greeley; the other was State Senator Terry Considine, who had aimed for the Republican nomination in the 1986 Senate race but missed. In conducting a statewide poll, Campbell was delighted to find himself well ahead of all other potential candidates. In fact, the poll showed that in a head-to-head race, he would be nine points ahead of Brown, the Republican front-runner at the time. "As a result of the poll," Campbell declares, "I was confident that I could win if I could get through my own party as a moderate."

But this was not to be. Since his first political race in 1980, Campbell had vowed to avoid primaries if he could. "In fact, I was once accused by a Democrat of not supporting democracy, because of my stand against primaries. The people who want primaries, however, are usually the ones who have never run for office themselves." Although most of the other

Democratic hopefuls interested in running for the seat graciously withdrew in favor of Campbell, former chairman of the Colorado Democratic party Buie Sewell saw no reason to stifle his political dreams. Having served as party chairman for four years, Sewell had a statewide network already in place and was determined to make a primary race of it even though a party poll indicated that Democratic leaders favored Campbell in a two-way race. To further complicate matters for the Democrats, Considine had dropped out of the race and gave Brown his support, thereby enabling the Republicans to unite and avoid a primary.

Meanwhile, as Campbell made his way around the state seeking support, he met with the same response from virtually all the leading Democrats. "We know Buie can't win," they said, "but we owe him for all the work he has done for the party and we can't ask him to stay out of the race." In more than a decade neither party had won an election in Colorado when it had first had to undergo a primary race and the other party did not. Since Sewell clearly was not going to move aside, Campbell saw it as a no-win situation for the Democrats unless he dropped out.

As soon as he did so, however, two other Democrats promptly entered the race making it a three-way primary, thereby sealing the party's fate. "All Democratic primaries are brutal," Campbell says, "and this one was no exception." By the time Sewell and his rivals had finished highlighting each other's negative qualities while depleting their finances, it was clear to virtually everyone that Campbell had been right. "The race was for the Democrats to lose, and lose they certainly did. To this day, I know in my heart that I could have won that election had the Democrats come together at the beginning."

Campbell, meanwhile, had entered his name as a candidate for his third term in the United States Congress. Since it was well known that he had been looking at the Senate race, several good Republicans gave thought to running for his House seat. One was his good friend Scott McInnis of Glenwood Springs. Another was Mike Strang. Once Campbell announced his intentions of seeking reelection, however, the field promptly changed. Strang chose to run for governor instead but failed even to get his name on the ballot; McInnis ran for majority leader of the

Colorado House of Representatives and won, then came roaring back to take the seat in 1992 when Campbell gave it up for the Senate.

Nonetheless, Campbell did not get a free ride to a third term. Two other Republican challengers surfaced, and Robert Ellis, an accountant from Montrose, finally made it to the ballot. "That race," Campbell claims, "was by far the meanest one I'd ever been in. Ellis didn't just distort facts, he invented them. He built his whole campaign around misrepresentation and outright lies." Much of the Ellis campaign rhetoric concerned his background as a CPA, which would supposedly help him balance the budget. Ellis, however, self-destructed when the press found out that he had failed to pay his property tax. The result was another landslide victory for Campbell, whose 70 percent win was again the widest margin of congressional races in the state.

Because of his success at the polls and his moderate voting record, the Republicans continued their blandishments for him to switch parties. "It's a running game between the Republicans and me," laughs Campbell. "They tease me because my voting record runs pretty moderate to conservative. They tell me I'm in the wrong party and we kid a lot about it, but there is no question in my mind that if I showed any serious interest, they would come after me in a hurry. I've had them tell me they would raise the money to repay any campaign debt I incurred, they would make sure that there would be no primary, they would clear the field for me."

Both John Sununu and Colorado Republican Bo Callaway have made serious attempts to get Campbell to switch, pointing out to him that he would no longer have to contend with the left-wing liberals in the Democratic party who are so unhappy with his moderate voting record. "That means," Campbell responded, "that I would always be fighting with the John Birchers and the right-to-lifers and the screwball right-wingers. If I've got to fight anyway, why change just to change the guys I'd be up against?"

Furthermore, Campbell had been pretty unhappy with the Reagan administration. "From my perspective," Campbell declares, "it was the most corrupt of any that I ever heard of. Everything was based on greed, avarice, and self-serving actions." You need look no further, he says, than at the ambassadors Reagan appointed. "Most of them couldn't find their ass with both hands when they got to their posts, but because they raised a million bucks for the administration they were suddenly qualified to be ambassador to whatever country they wanted. They didn't know the culture. They didn't know the language. It was blatantly run! Blatantly run! Appointing diplomats on the basis of how much money they raised for your election rather than their credentials for the post, that's a bad mistake for America."

Maybe it's true, Campbell says, that the United States went too far to the left before Reagan got elected. "Maybe the country needed someone like him, a real right-wing, narrow-minded guy. But one thing I do know, Reagan is not a particularly smart man. When he gave a prepared speech, he never missed a line, but at his impromptu press conferences he would step all over his tongue. I met Reagan on several occasions and was constantly aware of how uninformed he was without constant prodding from his aides. He didn't have a clue what was going on a lot of the time. I mean, here's a guy who once said that trees cause pollution, for Christ's sake. But give him the lines, give him the cue cards, then he has a masterful delivery. He was a packaging dream for the guys who sell commodities like toothpaste. In fact," Campbell claims, "I've often compared him to toothpaste. You can read the ads about it, but you really don't know what the hell is in the tube. That was President Reagan to me—a terrific image that was just glued to the outside of a toothpaste tube."

As if this were not bad enough, Campbell thinks Reagan hated Congress. Perhaps because he had never served in the Congress, he could not understand it. Whatever the explanation, says Campbell, "he used every opportunity in the most partisan fashion to blame virtually every bad thing that happened to our country on the Democrats. He spent so much of his time criticizing Congress it was only natural that, civilities aside, most of us did not work well with him."

Campbell also found Reagan's attitude toward minorities, particularly Indians, very offensive. This was reflected in many ways, but the one that sticks with Campbell resulted from a visit to Reagan's former office in the California capitol building shortly after Jerry Brown was elected governor. Brown wanted to do a series of ethnic art exhibits using the space in the governor's suite as the gallery. Indians mounted the first show because, Campbell believes, "Jerry loves Indians." As one of the participating artists, Campbell met with Brown, and his visit to the governor's suite was a real eye-opener. "I'll never forget it," he insists. "Reagan had not yet cleaned out the office except for his desk. In one of the little hallways between two rooms I noticed some old brown and white, sepia-toned, *Police Gazette*–type photographs. The pictures, which dated to 1890 or so, were of Indians being brutalized in one way or another—hanged, flogged, dragged around, and so on." As Campbell stared at the photographs, his mouth agape, Brown walked up to him and said, "That's Reagan's idea of Indian art."

It took a while, but Campbell eventually got an opportunity of sorts to call Reagan to task for his anti-Indian conceits. The occasion came after the U.S.-Soviet summit in May 1988 when Russian college students questioned Reagan about American Indian policy and he made a number of gross misstatements, among them the suggestion that the United States had "humored" Indians by giving them millions of acres of land for "preservations." His obvious ignorance of the facts infuriated Indians across the nation. Campbell relished the opportunity to provide the news media with his opinions on the subject. "I only wish the president knew as much about American Indians as he seems to know about the Russians," he told Associated Press writer Guy Darst. "It's incredible he knows so little. . . . He must have been learning [his history] from those old celluloid Westerns he used to act in."

President George Bush, Campbell insists, was as different as night and day from President Reagan. "I found Bush to be knowledgeable, friendly, and concerned about the issues. There was no question about his patriotism and commitment to what was right from his perspective. At least he was trying to be the best he could, but he had some right-wingers to contend with and some of those guys control the electoral process in the Republican party. He had to listen."

During his three terms in Congress, Campbell had to make hard decisions, but none was more difficult than his vote for Operation Desert Storm. "Congress," he says, "had passed several resolutions in support of the president and condemning Iraq, but to vote for actual conflict—putting American lives in jeopardy—was a much more difficult decision than I had ever before made. During the last few days before the vote, in fact, congressional telephone lines were literally burning up with calls from war protesters. In my offices alone, in the days preceding the vote we had 1,630 telephone calls against giving the president that authority and only 93 in favor. Although it appeared my constituents were against conflict, after a number of sleepless nights I decided to go against the flow and stand up for what I believed, even if it cost me a future election, which is exactly what most opponents of the so-called Solarz resolution threatened would happen to me. I voted my conscience, though, and never looked back. Interestingly enough, during town meetings which I held throughout my district during the month following that vote, the so-called silent majority did come forward and in fact did support my decision. I breathed a sigh of relief."

Dan Griswold, reporting on the 1992 Senate campaign in Colorado for the conservative *National Review,* described Ben as "an answer-the-mail and bring-home-the-bacon sort of guy." Rating the congressman as less liberal than Wirth, he nevertheless predicted Campbell would shift to the left once he represented the larger statewide constituency that included the urban areas of Boulder and Denver.

NINE

CUSTER, COLUMBUS, AND CAMPBELL

Ben Nighthorse Campbell occupied a unique niche in the U.S. Congress. As the representative from the Third District of Colorado, the state's enormous Western Slope, he was responsible for the needs and interests of a widespread and diverse constituency, few of whom were Indians. As the only American Indian in Congress, he also found himself, de facto, the representative of all Indians throughout the United States. Indians are among the most active lobbyists in our nation, and they quickly made Campbell their own. Few Indian leaders left Washington without stopping by Campbell's suite in the Longworth House Office Building at the corner of New Jersey and Independence avenues to pay their respects, tell him their troubles, or simply shake his hand, so they could return home and tell their constituents what "their" man in Washington had to say about per capita payments, Indian education, water rights, and the hundred-and-one issues that dominate Indian life today.

Campbell, of course, was not "their" congressman, but this mattered little to the Indians who came to him with problems. To them ethnicity transcends legal boundaries. Campbell is "one of the People," and they believed he would do for them what he could. They believed it, and he did it. When Clayton Lonestar, an Oneida Marine at the American Embassy in Moscow, was charged with dereliction of duty and espionage for certain high-jinks, his mother turned to Campbell for help and got it when other federal offices turned a deaf ear.

As a result of his strong feelings for Indian peoples, regardless of their tribal affiliation, Campbell did in fact do a considerable amount of work on their behalf. He carried their water, so to speak. When once questioned about this vis-à-vis his own constituents—"Don't they resent all the attention you pay to Indians outside of Colorado?"—Campbell simply shrugged his shoulders. "I'm pretty good at doing it quietly. My name doesn't get publicly associated with some of the things I am responsible for. One thing about the Congress, we all help each other. I can approach one of my friends to introduce a piece of legislation, which I can then cosponsor. No one can fault me for that," he smiles. "Besides, I plan to be out of office after my next term, and then it won't matter anymore what I did for Indians."

During his second term, for example, Campbell worked actively with Senator Daniel Inouye of Hawaii to enact legislation to build a Museum of the American Indian on the Mall in Washington, D.C., as part of the Smithsonian Institution. It was Inouye who spearheaded the drive to move the two-million-item Heye collection of American Indian artifacts from New York to Washington, but it took considerable behind-the-scenes activity, much of it by Campbell's staff, to ensure passage. "It took a lot of stroking of very large egos to get all the pieces in place," he says with obvious satisfaction regarding what he calls his "pride and joy" as a congressman. "Pablita Abeyta and Frank Ducheneaux of the Interior Committee staff, Kimberly Craven and Lisa Spurlock of my staff all did a terrific job of networking with other staffs. We also had to do some intense negotiating with the Congressional Black Caucus." The site, adjacent to the National Air and Space Museum, was the last unoccupied space on the Mall, and any building placed there would be the closest museum to the Capitol itself. "The Black Caucus for a number of years had looked at that piece of ground for a museum of American slavery. But we did talk them out of it and promised to support them in finding some other location if we could have that one for the Museum of the American Indian." The bill actually dealt with three buildings, the museum on the Mall, the renovation of the United States Custom House in New York City, and a restoration and research facility to be built in Virginia. The total cost was estimated at about $350 million.

But then again, Campbell wasn't called upon every time. "Russell Means wanted Congress to get guns to the Mesquite Indians of South America, but he didn't ask me specifically to help, and I'm glad he didn't because if he had, I would have said no. I don't want to be involved in some kind of doggone international incident."

Although Campbell has been sympathetic to the goals of the American Indian Movement, he has kept his distance from its activities. "I did help save Dennis Banks's ass once," Campbell continued. "He was under indictment in South Dakota, and he took off and ran to California, and the FBI asked Governor Jerry Brown to extradite him. At the time I was on the board of D-Q University, a little Indian-Hispanic college in Davis, California. That was the second place AIM took over after occupying Alcatraz Island in 1969."

The campus had been a military base, shut down but still owned by the federal government. "After the AIM guys left Alcatraz, they took it over in pretty much the same way, just defended it and hung on. The government got so much bad publicity out of Alcatraz that they didn't want the press there watching them shooting these Indians down or dragging them out. The Indians wanted the base for a school because it had dorms and kitchens and classrooms and all that. They worked out a long-term agreement that if they formed a school and ran it over a period of years, they would transfer title. And they do have it now. I was one of the original board members, there at the request of Dave Risling, who was a professor at the University of California Davis and also the president of D-Q U.

"Jerry Brown said he could turn down the extradition request on one condition, that Banks had a productive job. We gave him a job of teaching at D-Q U; then he could say that he had a steady source of income. So Brown refused to sign the extradition papers.

"I believe everybody has his own way of making change. Banks had his way and so did Russell Means, but it wasn't my way. I didn't condemn them in the early stages. The original concepts of AIM were to get rid of the booze, get rid of the alcohol, go back to a clean lifestyle, go back to traditional living, go back to cultural values, and those things are great. I agree with them all. The problem was, once the cameras started rolling and the news media started showing up, AIM began to attract a lot of what I call camp followers who were trash, just trash, and some of them weren't even Indians. They were the worst offenders in drug abuse, alcoholism, bullies, fighters, thieving rats, some of them. And it seemed like every one of the leaders of AIM—and there were four or five big leaders—each one developed his own little warrior following. The original principles of AIM started to suffer, and so I didn't have much to do with it. My way was to try to make change in the art world. I get along with Russell Means, but we're not in touch. I don't call him, and he doesn't call me. We see each other at things and we talk, but I've never donated money.

"Still, AIM said 'Enough is enough' and you can't really condemn Russell Means for that unless you're also willing to condemn Cesar Chavez and Martin Luther King and the guys that went into the restaurants and got on the buses and wouldn't sit in the back. The founders of this country said 'We've got to fight back.' But violence isn't my way."

Campbell is proud of the fact that in 1988 he was named as a Colorado delegate to the Democratic National Convention in Atlanta. "During that convention," he recalls, "we had a total of fifty-one Indian delegates from all over the United States, and we formed the first Democratic American Indian Caucus as an official entity of the Democratic party. The majority of Native Americans are registered as Democrats if they are registered at all, so we followed the lead of the Hispanic Democrats and the black Democrats, who had organized years before within the party. Our first chairman was Frank LeMare, a bright young Indian from Nebraska."

The highlight for Campbell was being asked to address the convention on behalf of American Indians. "While I was speaking," he says proudly, "all fifty of my Indian brothers and sisters stood before the podium wearing their traditional Indian dress to lend me moral support."

In a political sense, for Campbell this convention address was a step out from behind the scenes in national Indian affairs. Before then he had been rather circumspect with regard to advocating Indian causes, but thereafter he became increasingly public and vocal as an Indian champion. In 1991 the congressman found himself at center stage of two very noisy pieces of political theater. Indeed, the spotlight could not have been brighter than for Campbell's performance as co–grand marshal and the

Indian "counterpoint" for the Tournament of Roses on New Year's Day in 1992, the quincentennial anniversary year of Columbus's arrival in the Americas, with Cristóbal Colón, a direct descendant of Christopher Columbus. Lest anyone fail to recognize him, Campbell rode at the head of the parade on Black Warbonnet, his splendid black and white paint, in full tribal regalia of beaded buckskins and an eagle-feather headdress with two trailers.

Less visible but no less laden with symbolism was Campbell's role in the controversy surrounding the site of the famous battle of the Little Bighorn, arguably the most well known yet least understood engagement in the four centuries of struggle between red man and white man for control of North America. Here Campbell challenged the ghost of General Custer as well as active and vocal Seventh Cavalry "would-have-beens and wannabes" who still cherish the romantic imagery of "Custer's Last Stand." Emulating the exploits of Black Horse, his Cheyenne forebear, Campbell counted coup on each opponent who stood between him and final victory. Thanks largely to his efforts, the Congress changed the name of the site from Custer National Battlefield Monument to Little Bighorn National Battlefield Monument and authorized a memorial to the Indians who fought there as well.

The fascination with the battle of the Little Bighorn is not difficult to understand, even though it is remembered most for the person who lost it. Lieutenant Colonel George Armstrong Custer, a hero of the Civil War, hoped to use a major victory over the last free-roaming bands of Sioux, Cheyenne, and Arapaho Indians as a catapult to the presidency but, instead, gained immortality by getting himself and some 265 soldiers and civilians killed. This catastrophe happened in our nation's centennial year. While at one end of the country Americans were thumping their chests over the rise of the United States as a world power, at the other end another group of Americans were thumping one of the most efficient and glamorous military units ever fielded by the United States. The impact on the public of the loss of the colorful Custer brothers—Tom Custer won two Congressional Medals of Honor during the Civil War—is probably best likened to the Kennedy assassinations a century later.

Justification can be found for both sides in that awful encounter, which took place on a hot afternoon in June along the banks of the Little Bighorn River in the southeastern corner of present-day Montana. Custer and the soldiers who fell with him were following orders and died in the service of their country. They were not policy makers, they were policy enforcers. Custer himself considered the handling of the nation's Indian affairs misguided and corrupt.

Arrayed against the Seventh Cavalry were the followers of Sitting Bull, Crazy Horse, Lame White Man, Gall, Two Moon, and a score of other Sioux, Cheyenne, and Arapaho leaders who happened to be camped there that day and who were guilty of nothing more than a refusal to step aside so that the Manifest Destiny—they would have called it Manifest Greed—of an impatient United States could continue to unfold in an orderly and systematic fashion. The Indians did what anyone would do when attacked without warning and without provocation. They defended themselves. They fought to protect their families and their way of life. Their stunning victory, ironically, was also their undoing, because the armies of the United States wreaked swift and brutal vengeance. Before another year had passed, most of the Indians camped on the Little Bighorn that fateful day were either dead, confined to reservations, or in exile with Sitting Bull in Canada, where a handful of followers remained with the Sioux patriot until 1883, when they, too, finally acceded to a way of life they neither wanted nor understood.

Viewed in that light, the Little Bighorn battlefield deserved to represent something far bigger, more symbolic, than a needless skirmish no different than the hundreds of other fields that mark the bloody transition of ownership of the North American continent. A battlefield can become a place of healing, but instead of adopting the successful models offered by Gettysburg and a score of other Civil War sites that honor both the blue and gray combatants who died on them, the United States chose to make the Little Bighorn battlefield a memorial to the fallen of only one side. The U.S. Army designated the site a national cemetery in 1879, three years after the battle, but did not transfer it to the Park Service until 1940. The ultimate indignity to the Indian victors occurred in 1946, when the government named it the Custer Battlefield National Monument, thereby making it the only federally administered military battlefield in the United States named for an individual, and the loser of the battle at that. Little wonder then that the battlefield and what it stood for became a source of increasing bitterness and frustration to Indian peoples throughout the nation.

The idea for an Indian marker at the site first surfaced in July 1925 during the planning for the fiftieth anniversary commemoration, when surviving Indian participants and members of the Seventh Cavalry were brought together at the battlefield for several days of fellowship and reconciliation. The suggestion came from Mrs. Thomas Beaverheart, a Cheyenne woman whose father had died in the fighting. "My father . . . was a Cheyenne chief," she wrote, "and there are two men living who know where he fell and where he was buried. We would be glad if you could help us get the places marked, so that the place might be remembered on the next anniversary." The Army ignored her request, and nothing more was done about acknowledging Indian participation until the Park Service in 1958 authorized the placing of a wooden marker to denote the spot where Lame White Man, a Cheyenne chief, died in the closing moments of the fight as he led a charge against the handful of soldiers clustered with Custer at the top of Last Stand Hill.

Despite widespread Indian resentment and cynicism about being overlooked at the site of their best-known triumph over the U.S. Cavalry, few did more than grouse and grumble among themselves or remark with typically Indian sarcasm: "We don't need our own memorial; each of those white tombstones is a monument to our people."

Indian passivity about the issue, however, changed in the 1960s as the Custer battlefield got caught up in Red Power activism. In seeking sites and issues that could capture media attention, members of the American Indian Movement, led by Russell Means, found the Custer battlefield an ideal place to draw attention to Indian grievances. Three times—in 1972, 1976, and 1982—Means attempted without success to install a plaque at the battlefield before he finally prevailed on June 25, 1988, the 112th anniversary. The plaque, now on display in the park's visitors' center, is a steel plate roughly three feet square, with the following message inscribed with a welding rod:

> IN HONOR OF OUR INDIAN
> PATRIOTS WHO FOUGHT AND
> DEFEATED THE U.S. CAVALRY
> IN ORDER TO SAVE OUR
> WOMEN AND CHILDREN
> FROM MASS-MURDER, IN
> DOING SO, PRESERVING RIGHTS
> OF OUR HOMELANDS, TREATIES
> AND SOVEREIGNTY. 6/25/1988.
>> G. MAGPIE
>> CHEYENNE

Means succeeded on his fourth attempt largely because park officials wanted to avoid an ugly confrontation. With most of the staff and park visitors sympathetic to the idea of a suitable memorial to the Indians who had fought at the Little Bighorn, it seemed unwise to provoke an incident by trying to prevent Means and his followers from conducting their peaceful demonstration. As a result, the staff and curious visitors watched in respectful silence as Means and about 150 companions including Austin Two Moons, who had conducted a sunrise prayer service at his ranch near Busby and then led the group in a prayer for world peace on a slope near Last Stand Hill, proceeded to place the plaque in a bed of fresh cement at the foot of the monument over the mass grave containing the bones of Custer's troopers. As several men dug the hole for the plaque, Means, pointing to the monument, addressed the onlookers. "We are told we are citizens of the United States and that we're treated like the rest of the citizens, but these men came to kill our women and children. Can you imagine a monument listing the names of the S.S., of the Nazi officers, being erected in Jerusalem? A Hitler National Monument?"

No matter that such a plaque was long overdue or that the park authorities had exercised considerable wisdom in letting events proceed peacefully, official reaction was quick and unsympathetic. Park superintendent Dennis Ditmanson, for one, lost his job as a direct result. "It was pretty obvious a monument would be placed today," he admitted in an interview published in the *Billings Gazette*, "but I didn't . . . know where they were going to put it until they went over with shovels and started turning the soil. We weighed the alternatives and decided to take the course we took."

Leading the outcry against Ditmanson and the Park Service was William Wells, a member of the board of both the nonprofit Custer Battlefield Historical and Museum Association and the Little Big Horn Associates, whose goal is to promote the memory of Custer and the Seventh Cavalry. Wells, a witness to the event, described it as "a sad and disgusting sight" and dismissed the Indian participants as "a group of thugs." Writing to William Penn Mott, director of the National Park Service—with copies to various senators and Custer organizations— Wells threatened, blustered, and demanded: "Have that silly steel plate removed immediately, prosecute to the fullest extent those who violated the law and restore some respect for the National Park Service in the eyes of those who have concern about the Battlefield and the preservation of the law. There should be no ifs, ands, or buts. There are no gray areas, no variables and no mitigating circumstances. I was there—I saw it and heard it. If you want a witness for the prosecution, I'm your man. As many hearings as it takes—I'll be there."

As a result of such indignation, perhaps even inspired by it—Wells himself suggested that "if a legitimate, responsible group representing Indian Americans wants to place an unbiased and historically correct monument to their forebears who fought and died at the Little Bighorn, it is my feeling that they should get all the help they need, including full government funding"—the Park Service at last stirred itself to action on the issue of an Indian memorial. Little, however, did Wells and his colleagues imagine that their vitriolic attacks on the superintendent and the National Park Service would be just one gust in a gale of change that would alter the status of the Custer battlefield, namely to take it out of the hands of the military historians who had traditionally managed it and

265

to change its name, as well as to erect the monument Indian activists had long demanded.

The process of change began innocently enough with Ditmanson's official report. "Since the event," he wrote, "we have been informally monitoring visitor reaction. Not surprisingly, there is almost universal support for an Indian monument and, in fact, surprise that such did not already exist." The visitors, however, were also unanimous in their desire to see something more appropriate—artistically as well as linguistically—erected to honor the Indian participants. "These findings reinforce our view that you cannot honor one people by dishonoring another," wrote Ditmanson, who urged the following course of action: remove the plaque and display it in the visitors' center with an appropriate label detailing the circumstances surrounding its creation and at the same time organize an independent panel of spiritual and political leaders representing the tribes that fought at the Little Bighorn and charge it with designing a memorial that would be placed on the battlefield in the summer of 1990, the fiftieth anniversary of National Park Service administration of the national monument. Hoping to make his suggestion even more attractive, Ditmanson added: "U.S. Congressman Ben Nighthorse Campbell has already indicated an interest in this process and may be willing to head the group."

Campbell, in fact, relished the opportunity. If truth be known, he fully supported Means and his associates in the plaque laying and helped plan the event. George Magpie, the person who made the plaque, was—with Campbell—a member of the Council of Forty-four Chiefs, leaders of the Northern Cheyenne; Austin Two Moons was their spiritual adviser. Inviting Campbell to head the panel was much like giving the fox the key to the henhouse.

Campbell, in turn, soon had a willing and strategic ally in the person of Barbara Booher, the superintendent who replaced Ditmanson in June 1989. Booher—attractive, dignified, articulate, and Indian (part Cherokee and part Ute) to boot—had been with the Interior Department in Alaska for seventeen years before her selection as battlefield superintendent. Nonetheless, her appointment triggered a torrent of protest, most of it from Custer buffs who challenged her fitness for the position. "I think Barbara was selected for all the wrong reasons, because she is a woman and an Indian," charged Wells, who continued to monitor activities at the battlefield park seemingly on a daily basis. "I don't think she was qualified, and she was ill prepared. I think she is way in over her head," he insisted to a reporter with the Associated Press at the time of her appointment.

Indian leaders, on the other hand, were delighted with her appointment. "Barbara's a breath of fresh air," remarked Janine Pease Windy Boy, president of the Little Big Horn Community College at Crow Agency, which adjoins the battlefield park. "There's nothing more symbolic than an Indian and a woman to upset these so-called historians, who are mostly white and male."

Fortunately, Booher had Campbell in her corner. "I keep reminding the folks at the Interior Department of what a good job she's doing every time I see them. Those Custer buffs haven't got a chance of getting her removed as long as I'm still in office," he vowed. "She's also tough as nails. She's not the naive country girl they think she is, not by a long shot. She's got a red-hot black Porsche 944 that blows the minds out of most of the rednecked white cowboys around here. What a bomb that is! She likes to take it out at night and race around when nobody's looking. She's a real nighthorse herself."

Getting the necessary legislation passed proved much more challenging than anticipated, although it appeared simple at first. Campbell persuaded Republican Ron Marlenee of Montana, whose district included the battlefield, to introduce a bill in the 101st Congress authorizing an Indian memorial on the battlefield. There was no opposition to the bill, and it seemed headed for a quick and easy passage when, in the closing days of the term, Pat Williams, the other Montana representative, attached a rider that called for changing the name of the battlefield. Marlenee argued that he could not support a name change without public hearings in Montana, and the bill died.

Although Marlenee reintroduced his bill in the 102d Congress, Campbell offered two measures of his own, one calling for a memorial and the other calling for a name change. After all, a number of Indians informed Campbell, it was only right. Said Barney Old Coyote, a Crow elder: "Why should the battlefield be named for a military officer who spent only two days there, when Indians who had lived there for generations called it the Greasy Grass?" His sentiment was echoed by Bill Tall Bull, a seventy-year-old Cheyenne whose grandfather had fought at the Little Bighorn. "When you come into Montana from Wyoming," he declared, "there is a sign that says you are entering Custer Country. I want to see the sign say, 'You are entering Indian Country.' Custer isn't around anymore."

Campbell certainly liked the idea. Furthermore, as precedent he could credit Custer's wife, Elizabeth, affectionately known as Libby, perhaps the one person most responsible for creating the Custer cult. Libby had spent the rest of her long and productive life—she did not die until 1938 at the age of ninety-five—in promoting the memory of her handsome, dashing cavalier. Yet even Libby, who lost five relatives at the Little Bighorn, including her husband and two brothers-in-law, never called it the Custer Battlefield, a fact that elated Campbell when he learned it. "That's wonderful," he chortled. "She called it the Little Big Horn Battlefield herself. That's what we can call it, too, and we can say we are doing it in her memory."

For Campbell's bills, however, things were a little different this time around. Even the idea of a memorial to the Indians was considered offensive to some. Rush Limbaugh, the conservative radio talk show host, for instance, likened the idea to erecting a monument to the Japanese pilots who died at Pearl Harbor. Others were willing to concede the propriety of an Indian memorial but wanted it erected at some remote distance from Last Stand Hill. The preferred site was the valley below the main battlefield where the Indians were camped when Custer attacked and, not surprisingly, on land still in private hands. "This site," wrote one advocate, "would provide excellent employment opportunities for Native Americans, both locally and nationwide. Actual tepees and historic displays, living history demonstrations and crafts could [also] be a part of the encampment's program . . . [and] Superintendents, like Barbara

Booher, would find themselves content in an environment where they would not be trying to fit a square peg in a round hole." But, he continued, if the Indians were "just rattling sabers or ancient coup sticks [and were] . . . not serious, then my sympathies [for the memorial] will end with this letter."

Still others voiced concern about the impact the name change would have on tourism, not just at the battlefield but even in Custer's hometown, Monroe, Michigan, the lakeside industrial community where he met and married Libby. City fathers there appealed to Congress to preserve the Custer memory by not changing the name of the distant battlefield: "There is that fear," they wrote, "that Monroe's prominence in the history books will diminish because the Custer name on that battlefield will diminish."

Michigan Representative John D. Dingell agreed. "While I understand the reasons behind the legislation to establish a memorial at the Park to honor Native Americans," he wrote on May 29, 1991, ". . . I fail to see any logical reason for altering a name which is so deeply imbedded in our National consciousness for 110 years." In this request, Dingell was supported by Colonel George A. Custer III, the great-grandnephew of his namesake, who had returned to Monroe to help with the fight.

The very evening, however, after meeting with Dingell to discuss the strategy for blocking the name change, George Custer III died suddenly and unexpectedly. Custer had been one of the most vehement opponents of the name change and, in fact, had argued about it with Campbell on several occasions. Although his opposition had not worried Campbell, his death nonetheless removed an obstacle just a few days before a round of scheduled hearings on the subject. "Some people, in fact, might even see an omen, in the Indian sense, that he passed away at just this time," Campbell suggested upon hearing the news.

Campbell could understand and sympathize with the members of the Custer family who opposed the name change, but he had little patience with those who feared its impact on tourism. "I have two comments to that," he told a gathering of staff and faculty at the Little Big Horn Community College in May 1991. "First of all, the National Park Service says it won't hurt tourism. They've done a study which says, if anything, it will increase tourism." But the more important issue, Campbell told his Crow listeners, is the dignity of a race of people. "Should immediate profits be more important than that? Some people tell me that the monument and name change are not important because they're only symbolic and that we should be doing more for child nutrition or education. The fact is," declared Campbell, "symbolism is important. The American flag is important to millions of people; so is the Statue of Liberty. The monument we're going to build over there is going to be the Indian Statue of Liberty."

Although media reports made it appear that opposition to the legislation was widespread, the fact is opposition came from a very small though vocal minority. Barbara Booher, for instance, eventually received more than six hundred letters concerning the name change but no more than a dozen against it; three came from the same person. Nor were all those opposed passionate about the issue. For example, one local rancher, whose grandfather had been a homesteader near the battlefield in the late nineteenth century, had no real reason for opposing the name change other than nostalgia. "I've been going by here and visiting for sixty years," he wrote. "Sure would like to see it stay somewhat the same."

Typical of the letters in support was one from a woman in Christchurch, England, to a Custer descendant. "It is," she wrote, "my belief that General Custer would have raised objections to naming a sacred part of Indian territory after him, because of his deep belief in the basic rights of the indigenous people of the interior, the Sioux and Cheyenne." Furthermore, "it was the only major victory of an increasingly oppressed people and a monument to the Indian nations would not demean the name of Custer. Should you compromise on this issue Old Yellow Hair would have the last laugh on the corrupt officials who sent him to his defeat."

Nonetheless, the opposition was strong enough to jeopardize passage of the legislation, a fact that caused Campbell more than his share of anxious moments during the first session of the 102d Congress. "This says something about America," he grumbled at a critical moment.

"Look at the history of this country. Very little social change has ever come about without violence occurring first. You can try to do it peacefully and by golly, that's what you're up against. You've got to get somebody's throat to get their attention. The blacks found that out a hell of a long time ago. Indians, of course, got beat down so bad a hundred years ago, they don't understand that they now have political power. Although I don't condone the anger and the burn-it-down attitude," Campbell continued, "I know they focus attention on things. As long as you just keep talking, shit, nobody listens. They don't have to. No one starts listening until you start swinging. That's a weakness of our government. People in control will not change unless they're forced to. Our bill died in the House simply because Marlenee and Williams were at odds with each other. Now we got the damn thing past the House and it's killed in the Senate. Crazy, isn't it?"

Such laments were the norm for Campbell as he struggled to get his legislation through what became a Senate minefield. Invariably, as soon as an old hurdle was cleared a new one appeared. Having seen the bill finally sail through the House, he understandably felt confident that the same thing would happen in the Senate. After all, his problems the year before had all been with the House. Thus, when the bill came to an abrupt halt in the Senate, Campbell felt blindsided.

First to voice his opposition publicly was Senator Malcolm Wallop of Wyoming, the ranking Republican on the Energy and Natural Resources Committee. He demanded that the bill be referred to his committee for hearings. When pressed for an explanation, a Wallop aide told reporters, "The Senator said he doesn't see the need for Congress to run around renaming everything."

"Nonsense," retorted Campbell upon hearing this. "Congress doesn't run around renaming everything. It just renames the things that need to be renamed."

As soon as Campbell realized that his legislation was in trouble in the Senate, he took the offensive. "I'm going to go over and see all of them, every one of them," he announced. "I went over and saw Wirth yesterday, and I'm seeing Bradley tomorrow. I'm working on senators morning, noon, and night. Goddamn, they've got Custer County, they've got cemeteries, they've got museums, they've got high schools named after him. That's enough. Besides, we're going to leave the battlefield graveyard named after Custer so people will know where we planted him."

The only senator Campbell could not see was Wallop, who had opposed the legislation initially. When he could not reach him personally, Campbell decided the time had come to apply some outside pressure. Two people held keys to Wallop, he believed. One was Peg Coe, a wealthy and influential Wyoming Republican who had been a major benefactor of the Buffalo Bill Historical Center, the world-class museum in Cody. "She's the money, the brains, the guts, and the push behind that thing," Campbell declared, "and she is one of Wallop's biggest contributors. That lady's got power from beginning to end. She's quiet, and nice, and reserved. She's also very supportive of Indians. We had her give Wallop a call."

The other key was Wallop's Wyoming colleague in the Senate, Al Simpson—"a good friend and a good guy"—whom Campbell brought into his confidence. "Wallop has said that Russell Means will run the battlefield, if my legislation passes," Campbell told Simpson. "I don't know where he ever got that, but it's absolutely wrong. Russell Means isn't even going to be on the memorial commission. He's got a criminal record and the rules say that disqualifies you. He's going to have nothing to do with it," Campbell assured Simpson. "He can go there like any other American, and that's all. So, as a friend, will you talk to this guy for me, Al?"

"You bet I will," Simpson promised. "Your word is good enough for me, Ben. That's enough."

Campbell never learned which key opened the door, but shortly afterward one of Wallop's staff called over and said that the senator was not really against the legislation. True, he would still vote against it, but that would be the extent of his opposition. "We'll see," Campbell sighed. "My God, if they're smart, they wouldn't be against it in this day and age. But the simple fact is, forget about open public input and what's best—an awful lot of what happens around here has to do with who you can talk to, who knows you. Can you get somebody to talk to that guy, because you don't know him very well and if you go over there, it's just going to blow up. The best thing to do is to find an intermediary. Find someone you know, someone that person respects and likes. Maybe they've got a real close working relationship. Maybe they're good friends. Then you talk to this person. That's the way things are done on Capitol Hill. You get to somebody who can get to somebody. That's basically what it's all about."

Unfortunately for Campbell, Wallop proved to be but the first of many Senate headaches. Next in line as Custer defender of the day was Montana Senator Conrad "Jerry" Burns.

"Can you believe it?" Campbell growled upon hearing the news. "Senator Burns went the other way on the Custer bill. Now he won't support the name change. The Senate was supposed to vote this morning and he put a hold on the bill."

His explanation? "I've been getting a lot of calls from the Custer family," he told Campbell, who challenged him immediately.

"Wait a minute," Campbell retorted. "You mean the Custer family has got more input in the state of Montana than all the Indians who live there?"

"Well, some of the Chamber people are against it, too," Burns responded weakly. "They're afraid it will hurt business."

"This is not a dollar and cents issue. This is a human rights issue, Burns."

"Well, I just don't think I can support it. What would you think if we sent it back with just the monument and not the name change?"

"You'll kill the thing if you do that!"

Angry, disgusted, disheartened, Campbell gave up trying to reason with Burns. "You know what he's really saying, don't you? He's trying to cover both sides. He supports the monument without the name change. In other words, throw the Indians a bone. Give them something and satisfy those white rednecks, too. It's a damn shame. To me and to most Indians, the memorial and name change are linked."

273

When Campbell got only lukewarm encouragement from several Senate friends to whom he turned for help, he had a ready explanation: "They have a gentlemen's agreement in the Senate: I'll be a chicken-shit if you'll be a chicken-shit. That's the agreement. You know," he fumed, "I never saw such damn, gutless wonders as some of those senators. They won't stand up for anything. Some won't do anything if it makes somebody mad. That means any one of them can be an obstructionist and stop any bill. It also means that not one of them can make a bill go—because they're all reduced to the weakest link in a chain. Whoever says no stops everything."

Since the word patience is not in Campbell's vocabulary, he decided to strike back. "Besides calling a couple of senators I know, I also called around to the Montana tribes and asked them to raise hell with Burns. The Crows, the Cheyennes, everybody will be calling him." About all Campbell could hope for by this tactic was to make Burns uncomfortable, because the Indians could not really hurt him politically. "He knows they don't vote very much, so he can stick with the white rednecks and not have to worry about getting thrown out of office, and that," Campbell grumbled, "is the heart of the problem. It doesn't matter that the legislature supported it, that the governor did, that the county commissioner did. All it takes is two or three rednecks to oppose it to frighten you off a bill."

Scared or not, Burns would soon see the light, Campbell promised. "I've called Senator Baucus, his colleague from Montana, and I've called Bennett Johnston, the chairman of the Energy and Natural Resources Committee. He is supposed to call me this afternoon.

"It's a damn shame our country works this way. Americans overwhelmingly support what we're doing. The Park Service supports it. The administration supports it. It's only a few people who oppose this—those buffs who have built up a kind of Custer personality cult, the Custer family, and a few Chamber of Commerce groups worried about tourism. They're the ones writing letters to Burns. It's really discouraging that one family that doesn't even live in Montana can dictate the future of two million American Indians in terms of honor and respect."

Campbell did not blame Burns so much as the system. "It might seem amazing that a guy could back off when two or three rednecks light into him, but that's what happens in the Senate. That's why I didn't particularly feel like serving over there," Campbell claimed. "The more I learn about the Congress, the more I understand that we do have a House of Lords in this country—a house of gutless lords—and it's over there in the Senate. I really haven't been able to identify all that many senators who I think have demonstrated real courage. Wirth from Colorado is one. He went on the line for water projects and has taken some awful unpopular stands. Al Gore also has some real guts and so does Bill Bradley. He proved that with the introduction of that bill on the Black Hills. But too many of them over there can be scared off," complained an exasperated Campbell less than six months before changing his mind and deciding to run for the Senate himself.

After several anxious days, Campbell finally managed to get Burns to release the bill only to see another hold placed on it, this time by Ted Stevens, the prickly senator from Alaska. His opposition was short-lived, however. Campbell got to Stevens through Alaska Representative Don Young, whose wife is a Native Alaskan and who stressed to Stevens the bill's symbolic importance to native peoples throughout the nation.

Still the bill went nowhere because, it turned out, yet another senator had stepped forward to block it. By now Campbell was at his wits' end. "The darned thing is still deadlocked," he groused late in the afternoon on October 15. "We still haven't got it broken loose. We might not until next spring. I just don't know. The senior staffer on Energy and Natural Resources thinks Stevens is okay, but now someone up there in the Northeast is opposed to it. I haven't made the connection yet to get somebody to talk to him, but I'll do it. We got Wallop off it. We got Burns off it. We got Stevens off it. Now this one. Who knows, we may yet have to deal with Jesse Helms."

Then, miraculously, Campbell made the connection he needed—Larry Craig of Idaho. Craig had served with him in the House before being elected to the Senate, and Campbell, now just about desperate, appealed to his former colleague over a cup of coffee in the Senate

275

cafeteria for help in identifying the mysterious obstruction. "I've been having a hell of a time finding out who's got holds on my Custer bill and then getting them off," Campbell confessed. "Let's meet again for breakfast," Craig suggested. "In the meantime I'll do some snooping."

The following morning Craig handed Campbell an early Christmas present. Not only had he identified the culprit—Senator Robert Smith of New Hampshire—he had also convinced him to pull the hold. "The bill could pass as early as tonight," Campbell exclaimed, literally skipping with happiness. "Isn't that terrific? Larry may be a very conservative Republican, but he's done a lot of good for Indians. He's a prince of a guy. If that sucker passes, it will be back at the House by tomorrow and we'll fly it."

And fly it he did. With the procedural holds at last a thing of the past, the Senate passed the combined bill with a few slight modifications, which the House quickly endorsed. It then went to President Bush, who signed it on December 10, 1991. "Because of all your efforts as the sponsor of this legislation," Bush wrote Campbell in a brief note, "I wanted you to have this ceremonial pen to commemorate the signing of this bill into law." Campbell, in turn, had the pen, note, and a copy of the bill framed and sent to Barbara Booher, who placed them on display at the battlefield visitors' center.

Later, when questioned by reporters about his triumph, Campbell, who evidently had forgotten all his frustrations with the legislative process, said simply, "I'm absolutely elated. It's what America is all about—basic fairness."

Barbara Booher also had reason for elation, but hers was understandably muted. "What saddens me," she later remarked privately, "is that the name change came to overshadow the memorial. Indian people wanted the memorial, yet it got lost in all the hysteria over the Custer name. For example, we were to have a ceremony at the battlefield on the Fourth of July 1992 to present the legislation for the memorial, but the media focused instead on the name change and described the event as a rededication of the battlefield."

Even Russell Means, who had worked so hard to get an Indian

memorial for the battlefield, got exercised over the name change. "I want my son to grow up hating Custer as much as I do," he snapped to Booher in a moment of pique.

"Why would you want to teach hate?" she replied. "Don't we already have enough hate in the world?"

Moderation, restraint, dignity—that was Booher's approach throughout the controversy. "The Custer buffs and the rest of those opposed to Campbell and me wanted to skirmish. They thrive in skirmishes, but I wouldn't skirmish back," she smiled. "I tried to set high standards of conduct from the first, and I think I maintained them to the end, even though some of them have done hateful, hurtful things against me. It is incredible some of the things they have done to me in public and behind my back."

Perhaps what bothered her most was learning that the Custer buffs thought the only reason for her appointment was favoritism, that she was the special pet of the district supervisor who appointed her. "I hardly knew that person before then," Barbara said indignantly. "She wanted to give me a chance because I was both a woman and an Indian. Do you realize that of the 359 park superintendents, only 36 are women, and I am the only Indian? But I guess that contributed to all the commotion."

What gave Barbara Booher courage throughout the controversy was the support she received from Campbell, the Indian community, and, she believes, higher powers. After the first bill died in Congress, for example, she found an eagle feather on the road to the visitors' center as she arrived for work one morning. Another night a short time later, an eagle-bone whistle awoke her from a sound sleep. At first she thought she had been dreaming, but her cat was acting strangely as well, as though he had heard it also. "Something good was happening," she believed, and this gave her the heart to stand firm.

Barbara, however, may have misinterpreted these symbols. A Crow woman who worked at the battlefield insisted that the eagle feather and flute music were not signs from above but simply the work of an infatuated Crow man who was trying to gain the affections of the attractive superintendent through the use of Indian love medicine.

Be that as it may, there is no disputing the outpouring of support Booher received from both Indians and non-Indians around the country who rallied behind her. When Northern Utes holding a powwow in Ogden, Utah, learned she was in the audience, they called her to the podium and performed an honor dance for her. On another occasion she learned that Lummi tribal elders from Washington State visiting Japan as part of a cultural exchange program prayed for her welfare in a ceremony while there. "Not only were sweats being held in my honor, but tribal people from across the country were praying for me, writing me, and telling me that I am an inspiration to women everywhere. I even received two feathers in the mail."

Looking back on the controversy after most of the dust had settled, Barbara admitted it had been a difficult time for her. "Had I known what I was getting into, I probably would not have accepted the appointment," she confessed. "I was a real rookie coming in here." In fact, she pointed out, for each of the six previous superintendents—all male—this had been their first superintendency. "I told my boss that this must be the Park Service boot camp," she laughed.

Perhaps the last laugh belongs to the Custer buffs. The Park Service uses a code name composed of the two initial letters in the first two words of the title to identify its historic sites in official communications. Therefore, from now on, the Little Bighorn National Battlefield Monument will be officially known as LIBI—the name of Custer's wife.

At the very height of his frustrating difficulties with Senate procedures that delayed his Custer bill, Campbell became involved in yet another Indian war. Plans for the upcoming 1992 Tournament of Roses had been generating superheated, passionate controversy and unprecedented amounts of media attention. The invitation to a direct descendant of Christopher Columbus to lead the New Year's Day parade had ignited a firestorm of criticism. The choice was condemned from a wide range of ethnic and philosophical opinion, the most radical vehemently protesting what they viewed as the glorification of the person responsible for five hundred years of human and environmental catastrophe in the Western Hemisphere.

Campbell played no role in the early days of this drama, but once involved he demonstrated, as he had in the Little Bighorn battlefield controversy, an uncanny instinct for doing the right thing at the right time for the right reasons. He emerged increasingly appreciated by both Indians and the general public for his willingness to assume a leadership role on issues that others considered marginal or hopelessly messy and even politically destructive.

The first "tournament of roses" in 1890 was a modest affair that featured a few decorated carriages and horses that promenaded around a small park and was followed by athletic contests such as footraces, a tug-of-war, and jousting. Each succeeding year the parade got a little bigger and more elaborate, and in 1895 its promoters formed the Tournament of Roses Association, which still organizes the annual event. The first floats from outside Pasadena participated in 1897, and eastern newspapers covered it the following year, thanks to the endorsement of then U.S. President William McKinley. The first motion pictures of the parade date from 1900; two years later, an association president suggested a football game might be a way to finance the parade. How right he was! The first game netted three thousand dollars. The game now earns in excess of twenty million dollars, largely through television rights.

Today the Tournament of Roses is a media megaevent seen and heard by more than four hundred million people worldwide through a network of radio, television, and satellite communications. It is as much a part of American life as the celebration in Times Square on New Year's Eve. It is Macy's Thanksgiving Day Parade and the Super Bowl wrapped up in a single package. It features each year sixty spectacularly decorated floral floats, three hundred horses, twenty-two marching bands, and one grand marshal.

For most of the history of the Tournament of Roses, the position of grand marshal held little meaning or importance. Politicians have been steady favorites. So have sports figures, movie stars, and heroes of one sort or another—Medal of Honor winners, astronauts, admirals, generals. No matter that the first woman grand marshal—Mary Pickford—was not selected until 1933, forty-three years into the event; that the first black—Henry Aaron—was not selected until 1975; or that Republicans seem to be the political party of choice. Most folks, most years, paid little attention to the grand marshal. But when the selection for the 1992 parade was announced, it was clear that the tournament sponsors had landed in a new world.

The selectee was Cristóbal Colón, duke of Veragua, marquis of Jamaica, and the twentieth-generation descendant of Christopher Columbus. The choice belonged to Robert L. Cheney, president of the Tournament of Roses, who had also picked the theme for 1992—Voyages of Discovery.

Cheney had worked hard to reach the helm of the Pasadena Tournament of Roses Association, an organization unlike any other in the United States. It bears remarkable resemblance to an exclusive country club inspired with religious fervor. Members, who call themselves "white suiters" in recognition of the white suits and red ties they wear on parade day, are completely focused on making the tournament a success.

Turnover in the volunteer force of 850 men (and a few recently admitted women) is minimal, perhaps forty or fifty openings a year, and for those slots there is a long waiting list. Members must live in the immediate area—within seventeen miles of Tournament House in Pasadena—and applicants must be nominated by a current member and furnish two written references as well. It helps if an applicant is the son or daughter of an association member. Robert Cheney's father, for example, was a lifelong member; so were the father and grandfather of Cheney's wife, Ruthie. Their two sons are members as well. Membership in the association is like a treasured family heirloom that is passed down from generation to generation. Nonetheless, the duties are often menial, time consuming, and, except for a small salaried staff, entirely voluntary. Members even have to buy their own tickets to the Rose Bowl game.

The association is administered by a nine-member executive committee and the work is organized around twenty-nine committees, which have such responsibilities as concessions, crowd control, float construction, security, and the other often mundane but essential tasks required to ensure the glossy, smoothly run, high-quality production that the Tournament of Roses has become. Members start out as aides and then work themselves up the tournament ladder slowly and deliberately. To reach full committee status requires eight to ten years; another six to eight years of service is needed to become a committee chairman. Above the committee chairmen is the twenty-five-member board of directors (all male in 1991) and the nine-member executive committee. Once a member is elected to the executive committee he not only is assured of becoming president of the Tournament of Roses, but he is also privy to numerous perks and privileges, such as his own Tournament of Roses official car—a white limousine with red plush interior—quite a status symbol in Pasadena.

Cheney during his thirty years in the organization had demonstrated his ability to be an articulate spokesman for the Tournament of Roses. He began his tournament career solving problems on the parade route as a member of the Parade Operations Committee for the 1963 Tournament of Roses. Since then he served on eight committees, chairing five— Properties, Post Parade, Music, Community Relations, and Formation Area. In 1986 he was appointed to the executive committee.

Since selecting the theme and the grand marshal are special prerogatives of the tournament president, Cheney considered himself especially fortunate to rotate into the position in the quincentenary year of the Americas. "I thought about all the discoveries which have changed and improved our lives over the centuries and especially since Columbus took his three tiny ships to sea exactly five hundred years ago," said the fifty-three-year-old retired aerospace engineer. "I wanted to honor the pioneers who have pushed the boundaries of science, technology, the arts, and education."

Who would be a more appropriate grand marshal for the Tournament of Roses in the quincentenary year and with a theme like Voyages of Discovery than the direct descendant of Christopher Columbus? It made sense to Cheney and it made sense to the Tournament of Roses executive committee, but it outraged just about everyone else, not only in the Los Angeles area, but in the rest of the nation as well.

Within minutes of Cheney's announcement of his choice for grand marshal on October 7, 1991, black, chicano, and Indian protestors began assembling in front of Tournament House. Bearing placards that read "Who's the illegal alien, Pilgrim?" and "No 1492–1992 Quincentennial. Oppose 500 years of genocide and colonization," the protestors demanded that the Tournament of Roses rescind its invitation to Colón. "This man has no part in this land, much less the parade," declared Vera Rocha, chief of the Gabrielino Indians, a tribe native to the Pasadena region. "Columbus didn't discover America. We were already here, but wherever he set foot, his men spoiled the land and disgraced our people." Rocha's comments were echoed by Helen Anderson, chair of the California Alliance of Native Americans. "We don't like to come down on somebody's parade," she said, "but the fact of the matter is that a lot of our people are dead based on the era that man brought [to America]."

The protestors gained strong support from the Pasadena City Council. The very next day Vice Mayor Richard Cole fired off an angry letter to Cheney, blasting the Tournament of Roses—"an organization totally controlled by aging white men"—for its "extreme myopia" in selecting as a grand marshal someone who is "a symbol of greed, slavery, and genocide."

Immediately prominent Pasadena blacks and latinos stepped forward to support Cole. They argued that the tournament leadership "had lost touch" with the broader Pasadena community, in which minorities now constituted over half the population. For too long tournament leaders had exercised undue influence on city affairs, voiced one critic. "They throw their weight around and get what they want."

Not this time. The cozy, insulated world of the Tournament of Roses was being profoundly shaken. Typical of the intense feeling on the issue was the hearing held on Colón's selection by the Pasadena Human Relations Commission. The panel, whose role is to advise the Pasadena City Council on matters relating to discrimination, met on Monday, November 4.

The hearing, which was aired live on local television, attracted more than a hundred spectators, most of whom were violently opposed to the duke's appearance in the Rose Bowl Parade. "If they invite that man to insult us, we will be there to die like our ancestors," declared Cuahtemoc Paxtel, one of the speakers. Another threatened, "If Colón rides in that parade, then he better be prepared to die." Only one person, who suggested that "the attack on Colón is an attack on the concept of America," spoke in favor of permitting the duke to appear in the parade, but he was loudly hissed and booed by the crowd. Also rejected was the suggestion that a prominent American Indian be found to ride with Colón in the parade. "No way. I wouldn't get within six feet of him," responded Chief Rocha.

The commission wasted little time in reaching a decision. By a vote of 10 to 0, it passed a resolution recommending that the city council ask Cristóbal Colón to withdraw as grand marshal of the 103d Rose Parade. "There is enormous rage on the part of Africans, Latinos, and Armenians," commission member Bunny Nightwalker Hatcher, who is herself an American Indian, told reporters after the hearing. "They are all upset by the Eurocentric focus of the celebration and the fact that people of non-European ancestry were totally disenfranchised."

Although the almost universal criticism of Cheney's choice of grand marshal caught everyone on the tournament's executive committee by surprise, the initial reaction was to stay the course. After all, controversy was no stranger to the Tournament of Roses. During the Vietnam War, protestors objected to several grand marshals—Senator Everett M. Dirksen, the Reverend Billy Graham, actor John Wayne, and comedian Bob Hope—as being too conservative because of their prowar stance. Later, other critics objected to actor Gregory Peck as being too liberal because he had opposed the appointment of Robert H. Bork to the U.S. Supreme Court. Senator John Glenn had the misfortune to be linked to a savings and loan scandal the day after his selection (he was later cleared of any misdeeds); Frank Sinatra earned a chorus of boos for his alleged link to organized crime; and former President Gerald Ford took considerable heat for his pardon of former President Richard Nixon, who had himself been grand marshal on two occasions. Even someone supposedly as controversy-free as Shirley Temple Black caused tournament officials a little angst when she confessed to an allergy to roses after her selection as grand marshal in 1989. No wonder then that tournament officials at first chose to minimize the flap. "It's not the first time [we've had controversy] and it won't be the last time," remarked assistant executive director William Flinn.

Nonetheless, the continuing furor began to erode the confidence of Flinn, Cheney, and their associates on the Tournament of Roses executive committee. Although they insisted on supporting their selection of Colón as grand marshal, they were willing to accept the suggestion offered by various Indian militants that a prominent American Indian be invited to ride in the parade—"somewhere behind the grand marshal," according to the *Los Angeles Times.*

Qualifying the suggestion only served to increase the anger. Representatives of various American Indian groups insisted that any Indian who accepted the invitation must not ride behind Colón. "There should be a Native American as a sort of great-great-grand marshal," demanded Richard Blackbear Angulo, a Chumash leader.

By now even the duke of Veragua had become concerned. What had started out as a simple gesture of goodwill had turned into a personal nightmare. By nature a reserved, though extremely pleasant and charming, individual, Colón is cautious for his personal safety. Both his father and his uncle had been assassinated by Basque terrorists as a way of drawing attention to their grievances against the Spanish government, and since then he had avoided publicity lest he become a target of terrorists as well. To accept the invitation to be grand marshal of the Tournament of Roses was a remarkable step for him and one, by now, he doubtless regretted, as various militant groups promised demonstrations and worse along the route of the parade.

Speaking through Pedro de Mesones, his agent in the United States, Colón threatened to boycott the festivities unless tournament officials met Indian demands. "He'd be very pleased to ride along with a Native American representative," de Mesones told reporters.

At this point matters took a turn in Congressman Campbell's direction. Although his was a last-act appearance in the drama, Campbell was no stranger to the important question of the best stance for Native Americans to take toward the Columbus quincentenary. "Many people ask me personally how they as Indians should regard the nationwide Columbus celebration proposed for 1992," Campbell remarked in early 1991. "I have to remember many years of mistreatment and the continued tragedies facing Indian people. We have to look very hard for something to celebrate."

Nevertheless, in Indian affairs Campbell usually favors participation rather than opposition, education over confrontation. "There's some that will never get over fighting the old wars. You know, my philosophy has always been that we need to remember those tragedies to make sure that things like that don't happen again, but we also have to have a positive agenda. Otherwise how can we make it better? If you settle for exclusion instead of inclusion, it never gets any better."

In keeping with this philosophy, on the evening of October 24, 1991, Campbell gave a brief address at the black-tie opening of Seeds of Change, a quincentenary exhibition at the Smithsonian Institution's National Museum of Natural History. The exhibition focused on five "seeds"—sugar, corn, the potato, disease, and the horse—to explain the impact on the world of the Columbus voyages of discovery. Campbell, the only American Indian in Congress, uniquely embodies, with his Portuguese and Native American ancestry, what the events of 1492 really mean today.

That symbolism was not lost on Pedro de Mesones, who happened to be in the audience that evening. As soon as Campbell finished speaking, de Mesones was at his elbow. "How would you like to ride in the Rose Bowl Parade?" Colón's representative asked. "I told him that I would think about it," Campbell said the next morning, "but right now I don't see how it could work out. That is a hell of a mess out there, and the last thing I need is egg on my face, literally and figuratively."

But in the next few days, Campbell took several steps as a broker between the Indian community and the Tournament of Roses. "They have a nice event out there," he said, "and I would hate for it to get ruined because of a few hotheads." To help avoid a calamity, Campbell made phone calls to various Indian leaders—tribal chairmen, directors of various Indian organizations, lobbyists, militants—as he tried to find an appropriate person to participate in the parade with Colón. His first preference was Wilma Mankiller, chief of the Cherokees and one of the most respected Indian leaders in the country. She declined, as did just about everyone else with any stature. Yet no one wanted a token Indian, someone with little credibility in the Indian community. Such a choice would serve only to worsen matters.

Perhaps Campbell was the best person after all. "I would do it," he said, "only if I were a grand marshal myself and equal to Columbus."

Absolutely not, responded Caryn Eaves, public relations director for the Tournament of Roses, to the suggestion of coequal grand marshals. There was simply no way that idea would fly.

A minimal gesture, however, would be no solution. Once Campbell's name surfaced as a possible American Indian representative to ride in the parade, the pressure on Cheney increased a notch. On the evening of November 5, the Pasadena Human Relations Commission again met on the crisis and Campbell's participation was discussed. Although most of those present favored the idea, no one was willing to see him involved in any capacity less than grand marshal. "There seems to be a high level of sensitivity not only to the original selection decision but also with the resolution of the controversy," Vice Mayor Rick Cole informed Campbell the next day. "Any resolution which inflames the controversy by appearing to be tokenist or condescending would not be satisfactory to any of us. So I want to alert you to the local sentiment that believes that anything less than equal recognition falls short of reconciling those who feel hurt and angry about the original selection." Getting Cheney and his associates to see the wisdom of this would be difficult. "The exact protocol is one that needs to be worked out delicately with the Tournament of Roses Association but . . . [it] needs to recognize that a grudging response is in some ways worse than no response. We all have a stake in a graceful resolution in which all can claim participation and satisfaction."

Campbell heard the message loud and clear. Carol Knight, his press secretary, informed reporters that Campbell had decided against accepting the offer to ride in the parade. "It smacks of tokenism," she said.

Meanwhile, emotions continued to run high. Although few Indians threatened Colón with bodily harm, the same could not be said for individuals supposedly representing black, chicano, and latino groups. Each day Campbell received calls from across the country, offering advice, warnings, and supposedly inside information on this or that aspect of the affair. "I think it is going to be very dangerous for Colón to appear in the parade," Campbell said during one conversation. "Since no one else seems willing to address the issue, I would be willing to call him personally and suggest he develop an illness that will keep him away from Pasadena on New Year's Day. That way everyone can save face." When this idea was relayed to Cheney, he responded emphatically. "That simply won't do. I need to talk to Campbell."

The result of the conversation was a complete reversal on the part of the Tournament of Roses Association. Hoping to end the crisis so his beleaguered staff could get on with the business of hosting a parade and football game, Cheney offered and Campbell accepted an invitation to be co-grand marshal with Cristóbal Colón. The *Los Angeles Times* termed it "an unprecedented capitulation to critics." Indeed it was. Although there had been other occasions when more than one person served as grand marshal—in 1952 seven World War II Medal of Honor winners shared the position, as did Roy Rogers and Dale Evans fifteen years later—never before had the choice been forced upon the Tournament of Roses.

"Hurt is not what the Rose Parade is about," Cheney said November 11 at the hastily called press conference in Pasadena where he introduced his new grand marshal. "The very last thing we want to do is hurt or offend anyone. We feel that by selecting Representative Campbell we are initiating a healing process that will lead to even stronger relations between the tournament and the Native American community."

For his part, Campbell felt strongly that Indians would gain nothing by boycotting, disrupting, or blocking the event. "The buffalo are not coming back," Campbell said. "We need to participate and be able to tell

our story, and that simply can't be done if we drop out of the system."
What better way to draw attention to the needs of America's Indian
people? "The Tournament of Roses," he pointed out, "is the most highly
visible and popular pageant in America. Millions of generous Americans
offer their help throughout the world to those less fortunate than they. I
know if we can tell our story, those same Americans will help a people
who have lived on this land for thirty thousand years" but who "still have
the lowest standard of living and at the same time the highest rates of
unemployment, suicide, high school dropouts, fetal alcohol syndrome,
communicable disease, and substance abuse of all Americans. Too many
of our elders have no heat, electricity, or indoor plumbing. Too many of
our children have too little food. It is my hope," he said, "that we can
begin planting the seeds of harmony and understanding, of cooperation
and mutual respect, and above all, love and brotherhood, and have faith
that those seeds will grow into the tree of life of which Black Elk once
spoke, so that we may make a better life for all of God's children."

Initial response to the announcement was guarded but generally
positive. Colón, in a statement released in Madrid, announced his "delight" at sharing the honors as grand marshal with Campbell, because
"Indians are an important part of the evolution and development of the
United States." One of the most vocal of the early critics, Cristina
Guillen-Cook, a member of El Centro de Accion, a Pasadena community
organization, came out in favor of Campbell. "I would hope that it will
set the tone," she told reporters. "[Including] native people—it's a real
important concept." Less satisfied was Helen Anderson of the California
Alliance of Native Americans. "We knew they'd find an Indian somewhere, and [Campbell's] fine with us," she declared, but that did not rule
out a "major action" at the parade. "We're going to turn the tide in a way
that people will understand all the history that's been left out," she
promised. Another early critic who voiced support for Campbell was
Vera Rocha, leader of the Gabrielino Indians. "I appreciate their choice,"
she said, "because one Indian can represent all Indians. It was a surprise
that they did this," she admitted, "but they should have done this in the
first place."

Especially pleased was Vice Mayor Rick Cole, whose initial outrage gave real force to the controversy and whose behind-the-scenes work contributed much to its favorable resolution. "I am proud of the tournament," he told reporters at the press conference. "The officials have responded to the criticisms and made it possible to give the other side a chance to be heard. I said what I thought needed to be said and am pleased with the positive outcome."

Not so pleased was activist Manuel Valle of the Black Males Forum. "Just because they put an Indian guy in there doesn't improve the situation. That just makes it appear to be a slave–master kind of thing," he sneered.

The extent of the dissatisfaction that continued to surround the issue became evident the following day. It began with a telephone call from Human Relations Commission chairman James Lomoko to Campbell, who was now back in Washington. Lomoko suggested that there was a united front against him and he should reconsider his decision to participate. "What do you think I should have done?" Campbell asked him. "I don't think you should have agreed to be grand marshal," Lomoko replied.

Pent-up tensions finally erupted that afternoon at a meeting of the Pasadena City Council to discuss the Human Relations Commission recommendation that Colón be removed as grand marshal of the Tournament of Roses. The Pasadena *Star-News* described the two-hour meeting as a "war," as good a word as any to describe what happened as the council tried to conduct a hearing in chambers packed with representatives of Indian, black, and chicano groups as well as a good many officials and members of the Tournament of Roses Association, who termed themselves "goodwill ambassadors." Ambassadors they may have been but "goodwill" is not what they engendered. As various speakers voiced decidedly negative opinions about Colón, the members of the Tournament of Roses delegation expressed their own opinions in the form of boos, hisses, and catcalls.

As Indian drummers and singers provided musical background in the foyer, Native American representatives talked of peace but threatened violence if Colón appeared in the parade. "You want a war, you'll get one," threatened one speaker who said his name was Wolf-That-Is-Black. "You want to walk in peace, we will." His sentiments were echoed by other Indian speakers who pointed at the centuries of injustice they had suffered at European hands and threatened to redress their grievances on New Year's Day. Even Vera Rocha, who only the day before had endorsed the compromise, now spoke against it, claiming she had thought Campbell would be the grand marshal instead of Colón.

Efforts on the part of the city council to ease the resentment toward the Tournament of Roses largely fell on deaf ears. "Healing begins when people share power," explained Councilman Bill Thompson, as he tried to calm the crowd. "I think the choice of Ben Nighthorse Campbell is a major step forward. I'm proud of the tournament for doing it." Vice Mayor Cole also struck a conciliatory note by urging the largely Indian opposition to "walk a mile in another person's moccasins."

Tournament officials were not the best advocates of their cause. "Our organization is devoted to helping people," declared Robert Monk, a member of the executive committee. "When is the healing going to start and the hostility stop?" Yet when one of the council members pointed out that the tournament leadership was all white and all male, it was Monk who ridiculed and challenged him.

Cheney, on the other hand, accused Jim Lomoko of the Human Relations Commission with sabotage for calling Campbell and trying to undo the compromise. "I'm upset, hurt, and livid," Cheney declared. "This has gone beyond the breaking point. I'm asking for an apology from the City Council for his despicable actions."

When questioned about it by one of the council members, Lomoko admitted calling Campbell. "When I read the newspaper this morning and realized he had agreed to ride in the parade, I couldn't believe it." Although Lomoko denied trying to dissuade the congressman from participating, he made clear where he stood on the issue. "Campbell's putting on a warbonnet and turning the parade into a wild west show."

With that Cheney challenged the city council to take a stand. "Are you for or against the Tournament of Roses? If you are for us, we need to hear it and we need to hear it now!"

Caught between the proverbial rock and a hard place, the city council ducked the issue entirely. Later, after the public hearing had ended, the council members voted 6 to 1 to approve a motion declaring its continued support for the Tournament of Roses and for "the leadership it has shown on this issue." The council also commended the tournament for "the goodwill and international acclaim it brings to Pasadena. Without it, Pasadena would not be the community it is." Perhaps it is no surprise that the council ignored the question of whether or not to oust Colón, the reason for which the hearing had been held in the first place.

Reaction to the compromise was mixed. Robert A. Jones, in his *Los Angeles Times* essay "Raining on More Than a Parade," asked the question "When did the concept of 'America' finally roll over and die? At what point did it become impossible to celebrate any aspect of America that suggested unity or common purpose? Let me suggest that Monday's capitulation to the Columbus haters may turn out to be the front runner."

The *Denver Post,* on the other hand, endorsed the compromise. In an editorial titled "Riding Tall" published on November 13, it gave the Colorado congressman high marks for his readiness to help the Tournament of Roses proceed with its celebration. "There's a fine line between tokenism and symbolism, and U.S. Rep. Ben Nighthorse Campbell has shown this week that he perceives the difference." Certainly he could have dismissed the offer as insincere and expedient, knowing full well that the parade organizers were seeking to forestall protests on New Year's Day. "But to his credit, Campbell decided not to get up on that high horse. In accepting an invitation to serve as co–grand marshal of the Rose Bowl Parade, along with a descendant of Christopher Columbus, the congressman from Colorado has seized an opportunity to underscore the role of Native Americans in forging the nation's cultural heritage."

Perhaps the best comment is the one that appeared in an editorial in the *Los Angeles Times.* "On the first day of 1992, the year that marks the 500th anniversary of Columbus's arrival in America, a few million people will gather in Pasadena for the Rose Parade." This time, noted the writer of "Thorny Rose," there will be two grand marshals, one a descendant of Columbus, the other a congressman who is a descendant of a Cheyenne warrior named Black Horse. To some, Columbus symbolizes imperialism and genocide; to others, he symbolizes heroic adventure, opportunity, new beginnings. "The problem with symbols is that they don't allow for subtlety, for shades of gray." If Colón can only represent the explorer who began the processes of change in America, then someone had to represent the American Indians and all the others who had a new way of life unwillingly thrust upon them. "Enter Ben Nighthorse Campbell, the only American Indian in Congress and great-grandson of a man who fought Custer at Little Big Horn. Alongside Colón, in a parade open car, will ride Campbell on horseback. The symbols are powerful—the issue serious. Tournament officials came to a wise and sensible compromise."

No one was more aware of the symbolism than Campbell himself. He decided to wear tribal regalia and ride his horse in the parade because of their symbolic importance. An eagle feather warbonnet is known the world over as an American Indian emblem. No more appropriate symbol exists for Indian people themselves than the horse, which they view as a gift from the Creator and which still represents the spirit of freedom and independence so much associated with their lifeways. It is the import from Europe that Indians came to value most. Even Campbell's placement in the parade ahead of Colón was symbolic. "We were here first," he insisted to Cheney in a take-it-or-leave-it ultimatum.

By the day of the parade only a few Indian hard-liners still objected to his appearance, thanks to the hard work of Bunny Nightwalker Hatcher, who organized a reception for Campbell upon his arrival in Pasadena with local community leaders. Open and candid as usual, Campbell told the skeptics he was participating in the Tournament of Roses in order to help them and their kinsmen across the country. After his brief remarks he gave away a stack of autographed posters of himself in full regalia mounted on Black Warbonnet. Who could resist his candor, warmth, and posters? "I knew you could persuade them!" an ecstatic Hatcher wrote the following day. "I've already gotten a lot of feedback, & even those who came to the reception strongly opposed to your participation are now 100 percent behind you."

Not quite. At the reception Campbell received a petition from the local chapter of the American Indian Movement with thirty-one signatures. "We are puzzled and dismayed that you have agreed to be the co–Grand Marshal of the Rose Parade, with its theme of 'Voyages of Discovery,' " the petitioners declared. "Millions of people around the world will see this parade and with you, a Native American, in the role of co–Grand Marshal, they will surely get the impression that you believe it is appropriate to honor Cristóbal Colón in this way. We cannot believe that this is your intent." Therefore, they urged, "withdraw . . . and join us in our protests against Cristóbal Colón as Grand Marshal."

Campbell had no intention of withdrawing. In his mind he had found the ideal forum to bring the world's attention to the problems that beset America's Indians. For example, one of his terms for accepting the role as co–grand marshal was the right to speak out about American Indian issues in all interviews with the media. Although Cheney had readily agreed to this, the media had not, and this led to a few awkward moments like the one with the NBC film crew that held up a cue card—"Happy New Year. Let 1992 be the year we plant the seeds of understanding, peace, and brotherhood"—and told Campbell to read it on camera.

The congressman refused. "My deal with the Tournament of Roses," he informed the startled producer, "calls for in-depth interviews in which I can address issues of concern to American Indians." The producer, in turn, told him that would be impossible; all NBC wanted was a brief soundbite to use during commercial breaks. "They don't need me, they need a trained parrot!" Campbell muttered as he stomped away from the camera and sat down.

Obviously flustered, the producer turned to Colón and asked if he had any objections to reading a prepared statement on camera. "Not at all," he smiled, as he took his seat. Colón quickly changed his mind, however, when he read the innocuous statement prepared for him. "I much prefer the one you wrote for Congressman Campbell," he said.

Then he excused himself and walked over to Campbell. "Do you mind if I read your statement? I think it is much more suitable than the one they prepared for me."

"It's all yours," growled the still angry Campbell. This exchange took place at Tournament House during the second of a lengthy series of tightly scheduled interviews between the grand marshals and various radio, television, and newspaper reporters.

Meanwhile, as Campbell fumed and Colón struggled to read his cue card, a bevy of red-faced, white-suited association volunteers tried to remain calm as they struggled to extricate themselves from an impending media disaster second only to the selection of Colón as grand marshal. This time the outcome was more satisfactory. Cheney and his media committee chairman, Don Reeves, met in the lobby with the remaining television teams and advised them that Campbell expected a real interview.

What could have been a succession of difficult situations turned into rather humorous exchanges as various producers entered the room with a ready quip, like "I understand you have something to say" or a placating "Whatever you want is fine with us." As a result, Campbell in the subsequent interviews managed to express his strong opinions on contemporary American Indian issues and at least one major network—CBS—carried his statement virtually intact.

The deep-seated resentments that surfaced because of the choice of Colón as grand marshal encouraged the Spanish government to consider a public statement toward reconciliation with the Indian peoples of the Americas. By coincidence the National Congress of American Indians held its annual convention in San Francisco during the height of the controversy, and the Tournament of Roses was a topic of hot debate. Seizing the opportunity to extend the olive branch, King Juan Carlos of Spain sent the conferees a goodwill message that was delivered by the consul general of Spain in Los Angeles. "I would like to convey to . . . all the representatives . . . my best wishes and congratulate you for the outstanding work that the National Congress of American Indians has been achieving in preserving the important Indian heritage in North

America," the king wrote. "As we are drawing close to a new era, we must enhance the decisive contribution of the Native American philosophy to the western world in their respect for the environment and their understanding of nature. I believe that it is important to preserve this beautiful common heritage, and walk together into the future in a trail of peace and understanding."

Campbell, working hard to reduce the Indian resentment toward the Tournament of Roses, also took advantage of the NCAI meeting by addressing the convention in person and speaking privately with fourteen tribal chairmen. Although the advice he received was not unanimous, most whose counsel he sought welcomed the idea of his participation, but with certain qualifications—he should do nothing to suggest he validated Colón's selection as grand marshal; he should use the parade as a forum to promote awareness of past tragedies; and, most important, he should not ride with Colón in the parade. Many also urged him to wear traditional dress—"symbolism being important"—rather than a three-piece suit, a decision he had already reached on his own.

Despite Campbell's best efforts as well as those of a host of community leaders, the tension level remained high in the days immediately preceding the parade. No one could feel absolutely certain about the safety of the grand marshals, although all agreed that the only person possibly at risk was Colón. Campbell, on the other hand, was confident that the worst anyone would do to him was throw something or frighten his horse with a firecracker. Asked if Black Warbonnet spooks easily, Campbell laughed. "Well, I'm a pretty good rider. He's a nice little pony, very well mannered and trained. The fact is, you don't want an old deadhead in a parade. You want a horse that's got some pride and holds up his neck and prances a little bit. That's what makes them look good. You can't have some plodding thing carrying his head down. I mean, warriors don't ride that kind of horse."

Heads up was also the motto for the Pasadena police, who felt prepared for any eventuality. A contingent of more than one thousand law enforcement officers lined the parade route, many of them in civilian dress (including eight who walked alongside the carriages carrying the

Colóns and the Campbells), and several helicopters continually circled overhead throughout the parade. In addition, three 32-member SWAT teams—on alert for possible volatile incidents—were a discreet distance from the parade route.

Since it seemed impossible to bar peaceful protestors, the Pasadena police provided a space for them along the parade route at the corner of Colorado Avenue and Garfield Street. It was here that the Los Angeles Indigenous Peoples' Alliance held a candlelight vigil throughout the night preceding the parade. Supposedly representing some twenty organizations, among them the Aztlan Underground, the Chicano Moratorium Committee, the International Indian Treaty Council, and the Lafayette Community Kitchen, the alliance distributed hundreds of flyers across the Los Angeles area calling upon blacks, Hispanics, and Indians to join in the vigil.

The flyers attracted about fifty protestors, many of them in traditional dress, who spent a chilly night appealing to curious onlookers for support and waiting for their moment to harass Colón and Campbell. If the group had a leader, it was Vera Rocha of the Gabrielino Indians, who was one person Campbell failed to win over. She organized the protest, and she served as master of ceremonies, which included a dramatic sunrise prayer service that featured incense, three drums, and the Cuahtemoc–Danza Azteca dance troupe in Aztec costume. But despite her best efforts, the protestors failed to attract much of a following in the burgeoning crowd. Indeed, some bystanders heckled them by slapping their hands to their mouths in mocking war-whoops, prompting one young protestor to spray them with Silly String. "I only spray the ones who are ignorant," he told a reporter from the *Los Angeles Times*. Most of the onlookers, however, had little interest in either the Indians or their anger at Colón: "I'm not for it and I'm not bothered by it," remarked one young man waiting for the parade to start. "It's just another guy riding in a car to me."

Finally, at 8:10 A.M. on New Year's Day 1992, after weeks of anticipation—and considerable trepidation—the Tournament of Roses Parade began under a welcoming sun and before an approving crowd.

The sun was particularly welcome; torrential rains had fallen for two days, and another downfall had been predicted for parade day. Although drought-stricken Los Angeles had been blessed with more water than normally falls in a year and a half, even the most apathetic residents of Pasadena were loath to see it rain on their parade. (Cheney, in part because of all the controversy and in part because, in the past, it had usually rained on tournament events he organized, was dubbed—ironically—Chief Black Cloud by his associates, and he fully expected it to pour.)

When the sun broke through the glowering clouds early that morning, Cheney took it as a good omen, and a good omen it proved to be. From the moment the parade began it was obvious that all the hostility, all the anger, all the dire predictions, all the adverse publicity would have no impact on the crowd. Campbell, as he had insisted, preceded Colón and his wife in their open carriage and his own family—Linda, Colin, and Shanan—in theirs. He looked resplendent in his eagle feather headdress and double trailer—each of the seventy-two golden eagle feathers representing a victory in international judo competition—as did his black and white paint Black Warbonnet, who was equally resplendent in beaded parade dress. The beautiful spotted pony seemed to sense the symbolism of that special moment, perhaps knowing he bore two burdens—not just Congressman Campbell, U.S. representative from Colorado, but also Ben Nighthorse, a Cheyenne warrior representing millions of Indians across the Americas, not only those who were here in 1492 but also those here in 1992.

Campbell also seemed to sense the burden he carried, for his demeanor was not that of a politician at a pep rally. Carrying a lance and shield, wearing beaded buckskins and his magnificent headdress, astride his proud and handsome paint, he truly resembled a warrior of times past as he set out on his five-mile journey along Orange Boulevard and Colorado Avenue. This was no lark, as one of the few hecklers in the crowd discovered. "Why aren't you walking like your ancestors did?" he yelled as Campbell came alongside.

"Fuck you!" Campbell snapped back. "You should have seen his jaw drop," Campbell said afterward. "He never expected a congressman to say something like that to him, but I wasn't about to take any crap from a jerk like that."

Fortunately, there were very few hecklers or troublemakers along the parade route. One youngster did throw a marshmallow at Campbell—a traditional missile usually reserved for motorists who drive along the parade route the night before—and hit Black Warbonnet in the head, but the pony did not seem to notice. Otherwise, the crowd roared its approval until Campbell and Warbonnet reached Vera Rocha and her cohorts at the corner of Colorado and Garfield. There things got a little nasty. As the drummers tried to spook the horse and protestors waved their placards and screamed insults, a young woman attempted to rush forward and hurl a plastic bag filled with red dye at Campbell. But before she could lift her arm two plainclothes policemen wrestled her to the ground. "She never got past the curb," the head of parade security proudly said.

By parade's end everyone involved with the Tournament of Roses was ecstatic, especially Bob Cheney. "I am on an absolute high," he told a reporter. "I cannot believe the number of people on the parade route who were supportive. They were saying 'Nice job. Tough year, but a great parade.' " His feelings were echoed by a headline in the *Los Angeles Times* the following day: "Controversial decision to have both a descendant of Columbus and an American Indian is a hit."

Indeed so. To the crowd, Colón and Campbell were "Chris" and "Chief." Ironically, of the few people who did boo Colón, most directed their ire at the wrong person—they mistakenly booed Campbell's son, Colin, who resembles the duke, since he was riding in the carriage with his mother and early plans had been for Colón and Linda to ride together in the parade as a gesture of friendship and goodwill. At the last moment, however, the duke decided to ride with his own wife and, in so doing, missed some of the hecklers. Colin, on the other hand, thoroughly enjoyed the moment of fame, especially since it shielded Colón from the smattering of ill will that still lingered on parade day.

In fact, the duke's warmth, sincerity, and charm had won the heart of everyone involved in the tournament—especially the members of the

Campbell family—and no one wished to see him embarrassed in any way. Campbell himself squelched one rather cheeky interviewer who tried to suggest that, as an Indian, he might later regret having been associated with Colón as a co–grand marshal. "Indians," he pointed out, "respect courage, and the duke has demonstrated his courage on more than one occasion. As a helicopter pilot in the Spanish Navy, he received Poland's highest decoration for rescuing eight Polish sailors from a sinking ship in the height of a terrible storm at sea. Whatever they might think of his ancestor, all Indians respect a military hero."

Equally ecstatic at day's end were the Pasadena police. There had been no serious incidents and only a few minor disturbances. In fact, the number of arrests—seventy—for crimes of any sort were greatly below the total for previous parades, little more than half the number from the year before (when two spectators were stabbed to death in fights) and far below the hundreds arrested each year during the height of the Vietnam demonstrations. "This is the lowest total that I remember in twenty-seven years with the Pasadena Department," marveled one police officer.

Perhaps the most serious casualty of the parade was Campbell. "That was the hardest five miles I ever rode," he grumbled. "That Indian saddle is a killer. I used extra padding, but it was still like sitting on rocks!"

TEN

SENATOR BEN NIGHTHORSE CAMPBELL

When Campbell gratefully dismounted from Black Warbonnet on New Year's Day 1992, he fully believed that the spotted pony's parade days, like his own political campaigns, had come to an end. Not in his wildest dreams did the congressman think that, a year later, he would again be astride his prancing tobiano paint, opening still another chapter in an already eventful life. Yet on January 20, 1993, Campbell and Black Warbonnet once again donned their parade finery. Their route this time was not Colorado Boulevard in Pasadena but Pennsylvania Avenue, the Avenue of the Presidents, in Washington, D.C. In Pasadena Campbell rode alone, a solitary symbol of hope and pride for Native Americans in America's quincentenary year; in Washington a year later, as Senator Ben Nighthorse Campbell, he had company. Riding with him in full regalia were a score of men and women representing tribes from across the United States.

Six of the riders were Northern Cheyennes, who had bankrupted themselves to show the world that Campbell was one of their own. Here were descendants of the warriors who fought Custer—Dennis Limberhand, Charlene Alden, Gilbert Little Wolf, Lee Lone Bear, Levando "Cowboy" Fisher, and Johnny Joe Woodenlegs—riding down Pennsylvania Avenue in the inaugural parade of President Bill Clinton. The Cheyennes were delighted with the Democratic victory in the 1992 presidential election, but their real reason for celebrating was Ben Nighthorse Campbell's election to the Senate, a milestone in Cheyenne history. Jimmy King, the tribe's elderly historian, put it all in perspective: "Lots of tribes have educated and famous members, but we Northern Cheyennes have the only U.S. senator."

Although not the first Native American senator, he is the first to make a statement with his Indianness. Indeed, just prior to making the decision to run for the Senate he also decided to again let his hair grow. Although friends and advisers urged him to cut his hair, he refused. "I intend to be wearing braids when I take the oath of office," he promised. By the time Campbell did get sworn in as the junior senator from Colorado on January 5, 1993, his hair was not yet long enough for braids, but no one could miss his ponytail.

Campbell's decision to run for the Senate stunned his family, his staff, and his friends. Nothing, in fact, was further from anyone's mind the first week of April 1992, when popular and highly respected Colorado Senator Tim Wirth confounded the experts by abruptly announcing he was not going to run for reelection. Upon hearing the news, Campbell's chief of staff, Ken Lane, went into the congressman's office, told him what he had heard, and jokingly remarked, "Hey, Ben, if Tim really doesn't run, why don't you?" It was as if a light bulb suddenly went on in Campbell's head, Lane recalls. "I will," was his immediate response.

Although Campbell said he had to talk it over with his family, he had already made his decision and stuck with it. His sole caveat concerned Colorado Governor Roy Romer. Only if Romer decided to run for the seat would Ben stay out of the race. When Romer chose not to run, Campbell never hesitated, even though two other formidable opponents had announced their candidacies: Josie Heath, who had run for the Senate once before and lost; and Dick Lamm, who had been the most popular governor in modern Colorado history. No matter. "I have *never* in the seven years I've known him," claims Lane, "seen such a fire in his eye, such a fierceness of spirit. It was kind of scary. He was smelling blood. It was almost as if some latent animal instinct had gripped him. Ben saw the quarry and was not going to be deterred."

What Lane glimpsed was the competitive spirit that boils within Campbell. It had made him a judo champion, and it has continued to enable him to triumph time and time again against seemingly overwhelming odds. It was not the Senate seat that Campbell wanted as much as the opportunity once again to experience the exhilaration of competition. As he has said more than once, the world consists of winners, losers, and spectators, and Campbell is neither a spectator nor a loser—as Lamm, Heath, and the political experts of Colorado were soon to learn.

Campbell had no statewide organization at all, not even a semblance of one, because he had never before run for a statewide office. The pundits at first dismissed him as a hick with a bad temper from southwestern Colorado, a politician in polyester suits with a mediocre legislative record. Moreover, both his opponents could campaign full time while Ben had to tend to House duties. About the only thing in his favor was his charisma.

Nonetheless, the polls had Campbell a ten-point favorite going into the Democratic primary. Although no one really expected that lead to stand up, it did. He took almost 46 percent of the vote to Lamm's 36. Campbell pulled ahead very early on election night and stayed there, prompting one admiring Denver TV commentator to remark, "Nighthorse is a racehorse! " The Grand Junction *Daily Sentinel* echoed the sentiment the following morning with the banner headline: NIGHTHORSE IS NO DARKHORSE.

Campbell was now halfway to the Senate and most observers were ready to concede the seat to him. Some polls claimed he was thirty points ahead of his Republican opponent, Terry Considine, a wealthy former state legislator who had made a bid for the same Senate seat that Wirth won in 1986. In the minds of many people, the Senate race had been the Democratic primary.

Once again, however, the prognosticators were wrong. Ben had charisma, but his Republican opponent had money. Considine immediately began a media blitz that went unanswered for six weeks because Campbell's campaign was flat broke.

Considine also ran a brilliant race, while Campbell's campaign stumbled from one miscue to another. The worst blunder occurred when two of his campaign staffers called a radio talk show that featured both Campbell and Considine. The staffers, who both lied about their identities, asked Considine leading and embarrassing questions. Although Campbell, who was on a telephone hookup from his ranch, had no idea

302

the two callers were members of his campaign staff, their voices were recognized by a reporter for the *Rocky Mountain News* who made this charade a major story for days. Considine and his backers also dredged up a seemingly endless list of unsavory and largely baseless accusations. Ben was charged with being too liberal, being a Washington insider, having a poor voting record, trying to avoid debates, and lacking legislative accomplishments. Considine's campaign also planted stories suggesting that Ben was not really an Indian, that he had beaten his first wife, that it was wrong for him to be making jewelry while holding public office, and that he had an illegitimate son in prison. The inmate, when questioned about his parentage, readily acknowledged that his father was named Campbell, but not Ben Nighthorse Campbell.

Even Campbell's most ardent supporters, however, had to admit that the most difficult part of the campaign were the ten televised debates with Considine. "They were an agony," Lane admits. Some staffers even dared to call them a "disaster." Considine was an excellent, well-coached debater. He punched all the right buttons in attacking Campbell, who is not at his best in this format. Campbell is not polished, he angers easily, and he sometimes comes across as uninformed. None of this seemed to matter to the Colorado electorate, however. They evidently saw a diamond in the rough. As Lane points out, "His answers were not canned or calculated. He was open, he was angry, he was honest. The contrasts with Considine were glaring."

Nonetheless, from a thirty-point lead the day after the primary, Campbell's cushion sank steadily during the campaign until—two weeks before the election—it hit rock bottom. A poll by the *Denver Post*, the same newspaper that had predicted Campbell's ten-point victory in the primary, showed the race dead even at 44 percent each. Campbell's own poll actually showed him behind Considine by a point or two.

By then even Campbell had become discouraged. Everything seemed to be going wrong. The first ominous portent concerned Linda. Normally tough and tireless, she had become increasingly short of breath and energy. Soon after Campbell had announced his candidacy, Linda learned she had a congenital heart defect that required immediate, open heart surgery. The operation kept her out of action for several weeks at a critical juncture in her husband's Senate campaign.

Although she made a complete recovery, Linda for once was not there to pick up the slack for her husband, and things seemed to go from bad to worse. "We couldn't raise the necessary financial support to counter Considine's media barrage and everything seemed to be going wrong," Campbell admits. "I was working as hard as humanly possible. I was away from home weeks at time. The entire family—Shanan, Colin, even Linda after she recovered her health—were stumping the state for me, yet nothing seemed to be working."

Even Campbell began to have self-doubts, to think he had made a serious mistake in jumping into the Senate race. He was depressed, tired, and discouraged. The sad state of his spirits was reported to his friends and relatives at Lame Deer by Joyce Knows His Gun and her sister Rosalie Tall Bull. Joyce and Rosalie, who are members of the Limberhand family, had been working with the campaign and they saw the change in Campbell.

Immediately, the various warrior and religious societies of the tribe began praying for him and holding sweats on his behalf. It was obvious to them that some sort of evil was surrounding Campbell and that he should take certain precautions to protect himself and save his campaign.

Johnny Russell, a Vietnam veteran who is active in the Chiefs' Society and schooled in the traditional ways of the Cheyennes, called Campbell. He told him to carry the tuft of an eagle feather he had received upon becoming a member of the Chiefs' Society and to apply a special red paint daily to specific parts of his body. Russell even faxed Campbell a sketch showing him the exact places to put the paint—a dot in the palm of each hand, one on the top of his head, and another over his heart. When Campbell told Russell he did not have the proper paint, a container arrived the next day by express mail.

Meanwhile, Campbell had told Linda about the Cheyenne's fears and advice to him. "Do you think I should do what they are recommending?" he asked.

"Why not?" she replied. "What have you got to lose?"

"That's what I thought, too," Campbell says, "so I did everything just as they told me. I know most people will find all this hard to believe, but I have to admit that almost immediately things got better. Just like that, money started to pour in, I began feeling better, and my standing in the polls began to climb. By the night of the election we had reversed the skid and were even pulling away from Considine."

Campbell won by a 9.6-point margin over his opponent. "It was a landslide by Colorado Senate race standards," insists Carol Knight, "and appears to be a Democratic record." He won all but seventeen of the state's sixty-three counties. All of western and most of northern and southern Colorado went for him. He swept all of the Denver metropolitan counties, and he won big in Boulder with more than 60 percent of the vote.

Among the congratulatory notes he received was one from Jose Quintero, town manager of Ignacio. "Thirteen years ago when you submitted your name to the Ignacio School Board for consideration to the vacated position . . . and were unceremoniously rejected, no one on that Board including the two of us that did support your appointment ever imagined the possibility of you being our national representative some day. You have truly awed us since that day. Senator Campbell, you have done us proud."

No one was more proud than the Northern Cheyennes, who claim a share of the credit for Campbell's victory. "Ben put that eagle feather in his pocket and never took it out, and he put his chief's paint in the prescribed places. It was just like a shield," declares Dennis Limberhand. "It gave him strength, a new beginning. Ben started digging in, fighting back, and everything started to change and work out for him."

Little wonder then that the tribe almost immediately began clamoring for Campbell to come home so they could share in his good fortune. Although several carloads of Cheyennes—including Austin Two Moons, who prayed privately with Campbell after his victory was confirmed—were with him in Denver on election night, they insisted he come to Lame Deer so they could host an old-fashioned victory celebration for him.

Campbell was honored to comply. The first thing to strike his eye upon reaching the Lame Deer city limits was a boldly lettered, freshly painted plywood sign: HOME OF U S SENATOR BEN NIGHTHORSE CAMPBELL. "We made it and put it up last night," remarked one of the Cheyennes.

Although the weather that late November weekend was bitterly cold, it was more than offset by the warmth of the people, who mobbed Campbell everywhere he went. It is doubtful he had a more intense forty-eight hours on the campaign trail. Interestingly, the welcome-home party was covered by television crews from Japan, Sweden, and France, but not the United States.

The first day opened with a luncheon and speeches at Dull Knife Memorial College attended by Crow tribal chairwoman Clara Nomee as well as a roomful of Northern Cheyenne and state dignitaries; the day closed with a sweat and traditional meal at the home of Dan Foot and his wife, Bird Woman. As everyone sat huddled in the steam-filled blackness of the sweat lodge—eight men and six women, including Little Bighorn Park Superintendent Barbara Booher—Campbell could not resist thinking that this probably was a first for a U.S. senator.

Squeezed in between the luncheon and the sweat were a visit to the elementary school and a parade on the main street of Lame Deer. Led by tribal president "Cowboy" Fisher and Campbell riding a borrowed horse, the parade was the longest in Lame Deer history, according to a number of the spectators who braved the biting cold to cheer their new senator and wave and laugh at friends and relatives riding by on horseback or in the twenty or so decorated wagons, cars, and vans.

At the school were roughly five hundred Cheyenne youngsters who had waited more than two hours for his arrival. Waving signs that read YOU MAKE US PROUD and WE HONOR YOU, the children listened in respectful silence as Campbell spoke briefly about the importance of education. "With an education," he told them, "you can still sing and dance and preserve those traditions that are so important to our people. Sure, as you go along in life, you might be criticized for not doing better and, being Indian you will be criticized, but you don't have to be the best in the world. The only thing you really have to do is be the best *you* can be! Just be the best you can be. Take each day a step at a time. At the end of the day, look back and ask yourself, 'Did I do the best I could today?' If you do that, you will succeed. You will move forward. You will be an asset not only to this Indian community but to all America."

At least one youngster was paying attention. That evening after the parade had ended and we were on our way to the sweat lodge behind Dan Foot's house, Campbell, as usual, was hungry. He stopped at the only "restaurant" in Lame Deer, a store that featured video games, sodas, and microwave-ready sandwiches. The street was alive with youngsters scampering about, most of them wearing only T-shirts, tennis shoes, and blue jeans, while Campbell and his companions were shivering in their sheepskin-lined jackets. As Campbell was about to enter the store, a short, stocky boy about twelve years old yelled out, "Hey Ben, I heard you talk at my school today!"

Campbell called him over, put his arm around him, and asked, "Well, how are you doing in school? Are you getting all As?"

"No sir, I'm not," he grinned, "but I want you to know that I'm being the best I can be."

The highlight of the weekend was the victory celebration on Saturday night at the Lame Deer high school gymnasium conducted by the various warrior and religious societies. It was a night of dancing, singing, drumming, and friendship. Campbell received a new name—the name of his Cheyenne forebear, Ruben Black Horse—and he received the plaudits of people from across the reservation. The celebration put to rest, hopefully for the last time, any doubts that he was a Northern Cheyenne and that these were his people.

When the Cheyennes learned that Campbell planned to ride his horse in the inaugural parade, they besieged him with requests to join him as did Indian friends from across the country. By inauguration day, he had received over a hundred such appeals but parade officials limited the total to thirty. All the riders, except Campbell, were to be mounted on appaloosas. As luck would have it, not all the necessary horses were delivered to the parade on time, so only about two dozen Indians, including movie star Rodney Grant and the six Northern Cheyennes, actually escorted Campbell up Pennsylvania Avenue from the Capitol to the White House.

Accompanying the Northern Cheyenne riders to Washington was a cheering section that consisted of two dozen relatives and tribal representatives including five chiefs and Austin Two Moons, their elder statesman. Campbell was able to arrange for a small section along the parade route at about 6th and Pennsylvania Avenue to be cordoned off for the Cheyennes, who came dressed in regalia and were prepared to sing a chief's song and honor song for the senator and their kinsmen as they rode by.

The group had to be in place by 8 A.M. There were no chairs, no restroom facilities, no food, but nothing could dampen their ardor or their excitement. Even as the continually surging crowd threatened to engulf them—few in the record-setting throng had any understanding or appreciation for the unique circumstances that had brought the Cheyennes to Washington at great cost and personal sacrifice—the group sang and danced and passed the time until the Indian riders came and went at about 3:30 P.M. Everyone in the group was so excited at that moment, which lasted only a few seconds, that little drumming or singing was actually done. And once Campbell and the riders had passed, the Cheyennes immediately gathered their belongings and fled the scene, anxious to find restrooms, chairs, and food.

But while they were there it had been a special moment in the history of the nation's capital. When President Clinton and Vice President Gore passed in their limousines at the head of the parade, the Cheyennes—the women in dance dress and the men in buckskins and war bonnets—wildly waved their American flags.

No one was more enthusiastic on Inauguration Day than Austin Two Moons, Campbell's mentor and spiritual adviser. Despite a crippled leg, the result of an injury suffered as a bronco rider on the rodeo circuit, Austin seldom sat in the wheelchair that had been provided by a sympathetic Washingtonian. "We need to let that wheelchair rest," he would joke. Throughout the long day Austin stood tall and erect, clutching an American flag in one hand and an eagle-wing fan in the other. The fan had once belonged to the famous Sioux chief Red Cloud and had been given to him by the chief's son, Jack Red Cloud.

As first Clinton and Gore and then Campbell passed, Austin vigorously waved both his fan and the flag. At one point, he turned to me and said, "You know, we have a right to this flag. When Custer came to drive us from our land, he carried it. My grandfather told me that at the Little Big Horn Custer dropped the flag and the Cheyennes picked it up. We have kept it ever since. Now the flag unites all of us in this great country. Now we are all friends and we need to work for world peace. Put that in the book."

EPILOGUE

Much has changed—in the world, in Washington, in Campbell's life—since the newly elected senator paraded Black Warbonnet, his painted pony, up Pennsylvania Avenue as part of Bill Clinton's inaugural festivities in 1993. Gone is Austin Two Moons, his Cheyenne mentor and spiritual adviser, who died in 1994 at age sixty-seven. His death was a tremendous loss to the entire Northern Cheyenne community, but especially to Campbell, who wrote: "Austin is a part of history now. He has been the conscience and guiding spirit of the Northern Cheyennes and an emissary of peace for our nation and the world. He now carries the dreams of the Cheyenne people to Maheo."

Gone, too, is Black Warbonnet. The Clinton inaugural was one of his last public appearances. At age twenty-four, Black Warbonnet had to be put to sleep when he could no longer get up. Campbell still rides, but now his horse of preference is made of iron, a Harley-Davidson motorcycle, which has become an integral part of his senatorial persona. For him, the motorcycle is a logical progression. "I think bikers are a reincarnation of the trappers, Indians, and cowboys of the old days when they could do anything they wanted. There are unbelievable similarities," he says, "some obvious, some subtle."

Campbell has owned motorcycles since his teenage years. He later got his wife Linda hooked on them as well. They each had their own bike until the kids grew up and other needs prevailed. They then sold their bikes. Upon winning the Senate race, however, Ben got back onto motorcycles thanks to Linda, who bought him a blue Harley-Davidson Electraglide as a victory present. Linda rides a Harley Heritage softail and, until recently, was part of a twenty-two-member all-woman Harley-Davidson drill team that rides in national parades and fairs. Campbell also owns an old-style chopper with the ape-hanger handlebars and no front brakes made famous by Dennis Hopper in *Easy Rider*, and an FLHT tourer, the kind called "couches" in California, with cruise control, stereo tape deck, and saddlebags.

Capitol Hill is populated with cookie-cutter, three-piece, button-down interns, staffers, and congressmen, but Senator Campbell is not one of them. "I may be part of the establishment," he declares, "but I'm no conformist. As a senator I am required to wear a coat and tie, but nothing is written about pants, which is how I get away with the black jeans and cowboy boots." Also nonregulation is his long ponytail.

Campbell's motorcycle and unique dress code have raised some eyebrows on Capitol Hill, but most legislators are more charmed than offended by their unorthodox colleague. One of his fans is Senator Kay Bailey Hutchison of Texas. "After God made Ben, he threw away the mold," she laughs. "On Capitol Hill, Ben has proven himself to be a solid ally, somebody you want in your corner, and I can always rely on his word. He is one of my favorite people in the Senate." Another Campbell backer is friend and fellow Republican, Senator Orrin Hatch of Utah. "Ben is a maverick," Hatch admits, "but I also say he's a leader, not a follower, and woe be to those who don't get out of the way when Nighthorse charges up Capitol Hill on his Harley."

As soon as Campbell got his Harley, he began seeking opportunities to combine business with pleasure. In the late summer of 1993, he launched the Annual Four Corners Iron Horse Motorcycle Rally, a charity fund-raiser held on Labor Day weekend in his hometown of Ignacio. The first rally attracted some seven thousand bikers; in 2001 over thirty thousand registered. "Where else can a biker go and pay a ten-dollar admission fee and visit with his senator?" chortled one rider.

Now Campbell participates in charity rides across the country. Whether it is for the March of Dimes, the Ride for the Cure for Breast Cancer, or a ride in New York that raised money for the families of the fallen firefighters and police officers after the Twin Towers disaster, he can be counted on to participate.

A ride of special importance to Campbell is Rolling Thunder, which honors the dead and missing soldiers who fought in Vietnam. The rally attracts some 250,000 participants to Washington, D.C., every Memorial Day weekend. The bikers assemble in the Pentagon parking lot and then, led by Campbell, parade in formation to the Vietnam Memorial on the Mall. Thanks in part to Campbell's participation, the Rolling Thunder ride has raised the profile of its participants, helping to gain mainstream media attention as well as corporate sponsorship while promoting the bikers' POW/MIA cause. In return, Campbell has received just about every possible award from veterans' groups nationwide.

Campbell has also become a staunch advocate for bikers' rights. He is always the first in the Senate to go to the mat for those who ride on two wheels. He helped defeat the effort to make safety helmets mandatory for motorcyclists and he has also championed biker health care. Thanks to his seat on the Appropriations Committee, Campbell also managed to secure funding to allow the Capitol Hill police to replace their foreign-made motor-cycles with American-made products. "I wanted tourists who come to the nation's capital to see American bikes," Campbell says. "Besides, it also instills pride in those officers."

The biker community is a rising political force whose political philosophy resonates nicely with the Republican message. According to Mike Russell, Campbell's former deputy chief of staff, the Federal Government's growing involvement with helmet laws in the late eighties and early nineties galvanized bikers across the country into a national movement. Traditionally, most bikers were libertarian and politically inactive, but that began to change in the mid-nineties. "Bikers today, in contrast to those of a couple of decades ago, are more upscale and come from all walks of life—they're doctors, lawyers, CEOs, and elected officials. In fact, over 25 percent of the governors today ride motorcycles," Russell says. "And the majority of them relate clearly to the Republican message of lower taxes, limited government, individual freedoms, second amendment rights, and a strong national defense. In fact, many bikers are former veterans and supporters of the POW/MIA cause."

The editors of Street Rodder magazine would certainly agree. In the December 2001 issue, in an item titled, " 'Our' Kind of Senator," the editors affirmed: "Needless to say, with his love for horsepower, his ponytail, and his flashy jewelry, he's not what you think of when you picture a United States Senator. Actually, Campbell is one of us, and that makes him a tremendous ally on Capitol Hill." He supports the efforts of bikers and rod and custom enthusiasts "to keep the government 'out' of your garage" and, as far as the editors of Street Rodder are concerned, "it's a huge relief to know that a free thinker … like Ben Nighthorse Campbell is helping to run our country."

An example of the GOP change of heart is indicated by the bike rally Campbell helped organize for the party's 1996 presidential nomination convention in San Diego. Campbell mobilized thousands of bikers for a "Dole for President" rally, the first in American political history. Newt Gingrich, Larry Pressler, Dick Armey, Trent Lott, Duke Cunningham, and other members of the House and Senate as well as other elected officials led the motorcade into the huge parking lot of the San Diego Convention Center where Campbell then addressed them. Campbell later organized a similar ride for Dole in Ames, Iowa.

This is not to suggest that Campbell's motorcycle "biker" persona has met with universal approval. An early and vocal critic of then Democratic Senator Campbell's love affair with Harleys was Don Bain, the Colorado State Republican chairman. "I don't think Campbell's setting the kind of example we want," Bain huffed. "I don't think we want our kids to grow up to be bikers. His lifestyle is totally inappropriate for a U.S. senator." Bain also went on record to predict Campbell would be a one-term senator, calling him a decent, honest person but an undistinguished elected official.

Colorado bikers immediately rushed to Campbell's defense. Wrote Gayle Bishop of Denver: "Ben Campbell represents quite a hope for many. His life, his position as a United States Senator says to the kid who isn't interested in growing up to be a Don Bain clone, that it's OK not to." Ditto, echoed Debi Craig of Aurora. "My husband and I are bikers ... [and] my children are growing up to respect bikers and I, for one, am not ashamed of that."

Another defender was the *Rocky Mountain News:* "We frankly don't know what most 'bikers' do during their working hours. We wouldn't be surprised, though, if their numbers included, besides the occasional senator, even a few bigtime lawyers like Bain. Finger wagging is often a risky proposition, unless the object of scorn is so far beyond the pale that only a barbarian would stand in his defense. This is far from the case with Sen. Campbell, most of whose biking activities are perfectly harmless." To show Bain he held no hard feelings, Ben presented the Republican state chairman with a black Harley-Davidson T-shirt when he later switched parties.

Then there was the *Denver Post* story about Campbell's sometime presence at the Crow Bar, a D.C. watering hole popular with the biker crowd.

According to the *Post* reporter, the bar was also said to be frequented by hookers, strippers, and other unsavory types—certainly not the sort of folks with whom a U.S. senator should fraternize.

Nonsense, Campbell retorted. The Crow Bar is, in fact, frequented by a cross-section of the D.C. population, including politicians, pundits, lawyers, doctors, and blue-collar workers, although it has long been known as a gathering place for riders of Harley-Davidsons. "You also imply that the Crow Bar is a hangout for hookers and strippers," Campbell wrote. "You must know a lot more than I do from my twice or three times per month Coca Cola drop by because no one ever introduced themselves to me by saying their profession was either hooker or stripper. It's not hard to find trouble in our nation's capital, especially if you are looking for it. I also go to the White House," he informed the *Post*, "but that doesn't mean I'm having sex with interns."

Campbell says his association with outlaw bikers is more hype than fact. "The Hell's Angels used to be the image of the average biker, but not anymore," he insists. "I've attended bike rallies in California and my riding partners were Otis Chandler, owner of the *Los Angeles Times*, or Peter Fonda, or Larry Hagman, or some other movie actor. I've seen more corporate execs and doctors at bike rallies than anyone could imagine. For me, it's a legitimized form of therapy to get away from a high stress profession, but what's interesting to me is that you see people at these rallies about whom you know nothing. They don't talk about their other life. The rider next to you might be a corporate exec or a housewife or a farmer or an ex-convict, but all of them are enjoying talking about cubic inch displacement and belt drives versus chain drives, carburetors. Nobody talks about what they do in their other life hardly at all."

Biking may be therapy, but it is potentially dangerous therapy. In 1995, Ben and Linda were enjoying a pleasant ride on a Colorado back road that follows the Delores River through the Mancos Valley from Mancos to Telluride and were up in the hills just above a little wide spot in the road called Rico, a little mining town. As Campbell recalls, "there was a curve there and a gravel pit down by the river and the trucks were pulling out on the road and a couple of them pulled out on the curve and spilled some gravel off the top. I didn't see it, but I guess the guys in front of me did because they moved over by the center line. I came around wide and kind of on the outside and hit that damn gravel and—bam—went right into a slide. I slammed into a guardrail at fifty-five or sixty miles per hour and knocked the shit out of me. I hit the rail and bounced back. Me and the bike flew through the air. I was thrown back onto the highway. If I'd gone over the rail it was an easy 125 or 150 feet right straight down to the river. I could have gotten really hurt had I gone over that baby. I didn't get hurt at all except for my right arm, but I hit so damn hard they found patches of leather from my jacket torn and sticking on the guardrail bolts. My friends pulled them off and I had them sewn back into my leather jacket, which was brand new. I didn't have any bruises anywhere, but my right arm took the full force of the blow. It had eight breaks—five in my forearm and three in the back of my hand. One finger is still crooked. When I pointed it out to the doctor that somehow my finger had healed crooked, he said, 'Oh, I can fix that easy enough. I just have to rebreak it and straighten it out.' No way, I told him, I've had so many broken bones in my day, I'd rather live with it this way than go through that again. Besides, it's not that bad, it just makes it a little more difficult working on jewelry. But man, that was an expensive accident—about $42,000 for the arm, $27,000 for the hospital, $10,000 for the doctor, and $5,000 for the bike—everything from the frame forward was crushed and had to be rebuilt."

Another near disaster for Senator Campbell was changing political parties. He joined the Senate ranks as a Democrat; in March 1995 he became a Republican, a switch made after considerable soul searching. At the time, the tempest threatened his political career, but in true Campbell fashion, he has emerged more popular and more effective.

His reason for the change? Anger at President Bill Clinton's attempts to muster Democratic support against the Republican balanced budget amendment. "Clinton made the balanced budget amendment an absolute test of party loyalty," Campbell says. "That may have worked with some of my Senate colleagues, but not with me." Campbell announced his switch the day after Democrats blocked by one vote what the GOP had proclaimed its top priority—a balanced budget amendment to the Constitution.

Clinton arm-twisting was certainly an issue, but associates and friends had long known of Campbell's ambivalence about party loyalty. Colorado

Senator Wayne Allard, a fellow Republican whose niece is married to Ben's son Colin, said Campbell's switch did not surprise him. "He had been talking about it since we were both in the Colorado statehouse."

Campbell's staffers and other insiders knew that he had other issues as well. According to Dave Devendorf, state director for the senator, Campbell had initially supported Clinton's candidacy for president since he had run as a moderate, "a new kind of Democrat." Moreover, Campbell identified with the fact that Clinton had come from humble origins, raised in poverty by a single mother, like himself. But, Devendorf recalls, "Ben became sorely disappointed when Clinton surrounded himself with a bunch of twenty-something liberals and pushed a very liberal agenda that was counter to the platforms he had run on." Campbell tried to remain a team player, but it became increasingly difficult given Clinton's agenda, especially the attacks on public lands and water issues, which were the lifeblood of Colorado and other western states. Devendorf agrees that the balanced budget amendment was the straw that broke the camel's back. "He could have played it safe and been known as a 'conservative Democrat' trying to preach fiscal sanity within his party. Instead, declaring 'I can no longer carry the water for the Democratic party,' he took the major risk and switched."

One of the most telling factors in his decision was the grudging acceptance of its maverick senator by the state Democratic party machine. Campbell always felt that he and his wife Linda were tolerated, but not accepted, by state Democrats.

This is confirmed by Campbell's Colorado staff. "We saw first hand the way Ben was being treated by the Democratic establishment in Colorado," says senior aide Alton Dillard. "That is why, speaking for myself, I did not have a huge problem with the party switch. Trust me," he confides, "if the Colorado Democratic establishment could have had its way, Dick Lamm [Campbell's opponent in the 1992 Democratic primary] would have been our senator. It was interesting to us that the so-called party of the people preferred the Anglo, highly educated, Ivy League, Brooks Brothers male kind of types and regarded the outspoken, San Jose State grad with a ponytail and the motorcycle to be some kind of threat. Despite the switch," Dillard insists, "his popularity among John Q. Public remains as high as ever. You need to make a differentiation between the people who live, eat, drink, and breathe politics and the ordinary citizens because they are not one and the same."

Dillard's analysis is confirmed by Devendorf, who has been on the Campbell staff since his days in the House of Representatives. "As a rural moderate, Ben was truly a 'man of the people,' but not a darling of the leadership of the Democratic party, which was more urban and liberal-minded. They owed a lot to the Dick Lamms of the world and they were less than thrilled to have this moderate Native American rancher as their new senator. Worse yet," Devendorf says, "Ben was charismatic, popular, independent, and stubborn. He was not one to look to them for advice or guidance, and since he was of the mind that 'the people' had elected him, he saw himself accountable 'to the people.' The party did not."

In discussing the switch several years later, Campbell made no bones about the difference in attitude expressed publicly and privately by Republicans from the top down. "Linda and I were welcomed warmly and sincerely by everyone. I only wish I had made the change years earlier."

The Republicans expressed their appreciation to Campbell by placing him on two key Senate committees: Appropriations and Indian Affairs, the latter of which he chaired. This chairmanship was an important milestone because he is one of only two Colorado senators to chair a full Senate committee. It is also the only time in the history of the Senate that an American Indian held that seat. Indeed, he was the first Colorado senator to chair a full committee in over forty years, and the first to sit on the powerful Appropriations Committee in nearly thirty years. As a result, he is arguably one of the most powerful Colorado senators in state history.

For the people of Colorado, Campbell's seat on the Appropriations Committee has been especially beneficial. "I pork barrel the hell out of this place, and I make no bones about it," he admits. "We are a donor state. Even now we get back just ninety-two cents for every dollar we pay in. My first goal was to get the taxes reduced. Failing that, I went to plan B, to get it back through the appropriations process. We now average $150 million a year in appropriated funds; last year we got $180 million. That money has gone to our universities, our transportation needs, to our public lands efforts, our hospitals. We need big money in all those areas. I don't fool around with word games. I'm proud of what I have accomplished. Critics can call me anything they want. The expression 'pork barreling' is often used around here to describe the process. When I do it, I'm pork barreling. When others do it, they're getting jobs and economic development for their constituents. That is the game that is played around here, but I don't care what they call it. I'm going to get all the money I can for my state. And I tell you what, the people of Colorado love me for it."

One fan is Elizabeth Hoffman, president of the University of Colorado. Thanks to Campbell, she obtained 65 million federal dollars to launch a capital campaign that raised $650 million to move the medical arts center from the CU campus to a closed military base nearby. "That's why it's so important," Campbell says. "It's like seed money. When the federal government makes a commitment like that, all kinds of people out there—medical doctors, scientists—they all come in with private sector money. And don't forget that the university is a very liberal organization. Probably nine out of ten professors and students are Democrats. Of course," he adds with the hint of a smile, "the fact that the university is going to open a building named the Ben Nighthorse Campbell Indian Diabetic Research Center is kind of nice, too."

Another Campbell enthusiast is Tom Norton, director of the Colorado Department of Transportation. Colorado desperately needs transportation improvement, and Campbell has been able to help fill the need. Colorado is the third-fastest growing state in the nation, behind Arizona and Nevada. This places real stress on parks, schools, and highways. Indeed, at one point Colorado had the number one and number three fastest growing counties in the nation. Traffic congestion up and down the front range continues to worsen. Campbell has been able to funnel federal monies back to the state to expand roads, build bridges and ramps, create bicycle lanes, and conduct feasibility studies on the use of light rail to ease traffic woes. "We need the federal money," he says, "for the simple reason that we don't have the tax base to deal with the burgeoning population."

What makes this largesse possible is senate seniority. "If you look at the billions and billions of dollars that we appropriate every year, look at where the money goes," says Campbell. "The biggest chunk goes to the states of the most senior members, as simple as that, West Virginia and Alaska, Senator

Byrd and Senator Stevens. The three who have the biggest voice in where that money goes are Senator Byrd, Senator Stevens, and Senator Inouye, who are number one, two, three in seniority. I am not denigrating it. I'm just saying that is the political reality of things around here. Seniority counts, and if you are on the Appropriations Committee, it's a very important seat."

One of the most vocal critics of the current system, however, is Senator John McCain of Arizona. "Again, I find myself in the unpleasant position of speaking about parochial projects in yet another conference report," he declared from the Senate floor on December 20, 2001. "Pork barrel spending … is outrageous, disgraceful, and it is an abrogation of the process of legislation. Again, I will continue to oppose this and try to bring this to the attention of the American people. … The power is now in the hands of the Appropriations Committee and those members of the Appropriation Committee," he railed, but "I will propose a change in the rules of the Senate [next year]. I hope it will be considered by many of my colleagues. I know it probably won't be [considered by] those on the Appropriations Committee because now they have all the power."

No one is more aware of that power than Campbell, who thinks his seat on the Appropriations Committee is a reward for switching parties. "It is a plum," he admits. "When the Senate leadership offered it to me, I could not believe it. When I discussed the party switch with Bob Dole, I said I do not want anything and I do not want to be offered anything because I did not want to be accused of selling out. Changing parties often causes a major change in the political structure and you ought to do it based on some principles and beliefs, not based on what you are going to get. Others who have changed parties usually cut a deal, but that is not my style. I didn't care if they gave me something or not. I changed because of philosophy. They didn't offer me a damn thing and I didn't ask for a damn thing, but about a year later they said there is a seat on the Appropriations Committee. A senior member had retired so there was an opening. I had the seniority so they offered it to me and that is how I got it."

Although the rancor caused by his switch has largely passed over—even former Democratic colleagues like Barbara Boxer and Dianne Feinstein seem to have buried the hatchet, Campbell says—the switch certainly disrupted and angered his staff. Those hurt most were in his office on Capitol Hill. The staffers in Washington had not yet been briefed about the change, perhaps in the hope that, thanks to the two-hour time difference, there would still be time in the morning before issues of the *Denver Post*, breaking the story, would hit the streets in Colorado. Instead, word leaked out in the middle of the night, as the early edition was first being printed, and some of Campbell's staff were awakened around 4 A.M. by phone calls informing them of the switch. Their shock at the change was compounded by the hour and manner in which they learned of it. None of them had the least inkling that their boss was about to switch parties; Jane Wilson, his appointment secretary, quit immediately.

As Press Secretary Carol Knight said at the time, "Ben tried to assure us there would be no change except for party affiliation. He would be the same person, with the same independent philosophy. That was easy for him to say, but I found it impossible to think that now I would have to write nice things about Newt Gingrich."

Knight had already announced her intention to return to Colorado within a few months, but for the other staffers in the Capitol Hill office, it was a bitter pill to swallow. Most were young, idealistic, and staunch Democrats. Even Chief of Staff Ken Lane left, taking his pictures of John and Robert Kennedy with him.

Of the pre-switch staff in Washington only Larry Vigil stayed with the senator, whereas the Colorado team remained largely intact. As several of the Colorado staffers pointed out, they have other lives besides politics. "Work hard, but have a life" is Campbell's mandate to his Colorado staff, says Alton Dillard. But for the Washington staff politics was their entire life; they lived and breathed Democratic politics. The Colorado staff went home each day to family, Little League baseball, and church and school activities. As one staffer says, "We all knew Ben would not change regardless what party he espoused. That's all that mattered to most of us."

The media and state Democratic party leaders made more of the switch than the people of Colorado. Representative Pat Schroeder, for one, challenged Campbell to resign from the Senate and see if he could be reelected as a Republican. Responded Campbell: "I will resign on the spot if you run against me!" Schroeder declined the invitation. No matter. Five years later Campbell did, in fact, win as a Republican by swamping Dottie Lamm, wife of former Colorado governor Dick Lamm.

For the most part, however, rank-and-file Colorado Democrats had little difficulty with the party switch. Perhaps it is the realization that Campbell is a Democrat at heart. "The fact of the matter is, in some respects, I still have some Democratic tendencies," he confesses. "I tend to be very pro–organized labor, for example. I am a real soft touch for people in need or someone who is hurting, a trait most people associate with Democrats, rather than Republicans. So even though I switched parties and I really believe in fiscal responsibility, national defense, and all that, I have some residual Democratic leanings inside me. It was the way I was raised."

Whatever the explanation, the voters, like his Colorado staff, were happy. "Ben is Ben. He won't change," seemed to sum up the general reaction. Campbell indeed did not plan to change. At a Republican gathering in Grand Junction, two days after he announced his switch, Campbell declared: "I really apologize to those I disappointed, and for those who are really thrilled, they should remember I'm an independent cuss."

The test would be whether Campbell could get reelected as a Republican. Naysayers had been confident that Campbell would get soundly trounced, possibly even in the Republican primary. Campbell, as usual, was not worried. As he confided to the author in a conversation in 1997, for some Colorado Republicans he had not been right wing enough, just as he had not been left wing enough for some Democrats. Democrats were hoping for a Republican primary, which would weaken the party and perhaps make it possible for a Democrat to regain the seat. "Those Democrats who were mad at me," Campbell declared, "were the same Democrats who were mad at me when I was in the party. I could not live with them then, so I said the hell with it and switched. Naturally, I want to win this election," Campbell continued. "I am as competitive as hell, but if I lose, what have I really lost? I'll go home to a great wife and family, I'll have more time than I'll know what to do with to ride my bike, ride my horses, and enjoy the sunshine. I'll be able to work in my jewelry shop and make three times more money than I can in public office, and I will be able to sleep in on Sundays. Shoot, losing would be great for me personally."

Campbell's Democratic opponent was Dottie Lamm, wife of the former three-time governor (whom he had defeated in the Democratic primary for his senate seat six years earlier). Not only did Campbell win his senate reelection—considered impossible by the so-called experts because the party switch was supposed to be political suicide—but he won by a much larger margin. In 1992 his margin of victory had been 10 percent; in 1998 it was 31 percent. In the process he had also defeated—by a three-to-one margin—a conservative primary opponent who ran on the premise that Campbell was not conservative enough for the GOP.

How was this possible? "Because," says Dave Devendorf, "Campbell resonates with so many constituencies. In the Senate he is the only Native American, the only jeweler/artist, the only former Olympian, and one of only a few ranchers. He also has been a schoolteacher, a law enforcement officer, a cross-country truck driver. He is the only veteran in the Colorado delegation. He is a teamster, the only licensed commercial truck driver. He was both a high school dropout *and* a college graduate. He rides a Harley and he has a ponytail, not for the notoriety but because it suits him. He can talk to anyone on any subject in any part of the state, be it a town meeting or a truck stop, and he identifies with them and they with him because he has been there and done that and gotten his hands dirty in the process. He shoots straight with folks and he doesn't sugarcoat his answers. They may not always agree with him but they respect his honesty."

Ginnie Kontnik, Campbell's chief of staff since 1995, says his reelection victory should have been no surprise. "A majority of the Republicans in Colorado are his kind of folks—small business people, cops, firefighters, and his message of fiscal conservity and social moderation still rings with them. They are a different breed from the state farmers and ranchers and the hard-core conservatives. Besides, what gets votes is constituent services and his staff excels at that."

Devendorf agrees. "In state offices, our primary function is to assist people who are having problems with federal agencies. We don't ask or care about their party affiliation. If someone's Social Security check is missing, that person simply needs help cutting red tape to the money needed to pay bills. Most of us in the state offices felt that our allegiance was to Ben and his efforts to help Coloradans rather than to a party. That is why so many stayed. Most changed their affiliations as well even though he never requested it. He said he did not care what party we belonged to when he hired us and he still does not care, just as long as folks do their job."

Whatever the explanation, Campbell has an uncanny ability to come out on top whatever the issue or controversy. Marvels Ann Brown, a staffer with Ben from his first campaign for the state house in his district through his first Senate race: "Campbell's like a cat. No matter how rough things get, he will always land on his feet."

An indication of Campbell's remarkable popularity is found in a poll taken by the *Rocky Mountain News* and the Denver NBC affiliate, News 4, in late May 1999. The poll compared then President Bill Clinton and five prominent Colorado public figures. In addition to Campbell, these were Governor Bill Owens; Charleton Heston, actor and president of the National Rifle Association; Wayne Allard, Colorado's junior U.S. senator; and John Elway, quarterback of the Denver Broncos professional football team, who was still basking in a Super Bowl victory and who had just announced his retirement. Excluding President Clinton, Campbell, at 93 percent, came in second to John Elway (at 99 percent) in terms of name recognition and second also to Elway with respect to positive name identification: 58 percent for Campbell; 83 percent for Elway.

Shortly after the poll came out, Ben and Linda were in the San Luis Valley for town meetings when an admirer approached him and said, "I couldn't believe you got beat out by John Elway as the most popular person in the state. You'll always be Number One with us." Campbell's reply was perfect, recalls one of his staffers: "Well, I thought I did pretty good considering Elway has won two Super Bowls and has never had to take a position on abortion or anything like that. But, you know," Campbell said with a broad grin, "it's rumored he is considering politics, and if that happens, why I just might climb up on that list."

Another poll in which Campbell takes a measure of pride was published by *George* magazine, which tabbed him as one of the ten worst dressed on Capitol Hill. Cowboy boots, neck scarfs, and twill trousers are evidently not fashionable enough in the suit-and-tie world of D.C. No matter. Campbell took it as a supreme compliment and boasted about it in various speaking engagements around Colorado.

Some things have not changed, however. Campbell still has a salty tongue and he still has his periodic flaps with the press. For example, midway through his first Senate term, the *Denver Post* reported that Campbell had attended only two out of forty meetings of the Indian Affairs Committee, which he chaired at the time. "Some damn fool wrote that," Campbell snarls. "It was a total lie." The record shows he *missed* only two meetings. The *Denver Post* reporter had transposed the numbers. Then, to add fuel to the fire, a Washington newspaper ran the same statistic, citing the *Denver Post.* "Stuff like that is pretty frustrating."

Campbell is partly to blame because he has little time for reporters. "I don't go out and toot my horn much, and the damn press, they're too lazy to do the research to find out what you've actually done. They're more interested in how much you are going to spend on your campaign, that kind of crap. They don't want to get into the real deep stuff, I guess they're afraid the people reading it, their eyes will glaze over. The reporters miss the really meaningful things. All they want are one-liners, quotable-quote bullshit stuff, nothing with depth to it."

Alton Dillard, who served for a time as Campbell's press secretary, confirms the senator is no "media hound." Indeed, many is the time his staff has had to concoct some excuse when declining invitations for him to appear on a television program. "Catch him over a cup of coffee and he's fine, but he has zero interest in going to some soundstage," Dillard says with a laugh. "That is something the local media can't adjust to. Just about any time that they offer a politician airtime, no matter how inconvenient it is, most of them leap at the opportunity, but not Ben."

Perhaps that helps explain why reporters seem to have assumed that Campbell has been inattentive to his Senate duties. Criticism about his legislative record became such an irritant, in fact, that his staffers felt it necessary to silence the critics. "It was getting to the point that many questions were being asked about what Ben was doing for Colorado," admits one staffer. "The media was on the same kick. They preferred stories about motorcycles and ponytails. Although we have an excellent press team, we couldn't get our message out. Ben, for his part, just shrugged his shoulders. Granted that it takes a certain amount of ego to be a public official, Ben still is very modest and not one to toot his own horn or pat himself on the back even though he was responsible for more bills than the rest of the Colorado delegation combined."

Campbell's staff realized that there would be some risk in publicizing his legislative achievements. Nonetheless, the decision was made to go forward.

Campbell's legislative report card is little short of remarkable. In the 105th Congress, he introduced fifty-one free standing bills and seven resolutions. The Senate passed five of the resolutions and enacted nine of the free standing bills, which means they concern one subject and no other amendments have been added.

Campbell's record in the 106th Congress (1999–2000) is even more noteworthy. Of the 579 bills the Congress signed into public law, Campbell had twelve free standing bills enacted. The next highest number in the Senate—by Orrin Hatch—was nine. The highest number by a representative was eight. The Senate also passed nine of the fourteen resolutions Campbell introduced.

The explanation for Campbell's success is simple, says Mike Russell. "Ben is a rare member of the Senate who grew up in the fifties, went to war for his country, held numerous blue-collar or no-collar jobs, and paid his dues in life many times over. His legislative record reflects the same focus, tenacity, and strength that made him an Olympian."

Interestingly, Campbell ranks next to the bottom in the Senate for cosponsored legislation—99 out of 100—whereas some of his colleagues have cosponsored over three hundred bills in one cycle. "I don't want to be the king of cosponsors," Campbell informed his staff upon taking office. Indeed, if all bills were passed, says Russell, it would cost trillions more than it now takes to run the government. "As a fiscal conservative, Ben is extremely diligent in this regard."

With such a commendable scorecard why, then, is there so little publicity about Campbell's Senate record? Because, his staff believes, the bills and resolutions are not considered sexy enough by the media. They benefit the military, police officers, minorities, truckers, and other blue-collar causes.

This should come as no surprise considering Campbell's roots. He is the only veteran in the Colorado congressional delegation, and he is probably the only member of Congress who was a line law enforcement officer, having served six years as a deputy sheriff in Sacramento, California. Law enforcement has always been one of his top priorities. Since the September 11, 2001, terrorist attacks, of course, it has become especially popular to heap praise and support upon these groups, but Campbell was there much earlier.

A brief look at Campbell's law enforcement legislative activities shows his leadership in this area. In 1997, two Denver police officers asked him for help in introducing a bill to establish a matching grant to allow state, local, and tribal officers to purchase body armor. As a former deputy sheriff, Campbell had known officers who died because they could not afford to purchase the equipment needed to protect themselves. He agreed to go to bat for them. While working on the legislation, another Senate office asked if they could join Campbell. Bipartisanship is always helpful, so Campbell agreed. However, two days before the bill was to be introduced, another Senate office called to say they were going to introduce the bill without Campbell because he was not sitting on a committee of jurisdiction. This infuriated Campbell. "Let's kick ass," he declared. He told his deputy chief of staff Mike Russell to call their friends and get the bill moving through the process. "Campbell does not take no for an answer on legislation that is of special interest to him, like this one was. Whenever one of his bills hits a roadblock, he counts on us to exhaust every means possible, staff to staff, to move it along before calling the member with oversight." In this instance, Campbell was the first on record to have a bill of this magnitude introduced in the Senate. Signed into law on June 16, 1998, it authorized $25 million a year for the grant program; an amendment Campbell introduced two years later doubled the amount. What makes this program especially popular is the fact that it is user-friendly. A department can simply go on-line to place its order.

A similar initiative provided bullet proof glass for police vehicles. Campbell was moved to sponsor this legislation when a Colorado police officer, Dale Claxton, died at the hands of escaped convicts who killed him as he sat in his cruiser. The law is titled the "Police Officer Dale Claxton Bullet Resistant Materials Act."

Still another Campbell initiative of interest to law enforcement officers is his effort to see a law enforcement museum built in Washington, D.C. Campbell was approached about the idea in May 1999 by Craig Floyd, chairman of the National Law Enforcement Memorials Fund, after completing the Annual Law Motorcycle Ride that year. Floyd asked Campbell if he would sponsor a museum bill supported by fifteen national law enforcement organizations. According to Floyd, law enforcement groups had been watching Campbell and knew of his commitment and successful track record on their behalf. Campbell's strategy, as usual, was to build coalitions and consensus in a commonsense manner, while the D.C. government apparently saw the effort as an attack on its sovereignty and called upon all of its allies in the House and Senate in an attempt to derail the legislation. Remarked one House subcommittee staffer: "We refuse to be treated like a red-headed stepchild when it comes to our city."

After a year of head-knocking among D.C. judges, city officials, House and Senate committee members and staffers, and Campbell—"law enforcement officers will have their museum and nothing less"—a deal was crafted and the bill was signed into law on November 9, 2000. Interestingly, once the opposition saw the writing on the wall, they quietly fell in line. "In fact," says Larry Vigil, "some of the most outspoken opponents got so much flak from their local cops that they ended up cosponsoring the bill."

As a result of his efforts on behalf of law enforcement, Campbell is very popular with police officers, and he is equally comfortable around them. "There is nothing like watching Ben in a room full of law enforcement brass and the rank-and-file guys, chatting about changes in law enforcement theory," marvels Alton Dillard. "He is truly in his element just hanging out with the cops. In parades he chats with the cops around him, and they all know him. Sometimes when he gets inadvertently stranded somewhere by weather or miscommunication, he just has to go find a state trooper and he will get a ride to wherever he is needed."

Campbell also identifies with veterans, which is understandable since he is one of the few veterans of the Korean War remaining on Capitol Hill. In fact, one of his free standing bills enacted in the 106th Congress is titled "The Bring Them Home Alive Act." It offers refugee asylum status to any national from the former Soviet Union, China, North Korea, Vietnam, Laos, or Cambodia for finding and identifying a live American POW or MIA from either the Korean or Vietnam War.

The bill initially raised some hackles because, by its very existence, it refutes the assertion that no one was left behind. One stubborn Hill staffer stymied the bill in a subcommittee for months, prompting Campbell to confront the chairman of the committee of jurisdiction. The chairman knew nothing of the bill but, realizing its importance to Campbell, had it marked up out of the subcommittee and the full committee without any hearing whatsoever. It was signed into law in November 2000.

Campbell, still the only Native American in Congress, remains concerned about groups who are part of America's backbone but who are also sometimes marginalized and forgotten, like Indians and blacks. For example, when Campbell noticed that the American flag was not being displayed on Martin Luther King, Jr., Day, he had his staff look into the reason why. With some research, his staffers discovered that this holiday was somehow inadvertently omitted from the federal flag code, which authorizes the days upon which the American flag should be displayed. Troubled by such a glaring oversight, Campbell pulled in his legislative team. "Get me a bill to honor Martin Luther King with the American flag and let's push to make this happen."

This one required Campbell's personal attention because the idea had been discussed in other offices as well and had gotten nowhere. Campbell's first call was to his friend Orrin Hatch, who helped set the wheels in motion to have the bill marked up out of committee and reported onto the Senate floor. When Ben's bill went to the House for consideration, it was discovered that several House Democratic staffers were doing their best to kill the bill. They found the idea of a Republican attempting to honor Martin Luther King somewhat jarring. As soon as Campbell got wind of their behind-the-scenes machinations, he got on the phone and began enlisting the help of the House leadership, many of whom were still friends from his days as a representative. Campbell does not often call upon his friends and colleagues for help, but when he does he gets results. The bill was signed into law on October 25, 1999.

Campbell was equally involved when he read in the newspapers that the Martin Luther King papers were up for sale and that the Library of Congress was anxious to obtain them. On October 26, 1999, Campbell introduced the "Dr. Martin Luther King, Jr. Papers Preservation Act," to provide the funds necessary for their purchase. He then went down to the Senate floor and spoke to his good friend and colleague Mitch McConnell, then chairman of the Rules Committee, explaining to him the positive merits and legacy this kind of legislation could have. The bill passed the full Senate three days later. "I believe it was a record for us—from introduction to passage in three days," marvels one staffer. "Unfortunately, once the bill made it to the House, it fell into a political quagmire never to resurface."

On another occasion the African American community approached Campbell about sponsoring a bill to erect a memorial in Washington, D.C., to commemorate blacks who had served in the Revolutionary War. Once word got out that Campbell was willing to help, his office began to receive hate mail on the subject. That was the wrong thing to do. Campbell made passage of the bill a personal cause and, with the help in the House of his good friend J. C. Watts, the bill was passed and signed into law. Less visible but equally significant, Campbell pushed for and got through the confirmation process for the first African American on Denver's Federal District Court.

His efforts on behalf of the black community have not gone unnoticed. When the press was filled with criticism about his decision to switch parties, one of those who came to his defense was black syndicated reporter Ken Hamblin. "For his independent thinking and personal political savvy, Campbell is one American Indian who has won my admiration. If Campbell's switch from the party of the donkey to that of the elephant makes it possible for him to achieve the goal of free thinking and self-determination for poor Americans, no matter what color they are, then I salute him for being a true American warrior and I am honored to call him brother."

When Campbell changed parties, the Hispanic community became alarmed. "Tell my Hispanic friends that I will not abandon them," Campbell instructed. "That promise," his Hispanic liaison Ricardo La Fore declares, "was good enough for me. I stayed on for Ben the man, not Ben the Republican, and he kept his word."

Campbell, in fact, has more Hispanics on his staff than the rest of the Colorado delegation combined. According to La Fore, when Campbell ran for the Senate the first time, he promised to hire Hispanics, and he did. "Hispanics by nature are more impressed with what you do than by what you say you will do," La Fore points out, "so when Ben promised to hire Hispanics, he delivered in a big way. It says something to our community when you see someone who looks like you speaking on behalf of the senator or when Spanish speakers come to us for help and find Spanish-speaking people working on their cases."

La Fore's high regard for Campbell is echoed by Alberta Vega, who has been on Campbell's staff since 1987. Vega has been a Democrat her entire political life. When Campbell called to tell her he was switching parties, she recalls, he hoped she would stay but he also said he would understand if she quit because he was now a Republican. "I told him I didn't work for him because he was a Democrat but because he was the person he is. I knew that would not change. It has not. He is still the bright star, down-to-earth, hardworking man I first met and I hope to continue working for him until he is ready to call it quits."

It is no secret that Campbell prefers to meet constituents in less-than-formal settings and that he is more comfortable with small groups as opposed to large ones. Nonetheless, he has a quick wit and can deal easily with difficult situations. For example, when Campbell was once on stage at an American GI Forum, the elected official hosting the meeting tried to embarrass him for his stance against gun control. Evidently oblivious to the fact that the other individuals on the platform were combat veterans, the official suggested that all guns should be taken away from the American public. When Campbell got to the podium, he turned to one of the veterans and asked, "How about it, Gus, shall I take your gun away?"

"Yeah, Ben," Gus replied. "Over my dead body!"

"Case closed," Ben declared. "Next question?"

Campbell may prefer to avoid the limelight, but he does not hesitate to speak his mind when necessary. In December 2001, the Senate prepared to vote whether or not to accept an automatic pay raise of $4,900. The attempt to reject the raise failed, 65–33, although numerous members were made to feel guilty about accepting the raise in light of the economic downturn following the Twin Towers disaster. Ben was only one of two senators to take the floor—the other was Russell Feingold, Democrat from Wisconsin, who urged his colleagues to stop the "backdoor pay raise." Ben's comments were vintage Campbell. Characterizing it as "Vote no, but take the dough," he criticized those senators who voted against a pay increase, but then accepted it anyway. If they truly had qualms, he said, they could give the money to charity. "In the past, in fact, some have come to the floor to emphatically denounce the increase while letting other legislators shoulder the burden to pass the bill and they quietly pocket the money and sneak off in the night hoping nobody will notice that their outrage does not jibe with their actions," he commented.

Of Campbell's legislative achievements, he takes special pride in three: the Animas–La Plata project, the Black Canyon of the Gunnison National Park, and the Sand Creek Massacre National Historic Site Establishment Act.

Campbell has been working on the Animas–La Plata water project for more than twenty years. It was authorized in 1968, but opposition has been so strong—from states worried that the project will impact their water supplies—that it took until the 106th Congress to make it happen. According to the Bureau of Land Reclamation, the $350 million water project will be the last one built in the West. Brush clearing will begin in the summer of 2002. "I sometimes think that the people who get things done around here," says Campbell, "are not necessarily the smartest or the best, but the ones who won't give up. Just keep doing it, keep doing it. Get knocked down, get back up, and redo it again next year. Little by little, you'll get what you want, if you're willing to keep at it, keep at it."

Certainly that was the credo Campbell followed in getting Animas–La Plata funded and it also helped with getting the Black Canyon of the Gunnison National Park established. The Black Canyon of the Gunnison is so named because the sides of the gorge are so narrow and deep that the sun only hits the bottom a few hours each day. "It's got the best fishing in Colorado," Campbell declares, "probably because few people are willing to make the effort to climb down that steep slope." This accomplishment held special meaning to Campbell personally because the area around Black Canyon—

Montrose and Gunnison Counties—is where Linda's family homesteaded. Indeed, in the valley, in the small town of Cimarron, there is a roundhouse for the narrow gauge railroad that used to run through there. Linda's grandfather was an engineer on that railroad and he met his future wife at the roundhouse restaurant where she worked as a waitress. Near the dam, as a sort of monument, is the engine that her grandfather operated.

Credit for the idea of establishing the park, however, goes to Mike Strang, Campbell's predecessor in the Senate. Strang introduced the first bill, but it was much different and much smaller. Over the years, Campbell introduced perhaps five versions of his own, but he could never get consensus. "Water users were afraid it would detract from their water use; environmentalists wanted instream flow guaranteed to protect endangered fish. We just couldn't get all the parties to the table. Finally," Campbell says, "I set up a negotiating team that included Ken Gale, the former mayor of Montrose, and C. Wayne Keith, Linda's dad's cousin. Keith had been head of the Colorado state patrol. He had great credentials and he was a really good human being. When he retired to Montrose, I asked him if he would head up the committee to get the thing resolved. He worked at it four years, until he died. He really got most of them to the bargaining table. At the end, I just pushed the darn thing through. Clinton agreed to sign it, so I just went with it."

Campbell's reward came on a brilliant autumn day in October 1999 when, in front of Linda, her mother Nina Price, his children, grandchildren, and hundreds of spectators, he was recognized for his tireless effort to elevate the national monument to national park status.

There had been much confusion about its status as a national monument. "People thought the monument meant it was a big rock with an inscription, like a gravestone," Campbell says. "Now, as a park, they know it is a place they can enjoy, camp out, hike."

According to Ginnie Kontnik, Campbell's chief of staff, getting the national park established proved the senator had the mettle to bring together some very disparate groups to work cooperatively for a common good. "The process," she says, "which took over twelve years from start to finish, was one that few others could have accomplished. For Ben's supporters and staff, establishing the park proved yet again that anything to which he put his mind would come to fruition. Even his critics could find little to fault in the process, which required years and years of public meetings, the passing back and forth of draft management plans, environmental assessments, and countless studies."

Although Campbell would agree that it was one of his most significant senatorial achievements, he knows a lot of others deserve credit for their timely help. In fact, he tried to involve as many people as possible to gain consensus and avoid hard feelings, but, as he says with a shrug of his shoulders, "I have found from politics, no matter what you do, someone says, you didn't ask me, and that sure was true with the Black Canyon."

Consensus was easier to obtain for establishing the Sand Creek Massacre National Historic Site. Certainly few can dispute that what occurred at Sand Creek on November 29, 1864, was one of the darkest moments in our country's troubled relationship with its native peoples. At dawn on that awful day, Colonel John M. Chivington with a regiment of Colorado volunteers attacked a sleeping and unsuspecting village of Cheyenne and Arapaho Indians camped along Sand Creek. Their chief, Black Kettle, thought he had a promise of protection from federal army officers. When the attack began, Black Kettle raised an American flag and then a white flag over his tent, but Chivington wanted dead Indians, not prisoners. By day's end some two hundred Indians had been killed, most of them women, children, and the elderly. The volunteers, who then scalped and sexually mutilated many of the dead, later brandished their "trophies" to cheering crowds in the streets of Denver.

The legislation authorizing the site provides for the purchase of up to twenty thousand acres of land about a half-mile wide and several miles long in order to encompass the entire area involved in the massacre. This includes the site of the village and the route along the creek that fleeing Indians used in their attempt to escape the pursuing soldiers who hunted them down until sunset. The Northern Cheyennes expressed their appreciation to Campbell by holding an honoring celebration on their reservation in Montana for Campbell and Judge Bill Dawson and his wife, who were the first landowners to agree to sell their land back to the government.

Campbell envisions little difficulty acquiring the entire parcel, but it may take five or six years to complete the purchase. The land is worth $1,000 an acre, but some landowners think its importance as an historic site justifies $10,000 an acre. One reason so much land is needed is that no one knows the exact site of the village because of riparian changes over the years. The creek dried up years ago. Cheyenne oral history places the village at one site, near the Dawson ranch house, while archaeologists claim it was located elsewhere. "Let's take the whole thing," Campbell told the Cheyenne and Arapaho elders. "If you got the whole area, we can split hairs later whether the campfire was here or there. Nonetheless, despite the little dispute between science and oral history, the Cheyennes and Arapahoes are happy because the whole site will be protected, and there will be a certain parcel of land set aside for Indian religious and ceremonial events like the sun dance, memorial services, the reinterment of remains, peace events, and other spiritual activities."

I know establishing the historic site was of special importance to Campbell because in our very first meeting in 1990, when we discussed the writing of his biography, we also talked about Sand Creek. I asked then Congressman Campbell about his future plans. "I am not really sure," he replied, "but one dream is to become governor of Colorado. Can you imagine the irony, me, a Cheyenne Indian, the governor of Colorado, the state that massacred our people at Sand Creek? And you know what, Herman? There is a town out there named Chivington, and if I become governor I intend to burn that sucker down."

Another effort that met with almost universal approval was the Colorado Millennium Tree. Each year since 1964 the U.S. Forest Service has erected a large Christmas tree on the lawn of the Capitol Building—not to be confused with the White House Christmas tree, which the president and first lady light each year—and Colorado was chosen to provide the tree for the millennium year. Dubbed "the people's tree," Colorado's gift to the nation was a sixty-five-foot, perfectly formed blue spruce—the state tree—found in Pike National Forest, north of Woodland Park. Before the tree came down, Russell Box, an elder of the Southern Ute Indian tribe, blessed it with an eagle feather and tobacco, "so that it would go in a good way."

After the ceremony the large tree was taken to Peterson Air Force Base where it was shrink-wrapped and placed inside a covered wagon–style trailer.

From there it began the two-thousand-mile journey to Washington, D.C., in a seven-truck convoy on a path that roughly followed the historic Santa Fe Trail through Colorado.

As part of the publicity for the event, the Colorado Forest Service asked Campbell if he would care to drive the tree for a few miles since he had recently renewed his commercial trucking license. "Hell," Campbell replied, "why don't I drive it all the way?"

Although done during the Senate recess and not considered an official event, Campbell needed staff assistance along the way because people consider him on the job wherever he is and whatever he is doing. As Deborah Kalb, a Senate aide in the Pueblo office explains, "people are always asking him to speak or for information and it is difficult for him to keep track of all the requests, so there I was."

The first stop was Lathrop Park, near Walsenburg, a picturesque site in the shadow of the Spanish Peaks. The wind off the lake cut like a knife, but at 8:30 A.M. on a Sunday morning eighty-five people were waiting patiently in the cold to see the tree and hear a few words from Ben, who then joined a group of Indians in a circle dance: "You just want to keep from freezing," Kalb teased him. It was then on to Trinidad and a crowd of four hundred, where Campbell was given the key to the city. "The best was yet to come," Kalb recalls. "In between Trinidad and Las Animas is a whole lot of flat, empty prairie land, yet there were people waiting for the convoy alongside the road in their cars or standing by their mailboxes." Even more amazing, Kalb recalls, some 250 people were waiting at the Las Animas courthouse even though the Denver Broncos were on television at the same time. "Frankly, I was stunned. All those who went with us knew it was a once in a lifetime experience."

By the time the tree reached Washington, D.C., the convoy had made nineteen celebratory stops along the way including two in Kansas and one in St. Louis. Colorado's "gift to the nation" was planted on the west lawn of the U.S. Capitol Building on December 4, 2000. There it stood until January 2, adorned with ten thousand lights and four thousand ornaments made by Colorado schoolchildren.

During the nine-day trip, Campbell averaged six hours a day behind the wheel of the 460-horsepower Mack truck. Campbell shared time behind the wheel with a professional trucker, Jimmy Fika. The caravan included three Mack trucks provided by the company. One was a mobile museum telling the history of Mack Trucks, which also picked up the entire tab for the trip.

What shocked Campbell was discovering that the trees picked each year as the "national Christmas tree" have to be guarded night and day from vandals and environmentalists who are opposed to the practice. As a result, two state patrolmen and two forest service guards accompanied the convoy to the nation's capital. At each of the rest stops along the way the semi had to be parked in secure areas, like truck yards belonging to state departments of transportation.

"I loved it," says Campbell. "It was kind of like going home to my workingman roots. My staff wondered how my constituents would react to my doing this," Campbell laughed, "but I told them most people would be happy to hear that I was learning a new trade."

Actually, the experience renewed an old trade. "It brought back many fond memories of being on the road when I was in college driving trucks, the freedom of the road," he says. "There really is a calling to it, a calling that tugs at you to get on the road, to get away from everybody." Now, having renewed his commercial trucker's license, Campbell has taken to the road again. "I've been delivering beer out of Fort Collins for Budweiser and Coors breweries," he confides with a chuckle. "The trucks are eighteen-wheelers. I've had more damn fun. I pull in with a truckload of beer and these guys look at me not quite sure what to make of it. 'Are you Senator Campbell? What the hell are you doing delivering beer?' they say to me." He does it, he says, "to get out of the office, to get out with the real working people. And you know what I found out? There is an expression in politics, 'Joe six-pack.' Let me tell you they're all over the place, and they vote. They vote," Campbell declares with a hearty laugh. "I didn't do this because I wanted some benefit, but I have gotten more positive reaction from being out on the road with the truck drivers and the beer guys than you can possibly imagine."

Another special moment for Campbell was the honorary doctorate awarded to him by Meiji University, which he had attended while training for the 1964 Olympics. "I've been told the university has given only two such awards: one to Edwin O. Reischauer, who was U.S. Ambassador to Japan from

1961 to 1996, and me. It was great fun. For the event they brought back my old teammates and we had a terrific reunion. They all are still tough as nails. Even my old teacher was there, Sugata Sanchiro. He was ninety-two and had a pacemaker, yet he was still out on that mat slamming into those college kids. He was working out and roughhousing them like a man half his age. When he saw me he started talking. I couldn't translate it word for word, but the gist of it was, 'Get suited up and we'll do some mat work like the old days!' I pointed to my arm, which was still in a cast from my motorcycle accident, and managed to avoid getting on the mat with him, but I still had to suit up for pictures."

Much had changed in Japan since his judo days. Foreigners were all over the place, including more than a thousand who are members of the Tokyo-American Chamber of Commerce. "Everybody dressed western style and a lot of the Japanese people now speak fluent English," Campbell marveled. "It's like going to England except for all the Japanese faces."

Perhaps the biggest shock was seeing a woman practicing with the Meiji judo team. "What is she doing here?" Ben asked. The team captain laughed. "She kept coming around, so we thought if we beat her up enough she would go away. Now, she's a two-time women's world champion, but she only works out with men. If she gets on the mat with other women she just knocks the hell out of them."

One of the former judo players who came to welcome Ben was Toshiro Asada, the all-Japan-university champion Ben defeated in the pre-Olympic trials. Although Asada's judo career had been tarnished by his loss—his only defeat—to a foreigner, he seemed to hold no grudges. Ben had taken with him to Japan his popular warrior poster. It shows him on horseback wearing his warrior regalia, which features his warbonnet of seventy-two eagle feathers, a cherished gift to him from the Northern Cheyennes. Each feather represents an international judo victory. Asada listened carefully to Campbell's explanation of the significance of the warbonnet, then asked: "Which feather am I?"

Campbell has come a long way from the judo mats of Japan. Even he finds it hard to believe that today he is a member of the U.S. Senate. "I still look at my own lifestyle and where I came from and think it is kind of marvelous that someone like me, from the wrong side of the tracks, can even be here. It's wonderful."

Although the Senate as an institution is a little "ingrown," his colleagues have always made him feel welcome. "I think the world of them. They each bring something different. I've learned a lot from people like Byrd, who is kind of the conscience and historian of this place. I could sit for hours and listen to him even if it has nothing to do with this place. When he gets to talking about the Roman Empire or Greek times, I don't know how he fits all that in his head. He knows so much. It is wonderful for me just to listen to him. There are other people who don't say much, like Danny Akaka from Hawaii, just a prince of a human being. I'll always be enriched having known him. I learned a lot about other people, like Hillary Clinton, for example. I think I had a preconceived idea that she was kind of a dragon lady out of the White House, that kind of stuff. I was really amazed to find out she works so damn hard here, and that she's so approachable, easy to deal with and to talk to. I'm not into the big entourage thing that she likes, you know, with all the people following you around, lapdogging and all that business, that's just not me, but person to person, she is pretty easy to get along with and hard-working. It really surprised me. She's not trying to live on her laurels, having been first lady."

How then, with such rich minds and energetic people on board, does the Senate come across as a seemingly dull and stodgy place? "In some respects the reason this place is dull is that no one wants to risk criticism," Campbell believes. "They're all kind of status quo because they know the minute you do anything that is different, unusual, or forge ahead, someone is going to criticize you. It is the fear of criticism that holds back most initiatives in Congress, I believe."

INDEX

ABOUT THE AUTHOR

Herman J. Viola is a curator emeritus with the Smithsonian Institution. During his federal career, he has curated or served as a consultant for exhibits at the National Archives of the United States, the National Museum of American Art, the National Museum of American History, the National Museum of the American Indian, the Library of Congress, and the Corcoran Gallery of Art. From 1972 until 1987, he was the Director of the Smithsonian's National Anthropological Archives.

Viola was Director of Quincentenary Programs for the National Museum of Natural History, where he conceived and developed "Seeds of Change," a major exhibition that focused on the exchange of plants, animals, and diseases between the Old and New Worlds as a result of the Columbus voyages. He also conceived and developed the acclaimed "Magnificent Voyagers" exhibition, which told the story of the U.S. Exploring Expedition of 1838–1842.

Among his most important publications are *Thomas L. McKenney: Architect of America's Early Indian Policy*, *The Indian Legacy of Charles Bird King*, *Diplomats in Buckskin*, *The National Archives of the United States*, *Magnificent Voyagers*, *Exploring the West*, *After Columbus: The Chronicle of America's Indian Peoples Since 1492*, *Seeds of Change*, *The Memoirs of Charles Henry Veil*, *Warrior Artists*, and *Little Bighorn Remembered: The Untold Story of Custer's last Stand*. He has also written several books for young readers.

Herman Viola lives with his wife in Falls Church, Virginia.